The Oxford Picture Dictionary for Kids

Teacher's Book

Joan Ross Keyes
Dorothy Bukantz
Judith A.V. Harlan

OXFORD UNIVERSITY PRESS

198 Madison Avenue, New York, NY, 10016, USA
Great Clarendon Street, Oxford, OX2 6DP, England

Oxford New York

Auckland Cape Town Dar es Salaam Hong Kong Karachi Kuala Lumpur Madrid Melbourne Mexico City Nairobi New Delhi Shanghai Taipei Toronto

With offices in

Argentina Austria Brazil Chile Czech Republic France Greece Guatemala Hungary Italy Japan South Korea Poland Portugal Singapore Switzerland Thailand Turkey Ukraine Vietnam

ISBN-13: 978-0-19-434998-7
ISBN-10: 0-19-434998-5

Editorial Manager: Shelagh Speers
Senior Editor: June Schwartz
Production Editor: M. Long
Elementary Design Manager: Doris Chen
Interior Design: Silver Editions
Production Layout: Kristine Mudd, Doug Popovich
Art Buyer: Donna Goldberg
Production Coordinator: Shanta Persaud

Printing (last digit): 10 9 8 7

Printed in Hong Kong.

Special thanks to the following teachers who reviewed the Dictionary and contributed activity ideas for the Teachers Book, the Workbook, and the Reproducible Worksheets:
Ann H. Bell, Lori Chase, Elizabeth Manvell, Susan Sernau, and Susan Shalek White.

Special thanks to the following people for their work on the bibliographies
Charles Hirsch
Stephen Fraser
Margaret Simpson

Acknowledgments

To all my students everywhere whose appreciation and enthusiasm motivated me to create this book, its stories, dialogues, and Beats!

To the special people at Oxford University Press: the design and production staff for ingeniously putting all the parts together, to Shelagh Speers, the Editorial Manager, for her "go for it" encouragement, and most of all to my own editor, June Schwartz, whose patient labors got us through it all.

To Educational Activities, Inc. who first published my "Beats!" and granted rights.

And to my family, my daughter and sons, for understanding and giving me space...

I thank you all.

JRK

Table of Contents

Topic Lessons

Theme 1: Me and My Family

Theme 2: My House

Theme 3: My School

Theme 4: My Town

Theme 6: Vacation

Theme 7: Animals

Theme 8: Seasons

THEME 9: Earth and Space

Components

Picture Dictionary

The **Picture Dictionary** presents over 700 words in the context of 60 topics. Each topic is introduced with a beautiful full-color illustration that tells a story about or shows a situation from the lives of five characters and their families. The topics are organized into nine themes.

Teacher's Book

The **Teacher's Book** presents techniques and strategies for using each component of the program, along with specific instruction ideas for each topic, all within a simple easy-to-follow format. These ideas include notes about the words, stories, Beats!, and dialogues. The *Teacher's Book* also provides additional activities for each topic and bibliographies of recommended children's books for each of the *Picture Dictionary*'s nine themes.

Workbook

The **Workbook** offers activity pages for use with each topic in the *Picture Dictionary.* It contains a variety of word games, labeling and matching tasks, writing tasks, and other activities that enable the students to practice the words from each topic.

Cassettes

The **Cassettes** provide listening practice to accompany all the components in the program. They contain all the words from the *Picture Dictionary,* a short dialogue for each topic, and all the stories and Beats! from the *Reproducibles Collection.*

Reproducibles Collection

The **Reproducibles Collection** is a set of four books of reproducible pages:

- The **Word and Picture Cards** book contains pages for making matching word and picture cards for the words presented in each topic. The *Teacher's Book* tells you how to use the cards to reinforce and extend the student's understanding and use of the vocabulary.
- The **Stories** book contains one reproducible story page for each of the 60 topics. Each page is divided into four illustrated sections so that, when folded, it makes an individual mini-book. Students can color the page and take it home for individual reading practice.
- The **Beats!** book contains a playful rhythmic chant on each page. The Beats! provide language practice related to each topic. As in the *Stories* book, each page is divided into four sections so students can fold it into a mini-book they can color and take home.
- The **Worksheets** book contains two reproducible pages for each topic. These pages provide language practice through word games, writing tasks, and other activities.

Wall Charts

The **Wall Charts** are large poster-size reproductions of each of the 60 double-page illustrations in the *Picture Dictionary.*

Introduction

The Oxford Picture Dictionary for Kids is designed especially for young students, ages 5-7, learning English. The Dictionary can be used by itself or as the core of an entire language program with a variety of accompanying components (see p. viii).

About the Picture Dictionary

The *Picture Dictionary* presents over 700 words in the context of pictures that tell stories. Five characters and their families are introduced at the beginning of the book, and appear throughout in a series of 60 double-page illustrations, each of which introduces a topic. Most of the scenes take place in the town and city where these five families live. The topics reflect common experiences of children this age. The illustrations are filled with interesting details about the characters. Because of the high interest level of the illustrations, children at any stage of language acquisition will be motivated to develop their own language skills. The use of stories for presenting vocabulary allows students to obtain a better grasp of the language because they are learning language in the context of fun, familiar situations.

Organization of the Picture Dictionary

The 60 topics are organized into nine themes. The topics and themes progress from individual experiences at home and school, to the characters' explorations of other environments in their towns and cities, and out in the world. The situations depicted, and the vocabulary presented, are drawn from a range of content areas such as mathematics, social studies, and science.

The topics are self-contained so that they can be presented to students in any order. However, they do follow a logical sequence both in content and in language difficulty.

Each of the 60 topics is introduced with a double-page illustration. Twelve vocabulary words are featured under each illustration. Each of the 12 words is accompanied by a small illustration that duplicates the object or action in the larger picture. These *callouts* define the words. They allow children to isolate each item and search for it in the context of the picture story.

The number of words on each page has been kept to a minimum so that students can master the vocabulary more easily. Verbs and nouns are included together to help students more easily use the language in context. Verbs are grouped together on the page, and each is marked with a star.

An appendix at the back of the *Picture Dictionary* includes the alphabet, numbers, colors, shapes, days, months, and time.

Following the appendix are three lists: *Words, Verbs,* and *Subjects.*

- The *Words* list, arranged alphabetically, includes the words, labels, and key words from the topic titles. These are listed in black. Listed in red are other common words that do not appear in the text, but are pictured in the illustrations.
- The *Verbs* list is arranged by the topics in which verbs can be found.
- The *Subjects* list is a convenient cross-reference, by category, of words that can be found within several different topics and themes.

Organization of the Teacher's Book

The *Teacher's Book* offers a guide to general teaching techniques for use with any topic. This section contains strategies for presenting words, stories, Beats!, and dialogues, and suggestions for incorporating literature. It also includes ideas for assessment.

Following the guide to general techniques is a topic-by-topic presentation of teaching strategies and classroom activities (pp. 1–258). Each four-page topic unit contains suggestions for using individual elements as focal points for developing lessons. There are also specific teaching tips for the *Worksheets* and the *Workbook* pages.

The first page of each topic unit summarizes the content and language that can be developed through the topic. It also shows a small reproduction of the *Picture Dictionary* illustration along with a short descriptive paragraph. This page also includes a list of 12 topic words plus a list of additional words that are either related to the topic or found in the accompanying components.

At the end of the Teacher's Book is an alphabetical Word List of the vocabulary words (including nouns, verbs, labels, and title words) and additional words. There is also a separate list of all the verbs in the *Picture Dictionary*, and a cross-reference by common subjects.

Bibliographies of children's books
For each of the nine themes, the *Teacher's Book* contains an annotated bibliography of recommended children's books, both fiction and nonfiction, on subjects related to the topics found in each theme. The bibliography can be found on the overview page at the beginning of each theme section. The bibliographies make it easier to choose appropriate literature to create a theme-related classroom library.

Developing a program with the Picture Dictionary

The *Picture Dictionary* allows children the flexibility to engage in language development through exploring each picture, whether they are at the level of non-verbal response, identifying basic vocabulary, learning use of sentence structure, or developing more elaborate expressions for their thoughts and feelings. It also allows the flexibility of deciding how much time to spend on each topic and each activity according to the needs and interests of the students.

Each page presents opportunities for encouraging students to develop their listening, speaking, reading, and writing skills. The stories, Beats!, and dialogues bring the illustrations to life while offering models of language use. Fluency and comprehension will develop as the children listen to, read, and repeat the language patterns. These components can also be used as a basis for exploring verb tenses and grammatical structures, and for practicing conversational formats. Children will find that words introduced in one topic can be found in other pictures; this will enable them to grasp the vocabulary in different contexts and so expand their language use. The *Workbook* and the *Worksheets* allow the children to explore and reinforce language through individual reading and writing projects, enhanced by art activities, puzzles, and games to spark student interest and broaden their conception of language use.

Assessment

Two assessment forms are provided on the following pages as convenient tools for use along with other means of assessment, such as individual student portfolios. Use the first chart to keep track of the topics, and the elements within each topic, to which each student has been exposed. The second chart helps you create an overview of each child's development of language skills. Use it to record your observations of students' progress in listening, speaking, reading, and writing skills.

These are examples of observations recorded at different stages of language development:

Abdul pointed to appropriate callouts when named.

Suki correctly matched picture and word cards.

Marcela named five foods in the picture.

Estrella responded with partial phrases: "Alison on horse."

Ben identified location using prepositional phrases: "by the door, on the chair."

Noah answered questions using full sentences.

Miguel told about his trip in sequential order.

Katya wrote a story about skating.

Mateo read the story aloud.

Ivan and Tonio invented a dialogue based on the question-and-answer format: Do you like pineapple? Yes I do.

Kirsten wrote captions for her picture about summer.

Theme

Student Name

TOPIC	
TOPIC	Other
	Workbook
	Worksheet 2
	Worksheet 1
	Dialogue
	Beats
	Stories
	Picture Cards
	Word Cards
TOPIC	Other
	Workbook
	Worksheet 2
	Worksheet 1
	Dialogue
	Beats
	Stories
	Picture Cards
	Word Cards
TOPIC	Other
	Workbook
	Worksheet 2
	Worksheet 1
	Dialogue
	Beats
	Stories
	Picture Cards
	Word Cards
TOPIC	Other
	Workbook
	Worksheet 2
	Worksheet 1
	Dialogue
	Beats
	Stories
	Picture Cards
	Word Cards
TOPIC	Other
	Workbook
	Worksheet 2
	Worksheet 1
	Dialogue
	Beats
	Stories
	Picture Cards
	Word Cards

Student Name ____________________

	LISTENING	SPEAKING	READING	WRITING	OTHER NOTES
Topic ______ Component ______					
Topic ______ Component ______					
Topic ______ Component ______					
Topic ______ Component ______					
Topic ______ Component ______					

Techniques and Strategies

Refer to this section as you use the specific lessons for each Dictionary topic.

Words

Components: Picture Dictionary, Wall Chart, Cassette, Word and Picture Cards Reproducibles

Making word and picture cards

Photocopy the page so that cards can be colored and cut. To make sturdier cards, glue to poster board before cutting, or mount on index cards after cutting. If desired, laminate the cards. Many card games and activities work best with separate word and picture cards, but you can also make two-sided cards (words on one side, pictures on the other). Make a double-sided copy of the topic page; be careful to turn the book so that the words and pictures match up.

Getting Ready

- Display the Wall Chart. Listen to students' comments and ask questions to assess their prior knowledge.

  What do you see in this picture?
  What is this place?
  What's happening?, etc.

- Some students may ask questions *(What's that? What are they doing?,* etc.).

Listening

- Play the cassette or read each word so that students have a chance to listen to the pronunciation.
- During the reading, point to the object as it is named. The cassette contains enough space after each word for students to repeat the word.
- Invite individual students to take turns pointing.
- Divide the class into teams. Have team members take turns pointing to each object as it is named. For fun, make this into a game with scores.
- Evaluation: Have students open their books and point to each object as you call out the vocabulary words.

Speaking

- Replay the cassette, and ask the class to repeat each word as it is spoken. Then ask individual student volunteers to repeat the words.
- Have the class name each object as you point to it on the Wall Chart. Then give individual students a chance to do the same.
- Divide the class into teams. Have team members take turns pointing to and naming all the pictures.
- Evaluation: Circulate and point to specific objects in each student's book. Have students name the objects.
- Picture Card Project: Have students color and cut out the picture card Reproducibles. Practice language while you work. For example:

  First color the post office. Second, color the mailbox. Third ..., etc.
  What did you color first/second/third?
  What color is your/his/her mailbox?
  Who has a blue mailbox? How many people have blue mailboxes?

When the cards are finished, ask students to take turns placing their cards in the appropriate spaces on the Wall Chart in order to practice prepositional phrases. (The cards can be fastened temporarily with tape.)
Where does the mailbox go? (in front of the post office)

Where does the police officer go? (in the middle of the street)

- Play picture card games to reinforce vocabulary. (See the game ideas on this page.)

Reading

- Word Card Project: Have students make word cards to match the picture cards. Many of the same techniques used with the picture cards can also be used with the word cards. Have students repeat each word as they cut it out.

  What's that word again?
  What letter does it begin with?
  What letter does it end with?, etc.

  Invite students to match the words to the pictures on the Wall Chart or to the picture cards they have made. Continue to practice word-attack skills by using phonetic decoding and building sight-word vocabulary.

- Play games with word cards and/or picture cards to reinforce recognition of printed vocabulary. (See the game ideas on this page.)
- For a final "paste-up" project, make a poster or booklet with matching words and pictures.

Writing

- Have students write favorite words from the *Picture Dictionary* in a journal. Students can arrange these words by topic.
- Have students make personalized dictionaries with a page for every letter.
- Students can make their own personal word banks with index cards in an index file box or a shoe box. Have students make a card with a tab for every letter in the alphabet.
- New words that are not found in the Dictionary can also be added to word banks.
- Students can personalize their word banks or word journals by decorating cards or pages.

Word and Picture Card Games

The secret card: One student picks a card and stands in front of the class. Students take turns asking questions to figure out what the card is. The questions can be changed according to the level of the students. For example:
Is it a police officer? (No, it isn't./Yes, it is.)
More difficult:
Do you have a police officer? (No, I don't. / Yes, I do.)
More difficult:
Did you choose a police officer? (No, I didn't. / Yes, I did. I chose a police officer.)
More difficult:
Have you chosen a police officer? (No, I haven't. / Yes, I have chosen a police officer.)
The student who guesses correctly takes the next turn.

In a variation on this game, have two partners stand in front of the class. One student holds the secret card, and his/her partner knows what it is. The class directs questions to the partner who knows the card. For example:

Does he/she have a police officer? (No, he/she doesn't. / Yes, he/she does.)
Has he/she chosen a police officer? (No, he/she hasn't. / Yes, he/she has.)

You can also play this game by having a student sit in the front of the room, facing the class. Place the secret card on the Wall Chart so everyone but the student in front can see it. The student in front must ask questions, and the class answers in chorus. For example:

Is it a post office? (No, it isn't. / Yes, it is.)
Do you see a post office? (No, we don't. / Yes, we do.)

What's missing?: Place four or five cards on a ledge facing the class. Let one student come up and see the cards. That student then puts his or her back to the cards while another student removes one of them. The first student then asks questions.

Did you take away the mailbox? (No, I didn't. / Yes, I did. I took away the mailbox.)
Have you taken away the post office? (No, I haven't. / Yes, I have. I have taken away the post office.)

Word line-up: Line up the word cards on a chalkboard or easel ledge. Have students take turns choosing the correct word card as you call out the word.

Line up the word cards and the picture cards. Students can work with partners or individually. As you call out each word, the student picks the word card and matches it to the picture card. For pairwork, one partner picks the word card and the other picks the picture card.

Invite one student at a time to be the "word caller," while other students play, until all the cards have been removed from the ledge.

Adapting familiar card games: The cards can be used to play many familiar card games, and provide opportunities for students to use the words in conjunction with such additional verbs as *need/needed* or *find/found.*

"Concentration": Students can work with partners, in teams, or in groups of three or four for this game. Shuffle two sets of picture cards and lay them out facedown in rows. On each turn, a player turns over two cards. If the cards match, the player takes the pair. If there is no match, the cards are turned over again and everyone must remember where they are. Have players say the name of the picture each time a card is turned over.

The game can be adapted to use one set each of word and picture cards, or two pairs of word cards. Have students read each word card, or name each picture card. Sound out each word together if students need help matching the right word card to the picture card. If playing with word cards alone, use the opportunity to compare the cards by looking at each letter.

"Go Fish!": This game can have two players, or a small group. Use two, four, or six sets of cards shuffled together. Each student receives seven cards. Shuffle the remaining cards and lay them out facedown in a "fishing pool." The object of the game is to collect pairs. First, students take out the pairs they already have. In turn, they ask for matches for the single cards they hold. On each student's turn, he/she picks another student and asks, *Do you have a (ruler)?* If the answer is *yes,* the second student gives up the card and the first student gets the match. If the answer is *no,* the second student says, *No, I don't. Go fish!* The first student "fishes" for a card from the pool. If a match is made, he/she goes again. When everyone is out of cards, the player with the most pairs wins.

This game can be adapted to use either word- and picture-card pairs or word-card pairs, depending on the level of the students. Beginning readers may need help sounding out the words on the word cards.

Worksheet: Here's the Question! What's the answer?

This worksheet can be used at any point during or after the stories and dialogues. It involves all the skills — listening, speaking, reading, and writing — and it may be used with each of the 60 topics at any and all language levels, and in any and all verb tenses.

- Give each student a worksheet. Explain that the entire class is going to make up questions about the stories and/or the dialogues.
- Write the word *who* on the chalkboard. Model a question beginning with *Who* for the students, using the verb tense you wish to practice. Write the question on the board.
- Invite individual students to make up questions with *Who* as you write them on the board. If a question is grammatically incorrect, ask the class to help correct it.
- Ask for individual volunteers to answer the questions, and write their answers on the board. Ask for corrections from the class when necessary.
- Reread all the questions and answers and ask students to repeat them after you, either individually or as a group.
- Ask students to copy the question and answer they like best onto their worksheets. Advanced students may be able to work more independently and form their own questions and answers.
- Follow the same procedure for the other question words.
- As a review, divide the class into teams and have students take turns asking and answering questions, with or without worksheet prompting.

Here's the question. What's the answer?

1. Who ______________________________?

   ____

2. What ______________________________?

   ____

3. Where ______________________________?

   ____

4. When______________________________?

   ____

5. Why ______________________________?

   ____

6. How ______________________________?

   ____

Stories

Components: Picture Dictionary, Cassette, Stories Reproducibles

How to make story mini-books

Each of the four quadrants of the story page will become a page in the students' mini-books. Photocopy the story page. Fold the page in half so that story pages 1 and 4 are on one side, and pages 2 and 3 are on the other. Fold again so that pages 2 and 3 are on the inside. Students can color the pictures and take the books home.

Getting ready

- Look at the Wall Chart together. Take out the word and picture cards to review the words. Name each one together, placing either picture cards or word cards on the Wall Chart with students' help.

Listening

- Play the story section on the cassette, or read the story to the students. As children listen, point to the objects on the Wall Chart illustration that are mentioned in the story.
- Pantomime actions as necessary in order to aid student comprehension, and encourage students to join you.
- Discuss and explain the story as it progresses.
- Repeat the reading of the story as many times as you wish.

Speaking

- During the reading of the story, ask information questions using the question words *who, what, where, when, why,* and *how.* You may ask questions in any tense appropriate for the level of the students. For example:

  Where is Tommy going? (present continuous)
  Where does Tommy go? (present)
  Where did Tommy go? (past)
  Where was Tommy going when the taxi came? (past continuous)
  Where has Tommy gone? (present perfect)
  Where will Tommy go? (future)

Reading

- Give students their own copies of the story Reproducibles. Practice performing a choral reading with the cassette. After several choral readings, encourage individual students or pairs to take turns reading, prompting them whenever necessary.
- When students are familiar with the story, each one can illustrate a page. They can be added to make picture-book keepsakes. Picture books can consist of individual stories or a collection of stories from several topics.

Writing

- As a group, or with individual students, generate one or two more simple sentences to add to the story, on the same page or on a separate sheet. Some students may be advanced enough to retell the story in their own words. Have the class as a group write a retold story on chart paper, and have individual students help do some of the writing.
- The worksheet "Here's the question! What's the answer?" can be used at any time during the reading of the stories or dialogues. (See the worksheet instructions on this page xvii.)

Dialogues

Components: Wall Chart, Picture Dictionary, Cassette

Dialogues appear only in the *Teacher's Book* and not in the student materials, as they are meant to be listening exercises rather than reading exercises.

The following techniques can be used for any of the dialogues. You can find more specific ideas in the dialogue lesson for each *Picture Dictionary* illustration.

Because they are usually related to the stories, the dialogues may be either interspersed between the stories or done afterward.

Getting ready

- Look at the Wall Chart together. With students' help, describe the things that you can see, and name the characters that students will hear in the dialogue.

Listening

- Play the dialogue on the cassette while students listen. You may wish to interrupt the dialogue to question, discuss, or explain the dialogue, and to give students a chance to predict what will happen next.
- Replay the dialogue and question students on the content. Use whichever verb tense is appropriate for the level of the students. For example:

Why is Samantha saying that? (present continuous)
Why does Samantha say that? (present)
Why did Samantha say that? (past)
Why has Samantha said that? (present perfect)

Speaking

- Divide the class into two or three choral groups, one group for each character in the dialogue, and assign parts to each group.
- Choose a short segment from the dialogue to practice. lead each group in repeating the characters' lines. For example, if Tommy and Jim are having a conversation, model Tommy's first line. Have the "Tommy" group repeat it. Then say Jim's line and have the "Jim" group repeat it.
- Continue with the segment and practice it several times.
- When the groups become reasonably proficient, ask for two volunteers to role-play the dialogue as Tommy and Jim. Explain that they don't need to use the exact words from the dialogue. They may use their own words (with your help!). The play may be performed with two "Tommy"s and two "Jim"s, if students feel more comfortable that way. Encourage all students to perform. The dialogue can also be varied by reversing roles.
- More excerpts from the dialogues can be performed on the following days.

Reading

- If your students' reading skills warrant it, you may want to create a written script of a dialogue (or a portion of one) and have a "Reader's Theater" performance. Give each student a chance to read one of the character parts.

Writing

- The worksheet "Here's the question! What's the answer?" can be used at any time during the reading of the stories or dialogues. (See the worksheet instructions on page xvii.)

Beats!

Components: Cassette, Beats! Reproducibles

> **How to make Beats! mini-books**
> Photocopy the Beats! page. Fold the page in half so that Beats! pages 1 and 4 are on one side, and pages 2 and 3 are on the other. Fold again so that pages 2 and 3 are on the inside. Students can color the pictures and take their Beats! mini-books home.

Listening

- Play the cassette while students listen to the Beat. Show the *Beats!* Reproducibles book as an aid to comprehension.
- Play the Beat again, and encourage students to join in with the rhythm by clapping, snapping, or tapping, and repeating some of the words.

Speaking

- After the class hears the whole Beat, ask them to repeat each line as you say it. Keep the rhythm until they begin to feel comfortable with the rhythm and the words.
- Lead students through the entire Beat without repetition several times.
- Divide the class into two groups, one group for each character. Have each group perform their lines as you lead the rhythm and direct.
- Change the roles periodically so that groups can practice performing both of them. You may wish to divide the groups into boys and girls since the roles are often male/female. For fun, they can also perform the parts with the roles reversed.
- When the groups become proficient, ask for individual volunteers to perform as the Beat characters.
- Try tape-recording both group and individual performances. Many students love to hear their own voices on tape!

Reading

- Use the *Beats!* Reproducibles book at any time you deem appropriate during the lesson. Point to the words as the students perform, or ask students to identify specific words and specific passages.
- Make the Beats! mini-book. Give each student a photocopy of the illustrated Beats! page at any time during the lesson. The page may easily be folded into a "book" for the student to color, read, and practice.
- Using the *Beats!* Reproducibles book, try creating teams to do line-reading competitions.
- Set up a "Beats!" basket, and keep a few class copies of each Beats! mini-book in the basket. Add it to your class library so that children can read their Beats independently.

Literature

> **Theme Bibliographies**
> These literature ideas can be used with any book found in the annotated theme bibliographies at the beginning of each theme.

Getting ready

- Create a special reading area for your students and keep it filled with enticing literature selections. Baskets can be used to create a "portable reading center."
- Reinforce the concepts relating to how we hold and read a book written in English: front to back, top to bottom, left to right, beginning to end.
- Help students distinguish among letters, words, phrases, and sentences.
- Introduce your students to the words *author, illustrator,* and *illustration.*

Listening

- After the students are gathered and ready to begin, show them the story/poem you have chosen. Ask them what they see and what they think the story or poem is about.
- Read the selection all the way through while the students listen. Stop only briefly for questions or comments, to provide a complete listening experience. Try to save comments for the end of the reading.
- When you have finished, listen to the children's reactions and discuss the events and ideas.

Speaking

- Read the story/poem a second time, but this time stop at appropriate points to encourage questions and answers from the students. These may range from nonverbal reactions (such as pointing), to single words, to whole sentences.
- Encourage children to share events in their own lives suggested by the reading.
- Read the selection a third time. Move your finger under the words as you read and ask the children to join in wherever they can.
- Try an oral cloze technique. Leave specific words out of a sentence or phrase and see if the students can fill them in.
- More advanced students may enjoy memorizing parts of poems or play-acting stories, using their own words.

Reading

- Share the story/poem as many times as you wish.
- When the children are thoroughly familiar with the language, try written cloze exercises. On the chalkboard or chart paper, write words, phrases, or sentences from the reading. Read them together as you cover up letters, words, or phrases, and see if the students can guess what's underneath. Ask them to confirm their guesses: Does it make sense? Does it sound right? Does it begin with the right letter or letter cluster?
- Make word strips or sentence strips for students to match with sentences on the chalkboard or chart paper. Beginning readers can learn letter/sound correspondences in words and contexts they now know.
- Read the now-familiar selection together with students in a group reading.
- Provide an independent reading time.
- Have students read to you, or to each other in pairs. If they are not yet ready to read all the words, they can still benefit from retelling the story page by page in their own words.
- Let children pick books to take home so that they can share their reading with parents or friends.

Writing

- The same cloze techniques used for reading can be used for writing some of the words. As students are ready, have them write the missing word with help from you or from the class.
- Students can practice writing some of their favorite words from the story or poem and check their written words against the words in the book. These words can be added to a word bank or journal. (See "Writing" under Vocabulary: Presentation and Practice.)
- Give students a chance to retell in writing a favorite part of the story/poem — or to write and illustrate a related story about their own lives — either individually or as a group.
- A more advanced technique, which improves both oral and writing fluency, is to use some of the sentence patterns used by the author. Suggest a similarly patterned sentence to the students, and then compete to see who can create the most interesting or funniest sentence.

Worksheets

The worksheets in each topic can be in any order, independent of another. They can be done at any appropriate point when doing lessons for words, stories, dialogues, and Beats!

Activities

The activities section in each topic includes additional activities to enhance work with the components. Activities can be incorporated at any time in any of the lessons.

Theme 1: Me and My Family

Topic 1	Me	**Topic 4**	Big world!
Topic 2	My family	**Topic 5**	Where do you live?
Topic 3	Different faces		

Theme Bibliography

Chicken Sunday
written and illustrated by Patricia Polacco.
Paper Star Publishing, 1998. ISBN 0698116151
"Chicken Sundays" were those Sundays when Miss Eula, an African-American woman in Oakland, California, would fry chicken for her wonderful family dinners. The author, a Russian-American, recalls these special Sundays and weaves an ingenious story of interracial and intercultural friendship. While some paraphrasing of the story may be necessary for newcomers to English, the warm folk-art illustrations convey a rich cultural understanding of what makes up a true family.

Families: A Celebration of Diversity, Commitment, and Love
written by Aylette Jenness; photographs by the author.
Sandpiper/Houghton Mifflin Co., 1993.
ISBN 0395669529
This collection of personal stories from parents, children, and guardians celebrates the diversity that is reflected in your students' families. Most children will identify with the family stories and photo essays. You can encourage students to talk or write about the different faces that make up their families.

Family Pictures/Cuadros de Familia
written and illustrated by Carmen Lomas Garza.
English/Spanish. Children's Book Press, 1998.
ISBN 0892391529
In My Family/En Mi Familia
written and illustrated by Carmen Lomas Garza.
English/Spanish. Children's Book Press, 1996.
ISBN 0892391383
The vivid stories in these companion books convey the life of the author/illustrator, who grew up in a Mexican-American family in Texas. Each vignette is printed in both English and Spanish, and is accompanied by a photograph. These books are particularly recommended for classrooms with Latino students.

Fathers, Mothers, Sisters, Brothers: A Collection of Family Poems
written by Mary Ann Hoberman;
illustrated by Marylin Hafner.
Puffin Books, 1993. ISBN 0140548491
These twenty-six, lively, happy, and sometimes serious poems present all kinds of families and family life. You can find many of the Theme 1 vocabulary words in a number of these poems. In addition, the repetitive and cumulative structure of some poems provide many opportunities to reinforce language learning. These can also be used with various topics throughout the Picture Dictionary.

Father's Rubber Shoes
written and illustrated by Yumi Heo.
Orchard Books, 1995. ISBN 0531068730
Yungsu is a homesick young boy from Korea. His feelings of loneliness and dislocation match those of many children who emigrate to America. When his parents encourage him make friends, he begins by sharing his Korean food with another boy. Although the pictures may be somewhat abstract for very young children, they allow primary students to identify with Korean family life in our country. The vignettes about school, household items, and food help foster language acquisition.

How My Family Lives in America
by Susan Kuklin.
Simon & Schuster Children's Books, 1992.
ISBN 0027512398
Food and family life are the common themes in this photo essay. In this book, the author profiles three families, and shows how each family's distinct heritage influences their adaptation to American life. The expressive photographs can be matched with many of the word/picture cards to extend language acquisition. Family recipes are also provided as an added bonus.

If You Were Born A Kitten

written by Marion Dane Bauer;
illustrated by JoEllen McAllister Stammen.
Simon & Schuster Children's Books, 1997.
ISBN 0689801114

This book depicts twelve types of births, beginning with the birth of a kitten and ending with the birth of a human baby. Each accompanying description uses the construction, "If you were born ..." The repetitive language structure, along with the clear illustrations, make this book especially useful for read-aloud and read-along activities. This book may be used again with the Theme 7 topics (see pages 201-222).

I Like Me!

written and illustrated by Nancy Carlson.
Sundance Publications, 1996. ISBN 9996136914

This book is an excellent choice for helping children to learn to read, listen, and talk about themselves. *I Like Me!* has all the hallmarks of an easy reader: simple language and repetitive language structure. It is available in big-book format so you can read it aloud to the class. You may also wish to record the text so children can read along individually.

The Leaving Morning

written by Angela Johnson;
illustrated by David Soman.
Orchard Books, 1996. ISBN 0531070727

This portrait of inner-city apartment living is easy to read aloud to the class. It reaches children who are moving to a new home, especially children new to this country. The vocabulary is simple enough for emerging English-language learners, and the descriptive language is easy to paraphrase. Combining the book's sentence structure with your own reading strategies can help children either read along with you or read on their own.

One Hundred is A Family

written by Pam Munoz Ryan;
illustrated by Benrei Huang.
Disney Press, 1998. ISBN 078680405X

This illustrated poem provides a unique opportunity to combine learning numbers with learning about family life. The author counts—by ones and by tens—the loves, friendships, traditions, and communities that make up a family. The illustrations help students understand unfamiliar words, so they can move successfully to both partnered and individualized reading.

The Relatives Came

written by Cynthia Rylant;
illustrated by Stephen Gammell.
Aladdin Paperbacks, 1993. ISBN 0689717385

The relatives arrive for a gathering in the country. They enjoy themselves and are reluctant to leave. But who are they? We're never quite told. Students can work in small groups to retell the story in their own words, using word and picture cards to identify the different relatives. The animated illustrations provide additional context and can prompt children to incorporate new words into their everyday language.

The Wednesday Surprise

written by Eve Bunting;
illustrated by Donald Carrick.
Clarion Books, 1990. ISBN 0395547768

Anna and Grandma's "Wednesday surprise" is the gift of literacy. On Wednesdays, Grandma watches her school-age granddaughter, Anna, who in turn teaches her to read. You can use Anna's first-person narrative to prompt children to talk about their relationships with their family elders. The language patterns in the dialogue can be incorporated into role plays and small group discussions.

When I Am Old With You

written by Angela Johnson;
illustrated by David Soman.
Orchard Books, 1993. ISBN 0531070352

A young boy and his grandfather dream aloud about what they will do as they grow old together. The words and pictures work seamlessly to promote students' understanding. Students can use the repetitive structure "When I am old, I/we will ..." in building their own sentences.

Me

Content	Language
Making friends First and last names Ages	Exchanging greetings: *Hello, my name is Davy. What's your name? Hi, I'm Carol. Who are you?* Identifying first and last names: *What is his first name? My last name is Lawrence. What's his last name?* Exchanging salutations: *Hello, how are you? I'm fine, thank you. Nice to meet you.* Using numbers (one to ten) in reference to age: *I'm six years old. She's seven.*

The illustrations show the five main characters in the book. Tommy is a friendly five-year-old Caucasian boy. He is curious about everything. Ting is a smiling and outgoing seven-year-old Asian girl. She likes to be a leader. Diego is a six-year-old Hispanic boy who tries to appear very manly in all situations. Alison is a sweet, shy six-year-old Caucasian girl who is usually very correct about everything. Zoe, a seven-year-old African-American girl, is a good sport and lots of fun. Sometimes she can be a bit of a busybody.

Words

Tommy
Ting
Diego
Alison
Zoe

Additional Words

me
hello
hi
boy
girl
you
I
age
years
old
name
nickname

Words

Components: Topic 1 Wall Chart, Picture Dictionary (pp. 2–3), Cassette, Word and Picture Cards (Topic 1).

See page xiv for techniques and strategies for presenting and practicing words.

Me

Tommy Diego Zoe
Ting Alison

Notes

Play a name game. Begin by asking the children to raise their hands when they hear their names. Then call each child's name in turn. When everyone has had a chance, tell them it's their turn to say their own name. Point to each child in turn, encouraging each one to say his or her name aloud. This game helps the children to learn each other's names and gradually become less shy with their classmates. When the children have become familiar with each other's names, ask them to go around the circle introducing both themselves and the person next to them. Model the phrases: *I am ________. This is ________.*

Workbook page

Many children have a stock picture that they draw to represent themselves, but you may want to suggest that they look in the mirror before they begin. For children who are just learning to write, print their names and their ages (using numerals) for them and encourage them to trace over your writing.

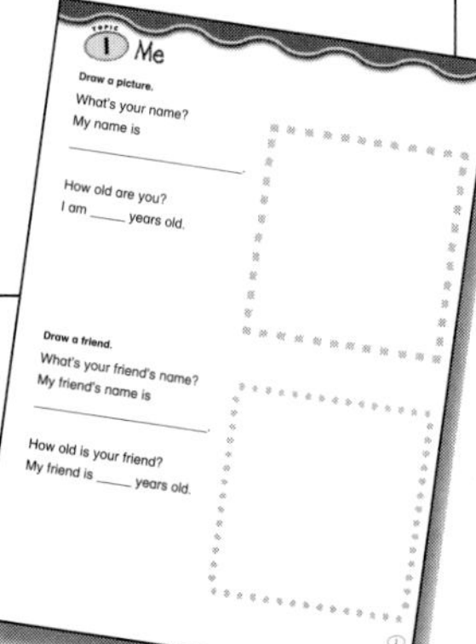

Stories

Components: Picture Dictionary (pp. 2–3), Cassette, Story (Topic 1)

See page xviii for techniques and strategies for presenting and practicing stories.

This is Alison.
Alison is her first name.
Her last name is Matthews.
She is six years old.

This is Ting.
Her last name is Cheng.
Ting Cheng.
She is seven years old.

This is Zoe.
Her last name is Jackson.
Zoe Jackson.
She is seven years old, too.

His name is Tommy Young.
He's five.

His name is Diego Lopez.
He's six.

Story notes

This is a good opportunity for children to practice exchanging greetings and introducing one another.

Ask about the story:
Who is this boy? Who is he? Is he Tommy? What is his first name? What is his last name? Is this boy's first name Diego? How old is he? Is this boy Tommy or Diego? Is this girl Zoe Jackson?

Ask about your students:
What's your name? Is your name ________? What is your first name? Is ________ your first name or your last name? What is her last name? How old are you?

Dialogue

Components: Cassette, Topic 1 Wall Chart, Picture Dictionary (pp. 2–3).

See page xix for techniques and strategies for presenting and practicing dialogues.

Narrator:	What's your name?
Zoe:	My name is Zoe.
Narrator:	What's your last name?
Zoe:	Jackson. Zoe Jackson, that's me!
Narrator:	How old are you?
Zoe:	I'm seven.
Narrator:	Hello!
Ting:	Hello! I'm Ting. Ting Cheng. Ting is my first name. Cheng is my last name. I'm seven years old.
Narrator:	Who are you?
Diego:	Diego. Diego Lopez. First name Diego. Last name Lopez.
Narrator:	How old are you?
Diego:	Six.
Alison:	How do you do?
Narrator:	How do you do?
Alison:	My name is Alison Matthews. I'm six years old.
Tommy:	Hi! I'm Tommy.
Narrator:	Hello, Tommy!
Tommy:	My real name is Thomas. Thomas Young. Tommy is my nickname. I'm five.
Narrator:	Nice to meet you!

Dialogue notes

Gather the children in a circle, and model the dialogue questions and answers. *What's your name? My name is ____. What is your first name? What's your last name? My first/last name is ____. How old are you? I'm _____. You are ____ years old.* Then ask the children to work in pairs practicing the phrases. Invite volunteers to invent dialogues with their own names and ages.

Beats!

Components: Cassette, Beats! (Topic 1).

See page xx for techniques and strategies for presenting and practicing Beats!

Hi! I'm Pete.
What's your name?
    My name is Joe.
Hello!
    Hello!

How old are you?
    Take a guess!

Are you five?
    No, no, no.
Are you six?
    No, no, no.

Are you seven?
    Yes! Yes! Yes!

Beat notes

Divide the class into two groups, one group to play Pete and one to play Joe. Perform the Beat in groups first, then in pairs. Then have the children replace Joe's and Pete's names with their own, and encourage them to walk around the room and greet each other.

Worksheets

Worksheet 1: Me (p. 1)

Have the children practice saying aloud the questions and answer phrases presented. Ask one child, *What is your name?* When that child has answered with a full sentence *(My name is _______)*, turn to a second child and ask, *What is his/her name?* Prompt the full-sentence answer *(His/Her name is ________)*. Then have the first child ask the same questions of two classmates. Continue in this way until everyone has had a chance to ask and answer. If needed, explain that the speech bubble shows what the boy in the picture is saying.

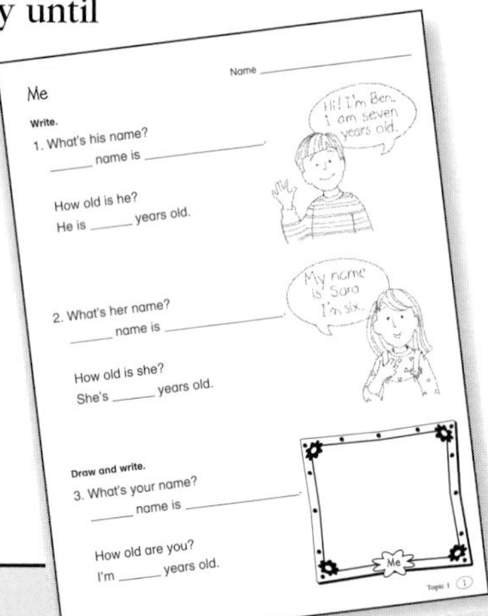

Name ____________

Me

Write.

1. What's his name?
   ______ name is ____________.

   How old is he?
   He is _____ years old.

2. What's her name?
   ______ name is ____________.

   How old is she?
   She's _____ years old.

Draw and write.

3. What's your name?
   ______ name is ____________.

   How old are you?
   I'm _____ years old.

Topic 1 (1)

Worksheet 2: Me (p. 2)

Write the first and last names of a famous or familiar person on the board or on chart paper. Say the full name aloud, and then underline the first name and say, *This is her/his first name.* Ask several students in turn, *What's your first name?* Then, on the board, circle the last name and say, *This is her/his last name.* Ask several students in turn, *What's your last name?* Help students who are learning to write fill in the missing words on the page. You might write the words *first, last, years, old, he, his, she, her, name,* and *my,* for the children to copy.

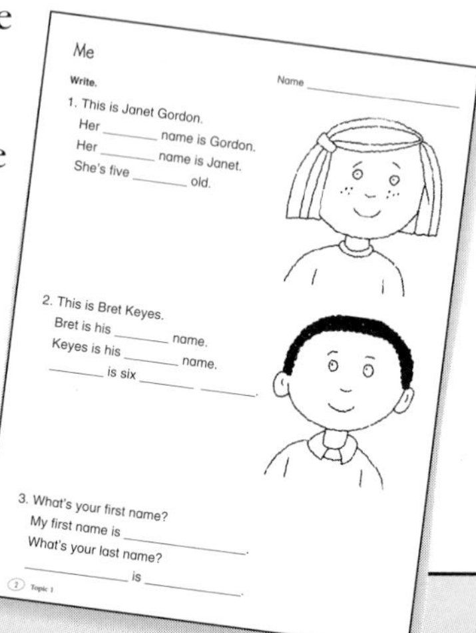

Me

Write.

Name ____________

1. This is Janet Gordon.
   Her ______ name is Gordon.
   Her ______ name is Janet.
   She's five ______ old.

2. This is Bret Keyes.
   Bret is his ______ name.
   Keyes is his ______ name.
   ______ is six ______ ______.

3. What's your first name?
   My first name is ____________.
   What's your last name?
   ________ is ____________.

(2) Topic 1

Activities

- Teach a naming song, to the tune of "Are You Sleeping?" ("Frère Jacques"). Make a chart of the song's words and touch each word as you sing. You might alternate voices (teacher and children, or two groups of children) whenever a line repeats.

  Where is _____? (student name)
  Where is _____?
  　Here I am!
  　Here I am!
  How are you this morning?
  How are you this morning?
  　I am fine!
  　I am fine!

  Expand this activity by replacing some of the words in the song with the words of the child's native language.

- Take a close-up photo of each child's face. Mat the photo and write the name of the child on the back. Write each child's first and last name on a card. Ask children to match the name to the picture. Continue to provide language models by saying: *Who is this? What's his/her name? Is this _____? Yes, it's _____. No it's not ____. Is this _____ or _____?* After this activity, use the photos in a display or hang them as part of a mobile.

- Ask children to bring in photographs of themselves at an earlier age for comparisons. Ask a child, *How old were you in this picture? How old are you now?*

- Roll out a long strip of paper and ask each child to lie down while you outline his or her body with pencil. Then encourage them to go over the pencil line with markers and add details: facial features, hair, and clothing. Use these pictures in a classroom mural. Have the children write their names under their pictures. Ask children: *Who is this? What's his/her name?*

TOPIC
2 My family

Content

- Family members
- Family relationships
- Family size

Language

- Identifying family members and relationships: *Tommy has a brother named Jim. Zoe is Marcus's sister. Their parents are Mr. and Mrs. Jackson.*
- Using comparative and superlative adjectives to describe relative ages: *Grandfather is the oldest person in my family. He is older than my grandmother. Jasmin is younger than Diego. Baby Rosa is the youngest person in Diego's family.*
- Using comparative and superlative adjectives to describe family size: *Diego and Ting have big families. Diego has the biggest family. Tommy has a small family. Who has the smallest family?*
- Describing family size using the numbers one to twenty: *There are ten people in Diego's family. There are three people in Tommy's family.*
- Asking and answering *how many* questions: *How many sisters do you have? I have one sister. How many brothers does he have? He has three brothers.*

The illustration presents the families of the five children featured in this book. Ting has a father, a mother, an eleven-year-old older brother named Henry, and two five-year-old younger twin brothers, Jo-Jo and Jackie. Jackie is hearing-impaired and wears a hearing aid. Their family name is Cheng. Alison has a mother and a stepfather. Their family name is Matthews. Tommy has a mother and a seven-year-old brother, Jim. Their family name is Young. Diego is shown with his extended family: mother, father, five-year-old sister Jasmin, grandmother and grandfather (father's parents), aunt and uncle (father's brother), cousin Vanessa, and a baby cousin, Rosa.

Words

1. sister
2. brother
3. mother
4. father
5. parents
6. children
7. grandmother
8. grandfather
9. aunt
10. uncle
11. cousins
12. baby

Additional Words

grandma
grandpa
grandparents
stepmother
stepfather
twins
younger
youngest
older
oldest

Words

Components: Topic 2 Wall Chart, Picture Dictionary (pp. 4–5), Cassette, Word and Picture Cards (Topic 2).

See page xiv for techniques and strategies for presenting and practicing words.

My family

1. sister	5. parents	9. aunt
2. brother	6. children	10. uncle
3. mother	7. grandmother	11. cousins
4. father	8. grandfather	12. baby

Notes

Encourage the children to practice using the words while following directions for coloring and cutting out the picture cards. Model sentences they can use: *Color the mother first. Who are you coloring? This is the mother. Color Diego's cousins.* Then ask students to arrange the picture cards to show comparisons between similar groups of people. First have them arrange the cards in response to *Which family is big/bigger/biggest?* Then ask the children to look at each family and respond to specific questions, such as: *Who is older, Diego or Jasmin? Who is the oldest child in Diego's family?*

Workbook page

Review the words for members of a family with the children. Suggest that students use their word cards as a reference, or write the words on the board. Then tell the children to draw a picture of their own family in the frame and label each member, either by given name or by family position.

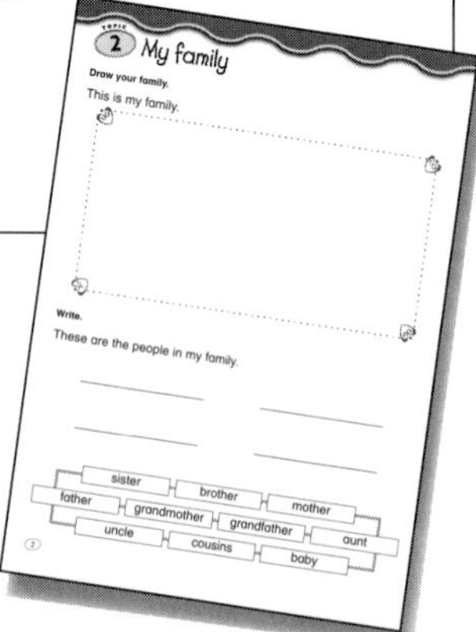

Stories

Components: Picture Dictionary (pp. 4–5), Cassette, Story (Topic 2).

See page xviii for techniques and strategies for presenting and practicing stories.

Diego has a big family.
He has a sister.
Her name is Jasmin.
Diego is her brother.

Diego has two parents.
He has a mother and a father.
Diego's father has parents, too.
They are Diego's grandmother and grandfather.

Diego has an aunt and uncle.
Diego's aunt and uncle have two children.
They are Diego's cousins.
One cousin is a baby.

What a nice family!

Story notes

Refer to the Wall Chart and help the children count the number of people in each family. Then focus on Diego's family, and point to each family member as you read the story.

Ask about the story:
Who do you see in the picture? Does Diego have a sister? Does Diego have a brother? Do Diego and Jasmin have a grandmother? Do they have a big family or a small family? How many parents does Diego have? Who are Diego's cousins?

Ask about your students:
Do you have a sister? How old is your brother? Are you older than your cousin? How many people are in your family? Is your family a big or a small family? Do you have a big family or a small family?

Dialogue

Components: Cassette, Topic 2 Wall Chart, Picture Dictionary (pp. 4–5).

See page xix for techniques and strategies for presenting and practicing dialogues.

Tommy:	Do you have any brothers, Diego?
Diego:	No. I have a sister. She's younger.
Tommy:	What's her name?
Diego:	Jasmin.
Tommy:	I have a brother. He's older.
Diego:	What's his name?
Tommy:	Jim. Who else is in your family?
Diego:	My grandparents. They live with us.
Tommy:	I have a grandma and grandpa, too, but they don't live with us.
Diego:	My aunt and uncle live with us, too. And my cousins.
Tommy:	How many cousins do you have?
Diego:	Two.
Tommy:	Are they fun?
Diego:	No. One is a baby, and the other one is a girl!

Dialogue notes

Discuss the exchanges between Tommy and Diego about Diego's sister. Start and stop the tape three or four times, and ask the students to repeat the lines with you. Then prompt them to ask one another questions based on the exchange: *Does Diego have a sister? What is Diego's sister's name? Is she younger or older than Diego?*

Beats!

Components: Cassette, Beats (Topic 2).

See page xx for techniques and strategies for presenting and practicing Beats!

Do you have any brothers?
Yes, I do.

How many brothers?
I have two.

Do you have any sisters?
No, not me.
I don't have any.

I have three!

Beat notes

Divide the group in half to practice this Beat as written. Then have the children form a circle and practice round-robin style, eliciting true responses. Be sure to keep the rhythm. Have the first child turn and ask his or her neighbor, *Do you have any brothers?* If the answer is *No, not me,* the child responding becomes the questioner, and turns to the next child to begin the pattern again. If the answer to the first question is *Yes, I do,* the first child should ask the second question, *How many brothers?* The child responding answers that question *(I have ______)* and becomes the questioner.

After completing the circle, you could repeat the pattern with a question about another family member, for example, *Do you have an uncle?*

Worksheets

Worksheet 1: My family (p. 3)

Refer to the picture of Ting and her family on the Wall Chart. As you point, identify each person in terms of the relationship to Ting. For example: *This is Ting's mother. This is Ting's father. These are Ting's brothers. This is Ting's family.* Ask: *Does Ting have any sisters? Does Ting have any brothers?* Now direct the students' attention to the worksheet. Help them complete the sentences regarding the picture of Tommy's family. To make it easier for them to complete the section on friends, help them practice asking questions about families (*Do you have any brothers? Do you have a sister?*).

My family

Name ____________

Fill in the blanks.

This is Tommy's family.

There are three people in Tommy's ____________.
Tommy has one ____________.
He doesn't have any ____________.
He has a ____________.

Ask a friend.
Write about your friend's family.

____________ has ____________.
____________ has ____________.
____________ doesn't have ____________.

Topic 2 3

Worksheet 2: My family (p. 4)

You might want to invite the children to work with a partner on this worksheet. Have them ask each other the first three questions. Then ask them to show their pictures to their partners and describe their families aloud. You may want to write the words: *there, are, family, big, small, sister,* and *brother,* for the children to refer to as they write the answers and fill in the missing words.

My family

Name ____________

Answer the questions.

How many people are in your family?
____
Do you have a big family or a small family?
____
Do you have any brothers or sisters?
____

Draw your family.

Write about your family.

There are ________ people in my family.
I have ____________
____________.

4 Topic 2

Activities

- Do a finger puppet song. Children can draw and color finger puppets for different family members, cut them out, and tape them to their fingers. Sing to the tune of "Are You Sleeping?"

  Where is Mother?
  Where is Mother?
  Here I am!
  Here I am!
  How are you this morning?
  How are you this morning?
  I am fine.
  I am fine.

  As the child responds with *Here I am,* he or she wiggles the finger with the appropriate puppet.

- Invite children to try on clothing and use props from the dress-up corner to role-play different family members. Ask each child to tell you who he or she is. Take this opportunity to ask the children questions about relationships within a family.

- Ask children to draw pictures of their families, including those they share a home with as well as siblings, aunts, uncles, cousins, and grandparents that live far away. Encourage them to dictate or write something about the people in their families. Be sensitive to children's feelings about discussing their family situation.

Different faces

Content

- Physical appearance
- Parts of the face and head
- Loose teeth

Language

- Identifying physical features: *I have two eyes; so do you. We both have hair. She has two eyes, a nose, and a mouth.*
- Using adjectives to describe physical appearances: *Diego has brown eyes. Tommy's nose is little. Alison has light skin. Ting's hair is black.*
- Describing size differences: *short, shorter, tall, taller, big,* and *little. Zoe is bigger than Alison. Tommy is not as big as Zoe. Diego is the tallest.*
- Using proper placement of adjectives (both before the noun and after the verb *to be*): *She has blond hair. Her hair is blond.*
- Introducing the use of apostrophe plus *s* to form possessives: *Diego's nose is big. Ting's hair is black.*

Words

1. eyes
2. ears
3. nose
4. mouth
5. tooth/teeth
6. chin
7. eyelashes
8. skin
9. hair
10. straight
11. curly
12. glasses

Additional Words

cheeks
forehead
eyebrows
lips
blue
brown
black
blond
long
short
big
little
tall

The five children, Zoe, Ting, Alison, Tommy, and Diego, are all happily comparing their faces. The girls are admiring one another. Zoe has removed her eyeglasses (which she hates!) and is laughing at herself. Diego and Tommy are playfully commenting on each other's faces. Diego is admiring himself in the mirror. He is proud of his two new white teeth and his big chin. Tommy is pulling at his own ears, wondering if they really are too big.

Words

Components: Topic 3 Wall Chart, Picture Dictionary (pp. 6–7), Cassette, Word and Picture Cards (Topic 3).

See page xiv for techniques and strategies for presenting and practicing words.

Different faces

1. eyes	5. tooth/teeth	9. hair
2. ears	6. chin	10. straight
3. nose	7. eyelashes	11. curly
4. mouth	8. skin	12. glasses

Notes

Invite the children to color the picture cards, using their own features as the model for eye, hair, and skin colors. Provide language models by saying: *Your hair is curly. My nose is short. His/her eyes are brown.* Prompt the children to point out the features and characteristics that make each of them unique, and to identify the similarities that tie all humans together. *My hair is brown and your hair is blond. We both have hair.* This is a good opportunity to encourage the children to appreciate diversity by comparing physical characteristics.

Workbook page

Ask the children to point to each word in the word box as you read it aloud. Then tell them that each word is a label for the pictures above. Direct their attention to the picture of the boy, and say the word *hair*. Ask, *Which line points to his hair?* Then say, *Write the word* hair *in the box with the line that points to his hair.* Allow children who don't yet write to dictate the correct word for each feature.

Stories

Components: Picture Dictionary (pp. 6–7), Cassette, Story (Topic 3).

See page xviii for techniques and strategies for presenting and practicing stories.

Diego has brown eyes.
Tommy has green eyes.
Diego's nose is big.
Tommy's nose is little.

Alison has light skin.
Zoe has dark skin.
Alison's hair is blond.
Ting's hair is black.

Diego has two big teeth.
They're new.
Tommy has one little tooth.
It's loose!

Everyone has two eyes,
two ears, one nose,
and one mouth,
but everyone has a different face!

Story notes

Talk together about the ways people look alike and the ways they look different.

Ask about the story:
Whose eyes are brown? Who has green eyes? Whose skin is light? Which child has blond hair? What color is Ting's hair? How many new teeth does Diego have?

Compare and name the characters. Provide descriptive clues and use sentences in discussion as models: *This girl has black hair and glasses. Her hair is curly. Is this Ting or Zoe?*

Ask about your students:
What color are your eyes? What color eyes do you have? What color is your hair? What color is your skin?

Ask children to draw pictures of themselves. Encourage them to show their pictures to the other children and use the vocabulary and language of the topic to describe themselves.

Dialogue

Components: Cassette, Topic 3 Wall Chart, Picture Dictionary (pp. 6–7).

See page xix for techniques and strategies for presenting and practicing dialogues.

Alison:	We all have different faces! I have blue eyes and you have brown eyes, Zoe.
Zoe:	Yup, and Ting's nose is little, and my nose is big.
Ting:	I like Zoe's hair. It's curly. My hair is straight.
Alison:	Your eyelashes are long, Zoe. They're pretty.
Zoe:	I'm not pretty with my glasses on!
Alison:	Yes, you are! I like your glasses.
Ting:	We're all pretty!
Diego:	I have a big chin.
Tommy:	You have a big mouth.
Diego:	You have big ears.
Tommy:	No, I don't. They just look big because I'm little.

Dialogue notes

Describe yourself to your students to model language: *I have ______ hair and ______ eyes.* Surprise your students by asking them to draw a picture of your face. Then ask your students to describe themselves. Ask questions and use sentences as models as you help them compare themselves to someone else: *Are you bigger or smaller than ______? My hair is straight. Is your hair straight? My hair is straight and your hair is curly.*

Beats!

Components: Cassette, Beats! (Topic 3).

See page xx for techniques and strategies for presenting and practicing Beats!

His nose is red.
His hair is green.
He's the funniest man
I've ever seen!

His ears are yellow.
His eyes are pink.
What's his name?
Mr. Rinky-Dink!

Her nose is orange.
Her hair is blue.
Her mouth is purple.
Her teeth are, too.

Who is this funny woman?
Who do you think?
What's her name?
Mrs. Rinky-Dink!

Beat notes

Make Rinky-Dink masks. Cut out of colored construction paper the features identified in the Beat: red and orange noses, green and blue hair, pink eyes, purple mouth and teeth. Give each child two paper plates and a complete set of facial features. Help them to glue the pieces to paper plates as they practice the Beat aloud. Allow them time to complete the masks by adding such details as a mouth for Mr. Rinky-Dink and eyes for Mrs. Rinky-Dink. Then repeat the Beat, pointing to each feature as it is described. Children might want to wear the mask and take turns acting out Mr. and Mrs. Rinky-Dink while their classmates recite the Beat. Display the paper masks around the room.

Worksheets

Worksheet 1: Different faces (p. 5)

Hold up an object that is brown and ask: *What color is this? What else do you see in the room that is this color?* Continue until you have reviewed all the color words used in this exercise. Compare an illustration of Zoe to one of Alison to review the words *curly, straight,* and *blond* for describing hair, and *light* and *dark* for describing skin. Read aloud the words at the bottom of the page, and suggest that if the question refers to eyes they will find words used to describe eyes in the group labeled *eyes.*

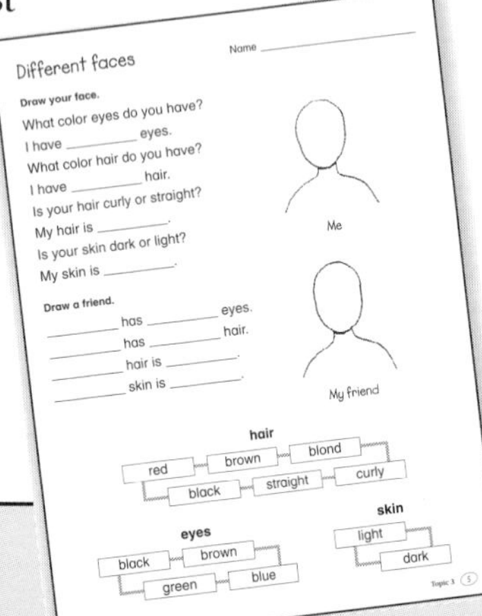

Different faces

Name ______

Draw your face.

What color eyes do you have?
I have ______ eyes.
What color hair do you have?
I have ______ hair.
Is your hair curly or straight?
My hair is ______.
Is your skin dark or light?
My skin is ______.

Me

Draw a friend.

______ has ______ eyes.
______ has ______ hair.
______ hair is ______.
______ skin is ______.

My friend

hair

red brown blond black straight curly

eyes

black brown green blue

skin

light dark

Topic 3 5

Worksheet 2: Different faces (p. 6)

Point to each of the children in the illustration on pages 6–7 of the Dictionary. Ask: *Who is this?* or *Is this Zoe or Ting?* When all of the children have been identified, encourage the students to color the uncompleted images on the page. You may want to write the words *straight, curly, glasses, red, black, brown,* and *blond* for the students to refer to as they work. Then ask the students to show their pictures and talk about them, for example: *This is Zoe. She has dark skin and curly hair.*

Different faces

Name ______

Color the hair and eyes.

Diego Zoe Ting Tommy Alison

1. What color hair does Diego have?
Diego has ______ ______.
2. Does Zoe have straight hair or curly hair?
Zoe has ______ ______.
3. Does Alison have red hair?
______
4. Does Ting have straight hair?
______
5. Who wears glasses?
______

6 Topic 3

Activities

- Make a chart to show the distribution of specific features, such as eye or hair color, among your students. Then model statements based on the chart: *Five people have brown eyes and three people have blue eyes.* Ask questions about the charts to elicit sentences: *How many people have brown eyes? How many more people have brown eyes than blue eyes?*

- Introduce a variation of the song "Head, Shoulders, Knees, and Toes." First, have children repeat after you as you point to the body part mentioned: *This is my head. These are my eyes.* Then repeat the song, pointing to each feature as you say it, for example:

  Eyes, ears, teeth, and mouth, teeth and mouth.
  Eyes, ears, teeth, and mouth, teeth and mouth.
  Eyes and ears and teeth and mouth.
  Eyes, ears, teeth, and mouth,
  teeth and mouth.

  Begin slowly. As students come to know the words, speed up the rhythm. Then ask the children to make up other verses using the other vocabulary words.

- Measure and record the height of each child. Help children measure a strip of paper or a string that is the same length as their height. Label the paper or strip with names. Hang them on the wall in order from the shortest to the tallest. Encourage the children to discuss height differences: *Who is tallest? Who is shortest? Is _____ taller or shorter than ______?*

- Cut a collection of facial "parts" from magazines, such as *eyes, ears, lips, chins, beards, mustaches, noses, eyebrows,* and so forth. After you've identified and discussed the features together, ask the children to glue the cutouts onto the page to make a complete face.

Big world!

Content

- Maps
- Continents and oceans
- Locations of countries
- Places of origin

Language

- Using a map to identify and name continents and oceans: *This is the Atlantic Ocean. Europe is next to Africa.*
- Asking and answering *where* questions: *Where is Peru? Peru is in South America.*
- Asking and answering questions about place of origin: *Where were you born? I was born in China. They were born in the USA. Where is your family from? His family is from Peru.*

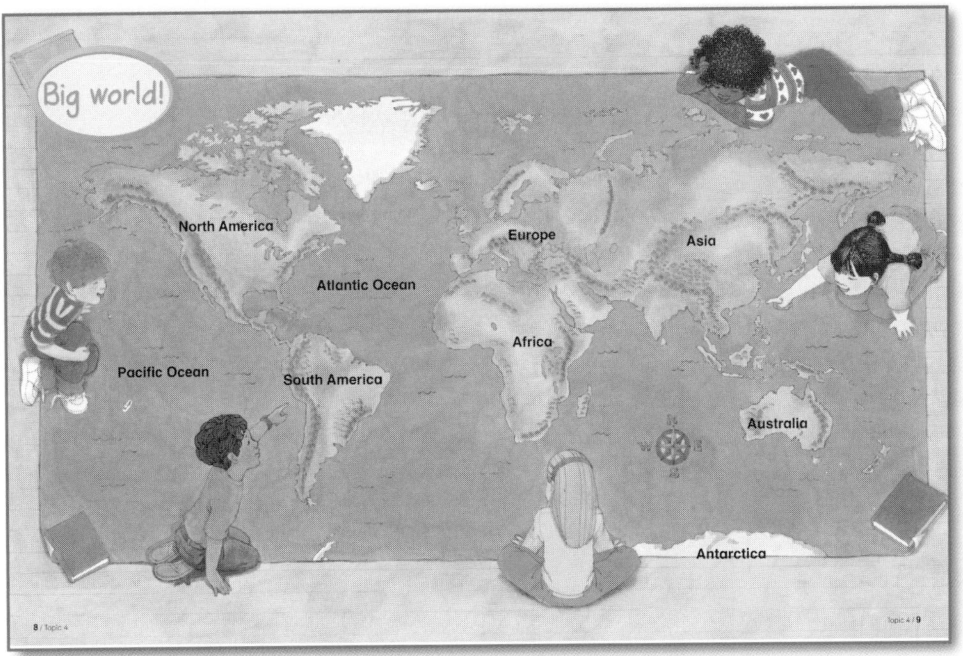

The scene depicts a large map of the world spread out on the floor. Tommy, Diego, Ting, Zoe, and Alison are gathered around the map. Diego is pointing at the South American continent because he is from Peru. Ting is pointing at China, in the continent of Asia. Ting and her family moved to the United States from China. Alison, Tommy, and Zoe were all born in the United States, in the continent of North America.

Words

North America
South America
Europe
Asia
Africa
Australia
Antarctica
Atlantic Ocean
Pacific Ocean

Additional Words

map
world
land
continent
ocean
born
Peru
Peruvian
China
Chinese
United States of America
USA
American

Words

Components: Topic 4 Wall Chart, Picture Dictionary (pp. 8–9), Cassette, Word and Picture Cards (Topic 4).

See page xiv for techniques and strategies for presenting and practicing words.

Big world!

North America	Asia	Atlantic Ocean
South America	Africa	Pacific Ocean
Europe	Australia	
	Antarctica	

Notes

Show the children as many different kinds of maps as you can to broaden their understanding of the concept of mapping. If possible, compare the map in the Dictionary illustration with a globe, pointing out its three-dimensional representation of the oceans and continents identified in the opening of this topic. The lesson may be extended to include the names of any countries that the children have come from or are familiar with. You may also want to introduce other words to describe the world shown on the map: *north, south, east, west, the equator, continent, the North Pole,* and *the South Pole.*

Workbook page

Invite the children to look at this map of the world, and to compare it to both the map in the Dictionary and other world maps. Ask for a volunteer to point to a part of the map that is an ocean. Ask a second volunteer to show which parts of the map are the continents. Review the words on the page. Then have students label the map with the appropriate numbers.

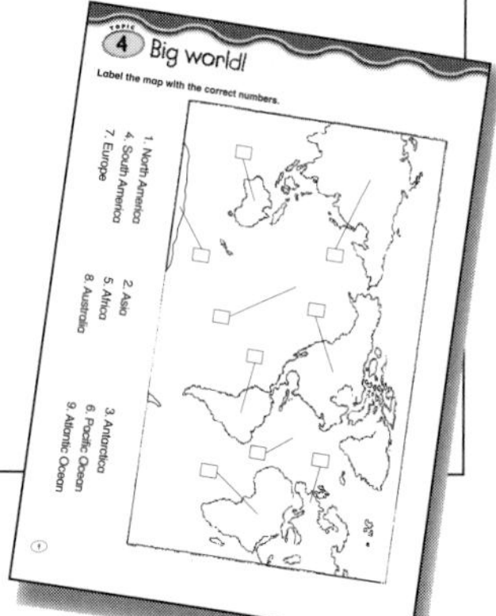

Stories

Components: Picture Dictionary (pp. 8–9), Cassette, Story (Topic 4).

See page xviii for techniques and strategies for presenting and practicing stories.

This is a map of the whole world.
It shows the land and the water.
It shows the continents
and the oceans.

It shows where people come from.
Where is Diego from?
He is from Peru.
Peru is in South America.

Where is Ting from?
She is from China.
She was born there.
China is in Asia.

Where are Zoe and Tommy from?
And where is Alison from?
They were all born in the
United States of America!

Story notes

Discuss the basic concept of mapping. If needed, make a simple map of the classroom on a piece of chart paper to reinforce the concept. Ask: *What is a map? What does a map show? How many continents are there?*

Ask about the story:
Where is Diego from? Where did Diego's family come from? Where was Ting born? Where is Peru? What continent is China in? Who was born in the United States of America?

Ask about the students:
This story presents an opportunity for the student to talk about her or his family's country and continent of origin and to find the locations on a map of the world. Model questions children can ask one another: *Where were you born? Where did you come from? Where is your family from?* Ask each child to say where a classmate was born, and to point out the place on the map. Post a list of all the countries and continents the children mention.

Dialogue

Components: Cassette, Topic 4 Wall Chart, Picture Dictionary (pp. 8–9).

See page xix for techniques and strategies for presenting and practicing dialogues.

Tommy:	Where do you come from, Ting?
Ting:	I come from China.
Tommy:	Were you born there?
Ting:	Yes, but I came here when I was a baby. Where were you born, Tommy?
Tommy:	I was born here.
Zoe:	Me, too!
Alison:	So was I!
Diego:	Not me! I'm from Peru. I was born there.
Zoe:	When did you come to America?
Diego:	When I was three.
Zoe:	It's such a big world! I'm glad we all came to the same place!

Dialogue notes

Have the children practice the opening exchange (Q: *Where do you come from, Ting?* A: *I come from China.* Q: *Were you born there?* A: *Yes, but I came here when I was a baby.*). Then invite volunteers to make up their own dialogues, asking the same questions and answering with information about their own lives.

Beats!

Components: Cassette, Beats! (Topic 4).

See page xx for techniques and strategies for presenting and practicing Beats!

Where do you come from?
    Take a guess.
Do you come from South America?
    Yes! Yes! Yes!

Where does she come from?
    I don't know.

Does she come from Antarctica?
    No! No! No!
    Take another guess!
    Take another guess!

Does she come from Asia?
    Yes! Yes! Yes!

Beat notes

Use this Beat at any point in the lesson, before or after the story or after the dialogue. Substitute continents that your students come from for those used. You may have the children nod or shake their heads vigorously to emphasize *no, no, no* and *yes, yes, yes,* and make a classic shrugging motion for *I don't know.*

Worksheets

Worksheet 1: Big world! (p. 7)

Ask several children in turn to say the name of the country in which she or he was born. Write each country's name and point to the country on a large map. Ask volunteers to answer the question *What continent is that country in?* Then ask the child, *In what continent were you born?* When the children are familiar with the pattern of questions and answers, have them fill in the missing words on this page. Provide maps of their countries of origin for them to copy or trace. You can find flags of the world in most encyclopedias for the children to use to color their home country's flag. Some children may want to color an American flag.

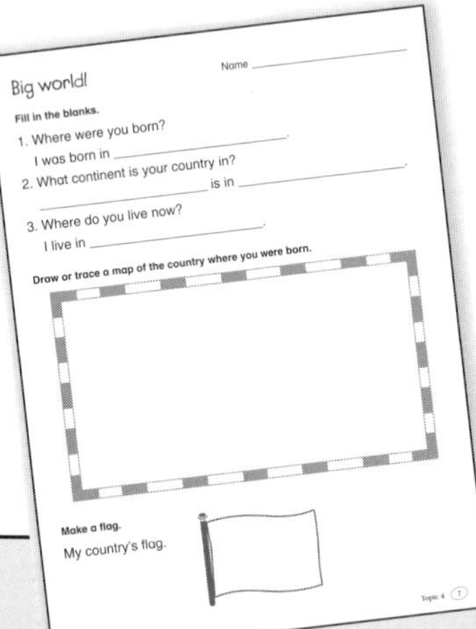

Big world! Name ____

Fill in the blanks.

1. Where were you born?
I was born in ____.
2. What continent is your country in?
____ is in ____.
3. Where do you live now?
I live in ____.

Draw or trace a map of the country where you were born.

Make a flag.
My country's flag.

Topic 4 7

Worksheet 2: Big world! (p. 8)

To prepare students to complete this exercise, ask a volunteer to say where he or she was born. For instance, a student might say, *I was born in Ecuador.* Ask the other students a series of questions: *Was he born in South America? Was he born in Africa?* Elicit full-sentence answers: *Yes, he was born in South America; No, he wasn't born in Africa.* Repeat the pattern, modeling a plural subject by identifying two children who were born in the same country. Ask questions about the children (for example, *Were they born in Asia?*), eliciting full-sentence answers: *No, they weren't born in Asia; Yes, they were born in North America.*

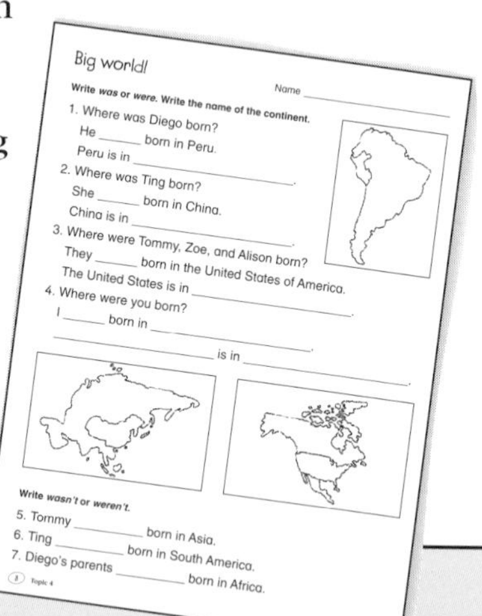

Big world! Name ____

Write was or were. Write the name of the continent.

1. Where was Diego born?
He ____ born in Peru.
Peru is in ____.
2. Where was Ting born?
She ____ born in China.
China is in ____.
3. Where were Tommy, Zoe, and Alison born?
They ____ born in the United States of America.
The United States is in ____.
4. Where were you born?
I ____ born in ____.
____ is in ____.

Write wasn't or weren't.

5. Tommy ____ born in Asia.
6. Ting ____ born in South America.
7. Diego's parents ____ born in Africa.

8 Topic 4

Activities

- On large pieces of colorful paper, write "Welcome" or an equivalent greeting in every language represented by students attending your school, including English. Label each poster to identify the language. Post them in the halls or in the classroom.
- Make postcards. Cut cardboard into large postcards and invite children to draw a picture on one side to illustrate a place on the map. Then have them write or dictate a message on the other side, including a reference to the place. For example: *This is South America. It has tall mountains.* Collect the cards in a box for children to look at or add to.
- Mount a large outline map of the continents on the wall. Help children draw in national borders. Ask each child to make a removable label for his or her country of origin. Make an arrow or pointer on which the child prints his or her name. Ask each child to place his or her marker on the map while telling the other children about it: *I come from ______. My family comes from ______.*
- Choose a country each week to highlight with a bulletin-board display. Include such things as posters, pamphlets, photographs, maps, books, art items, and games or toys from the country. Students and their parents can teach the other students a song or game, or prepare a favorite native dish. The family could prepare a recipe for the dish and the child could illustrate it for a class cookbook.

Where do you live?

Content	Language
Homes and neighborhoods Addresses and phone numbers	Using number patterns in addresses and telephone numbers: *333 Friendly Street. 465-9860.* Asking and answering questions about address and telephone number: *What's your address? I live at 98 Dahlia Drive. My address is 412 Redmond Road. My phone number is 723-2230.* Describing parts of a home: *My apartment has six windows. That house has a red roof. The apartment door is red.* Using the prepositions *in, on,* and *at* to identify locations: *I live in a house on Friendly Street. I live at 15 Hilltop Road.*

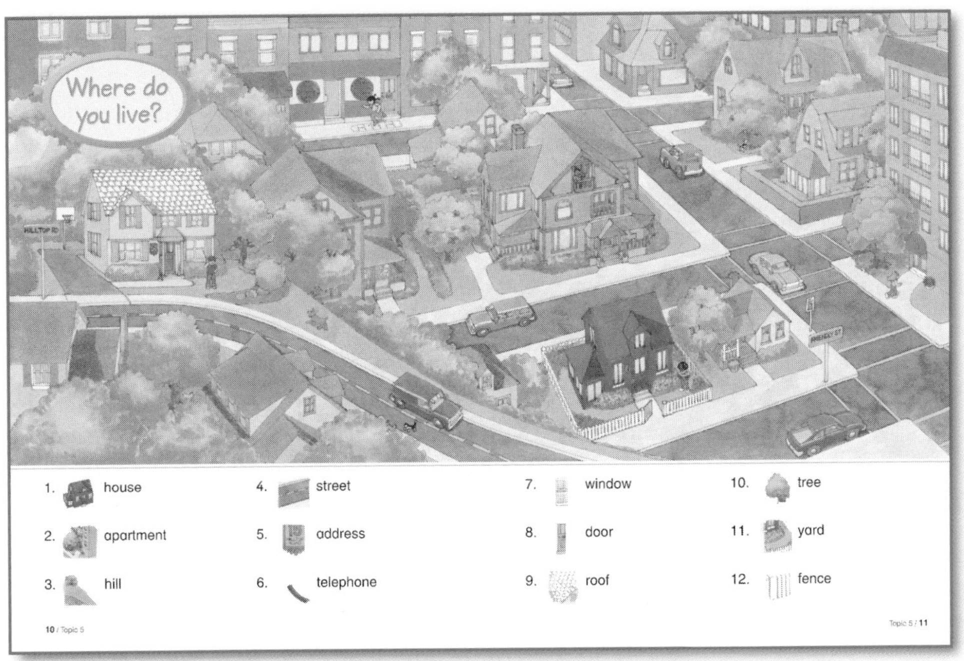

This scene is a panorama of the town and the neighborhoods where the five children live. The Jackson family lives near the center of town in the small red house on Friendly Street. It is number "6" and they have a small yard with a fence. The Cheng family lives in the second-floor apartment above their restaurant.The number "77" is on the bright green door leading up to it. The Lopez family lives in a big, rambling, blue house.The number "123" is on their front door. The Young family lives on the outskirts of town in a small yellow house with a white roof and picture windows. It's on top of the hill—number "15" Hilltop Road.The Matthews family lives in an apartment building with a big tree in front. Tommy and Diego are calling each other on the telephone. Tommy is on the front lawn of his house, using a cordless phone. Diego is looking out the upstairs window of his house as he talks on the phone.

Words

1. house
2. apartment
3. hill
4. street
5. address
6. telephone
7. window
8. door
9. roof
10. tree
11. yard
12. fence

Additional Words

town
restaurant
chimney
shutters
porch
driveway
(color words)
front
back
brick
sidewalk
gate
home

Words

Components: Topic 5 Wall Chart, Picture Dictionary (pp. 10–11), Cassette, Word and Picture Cards (Topic 5).

See page xiv for techniques and strategies for presenting and practicing words.

Where do you live?

1. house	5. address	9. roof
2. apartment	6. telephone	10. tree
3. hill	7. window	11. yard
4. street	8. door	12. fence

Notes

Talk with the children about the words *house* and *home*. Tape a piece of mural paper to the board and on it draw a large rectangle. Have the children choose partners. Shuffle the word cards and lay them facedown on a table. Invite each pair of children to select a card, say the word, and draw that part of the house on the rectangle until the house is complete. Tell the children who draw the word *address* to write an address for the house, and those who draw *telephone* to make up a phone number and write it on the paper. Ask the children to identify the parts of the completed house. Prompt them to ask and answer questions about the house.

Workbook page

Ask the children to point to and name as many parts of the house shown in the picture as they can before referring to the boxed words or to their word cards. Then review the words, having the children point to each word as you say it aloud. Tell them to write the words in the box with the line that points to the part of the house. The children should write the words *house, address,* and *phone number* to complete the sentences at the bottom of the page.

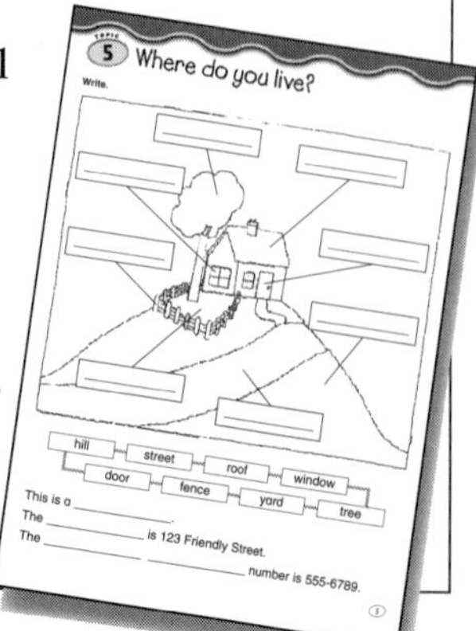

Stories

Components: Picture Dictionary (pp. 10–11), Cassette, Story (Topic 5).

See page xviii for techniques and strategies for presenting and practicing stories.

Everyone lives in the same town.
Diego lives in a blue house.
Tommy lives in a yellow house.
Zoe lives in a red house.

Ting lives in an apartment.
It is over her family's restaurant.
Alison lives in an apartment, too.
It has a big tree in front.

Zoe lives on Friendly Street.
Her house says number 6.
Her address is 6 Friendly Street.
She has a yard with a fence.

Tommy lives at 15 Hilltop Road.
His house has big windows and
a white roof.
He lives far away from Diego,
but he calls him on the telephone.

Story notes

This is an opportunity to use the prepositions *on, in,* and *at.* Compare the use of the prepositions in the following phrases: *in Smithtown, on Friendly Street, at 6 Friendly Street.*

Ask about the story:
What color is Diego's house? What color roof does Zoe's house have? Is the roof of Tommy's house blue? What is Zoe's address? Where does Ting live? Who lives on a hill? Who lives in a house with a fence? Who lives in an apartment? Does Alison live in a house or an apartment?

Ask about your students:
This is a good opportunity to be sure that every student knows his or her address and telephone number.

Where do you live? What's your address? What's your telephone number?

Many children know the name of their street and the street number. Help children learn to say and/or write their addresses and phone numbers.

Dialogue

 **Components:** Cassette, Topic 5 Wall Chart, Picture Dictionary (pp. 10–11).

See page xix for techniques and strategies for presenting and practicing dialogues.

(Sounds of touch-tone phone buttons as Tommy says each number)

Tommy: 493-1212.
Diego: Hello?
Tommy: Hi, Diego. It's Tommy. Can you come to my house?
Diego: Maybe. Where do you live?
Tommy: On Hilltop Road.
Diego: Where's that?
Tommy: It's on top of a hill. That's why it's called Hilltop Road.
Diego: I have to ask my mom. I'll call you back. What's your telephone number?
Tommy: 493-7348.
Diego: OK. Good-bye!

(Sounds of touch-tone phone buttons as Diego says each number)

Diego: 493-7348.
Tommy: Hello?
Diego: Hi. It's Diego. What's your address?
Tommy: It's 15 Hilltop Road.
Diego: What color is your house?
Tommy: It's yellow and it has a white roof. So, can you come?
Diego: No, I can't come today.
Tommy: Oh.
Diego: But I can come tomorrow.
Tommy: OK, great! Come tomorrow.
Diego: See you, Tommy.
Tommy: Bye, Diego.
Diego: Bye!

Dialogue notes

If possible, bring in two real or toy telephones for the children to use to practice dialing, and as props as they practice the dialogue. When the students are comfortable with the vocabulary, have each student work with a partner to invent a similar dialogue, substituting their own names, addresses, and telephone numbers.

Beats!

 **Components:** Cassette, Beats! (Topic 5).

See page xx for techniques and strategies for presenting and practicing Beats!

Where do you live?
On Noisy Street,
where the cars whiz by
and the horns go "beep"!

Where do you live?
On Quiet Road,
where the trees are tall
and the flowers grow.

Do you live in a house?
Yes, it's very small.
You can hardly see it
there at all.

I live in an apartment
way up high.
I can see the clouds.
I can touch the sky.

Beat notes

Ask students in which place they would like to live, Noisy Street or Quiet Road. When the children can recite the Beat with ease, invite them to take an imaginary walk, pantomiming the atmosphere of the places mentioned in the Beat. Have one group ask the questions and a second group answer, using loud voices and even adding sound effects (horns beeping, motor sounds) for Noisy Street, and using quiet voices for Quiet Road.

Worksheets

Worksheet 1: Where do you live? (p. 9)

Make a group list of children's addresses and telephone numbers. Practice saying them aloud. Then ask the children to copy their own addresses and telephone numbers on the worksheet. Have them draw pictures of their homes and help them to complete the sentences at the bottom of the page. You may wish to collect the pages and combine them into a children's address book. Students can help organize the pages alphabetically. Use the book to practice asking and answering questions *(Where does Maria live? What is Alexis's phone number?)* and to look up numbers. Children may also be interested in looking at a local phone book. Help them find their family names or the name of a friend or relative.

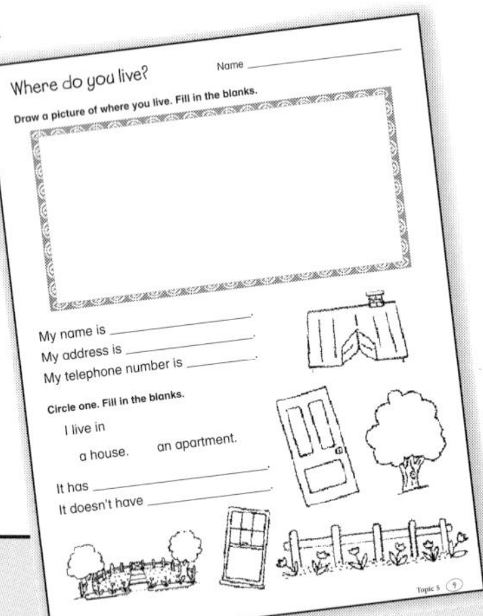

Where do you live? Name ______

Draw a picture of where you live. Fill in the blanks.

My name is ______.
My address is ______.
My telephone number is ______.

Circle one. Fill in the blanks.

I live in
a house. an apartment.

It has ______.
It doesn't have ______.

Topic 5 9

Worksheet 2: Where do you live? (p. 10)

Have children color the house and yard items. Then help them cut and assemble the houses. Pin a large sheet of mural paper to the wall or lay it on the floor. Draw a long winding road down the middle of the paper. Invite each child to place his or her pasted-up house on either side of the road. Encourage students to decorate their homes and yards with other details, such as flowers, bushes, sidewalks, shutters, and porches. Prompt the children to choose a name for their street and add addresses to each house. They can add seasonal or holiday decorations to the houses. Then invite volunteers to come forward to describe their houses and their locations.

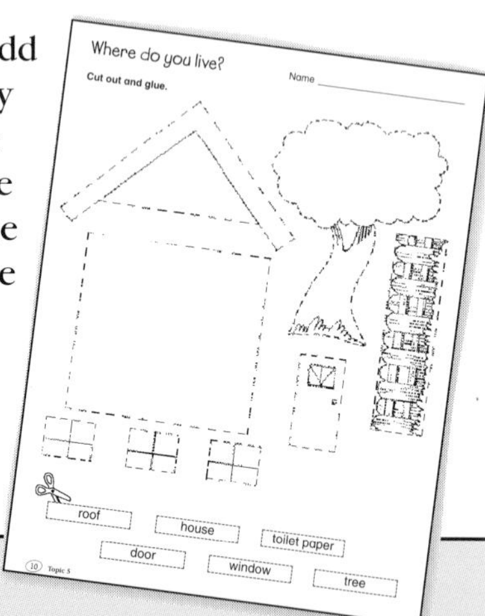

Where do you live? Name ______

Cut out and glue.

roof
house
toilet paper
door
window
tree

10 Topic 5

Activities

- Use a play telephone to model answering the phone, calling someone to the phone, or taking a message. Model what to say if a parent isn't able to come to the phone or is out. (Remind children not to reveal that they are alone.) Model when and how to make a 911 call. Work with two or three children at a time, and encourage them to practice different telephone-calling situations.
- Set up a telephone play area. Encourage the children to use play telephones to have real or imaginary conversations with friends. Prompt them to write or dictate the numbers and names of the people they call. Make a phone list to post next to the phones.
- Sketch a simple one-story house and a large apartment building. Generate a discussion about the similarities and differences between the two buildings. Write the words or phrases the children use. Ask: *Which building is bigger? Which one is taller? How many families live in this house? Is there more than one family in this building? Where do the children play? How do the families get up so high in the apartment house?*
- Ask children to bring in a photograph or draw a picture of the outside of their homes. Have them use the vocabulary to dictate or write a description of their homes. Be sensitive to students who may not wish to have their homes made subject to comparison. Or, you may have children draw pictures and describe a place where they would like to live.

Theme 2: My House

Topic 6 Good morning!
Topic 7 Busy bathroom!
Topic 8 What can I wear?
Topic 9 Who made breakfast?
Topic 10 Here comes the school bus!

Theme Bibliography

Bread Bread Bread
written by Ann Morris; photographs by Ken Heyman.
Mulberry Books, 1993. ISBN 0688122752
Houses and Homes
written by Ann Morris; photographs by Ken Heyman.
Mulberry Books, 1995. ISBN 0688135781
Each book offers a picture survey of the two staples of life: food and shelter. The poetic language and photographs can be used as story-starters or discussion prompts. The picture indexes and maps in each book provide helpful cultural information to help you tailor these books to your students.

A House Is a House for Me
written by Mary Ann Hoberman;
illustrated by Betty Fraser.
Puffin Books, 1993. ISBN 0140951164
This wonderfully silly and imaginative book reveals many different types of houses—not only of different peoples, such as the Eskimos and the Hopi—but also of animals and various inanimate objects. (A barn is a house for a cow. A glove is a house for a hand.) The repetitive structure "A house is a ..." facilitates both language learning and word acquisition.

How a House is Built
written and illustrated by Gail Gibbons.
Holiday House, 1996. ISBN 0823412326
Building a house requires many people with assorted skills, from the well diggers who first turn the earth to the painters who apply the final touches to the completed structure. This book reveals how these people work together, and shows the building process step by step. Students can use it for picture research when drawing or writing about building their own houses. You can also use this book with *Houses and Homes* (see above) to foster children's awareness of different houses and homes around the world.

How My Family Lives in America
written and photographed by Susan Kuklin.
Simon & Schuster, 1992. ISBN 0027512398
Three children—Sanu, Eric, and April—provide a window into the multicultural texture of American family life. The photographs underline the significance of food, art, and education. Using this book as a model, you can have students make a classroom album with family photographs of their lives in America. The text can be applied to other Dictionary themes, such as Me and My Family, My School, and The Weekend.

How My Parents Learned to Eat
written by Ina R. Friedman; illustrated by Allen Say.
Houghton Mifflin Co., 1987. ISBN 0395442354
This popular book has themes similar to those in *How My Family Lives in America* (see above). A young Japanese-American girl tells how her American father and her Japanese mother accommodate each other's respective cultures. "Some days we eat with chopsticks," she says, "and some days we eat with knives and forks." Although students will recognize key vocabulary, you may need to shelter the text in order to facilitate understanding.

Huggly Gets Dressed
written and illustrated by Tedd Arnold.
Cartwheel Books, 1998. ISBN 0590918192
Huggly Takes a Bath
written and illustrated by Tedd Arnold.
Scholastic Inc., 1998. ISBN 0590117602
Huggly is a cute little green monster that lives under the bed. These wonderfully humorous books, which recount his efforts to understand the human world, are good supplements to Topics 7 and 8. The story and illustrations provide good prompts for TPR activities about getting dressed or washing up.

I Got Community

written by Melrose Cooper;
illustrated by Dale Gottlieb.
Henry Holt and Co., 1995. ISBN 0805031790

This book starts "I got a neighbor, helps me near." It ends, "I got community. I belong right in the neighborhood, thick and strong..." This is an all-around-town book that uses simple words and rhyme. Some may object to the colloquial use of "I got." However, the book's message of sharing and caring makes it suitable to read aloud to students or to have them read it along with you.

Ira Sleeps Over

written and illustrated by Bernard Waber.
Houghton Mifflin Co., 1979. ISBN 0590099205

When Ira first sleeps over at Reggie's house, he finds himself in a quandary: He has never slept without his teddy bear, but he is afraid to bring it along for fear of being ridiculed. This story of childhood innocence and insecurity will resonate for many children. Shelter the English as you tell the story. The illustrations help you do so by featuring many everyday objects that students can identify as the text is read.

Night House Bright House

by Monica Wellington.
Dutton Children's Books, 1997. ISBN 0525454918

Ten frisky mice lead an all-night household rumpus in this wonderful story told in words and rebus. Clever wordplay abounds in this book ("'Who's up?' said the cup." "'Look out please,' said the cheese."), which makes it a fun book for English-language learners. The illustrations will help children learn everything they need to know about a house. It's a delightful literary supplement to the words and language in Theme 2.

Not Enough Room

written by Joanne Rocklin;
illustrated by Christina Ong;
and Math Activities by Marilyn Burns.
Cartwheel Books, 1998. ISBN 0590399624

Kris and Pat have to share a room because their parents are having another child. The siblings struggle with different mathematically-based room arrangements in order to come to terms with living together. The text's rhyme scheme helps language learners comprehend this story. The additional activities can be adapted to make cross-curricular connections to geometry and math.

A Picture for Harold's Room

written and illustrated by Crocket Johnson.
HarperTrophy, 1985. ISBN 0064440850

Harold decides he needs a picture for the wall in his room, and his attempt to draw one takes him on a journey. This book takes students into such subjects as transportation, geography, city, and town. The use of the past tense with common irregular verbs *(see/saw, come/came, go/went)* make this a welcome book for emerging language learners.

Potluck

written by Anne Shelby; illustrated by Irene Trivas.
Orchard Books, 1994. ISBN 053107045X

Alpha and Betty have invited a group of their friends to a potluck feast. Each person invited has a name beginning with a different letter of the alphabet, and each brings a dish that begins with that very same letter. The feast turns into an alphabetical smorgasbord, and exemplifies the cultural variety that makes up America. The initial-letter correspondence between names and nouns can provide some real fun with phonics.

Wheels on the Bus

written by Raffi;
illustrated by Sylvie Kantorovitz Wickstrom.
Crown Publishers, 1990. ISBN 0517576457

This illustrated version of the popular children's song contains both text and music. Encourage students to invent hand motions to accompany the repetitious and rhythmic text as they recite or sing the words. Use the illustrations to generate vocabulary as you help students identify foods, animals, articles of clothing, and other items.

TOPIC 6 Good morning!

Content

- Names and use of rooms in a home
- Household furnishings
- Morning activities

Language

- Naming each room in a house or an apartment: *This is the kitchen. The bathroom is between the two bedrooms. The living room is next to the kitchen.*
- Describing the use of each room: *We eat in the kitchen. He cooks in the kitchen. I sleep in the bedroom. They wash in the bathroom. We watch TV in the living room.*
- Identifying and describing familiar household furnishings: *We have a sofa and a TV in the living room. My bed is in the bedroom. There is a stove in the kitchen. They have two sinks, one in the kitchen and one in the bathroom.*
- Describing morning routines: *I wake up. She washes her face. I brush my teeth and comb my hair. I get dressed. We eat breakfast.*

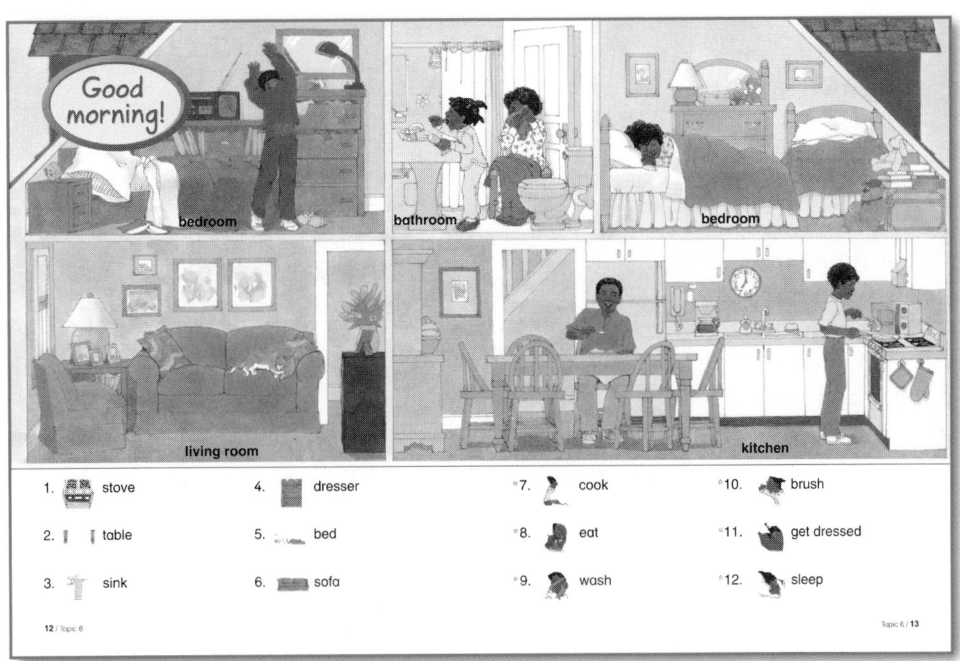

It's seven o'clock Monday morning at the Jacksons' house. Downstairs, Mrs. Jackson is busy cooking breakfast at the stove, while Mr. Jackson eats at the table, enjoying every mouthful. The cat is curled up on the living room sofa. Upstairs, Marcus is getting dressed in his bedroom, while in the bathroom Samantha brushes her teeth and Mariah washes her face. Where is Zoe? Still asleep in her bed!

Words

1. stove
2. table
3. sink
4. dresser
5. bed
6. sofa

Verbs

7. cook
8. eat
9. wash
10. brush
11. get dressed
12. sleep

Labels

bedroom
bathroom
living room
kitchen

Additional Words

TV
chair
refrigerator
upstairs
downstairs
attic
cellar

Words

Components: Topic 6 Wall Chart, Picture Dictionary (pp. 12–13), Cassette, Word and Picture Cards (Topic 6).

See page xiv for techniques and strategies for presenting and practicing words.

Good morning!

1. stove	3. sink	5. bed
2. table	4. dresser	6. sofa

Verbs

7. cook	9. wash	11. get dressed
8. eat	10. brush	12. sleep

Labels

bedroom bathroom living room kitchen

Notes

Tape four pieces of chart paper to the wall and label them *bedroom, bathroom, kitchen,* and *living room.* Lay the set of six noun word cards facedown on the table. Have a student choose a card and show it to the others. Then ask the child to place the card in the room where the illustrated furnishing would be found. Ask the child to say what he/she is doing or narrate for him/her: *I put the sofa in the living room. The sink goes in the bathroom.* When all the children have had a turn, repeat the process with the verb cards. Ask each child to point to the room and talk about the activity on the card: *I wash my face in the bathroom. I sleep in the bedroom.*

Workbook page

Tell the children to write or dictate the word for what each person is doing *(cooking, sleeping, washing, eating).* Then, for the writing exercise, review the words for different rooms by holding up a picture card and asking, *What room is this?* Ask the rest of the group to repeat the word. Point out that the first letter is given for each word as a clue. Finally, have children match the words and the pieces of furniture at the bottom of the page.

6 Good morning!

Write.

What are they doing?

1. He's ________ing.
2. He's ________ing.
3. He's ________ing.
4. She's ________ing.

Write.

b ________ l ________ k ________ b ________

Match.

sofa table sink dresser stove bed

Stories

Components: Picture Dictionary (pp. 12–13), Cassette, Story (Topic 6).

See page xviii for techniques and strategies for presenting and practicing stories.

It's seven o'clock. Get up!
The Jacksons are in the kitchen.
Mrs. Jackson is cooking at the stove.
M-m-m-m, it smells good!

Mr. Jackson is at the table.
He is eating his breakfast.
M-m-m-m, it tastes good!
Mrs. Jackson is a good cook.

Samantha and Mariah are in the bathroom.
Mariah is washing her face.
Samantha is at the sink.
She is brushing her teeth.

Marcus is in his bedroom.
He is getting dressed at his dresser.
Where's Zoe?
She is in her bed, sleeping!

Story notes

Encourage the children to retell the story in their own words and to talk about other things they see in the illustrations.

Ask about the story:
Is Zoe in the bedroom? Where is Marcus? Are Mr. and Mrs. Jackson in the kitchen? What room is Samantha in? Is Samantha in the same room as Zoe? Where is the stove? What is this piece of furniture? What is Mrs. Jackson doing? What is she cooking? What is Marcus doing? Who is getting dressed? Who is sleeping?

Ask about your students:
Does everyone in your family get up at the same time? When do you brush your teeth? Do you eat breakfast in the kitchen? Do you eat with other people in your family? Where is the stove in your home? Where is the bed? What room do you do your homework in?

Dialogue

Components: Cassette, Topic 6 Wall Chart, Picture Dictionary (pp. 12–13).

See page xix for techniques and strategies for presenting and practicing dialogues.

Mrs. Jackson:	Breakfast is ready! Where are the children? Are they in the living room?
Mr. Jackson:	No, they aren't. Nobody's in the living room, just the cat sleeping on the sofa.
Mrs. Jackson:	Samantha, come to breakfast!
Samantha:	I'm not ready.
Mrs. Jackson:	Where are you?
Samantha:	I'm in the bathroom with Mariah. I'm brushing my teeth.
Mariah:	I'm washing my face!
Mrs. Jackson:	Good girls! Well, hurry up! Both of you! Marcus! What are you doing?
Marcus:	I'm getting dressed!
Mrs. Jackson:	Where's Zoe?
Marcus:	She's still in bed.
Mrs. Jackson:	What?! Zoe! Get up!
Zoe:	(grunts sleepily)

Dialogue notes

After listening to the dialogue a few times, prompt the children to engage in similar dialogues. Tape four pieces of chart paper to the wall and label them *bedroom, bathroom, kitchen,* and *living room,* with a paper pocket under each word. Then invite a volunteer to put his or her marker—a card with a name or picture—in one of the pockets. Model the language: *Is she in the bedroom? No, she's not. Is she in the bathroom? No she's not. Is she in the kitchen? Yes, she is.* Prompt the children to take turns placing their markers and asking and answering the questions. You may have two children place markers together, in order to prompt a response using plurals.

Beats!

Components: Cassette, Beats! (Topic 6).

See page xx for techniques and strategies for presenting and practicing Beats!

Good morning!
    What time is it?
Time to get up!
    Wait a minute.

Breakfast is ready!
    What time is it?
Time to eat breakfast!
    Wait a minute.

Get up! Get dressed!
And brush your teeth!
    What time is it?
Time to go to school!

    School?
Yes!
Today is Monday.
    Why didn't you tell me?
    I thought it was Sunday!

Beat notes

Divide the class into two groups. One group can play the parent calling to the child, and the other can play the child responding. Then reverse the roles and practice until the children can recite the Beat. Then have the children form two lines facing one another— one line to say the parent's words, and the other the child's words. As all the children clap to the Beat rhythm, each line takes a step forward to speak, and a step back to listen as the opposite line takes a step forward to speak.

Worksheets

Worksheet 1: Good morning! (p. 11)

Begin by reviewing the rooms shown on the Dictionary page. Review the room names by asking questions: *What room is Zoe sleeping in? Where is Mrs. Jackson cooking? Is Mariah in the bedroom?* Help the children cut out the room labels and glue them on the worksheet. Then have them cut out the furniture images and labels, sort them, and glue them. Hold up the picture card for each item of furniture and have the children show you the word on their worksheets. As the children identify each piece of furniture, ask them to say where it belongs. Use different questions as models: *What room will you put it in? What room does the _____ go in? Where will you find a _____?*

Worksheet 2: Good morning! (p. 12)

Hold up one of the picture cards—for example, *stove*—and ask: *Will you find this in the bathroom? Will this be in the bedroom?* Prompt the children to respond with full sentences, including the word for the piece of furniture: *No, I won't find a stove in the bathroom. No, a stove won't be in the bedroom.* Then read aloud the first example on the worksheet and ask the children to name each piece of furniture. Then ask about each item individually. Have them circle the items found in the kitchen *(stove, sink)*. Point out that there isn't only one correct answer; some kitchens have a table, others don't.

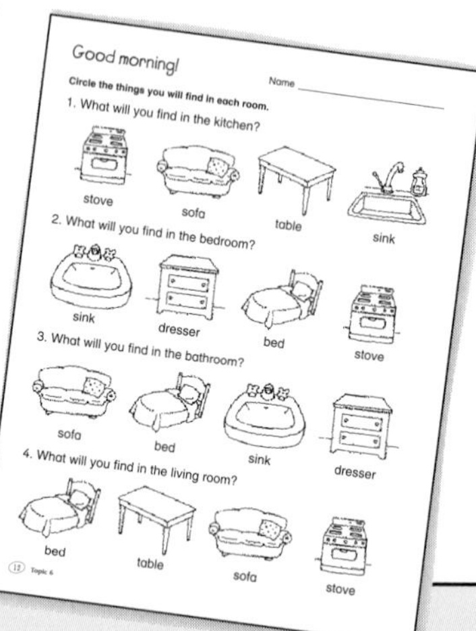

Activities

- On a large piece of paper, draw a house or apartment layout showing four rooms: kitchen, living room, bedroom, and bathroom. Put the children into four groups. Have each group work together to decorate one of the rooms by drawing or gluing pictures of appropriate furniture. Ask the children to draw a picture of a family member (on index cards or stick-on notes), place their family member in a room, and talk about what the person is doing.

- Have children cut pictures out of home-decorating magazines and use them to make a collage of one of the rooms depicted in the topic *(bedroom, bathroom, kitchen, living room).* Post the pictures and encourage the children to talk to one another about their work.

- Bring in a doll house with furniture. Let children take turns choosing a piece of furniture and placing it in the appropriate room. Encourage them to name the furniture and the room where it belongs. Then place a small doll in a room and talk about what the doll is doing there. Provide language models for questions and answers: *Where does this stove go? Put the stove in the kitchen. What is the girl doing? Where is she? The girl is cooking on the stove in the kitchen.* Allow time for the children to play with the figures, the furniture, and the doll house.

Busy bathroom!

Content

- Bathroom appliances
- Bathroom routines and activities
- Sinking and floating

Language

- Identifying appliances in the bathroom: *There is a bathtub and a sink. The shower is in the bathtub. The toilet is next to the sink.*
- Describing bathroom routines and activities: *I brush my teeth in the morning. My mother takes a shower. My little sister is playing in the bathtub.*
- Using possessives: *Is this their towel? This towel is theirs. Is it her comb? It's hers. Whose toothbrush is this?*

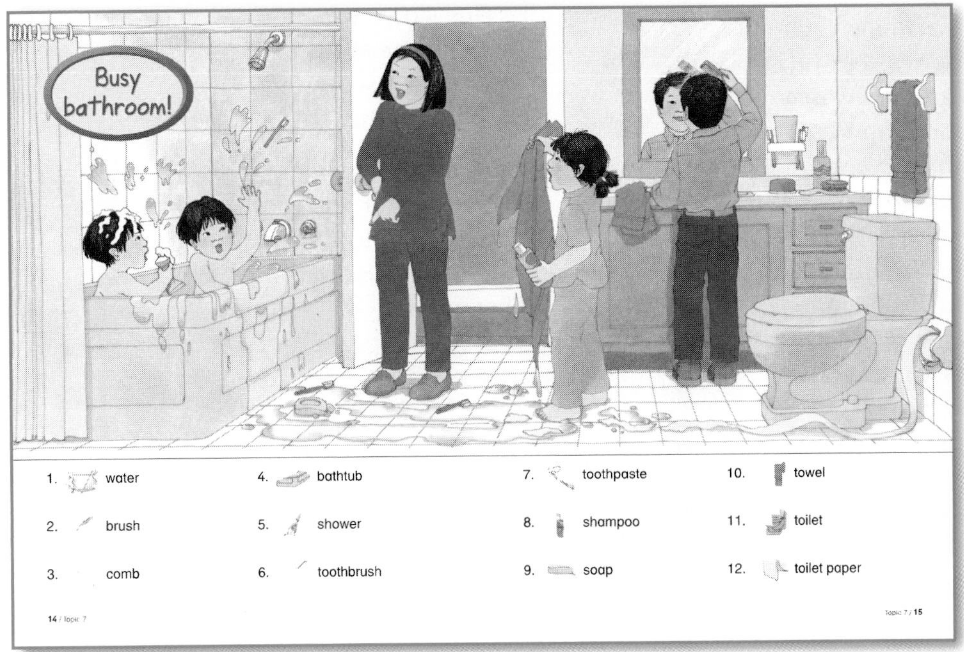

Words

1. water
2. brush
3. comb
4. bathtub
5. shower
6. toothbrush
7. toothpaste
8. shampoo
9. soap
10. towel
11. toilet
12. toilet paper

Additional Words

mine
yours
theirs
hers
his
water
hot
cold
warm
wash
sink
float
washcloth
dry
dry off

It's Monday morning in the Chengs' bathroom. The bathroom is busy and messy. The twins are in the bathtub splashing water. Jo-Jo has thrown four toothbrushes out of the tub onto the floor. Jackie has plastered his wet hair with toothpaste. Mrs. Cheng is pointing to the floor, where she sees the toothbrushes, a cake of soap, and some wet toilet paper. She is not happy. Ting is not happy, either. She's holding a dripping wet towel. It's hers! Henry is combing his hair at the sink. He is smiling, thinking himself very handsome, and ignoring the chaos around him.

Words

Components: Topic 7 Wall Chart, Picture Dictionary (pp. 14–15), Cassette, Word and Picture Cards (Topic 7).

See page xiv for techniques and strategies for presenting and practicing words.

Busy bathroom!

1. water	5. shower	9. soap
2. brush	6. toothbrush	10. towel
3. comb	7. toothpaste	11. toilet
4. bathtub	8. shampoo	12. toilet paper

Notes

Review the word and picture cards, naming each item aloud as the children touch the word or picture. Explain that the words *brush* and *comb* may be used as nouns and verbs. Then hold up each card again and model questions and answers: *What can you do with this brush? I can brush my hair.* Encourage the children to answer with pantomime and sentences or phrases. When the children are comfortable with the new words, invite them to play a riddle game. Ask volunteers to come forward and pantomime a bathroom activity. Let the other children guess what they are doing: *She is brushing her hair. He is looking in the mirror and combing his hair.*

Workbook page

Write the word *water* on the board. Then, while the children are watching, write the word again, letter by letter, scrambling the order. Point out that the pictures under each word provide a clue, and tell them to unscramble the letters and write one of the words under each picture. Direct their attention to the words at the bottom of the page, and tell them to draw a line from the bullet above each word to the part of the large picture that shows the word. They may want to circle each image first, and then draw the connecting lines.

Stories

Components: Picture Dictionary (pp. 14–15), Cassette, Story (Topic 7).

See page xviii for techniques and strategies for presenting and practicing stories.

What a busy bathroom!
Henry looks in the mirror.
He brushes and combs his hair,
and he smiles.

Jo-Jo and Jackie splash in the bathtub.
They have toothbrushes and toothpaste.
Jo-Jo throws the toothbrushes on the floor.
Jackie puts the toothpaste in his hair!

It's Ting's turn to wash.
She takes the shampoo.
Where is the soap?
She picks up her towel. It is all wet!

What does Mrs. Cheng see?
She sees water and toothbrushes
and soap and toilet paper on the floor.
And she sees Jackie's hair.
What a mess!

Story notes

If possible, provide various bathroom items for the children to handle: toothbrush, toothpaste, comb, brush, washcloth, towel, soap, shampoo. Ask the children to name the items as they examine them, take turns pretending to use the objects, and describe the way they are used.

Ask about the story:
Who splashed in the bathtub? What did Jo-Jo throw? Where did Jo-Jo throw the toothbrushes? What is Henry doing? Why does Mrs. Cheng say, "What a mess!"? How does the bathroom look? Whose towel is wet?

Ask about your students:
Where do you wash? Do you take a bath? How do you dry yourself? Do you like to play in the bathtub? Do you make a mess in the bathroom? Where do you put your toothbrush? What do you use to wash your face?

Dialogue

Components: Cassette, Topic 7 Wall Chart, Picture Dictionary (pp. 14–15).

See page xix for techniques and strategies for presenting and practicing dialogues.

Mrs. Cheng:	Oh, my goodness! Look at this mess! Boys, get out of the tub! It's Ting's turn to use the bathroom!
Ting:	Mom! My towel is all wet!
Mrs. Cheng:	Henry, please get Ting a dry towel.
Henry:	OK.
Mrs. Cheng:	Whose soap is that on the floor?
Jo-Jo:	It's mine!
Mrs. Cheng:	Whose toothbrushes are those?
Jo-Jo:	Mine!
Ting:	Mine!
Henry:	Mine!
Mrs. Cheng:	Oh no, Jackie, look at your hair! When Ting is finished, I'll have to wash it under the shower. Now, let's clean up this mess! Give me those toothbrushes! Pick up that soap! Pick up that toilet paper! And don't forget to flush the toilet!

Dialogue notes

After listening to the dialogue a few times, have the children extend it to include other objects:

Whose towel is that?
It's hers!
Whose brush is that?
It's his!
Whose toothbrushes are those?
They're theirs!

Beats!

Components: Cassette, Beats! (Topic 7).

See page xx for techniques and strategies for presenting and practicing Beats!

What happened to the soap?
I don't know.
It was right here
just a minute ago.

Did you look on the sink?
It's not there!

Did you look in the tub?
It's not there!

Here it is on the floor!
Well, what do you know!
I told you it was here
just a minute ago!

Beat notes

Continue the Beat with other bathroom objects: *What happened to the toothpaste? the shampoo? my toothbrush? the toilet paper?* Help the children invent new verses using a similar rhythm:

What happened to my towel?
It's all wet!
I'll get you a dry one.
Don't get upset!

Worksheets

Worksheet 1: Busy bathroom! (p. 13)

Open the Dictionary to pages 14–15. Hold up a picture card for one of the words. Ask a volunteer to say what it is and then find it in the illustration. Tell the children to find and circle each item on the worksheet, checking off each word as they find the matching picture. Point out that the first example has been completed; the brush is circled and there is a check-mark next to the word *brush*. Help them complete the sentences and read them aloud.

Busy bathroom! Name ____

Find and circle.

brush, toilet, shower, towel, water, toilet paper, soap, toothbrush, comb, bathtub, shampoo, toothpaste

Write.

What a mess! The girls are splashing in the ____.
The ____ are on the floor.
The ____ is all wet.

Topic 7 13

Worksheet 2: Busy bathroom! (p. 14)

Talk with the children about the things they use in the bathroom. Encourage them to use full sentences or phrases and as many of the vocabulary words as possible. Ask volunteers to read aloud the vocabulary words at the lower right of the worksheet. Explain that each of the unfinished sentences can be finished with one of these words. You may encourage children to work with partners to complete these exercises.

Busy bathroom! Name ____

Answer the questions. Match.

1. He is wet. What does he need? He needs a ____.
2. She has a toothbrush. What does she need? She needs ____.
3. Her hair is messy. What does she need? She needs a ____.
4. Their faces are dirty. What do they need? They need ____ and ____.
5. His hair is dirty. What does he need? He needs ____.

comb, toilet paper, water, soap, towel, toothpaste, shampoo

14 Topic 7

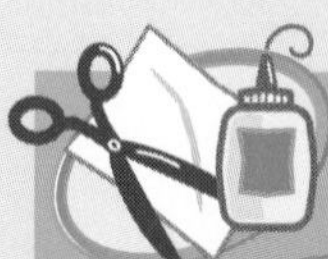

Activities

- Investigate sinking and floating. Set up a water table or bring in a pan of water, some objects that float (such as plastic bath toys or small wooden blocks), and some objects that sink (such as stones or coins). Explain that if the object *sinks* it drops down to the bottom of the pan, and if it *floats* it stays on top of the water. (Point out that the word *sink* has more than one meaning.) Pass each object and ask, *Do you think it will sink or float?* Ask a volunteer to place the object in the water as the children watch. Ask: *What's happening? What do you see?* Continue until all the objects have been tried. Ask the children to put things that float and things that sink in separate boxes or piles.

- Invite the children to play giving a toy a bath. Provide props such as a small stuffed animal, a shoe box or small rubber pan to serve as a tub, a small hand towel, a washcloth, a small bar of soap, a bath mat, and a soap dish. A bath plug is a nice touch. Ask them to tell the others in the group what they are doing. After everyone has had a chance to play, ask the children to dictate directions for washing the toy. Make a chart of the dictation. Touch each word as you read the directions.

- Invite the children to pantomime a bathroom activity such as brushing teeth. Encourage other children to ask questions in the tense you are practicing: *Are you brushing your teeth? Do you brush your teeth every day? Did you brush your teeth this morning? Will you brush your teeth tonight? How do you brush your teeth? What do you brush your teeth with?* Continue the activity with questions about other bathroom activities.

TOPIC 8

What can I wear?

Content

- School clothes
- Likes and dislikes

Language

- Identifying and describing what someone is wearing: *He is wearing jeans and a shirt. She has a dress on. Her shirt is purple. My shoes are wet.*
- Expressing likes and dislikes: *She likes to wear skirts. Her mother does not like jeans. I don't like that T-shirt.*
- Making and responding to requests: *Can I wear your black jeans? No way! Can she wear your black sweatshirt? Oh, all right.*
- Using polite language: *Please can I borrow your cap? Thank you for letting me wear your sweater. You're welcome.*

It is Monday morning in Jasmin's bedroom. Jasmin is in her pajamas. She has been trying to decide what to wear to school. Her underwear and a sweater are on the bed. Her baseball cap is on her lamp. She has already looked in her closet. She doesn't want to wear the red dress or the blue skirt her mother is offering her. She wants to wear her pink jeans, her orange T-shirt, her boots, and Diego's black sweatshirt. Diego is not really happy about it, but he gives her his sweatshirt.

Words

1. sweater
2. underwear
3. sneakers
4. socks
5. baseball cap
6. dress
7. skirt
8. sweatshirt
9. jeans
10. T-shirt
11. boots
12. pajamas

Additional Words

blouse
slip
stockings
suit
tie
shirt
collar
shoes
sandals
slippers
wear
wearing
mess
neat
picked up
nightgown
closet
hanger

Words

Components: Topic 8 Wall Chart, Picture Dictionary (pp. 16–17), Cassette, Word and Picture Cards (Topic 8).

See page xiv for techniques and strategies for presenting and practicing words.

What can I wear?

1. sweater	5. baseball cap	9. jeans
2. underwear	6. dress	10. T-shirt
3. sneakers	7. skirt	11. boots
4. socks	8. sweatshirt	12. pajamas

Notes

Distribute word and picture cards. Ask the children to color the clothing the same colors as the clothes they are wearing. If the children are wearing items of clothing that are not pictured, suggest that they make cards for those items. Help them name and label their new cards and share them with their classmates. Add these words to a list of clothing words on a chart. Have children give a show of hands in answer to questions such as: *Who is wearing jeans? Who is wearing a T-shirt?* Make a bar graph on the board or on chart paper to show how many children are wearing each category of clothing.

Workbook page

Each picture on the page has the corresponding vocabulary word beneath it. Point out that each word is missing at least one letter, and some are missing more. The children must fill in the missing letters. Encourage them to use their word cards to help them do so. Then invite them to color the pictures and write or dictate a short description of what they are currently wearing, using as many vocabulary words as they can.

Stories

Components: Picture Dictionary (pp. 16–17), Cassette, Story (Topic 8).

See page xviii for techniques and strategies for presenting and practicing stories.

Whose bedroom is this?
There is a sweater and underwear
on the bed.
There are sneakers and socks on the floor.
There is a baseball cap on the lamp!

It's Jasmin's bedroom.
She doesn't know what to wear to school.
Mrs. Lopez shows her a red dress.
Jasmin doesn't want it.

Mrs. Lopez shows her a blue skirt.
Jasmin doesn't want it.
Diego gives her his black sweatshirt.
Yes! That's what she wants!

She can wear her pink jeans.
She can wear her orange T-shirt.
She can wear her boots,
and Diego's black sweatshirt!

Story notes

Engage the children in a discussion about the concepts of *neat* and *messy*, using Jasmin's room as a focus. Model questions and answers: *Is Jasmin's room neat or a mess? It's a mess! Is your room at home neat or messy? I like the classroom to be neat. Today the classroom is a mess!*

Ask about the story:

What is Jasmin wearing? Can she go to school dressed like that? What is on her bed? Where is her baseball cap? What is Jasmin's mother holding? What does Jasmin want to wear to school? What will Jasmin wear to school?

Ask about your students:

Play a riddle game. Ask a volunteer to come to the front of the group. Choose an item of the child's clothing and describe it: *He is wearing something blue. What is he wearing?* Model the answer: *He is wearing blue jeans.* Invite volunteers to take turns giving clues.

Dialogue

Components: Cassette, Topic 8 Wall Chart, Picture Dictionary (pp. 16–17).

See page xix for techniques and strategies for presenting and practicing dialogues.

Mrs. Lopez:	Jasmin, why aren't you dressed yet?
Jasmin:	What can I wear?
Mrs. Lopez:	You could wear your red dress.
Jasmin:	I don't want to.
Mrs. Lopez:	You could wear your blue skirt.
Jasmin:	I don't want to. I want to wear Diego's black jeans.
Mrs. Lopez:	You can't wear Diego's jeans. They're too big.
Diego:	Come on! We're going to be late!
Jasmin:	Diego, can I wear your black sweatshirt?
Diego:	My black sweatshirt? No way!
Mrs. Lopez:	Diego, please let her wear your black sweatshirt. It's too small for you anyway.
Diego:	Oh, all right.
Jasmin:	Thank you, Diego!
Mrs. Lopez:	Now get dressed, Jasmin, as fast as you can! Or do you want to go to school in your pajamas?

Dialogue notes

After listening to the dialogue a few times, ask the children to choose partners and invent similar dialogues in which they practice making requests and responding to them using polite language. Provide language models:

Can I please wear your red shirt?
Yes, you can.
Thank you.
You're welcome.

Ask the children to take turns making requests and responding, and to vary the clothing mentioned.

Beats!

Components: Cassette, Beats! (Topic 8).

See page xx for techniques and strategies for presenting and practicing Beats!

Put on your blue jeans.
    I don't want to.
Put on your red jeans.
    I don't want to.
    I like the black ones.
All right! Put them on!
    OK.
Let's go!

Put on your green shirt.
    I don't want to.
Put on your red shirt.
    I don't want to.
    I like the yellow one.
All right! Put it on!
    OK.
Let's go!

Where's your belt?
    I don't have one.
Yes, you do!
    I don't need one.
Here's your belt!
    I don't like it.
Put it on!
    OK.
Let's go!

Put on your socks and
put on your sneakers.
What's the matter?
    I can't find them.
Where did you leave them?
    Here they are!
Put them on!
    OK.
Let's go!

Beat notes

Divide the class into two groups. One group speaks the parent's lines, and the other speaks the child's responses. Have children to suggest other articles of clothing while keeping to the rhythm of the Beat.

Worksheets

Worksheet 1: What can I wear? (p. 15)

Ask the children to color each of the clothing items shown on the bottom of the page. Invite volunteers to tell the group what they did: *I colored the shirt green.* Then help them cut out the articles of clothing and glue them to the figures of the boy and girl at the top of the page. Write the vocabulary words and any other words they request on the board as reference. They should finish the sentences with words that describe the two figures as they have dressed them.

What can I wear?

Name

Cut out and glue. Write.

He is wearing

She is wearing

Topic 8 15

Worksheet 2: What can I wear? (p. 16)

Invite volunteers to read the words in the word box as the other children hold up the picture cards that illustrate each word. Then have students draw the clothing in either the closet or the dresser. When their pictures are complete, ask them to write the words for the items they put in each storage place. Remember that there are no right or wrong answers about where clothes are kept, and that not all the children may have all of these items in their wardrobe.

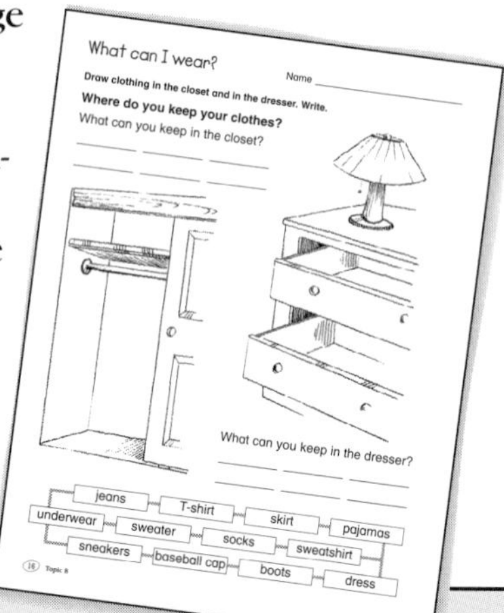

What can I wear?

Name

Draw clothing in the closet and in the dresser. Write.

Where do you keep your clothes?

What can you keep in the closet?

What can you keep in the dresser?

jeans, T-shirt, skirt, underwear, sweater, socks, pajamas, sneakers, baseball cap, boots, sweatshirt, dress

16 Topic 8

Activities

- Collect clothes for a dress-up box. Include school clothes, play clothes, sleepwear, and outerwear, and throw in a few outrageous pieces such as a dust mask, or a baby's bib. Ask the children to identify the clothing and encourage them to sort it into categories. For example, you could ask them to pack for a trip to a cold place, or pack clothing they would wear to school, on a camping trip, or to a fancy party. Invite the children to invent their own categories.

- Lead the children in chanting the following couplet, clapping once for each syllable:

  Mary wore a red dress, red dress, red dress.
  Mary wore her red dress all day long.

  Vary the words by singing the name of one of the children and an article of clothing he or she is wearing:

  _____ wore blue shoes, blue shoes, blue shoes.
  _____ wore blue shoes all day long.

- Make paper dolls. Trace and reproduce a picture of a popular character from literature, TV, or the movies. Paste the figure onto a piece of oak tag for strength. When the glue is dry, help the children cut out the character. Design and reproduce clothing with tabs to fold over in attaching the clothing to the doll. Then help the children color and cut out the articles of clothing. Model commands: *Put the sweater on Little Bear. Put some boots on Little Bear.* Invite the children to take turns giving directions to one another for dressing their paper dolls.

- Make a felt-board scene. Cut from felt the following items to be used on the board: symbols for weather conditions (for example, raindrops, a shining sun, and snowflakes), two children standing, and clothing cut to fit the figures of the children. Invite the children to take turns selecting the symbols for the weather conditions and choosing appropriate clothing.

TOPIC 9

Who made breakfast?

Content

- Breakfast foods
- Dishes and utensils
- Surprises

Language

- Identifying and describing the use of kitchen furnishings, dishes, and utensils: *We eat with a fork, spoon, and knife. Please put the milk on the table. He took eggs out of the refrigerator. She put the juice on the counter.*
- Identifying and describing breakfast foods: *I eat cereal for breakfast. He puts butter on his bread. The jelly is sweet.*
- Expressing likes and dislikes: *I like to drink milk for breakfast. I don't like to eat eggs in the morning.*
- Talking about surprises: *Was Mrs. Young surprised? Mrs. Young and Jim were surprised that Tommy made breakfast. He made breakfast as a surprise for his mother.*

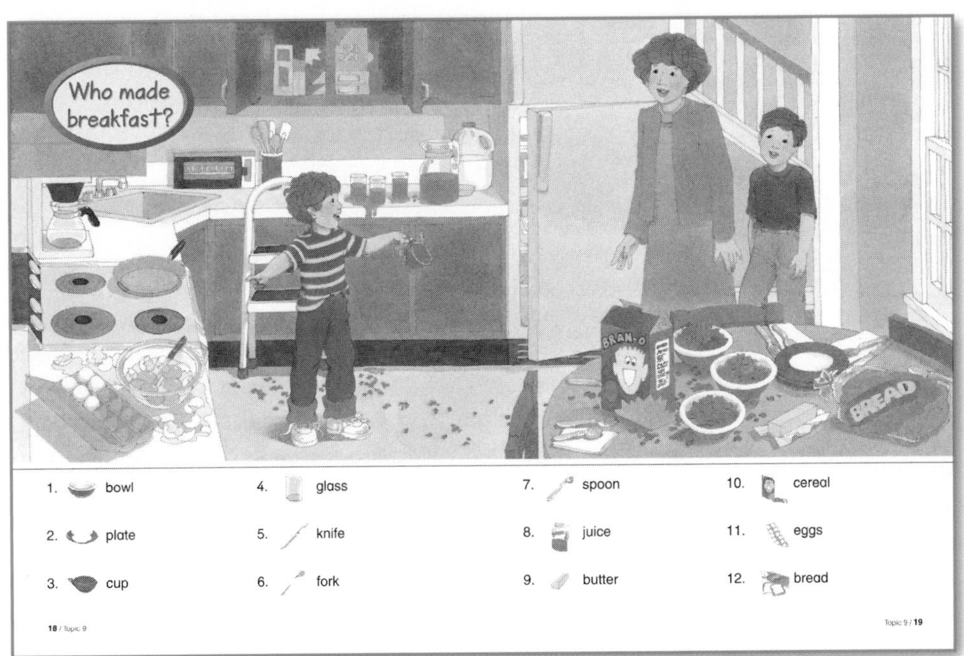

Words

1. bowl
2. plate
3. cup
4. glass
5. knife
6. fork
7. spoon
8. juice
9. butter
10. cereal
11. eggs
12. bread

Additional Words

eat
drink
milk
coffee
tea
fruit
jelly
toaster
stove
refrigerator
cabinet
counter

It is Monday morning in the Youngs' kitchen. Mrs. Young and Jim have just come into the kitchen and—"Surprise!" Tommy has made breakfast! He has fixed cereal, eggs, and juice, and he has set the table. Some cereal spilled onto the table and floor while Tommy was pouring it into the three bowls. There are some eggshells mixed in with the eggs that Tommy scrambled in the big bowl on the counter. There is also juice spilled on the counter where Tommy poured it into the three juice glasses. And the refrigerator door is still open, just a little bit. But Tommy is happy and proud.

Words

Components: Topic 9 Wall Chart, Picture Dictionary (pp. 18–19), Cassette, Word and Picture Cards (Topic 9).

See page xiv for techniques and strategies for presenting and practicing words.

Who made breakfast?

1. bowl	5. knife	9. butter
2. plate	6. fork	10. cereal
3. cup	7. spoon	11. eggs
4. glass	8. juice	12. bread

Notes

Ask volunteers to hold up cards that show pictures of food. On a chart write all the food words, draw a circle around them, and label it *foods.* Then have them hold up the word cards that name things that are not foods, and make a similar chart with the label *not foods.* Challenge the group to think of a category name for the topic items that are not foods. You may ask them to invent new categories for sorting the vocabulary words, or new words to place in the categories already defined.

Workbook page

It doesn't matter in what order the children write or dictate the words *(bowl, plate, cup, knife, fork, spoon).* Hold up a picture card (for example, *bowl*) and ask, *Is this a glass?* Then repeat the process, this time with a query that elicits the answer *yes.* Write the words *yes* and *no* so that the children can refer to them as they write. You may suggest that children who don't yet write circle the ones for which their answer is *yes,* and cross out those for which their answer is *no.*

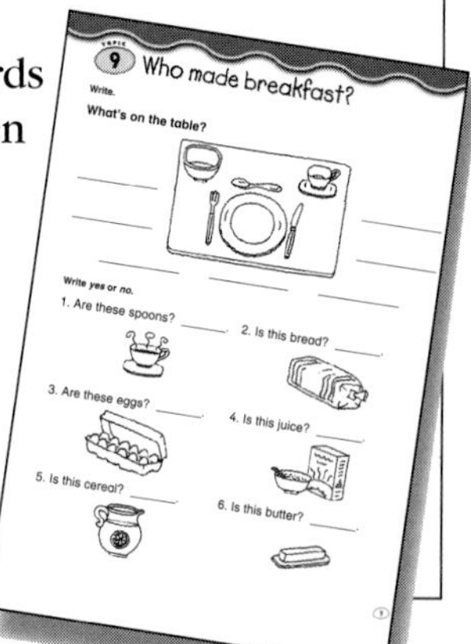

Stories

Components: Picture Dictionary (pp. 18–19), Cassette, Story (Topic 9).

See page xviii for techniques and strategies for presenting and practicing stories.

Tommy made breakfast!
He took the cereal out of the cabinet.
He poured it into three bowls.
A little bit spilled on the floor. Oh, well.

Then he took eggs out of the refrigerator.
He cracked three eggs open
and dumped them in a bowl.
Some eggshells went in, too. Oh, well.

Next he got out the milk and the juice.
He put them on the counter.
He poured some juice into three glasses.
Whoops! That spilled, too. Oh, well.

He put bread, butter, and plates on the table.
What else? Knives, forks, and spoons.
OK! Breakfast was ready.
What a nice surprise for Mom!

Story notes

This is a good opportunity to talk about the benefits of eating a good breakfast and about the variety of foods people eat in the morning. Ask the children to draw a picture of what they eat for breakfast, and then ask volunteers to show their pictures and talk about what they drew.

Ask about the story:
What did Tommy make? What did he take out of the refrigerator? Where did he get the milk? What happened when Tommy poured the juice? Was Mrs. Young surprised? Did Jim help Tommy make breakfast? Did Tommy make a good breakfast?

Ask about your students:
What did you have for breakfast today? What do you like to eat for breakfast? Do you eat the same thing every day for breakfast? When do you eat breakfast? Have you ever skipped breakfast? How do you feel when you don't eat breakfast?

Dialogue

Components: Cassette, Topic 9 Wall Chart, Picture Dictionary (pp. 18–19).

See page xix for techniques and strategies for presenting and practicing dialogues.

Mrs. Young:	My goodness!
Jim:	Tommy made the breakfast.
Mrs. Young:	So I see!
Tommy:	Look! Look! Orange juice, cereal, eggs, bread, and butter! Did you know I could make breakfast?
Mrs. Young:	No, I didn't.
Tommy:	But I don't know how to make coffee. Here is your cup, Mom. You'll have to do it. And you'll have to cook the eggs, too.
Mrs. Young:	That's OK.
Jim:	Did you set the table?
Tommy:	Yep! ... knife, fork, and spoon.
Mrs. Young:	Well, thank you, Tommy. This is a delicious breakfast! What a nice surprise!

Dialogue notes

After playing the cassette a few times, have each child work with a partner to invent similar dialogues about making breakfast. You can suggest that one child be the breakfast maker and the other child ask him/her questions about how the breakfast was made.

Beats!

Components: Cassette, Beats! (Topic 9).

See page xx for techniques and strategies for presenting and practicing Beats!

Who made this mess?
I didn't do it.
Who spilled this milk?
I didn't spill it.

Who dropped these cookies?
I didn't drop them.
Who made this mess?
Don't blame me!

Who broke this glass?
I didn't break it.
Who burned this pot?
I didn't burn it.

Who left these dirty dishes?
I didn't leave them.
Who made this mess?
Don't blame me!

Maybe it was Bill.
Maybe it was Lee.
Maybe it was Nancy,
but it wasn't me!

Beat notes

This Beat introduces a lot of useful verbs. As a warm-up or for extra drill on the verbs, the children can practice the Beat by repeating all the questions first (keeping the rhythm) and then repeating all the answers.

Worksheets

Worksheet 1: Who made breakfast? (p. 17)

Write the words *yes* and *no* on the board. Hold up the picture card for *cereal* and ask: *Do you eat cereal with a knife? Yes or no?* Ask a volunteer to answer and to point to the correct word on the board. Direct the children's attention to the second part of the page. Tell them to write the word for each picture on the line provided. Point out that the words they need are at the bottom of the page. Then tell them to circle the things they would use to eat each of the items named.

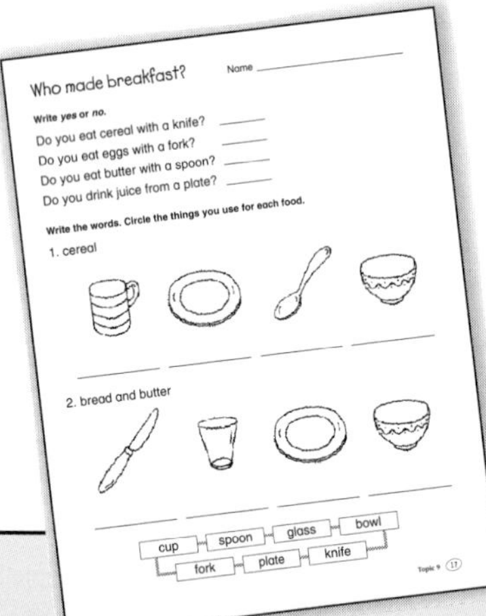

Who made breakfast? Name ____

Write *yes* or *no*.

Do you eat cereal with a knife? ____
Do you eat eggs with a fork? ____
Do you eat butter with a spoon? ____
Do you drink juice from a plate? ____

Write the words. Circle the things you use for each food.

1. cereal
2. bread and butter

cup spoon glass bowl fork plate knife

Topic 9 17

Worksheet 2: Who made breakfast? (p. 18)

Tell the children to write the missing words on the lines provided. Point out that the pictures below each set of sentences are clues. Encourage the children to color the pictures.

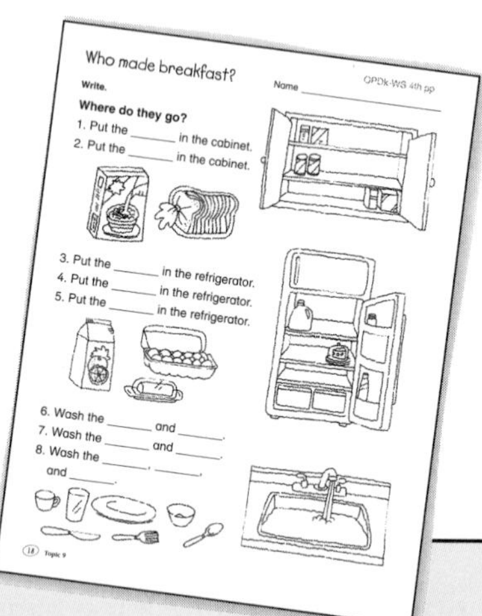

Who made breakfast? Name ____ QPDk-WS 4th pp

Write.

Where do they go?

1. Put the ____ in the cabinet.
2. Put the ____ in the cabinet.
3. Put the ____ in the refrigerator.
4. Put the ____ in the refrigerator.
5. Put the ____ in the refrigerator.
6. Wash the ____ and ____.
7. Wash the ____ and ____.
8. Wash the ____, ____, and ____.

18 Topic 9

Activities

- Practice setting the table. If possible, provide some props such as plates, cups, knives, forks, spoons, napkins, an apron, empty orange juice cartons, cereal boxes, egg cartons, and bread and butter wrappers. Model a way to set the table using a knife, fork, spoon, plate, glass, and cup. Then let children take turns setting the table, naming each item as they do so.
- Make a kitchen collage. Design and copy large-size pictures of a refrigerator, a stove, and a cabinet. Glue the pictures to poster board, leaving the doors free so that they can be opened and closed. Glue these pieces to mural paper. Spread out an assortment of magazines with food pictures or precut photos of food items. Help children work together to identify the foods. Encourage them to talk about what types of foods they like and to compare what they like with what other people eat. Invite the children to glue each picture in an appropriate place. Encourage them to add details to the scene, such as a table, counter, or large clock.
- Arrange for the group to visit the kitchen of the school cafeteria. Afterward, discuss with students how the cafeteria kitchen is the same as, and also different from, the kitchens in their homes. Have students draw a picture of the school kitchen.

Here comes the school bus!

Content

- School bus routines
- School bus safety rules
- Conduct on a school bus

Language

- Articulating school-bus safety rules: *Don't push people in line. Stay in your seats. Don't lean out the window.*
- Following directions and using commands: *Please sit down. Stand up. Go to your seat. Fasten your seat belt, please.*
- Describing school-bus routines: *The school bus stops at the corner. The children wait at the bus stop. They stand in a line with their backpacks. The bus driver opens the door.*

Words

1. bus stop
2. bus driver
3. corner
4. line
5. seat
6. seat belt
7. lunch box
8. backpack

Verbs

9. lean
10. push
11. stand
12. sit

Additional Words

please
excuse me
stoplight
stop sign
quiet
drive

The school bus has stopped on the corner near Alison's apartment. The bus driver has just opened the door. Several children have formed themselves into a line and are beginning to board the bus. The driver is sitting and talking with them, reminding them of some rules: line up, no pushing, move to the back of the bus. One boy is leaning out a window in the back of the bus. That's against the rules. The children sitting inside the bus are putting on their seat belts. Alison is running to get on the end of the line. Alison's mother is running after her, calling and holding out her lunch box. Alison forgot her lunch.

Words

Components: Topic 10 Wall Chart, Picture Dictionary (pp. 20–21), Cassette, Word and Picture Cards (Topic 10).

See page xiv for techniques and strategies for presenting and practicing words.

Here comes the school bus!

1. bus stop	4. line	7. lunch box
2. bus driver	5. seat	8. backpack
3. corner	6. seat belt	

Verbs

9. lean	11. stand
10. push	12. sit

Notes

After the children are comfortable with the words, sort the words into categories such as "things in the bus," "things you take on the bus," or "things outside." Practice the verbs by having students act them out.

Workbook page

Point out that some of the vocabulary words are written under an empty frame, while the other frames have pictures that show one of the words but no label. Tell the students that their task is to write the words for each picture that has no label, and draw an image for each word that has no picture. Tell them to cut out the appropriate image and glue it in the box.

Stories

Components: Picture Dictionary (pp. 20–21), Cassette, Story (Topic 10).

See page xviii for techniques and strategies for presenting and practicing stories.

The school bus stops at the corner.
The children wait at the bus stop.
They stand in a line with their backpacks.
The bus driver opens the door.

Stay in line. Please don't push.
Move to the back of the bus.
Sit down now. Put on your seat belts.
Let's be quiet. That's good!

One boy leans out the window.
Don't do that!
Keep your head inside.
Keep your hands in, too.

Wait! Here comes Alison!
Wait! Here comes Mrs. Matthews!
She has a lunch box in her hand.
Alison forgot her lunch!

Story notes

This is a good opportunity to discuss bus safety. Ask how many children ride a bus to school. Encourage those who do to talk about their experiences.

Ask about the story:

Where does the bus stop? Where is the bus stop? Who waits at the bus stop? Who is driving the bus? What is the boy doing? Why is Alison hurrying? Why is Mrs. Matthews trying to catch up with Alison?

Ask about your students:

Do you ride a bus? Where do you catch the bus? What are the rules on your bus? What do you bring to school with you? Do you sometimes forget things? Have you ever been late for the bus? Who rides on the bus with you?

Dialogue

Components: Cassette, Topic 10 Wall Chart, Picture Dictionary (pp. 20–21).

See page xix for techniques and strategies for presenting and practicing dialogues.

Bus driver:	Good morning, kids!
Children:	Good morning, Mr. Bower.
Bus driver:	Get in a nice line now. No pushing.
Children:	We know.
Bus driver:	Move to the back of the bus and take your seats. And what do you do after you sit down?
Children:	Put on seat belts!
Bus driver:	Good!
1st child:	Hey, Mr. Bower, look! Here comes Alison.
2nd child:	Here comes her mother.
Mrs. Matthews:	Alison, wait!
Bus driver:	Morning, Mrs. Matthews!
Mrs. Matthews:	Good morning, Mr. Bower. Alison forgot her lunch.
Bus driver:	Again?
Alison:	Thanks, Mom.
Bus driver:	I'm glad she didn't miss the bus!

Dialogue notes

Set up chairs to represent a school bus, and ask children to take roles as bus driver and passengers on the bus. Encourage them to invent dialogues as the students get on the bus and greet the bus driver. Have them take turns playing different parts.

Beats!

Components: Cassette, Beats! (Topic 10).

See page xx for techniques and strategies for presenting and practicing Beats!

Here comes the school bus
down the street.
    The red lights blink,
    And the door goes "Squeak!"

Hurry up! Hurry up!
Get inside.
    Hurry up! Hurry up!
    Ready for a ride.

Let's get to school!
It's not very far.
    Hurry up! Hurry up!
    Here we are!

Beat notes

Practice the Beat until the children are comfortable with all the words. Then set up a double row of chairs to represent the seats on the school bus. Ask one child to be the driver sitting in the front. Have the children recite the first stanza together. Then prompt the "bus driver" to recite the second and third stanzas as the rest of the children line up and take seats on the bus. Then have the entire group recite the final stanza together. Encourage all the children to take a turn playing the bus driver.

Worksheets

Worksheet 1: Here comes the school bus! (p. 19)

Show the children an example of any cartoon that has a character's words shown in a speech bubble. Explain that the words show what the character is saying. (You may want to explain the difference between a speech bubble and a thought bubble, and show an example of the latter if possible.) Then direct their attention to the pictures on the worksheet. Discuss the first picture. Ask someone to describe what is happening in the picture. Ask volunteers to tell what they think the school bus driver might be saying at that moment. Help children to write the words in each speech bubble, as needed.

Here comes the school bus! Name

Write.
What does the bus driver say?

Please ____ in your ____

No ____ ing!

Please do not ____ out the window.

Please stand in a ____

Topic 10 19

Worksheet 2: Here comes the school bus! (p. 20)

Explain that each sentence describes something in the picture. Ask a volunteer to find the part of the picture that shows the first sentence. Tell the children that they should write the number 1 on the line provided under that part of the picture, then do the same for the rest of the sentences. When the children are finished, invite a volunteer to show his or her picture and choose one of the numbered parts of the page. Ask that child to point to the picture and say the number he or she wrote. Read aloud the sentence with that number. Ask the rest of the children to say if the number is correct.

Here comes the school bus! Name

Number the picture.

1. The boy is leaning out the window.
2. The bus is at the bus stop.
3. The girl has a backpack.
4. The boy has a lunch box.
5. The girl is pushing.
6. The driver has his seat belt on.

20 Topic 10

Activities

- Make a bus safety book. Ask the children about rules on a bus, and write down their ideas. Prompt them to think about how to be safe when on the sidewalk, crossing the street in front of a bus, as well as getting on the bus. Ask the children to make pictures that illustrate safety rules. Ask them to write or dictate a sentence about the picture. Bind all the pictures into a book to share.

- Hold a bus evacuation drill. Explain to the children that sometimes in an emergency situation the passengers on a bus use a different exit than usual. Tell them that a drill is a chance to practice an emergency procedure. Ask students to set up a bus with a double row of chairs, and take a seat on the bus. For the first round, you can act as the bus driver, modeling simple, clear commands: *Please be quiet and listen. We will go out the back door. Don't push. One at a time. Go stand on the curb.* After the drill, invite volunteers to take the part of the bus driver and repeat.

- Teach the song "The Wheels on the Bus":

  The wheels on the bus go round and round,
  round and round, round and round.
  The wheels on the bus go round and round
  all through the town.

  Sing some other stanzas and encourage the children to invent new stanzas specific to riding a school bus.

Theme 3: My School

Topic 11	Time for school	Topic 16	Gym time!
Topic 12	What are you making?	Topic 17	What's for lunch?
Topic 13	Where's my homework?	Topic 18	Let's play!
Topic 14	Bodies and bones!	Topic 19	What's the matter?
Topic 15	What's new in the hall?	Topic 20	Music!

Theme Bibliography

Arthur's Chicken Pox
written and illustrated by Mark Tolon Brown.
Little, Brown & Co., 1996. ISBN 0316110507
Arthur's Teacher Trouble
written and illustrated by Mark Tolon Brown.
Little, Brown & Co., 1987. ISBN 0316112445
Arthur has problems not unlike any child in his or her first years of school. His sister always taunts him. A demanding teacher imposes tough requirements on him. When he gets chicken pox, he tries to get better in time to go to the circus. Both books are easy to share with primary-age children, who may identify with Arthur's problems. When practiced and modeled, the dialogue can be used to describe familiar everyday experiences.

The Body Atlas
written and illustrated by Mark Crocker.
Oxford University Press, 1994. ISBN 019520963X
This book, a collection of road maps to the body's various internal systems, is a fascinating introduction to the human anatomy. Topics range from everyday phenomena (e.g., why you sometimes feel sleepy after a meal) to the more complex (e.g., the principles of the immune system). The language is scientific and will require some sheltering. Every page is fully illustrated, providing an essential guide to the body's workings. Advanced students will find the glossary of key terms very helpful.

How Humans Make Friends
written and illustrated by Loreen Leedy.
Holiday House, 1996. ISBN 0823412237
A guide to human friendship, as "written" by an alien named Zork Tripork. Zork gives his(?) alien audience a guide to the things friends do, the things they talk about, how they get along, what they say. This complex subject is treated in a very light-hearted fashion. The illustrations resemble cartoon cells, and each is accompanied by a single sentence. The combination of graphic design and language helps students learn survival language and teaches them how to describe everyday feelings. It's an important book that encourages children talk about themselves in a world of others.

I Hate English
written by Ellen Levine; illustrated by Steve Bjorkman.
Scholastic Inc., 1995. ISBN 0590423045
Mei is so unhappy when her family moves from Hong Kong to New York that she refuses to speak or write English. But her teacher understands her struggle and helps her learn English. This book models the care and support teachers need to provide English-language learners with. It may resonate more with older students who are struggling with English, but it can benefit any classroom in which a newcomer faces similar problems.

I'm New Here
written by Bud Howlett; photographs by the author.
Houghton Mifflin Co., 1993. ISBN 0395640490
During his ten years of teaching and twenty-four years as an elementary school principal, the author developed a sensitivity to bilingual education and the problems of children new to America. In this book, he tells the story of Jazmin Escalante, a girl from El Salvador whose family moves to America. Through his photographs he focuses on the challenges Jazmin faces: adjusting to her new school, learning English, meeting new friends, and adapting to her new home. Latino children in particular will identify with Jazmin and her struggles. The text is above primary-grade reading level. The photographs provide prompts for discussion. You can use the book to model and practice both friendship and survival dialogues.

I Speak English For My Mom

written by Muriel Stanek;
illustrated by Judith Friedman.
Albert Whitman & Co., 1989. ISBN 0807536598

Lupe enjoys helping her mother by translating English into Spanish for her. She also helps with her mother's homework for evening English classes. Their experiences are common; in many families who emigrate to America, the children often act as interpreters for their parents. The relationship between Lupe and her mom is inspiring. For some children who are ashamed of their parents' lack of English skills, this book provides a positive role model to right that wrong.

King of the Playground

written by Phyllis R. Naylor;
illustrated by Nola Langner Malone.
Aladdin Paperbacks, 1994. ISBN 0689718020

Sammy is the self-proclaimed king of the playground. Whenever Kevin tries to play there, Sammy threatens to tie him up, stick him in a deep pit, or nail him shut in his house. Kevin is scared until his dad convinces him that Sammy can't actually do anything. There's a good ending to this story: Sammy and Kevin end up making a sand castle together and sharing the playground. In this story of young children's exaggeration in play, the dialogue is particularly useful in conveying the exaggerations, the subtleties—and the terrors—that young children use in their everyday language of play.

Konnichiwa! I Am a Japanese-American Girl

written by Tricia Brown;
photographs by Kazuyoshi Arai.
Henry Holt & Co., 1995. ISBN 0805023534

If any Japanese-American students attend your school, you can invite them to share this book—and by extension their own experiences—with your class. The book introduces us to the Kamiya family, and lets us see San Francisco's Japanese-American community through their eyes. Although the Kamiyas were born in America, they have maintained a sense of their own culture. Simple language and an abundance of photographs make this book easy to paraphrase in order to get at meaning. Furthermore, the photographs may be tied into the crafts, dances, and games that are presented throughout Theme 3.

Lilly's Purple Plastic Purse

written and illustrated by Kevin Henkes.
Greenwillow Books, 1996. ISBN 0688128971

Lilly, a young, impressionable mouse, admires her teacher Mr. Slinger so much that she wants to become a teacher herself when she grows up. This runaway best-seller has become a favorite in schools everywhere. Many teachers can relate to this beguiling story about reaching out to children, surviving the foibles of classroom management, and teaching the overzealous student. Shy newcomers may identify with Lilly's emotions, or with the "Lilly" in their classroom. You can model many of the book's scenes in the classroom to make further connections with students.

Meet Danitra Brown

written by Nikki Grimes;
illustrated by Floyd Cooper.
Mulberry Books, 1997. ISBN 0688154719

This book of poems explores the many different aspects of friendship through the relationship between Zuri and Danitra Brown, "the most splendiferous girl in town." All the hallmarks of true friendship (loyalty, empathy, trust, support, confidence, etc.) are evident here. Some poems are a little long, but others are short and sweet. Students may have some initial difficulty understanding the colloquialisms and slang. Nevertheless, this book is excellent for sharing the African-American experience with your class.

What's For Lunch?

written and illustrated by Eric Carle.
Cartwheel Books, 1998. ISBN 0590328425

This extremely short book chronicles an extremely finicky monkey's search for food. The "monkey" is actually a cardboard cutout that is suspended from a string inside the book. This lets the monkey travel from page to page to ask the question, "What's for lunch?" This is a very simple read for early learners. After learning the language in Topic 17, even the youngest students will have no problem reading this book.

Zin! Zin! Zin! A Violin,

written by Lloyd Moss;
illustrated by Marjorie Priceman.
Simon & Schuster, 1995. ISBN 0671882392

Using a sing-song rhyme, Lloyd Moss introduces us to assorted instruments and players, turning a solo act into a duo, then the duo into a trio, and so on. By the end of the book, a full orchestra has been amassed to perform. Some of the descriptive adjectives may be difficult, but you can use the illustrations and TPR to enable students to read along. This delightful book can reinforce the instrument and verb words learned in Topic 20, and provides additional words that can be easily added to a classroom word bank.

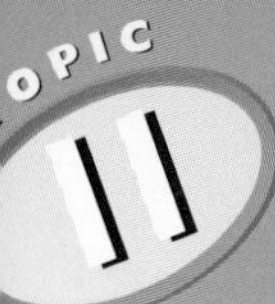

Time for school

Content

- People and places in school
- Ways of traveling to school
- Days of the week
- Telling time

Language

- Asking and answering questions about people and places in school: *Who is Mrs. Katz? She's the music teacher. What's this room? It's the office. Where is the teacher? The teacher is in the classroom. Where's the bathroom? The bathroom is down the hall.*
- Describing different ways of traveling to school: *How do you come to school? How did you get here today? I walk. I ride. I take the bus. I got a ride.*
- Identifying and using the names of the days of the week: *School starts Monday. Today is Thursday. Friday is a school day.*
- Understanding and using ordinal numbers in reference to location: *Go upstairs to the second floor. The gym is on the first floor.*
- Telling time and using expressions concerning time, such as *early* and *late: When is art class? [Art class is] In a half hour. Come early. Ping was late.*

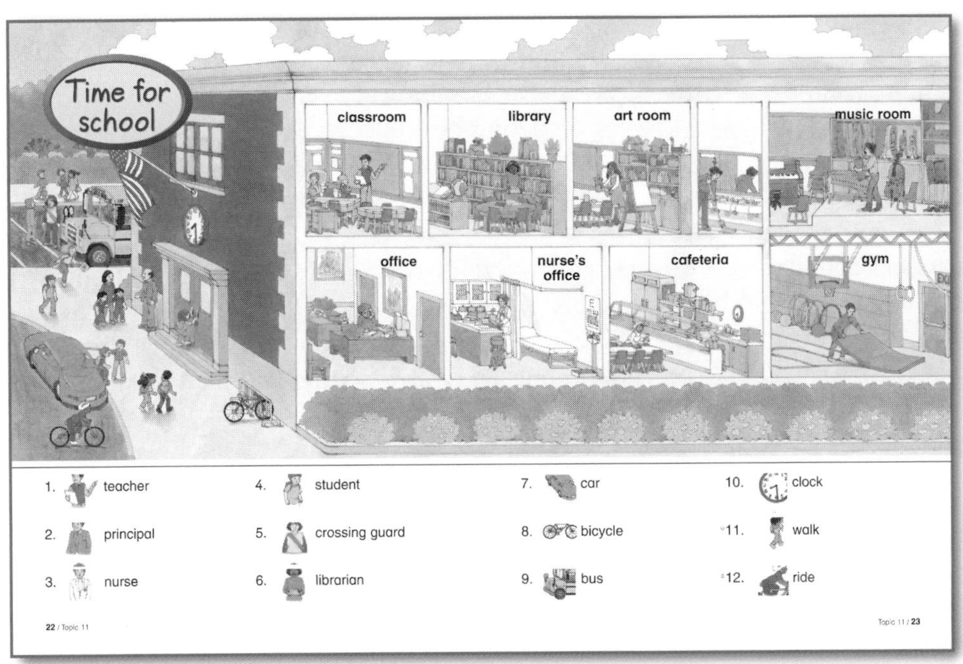

Words

1. teacher
2. principal
3. nurse
4. student
5. crossing guard
6. librarian
7. car
8. bicycle
9. bus
10. clock

Verbs

11. walk
12. ride

Labels

classroom	office
library	nurse's office
art room	cafeteria
music room	gym

It's 8:30 Monday morning. Students are arriving at school by bus, on bikes, in cars, and on foot. The crossing guard is there, helping the students. Alison is getting off the bus. Tommy and Jimmy are getting out of their car. Diego and Jasmin are walking, and Marcus is riding his bike. There is a bicycle rack by the front door. The principal is at the front door welcoming everyone. Mrs. Cheng is talking to him. She has the twins with her. The school has two floors. The first floor has an office, a nurse's office, a cafeteria, and a gym. The second floor has a classroom, a library, an art room, a bathroom, and a music room. Mr. Marino is in his classroom, the librarian is in the library, the nurse is in her office, and Mrs. Lee, the gym teacher, is in the gym.

Additional Words

first/second floor	inside/outside
upstairs	next to
downstairs	between

Words

Components: Topic 11 Wall Chart, Picture Dictionary (pp. 22–23), Cassette, Word and Picture Cards (Topic 11).

See page xiv for techniques and strategies for presenting and practicing words.

Time for school

1. teacher
2. principal
3. nurse
4. student
5. crossing guard
6. librarian
7. car
8. bicycle
9. bus
10. clock

Verbs

11. walk
12. ride

Labels

classroom	art room	office	cafeteria
library	music room	nurse's office	gym

Notes

Set apart the picture cards that depict people who work in the school. Invite a volunteer to select a card, look at it, and keep it hidden. Then prompt the other children to ask him or her questions: *Is this person usually in the gym? Does this person help children in the library?* Encourage them to make picture cards for other people at school (such as the secretary, custodian, or art teacher). You may want to extend this activity by using the names of the people who work in your school.

Workbook page

Tell the children to refer to their word cards, or write the words on the board. Read the question aloud: *Where are they?* Point out that the completed sentences answer this question for the people shown in each picture. At the bottom of the page, tell the children to look at each picture in the set and write the word for how the child shown is going to school.

11 Time for school

Write.

Where are they?

1. The ______ and the ______ are in the classroom.
2. The ______ is in the nurse's office.
3. The ______ is in the office.
4. The ______ is in the library.

How do you go to school?

Stories

Components: Picture Dictionary (pp. 22–23), Cassette, Story (Topic 11).

See page xviii for techniques and strategies for presenting and practicing stories.

It's Monday.
The school clock says 8:30.
The students are coming to school.
Here comes Marcus,
riding his bicycle.

Diego and Jasmin are walking.
Alison takes the bus.
Jim and Tommy come by car.
The crossing guard helps everyone.

School is ready to begin.
The teachers are in their classrooms.
The nurse is in her office.
The librarian is in the library.

Where is the principal?
He is standing at the door.
He is smiling at everyone.
Don't be late!

Story notes

This is a good opportunity to have the children practice telling time (to the half hour). Use a toy clock with movable hands, and encourage the children to take turns setting and reading the time.

Ask about the story:
What time does school begin in the story? How did Marcus come to school? Were Diego and Jasmin walking or riding? Who rode on the bus? What did the crossing guard do? Where are the teachers? Who is in the library?

Ask about your students:
What time does our school day begin? Do you try to come on time? Were you on time today? Are you ever early for school? How do you get to school? Who helps you cross the street?

Dialogue

Components: Cassette, Topic 11 Wall Chart, Picture Dictionary (pp. 22–23).

See page xix for techniques and strategies for presenting and practicing dialogues.

Mrs. Cheng:	Excuse me, please. Where's the nurse?
Principal:	She's in her office, Mrs. Cheng.
Mrs. Cheng:	Where's that?
Principal:	The nurse's office is on the first floor. It's between the office and the cafeteria.
Mrs. Cheng:	And where is Mr. Marino?
Principal:	He's in his classroom.
Mrs. Cheng:	Is that upstairs or downstairs?
Principal:	It's upstairs on the second floor, next to the library.
Mrs. Cheng:	Oh, thank you. Can I go up?
Principal:	Of course you can.
Boy:	Mr. Marino, where's the bathroom?
Mr. Marino:	It's right down the hall. It's between the art room and the music room.
Boy:	Thanks!

Dialogue notes

Have the children point up when they hear *upstairs* and point down when they hear *downstairs*. Have the children work in pairs, practicing an exchange based on one of the two exchanges.

Beats!

Components: Cassette, Beats! (Topic 11).

See page xx for techniques and strategies for presenting and practicing Beats!

Walk a little faster,
We're going to be late!
　　No, we're not!
　　We're going to be early.

Walk a little faster,
It's half past eight!
　　No, it's not.
　　We're going to be early.

　　Why oh why are you
　　walking so fast?
I don't want to be last.

Why oh why are you
walking so slow?
　　I don't want to go!

Beat notes

Have the children choose a partner and take turns reciting the two roles while acting out the words. Suggest that one child walk slowly while the other walks fast.

Worksheets

Worksheet 1: Time for school (p. 21)

For each job listed on the page, say the name of the person in your school who has that job. Ask volunteers to choose the appropriate picture card and hold it up. For example, if your principal is Mr. Gajewski, the children should hold up the card for *principal* when you say his name. Tell them to write the names of each person who works in your school on the lines provided and draw a line to each job description. Write their names on the board so the children can spell them correctly.

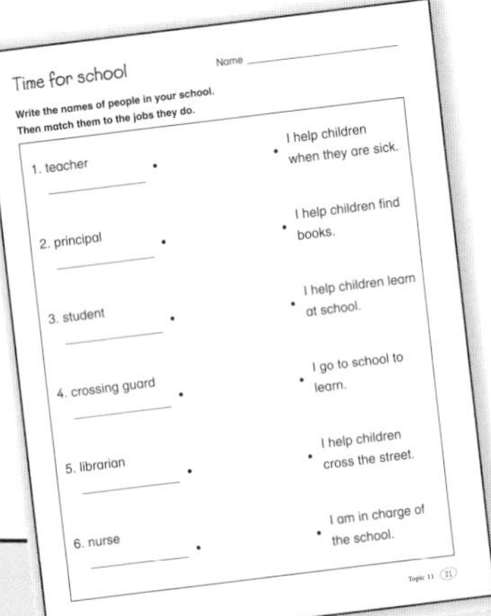

Time for school Name ____________

Write the names of people in your school.
Then match them to the jobs they do.

1. teacher ______ • — • I help children when they are sick.
2. principal ______ • — • I help children find books.
3. student ______ • — • I help children learn at school.
4. crossing guard ______ • — • I go to school to learn.
5. librarian ______ • — • I help children cross the street.
6. nurse ______ • — • I am in charge of the school.

Topic 11 21

Worksheet 2: Time for school (p. 22)

Generate a discussion about the different ways students get to school. Tell the children to circle the picture that shows how they get to school most days, and write a sentence that gives the same information. To fill in the chart at the bottom of the page, have each child ask at least three classmates how they get to school. You can make a class chart that shows the results.

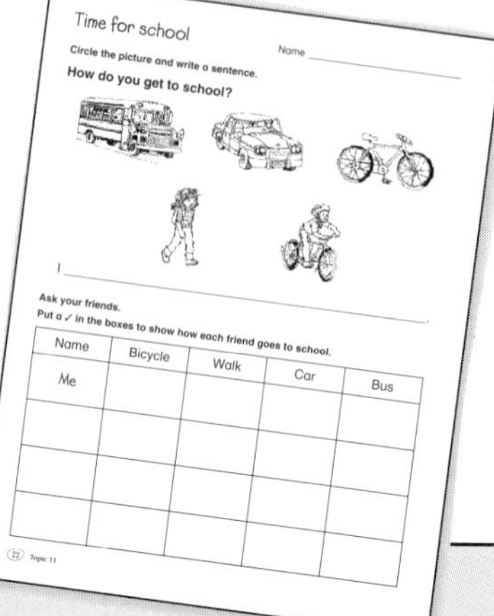

Time for school Name ____________

Circle the picture and write a sentence.
How do you get to school?

I ______________________________.

Ask your friends.
Put a ✓ in the boxes to show how each friend goes to school.

Name	Bicycle	Walk	Car	Bus
Me				

22 Topic 11

Activities

- Lay on a table a row of three of the picture cards that show people. Have the children take turns asking and telling where each person's card is in order from left to right: *Is the teacher first? Who is second? The principal is second. The third one is the nurse.* Change the cards around and repeat the activity. Then vary the activity by giving a child the three cards, and asking him or her to put them on the table in the order you dictate: *Put the nurse first, put the crossing guard second, and put the librarian third.*

- Have students make a model of an imaginary three-story school building by stacking empty shoe boxes. Help the children make labels for the rooms on each floor, and encourage them to add detail (such as cardboard furniture and clay people). Explain that the convention for numbering floors is different in the United States from that in most other countries: The street-level floor is called the first floor, and one flight up is called the second floor.

- Help the children brainstorm a list of people who work at school. Record these on a large sheet of chart paper. Discuss and list on the chart the children's ideas about what these workers do on the job. Tour your school, taking pictures of the people who work there. Then make a large poster labeled "Workers in Our School." Put each photo on the poster and help the children label each photo.

- Ask the children to draw pictures of themselves on their way to school. As they draw, encourage them to add detail by asking questions: *Do you ride a bike? walk? ride a bus or car? What are you wearing? What is the weather like? Is there a lot of traffic? Are there other people with you? Are you hurrying to be on time?* After the pictures are done, have the children write or dictate a description. Bind the pages together to make a class book. Make a chart that shows how the children in your class get to school.

What are you making?

Content

- Classroom supplies
- Classroom activities
- Classroom routines

Language

- Identifying classroom supplies and describing their use: *I can write with a pencil. She built a tower with blocks. Use scissors to cut out the cards.*
- Asking about and describing classroom activities: *What are you making? I am painting a house. It's cleanup time.*
- Expressing likes and dislikes: *She likes to build with the blocks. I don't like to paint. I like to glue pictures.*
- Calling for attention: *Stop! Look! Listen! Clean up! It's time to clean up now!*
- Understanding and using words that can be nouns or verbs: *I spilled the paint. Can I paint this box? Where's the glue? Glue the hair on the puppet.*

There is a lot going on in this kindergarten classroom. Jo-Jo is very proud because he has his own pencils and markers. He loves school! Zoe is painting blue trees. Some have fallen to the floor. Jasmin is making a house. She's using crayons and markers. Jackie is using the scissors (very carefully) to make a cutout. Tommy is building a tower with the blocks. The tower is already very tall, and he is putting another block on top. Is it going to fall? Mrs. Diaz is trying to get everyone to listen because it's cleanup time.

Words

1. picture
2. markers
3. pencil
4. crayons
5. scissors
6. glue
7. blocks

Verbs

8. build
9. listen
10. look
11. paint
12. cut

Additional Words

clay
color
paintbrush
building
tower
paste
cleanup

Words

 **Components:** Topic 12 Wall Chart, Picture Dictionary (pp. 24–25), Cassette, Word and Picture Cards (Topic 12).

See page xiv for techniques and strategies for presenting and practicing words.

What are you making?

1. picture
2. markers
3. pencil
4. crayons
5. scissors
6. glue
7. blocks

Verbs

8. build
9. listen
10. look
11. paint
12. cut

Notes

In this unit, *glue* has been introduced as a noun and *paint* as a verb. Your students may wonder why the same words are used in different ways. You can talk to the class about words for things (nouns) and words for actions (verbs). Point out that *glue* and *paint* are both things and actions. Model questions and answers: *What is this? It's glue. What do you do with it? I glue paper. What is she using to paint? She is using paint.*

Workbook page

Ask the children to match the pictures on the page to their picture cards. Then have them trace over the words that name each item and read the sentence aloud. You can read the first two sentences with the class as models. Then tell the children to write the verbs in the missing spaces at the bottom of the page. If needed, prompt them by asking, *What is he/she doing?*

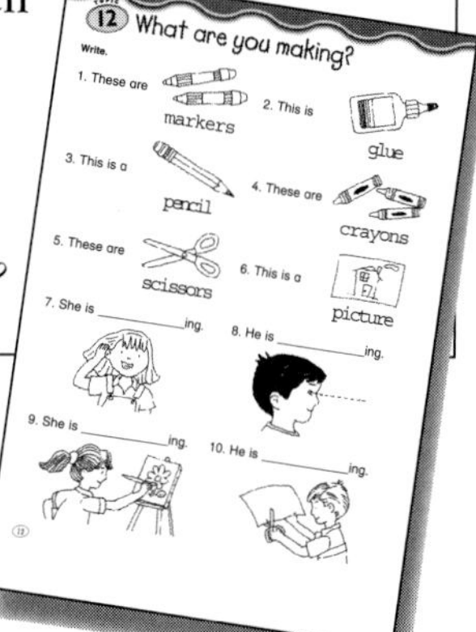

12 What are you making?

Write.

1. These are markers
2. This is glue
3. This is a pencil
4. These are crayons
5. These are scissors
6. This is a picture
7. She is ____ing.
8. He is ____ing.
9. She is ____ing.
10. He is ____ing.

Stories

 **Components:** Picture Dictionary (pp. 24–25), Cassette, Story (Topic 12).

See page xviii for techniques and strategies for presenting and practicing stories.

Jo-Jo loves school.
He has his own pencil and markers.
Tommy loves the big blocks.
He is building a tall tower.

Samantha likes painting
lots of pictures.
Swish! There they go!
All over the floor!

Jackie is using the scissors.
He is cutting very carefully.
Jasmin has crayons and glue.
She is making a house.

Look at Tommy's tower!
Is it going to fall?
Listen, everyone.
It's cleanup time!

Story notes

This is a good opportunity for children to express their likes and dislikes. Read one line of the Story (for example, *Samantha likes painting*) and then ask an individual, *Do you like to paint?*

Ask about the story:
What is Samantha painting? What is Tommy building? Who is making a picture? Why is Jackie cutting carefully? Why did the teacher say, "Listen"? Why is Tommy's tower going to fall? Who painted a blue tree? What did Jo-Jo have?

Ask about your students:
What did you use to make your building? What will you use to make a picture? How can you make a picture? What do you do at cleanup time? Where do we put the markers?

Dialogue

Components: Cassette, Topic 12 Wall Chart, Picture Dictionary (pp. 24–25).

See page xix for techniques and strategies for presenting and practicing dialogues

Samantha:	What are you making, Jasmin?
Jasmin:	I'm making a house.
Samantha:	How are you going to put the roof on?
Jasmin:	With the glue.
Samantha:	Oh.
Jasmin:	What are you painting, Samantha?
Samantha:	I'm painting trees.
Jasmin:	Why are they all blue?
Samantha:	I like blue trees.
Jasmin:	Oh. You better pick them up off the floor. Someone will step on them.
Mrs. Diaz:	Listen, everyone! Stop what you're doing, and put everything away. It's cleanup time!
Tommy:	Look, Mrs. Diaz! Look at my tower!
Mrs. Diaz:	Oh, it's so tall, Tommy!
Samantha:	Don't put that block on top, Tommy.
Other kids:	It's going to fall!

Dialogue notes

Have the children choose partners and invent their own dialogues based on the exchange between Samantha and Jasmin, beginning with *What are you making?* and using other questions (such as *How will you do that? What will you do next?*) to elicit more responses that use vocabulary words.

Beats!

Components: Cassette, Beats! (Topic 12).

See page xx for techniques and strategies for presenting and practicing Beats!

Who's got the glue?
I've got the glue.
I need the glue.
You can have it next!

Who's got the paint?
He's got the paint.
I need the paint.
You can have it next!

Who's got the scissors?
She's got the scissors.
I need the scissors.
You can have them next!

What are you making?
A house, I guess.
But if I don't get the glue,
and the paint,
and the scissors,
it's going to be a great big mess!

Beat notes

Explain that *Who's got …?* means the same as *Who has …?* Have the children practice the Beat together until they are comfortable with the words and phrases. Then have them choose one of the items mentioned: *glue, scissors,* or *paint.* Tell them that each time the question *Who's got the …?* is asked and the item they've chosen is named, they can jump up to answer, *I've got the …* .

Worksheets

Worksheet 1: What are you making? (p. 23)

Read aloud the labels on the storage areas. Have the children hold up the picture card that goes with each area. Then ask them to name each item shown at the bottom of the page. Help them cut out the pictured items, and tell them to glue each one in the storage area in which they think it belongs.

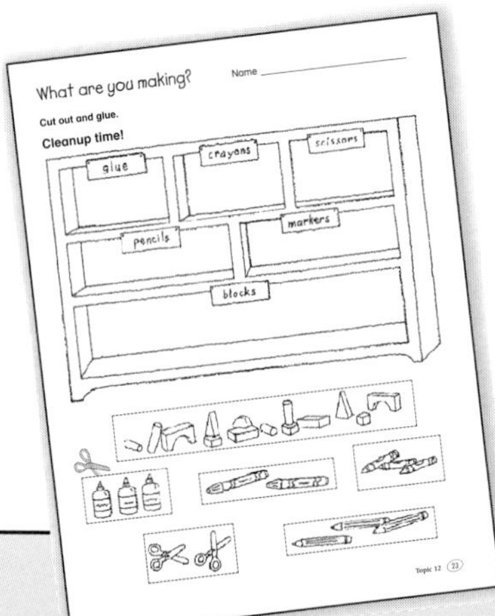

What are you making? Name ______

Cut out and glue.

Cleanup time!

glue
crayons
scissors
pencils
markers
blocks

Topic 12 23

Worksheet 2: What are you making? (p. 24)

Review the words at the bottom of the page with the class. Tell them to look at the picture for each numbered item at the top, and then write the word that is missing from each sentence. All the words they need are among the words at the bottom. (There is one extra word.) When they have completed the page, ask *What word did you not use?* (crayons)

What are you making? Name ______

Write.

1. I like to ______.
I build with ______.

2. I like to ______.
I cut with ______.

3. I like to ______.
I paint a ______.

4. The teacher says ______.
It's cleanup time.

5. ______ at my picture!
I made it with ______.

blocks crayons scissors cut paint listen picture build look markers

24 Topic 12

Activities

To the tune of "This Is the Way We Wash Our Clothes," sing a song about classroom rules and activities:

This is the way we cut with scissors. …
This is the way we put away markers. …
This is the way we walk in the hall. …
This is the way we wash for lunch. …

Talk with the children about why the classroom rules are important, and prompt them to list the all the rules they can on a chart. Then invite them to work individually, or in pairs or small groups, to make a poster reminding the class of one of the classroom rules. Display their posters.

Tell the children you have hidden a pencil somewhere in the room. Say: *Where is the pencil? Look for the pencil.* When they have found the hidden pencil, model questions and answers: *What did you/she/he find? I/She/He found the pencil.* Then invite a volunteer to hide a different classroom object and direct the activity. Play this way until everyone has a chance to hide, find, and say the vocabulary words.

Play a pantomime game. Help the children invent motions for some of the vocabulary words, for example, *look* (hand above eyes), *listen* (hand behind ear), *paint* (make brush strokes), *cut* (make cutting motion with imaginary scissors), or *build* (make motions of stacking). Tell the children to walk around in a circle until you call out a word. Then tell them to stop and pantomime the word. Invite volunteers to take turns calling out the words.

Where's my homework?

Content

- Classroom activities
- Classroom objects

Language

- Identifying and describing the use of classroom objects: *Mr. Marino was writing on the board with chalk. They put their homework on the teacher's desk. She threw her old paper in the wastebasket.*
- Asking and answering questions about classroom work: *Who is reading? What are you writing? She is thinking about what she wants to write. He drew pictures of dinosaurs.*
- Telling time to the quarter-hour: *It's 9:15. It is a quarter to ten.*
- Using prepositions *in, on,* and *under* to describe location: *The book is on the desk. The notebook is under the chair. Is there paper in your notebook?*

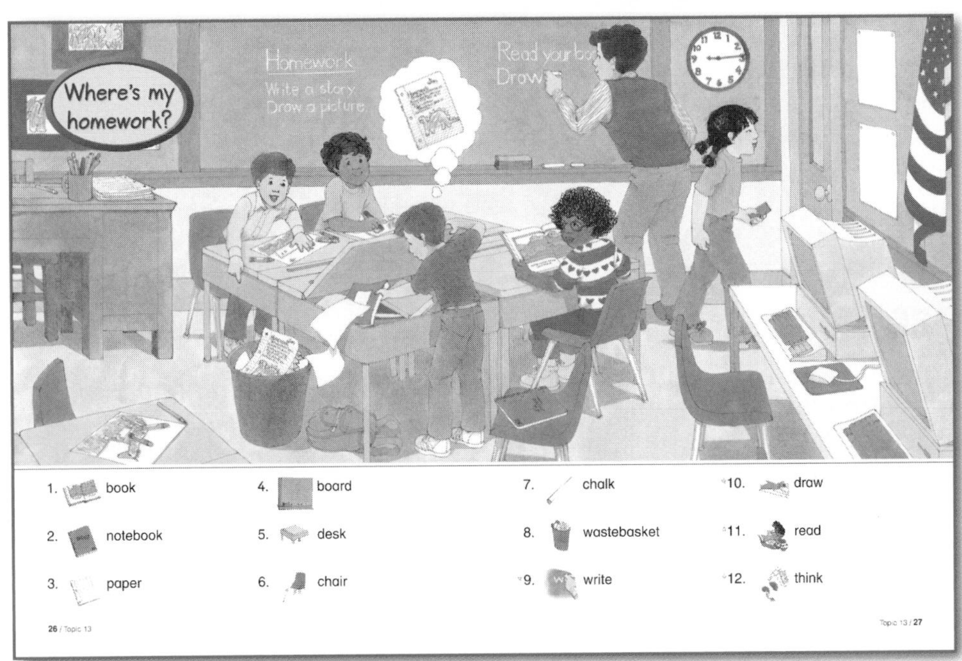

The classroom clock says 9:15. Mr. Marino's second-grade class is in full swing. The students have put their homework papers on their teacher's desk. Mr. Marino is writing on the board. Zoe is reading a book. Jim's friends are drawing pictures, and Ting is on her way to the bathroom. But Jim is still looking for his homework. He has looked in his backpack, which is now on the floor, and in his notebook on his chair. He has been frantically looking in his desk. He is thinking. Jim's friend Paul points to something in the wastebasket next to Jim's desk. It's Jim's homework. Thank goodness!

Words

1. book
2. notebook
3. paper
4. board
5. desk
6. chair
7. chalk
8. wastebasket

Verbs

9. write
10. draw
11. read
12. think

Additional Words

homework
coat hook
chalkboard
eraser
bulletin board
shelf

Words

Components: Topic 13 Wall Chart, Picture Dictionary (pp. 26–27), Cassette, Word and Picture Cards (Topic 13).

See page xiv for techniques and strategies for presenting and practicing words.

Where's my homework?

1. book	4. board	7. chalk
2. notebook	5. desk	8. wastebasket
3. paper	6. chair	

Verbs

9. write	11. read
10. draw	12. think

Notes

Invite the children to make signs to label classroom objects. Introduce the verbs one at a time, and model asking and answering questions, incorporating as many of the vocabulary nouns as possible: *What do we do with a book? We read a book. Where can we write? We can write on paper/the board.*

Workbook page

Offer the children a variety of strategies for unscrambling words. Write the word *koob* on the board. Tell them to count how many letters the word has. Ask them to name all the vocabulary words that have the letter *k*. Ask: *How many letter "o"s do you see in* koob*?* Then have them look at all the words and find the word that has the letter *o* twice *(book)*. Have them check to see that the scrambled word has the letter *b*. Have the students write the unscrambled words on the lines. Remind them to check that each letter is in both words. Tell them to circle (or draw a line to, or color) the picture of each word they unscramble.

Stories

Components: Picture Dictionary (pp. 26–27), Cassette, Story (Topic 13).

See page xviii for techniques and strategies for presenting and practicing stories.

Hand in your homework, please!
Put it on Mr. Marino's desk. Good!
Was everyone's homework there?
No, not Jim's.

Squeak! went the chalk.
Mr. Marino was writing on the board.
Zoe was reading her book.
Jim's friends were drawing pictures.

But Jim was looking in his desk.
Where was his homework? Think!
Was it in his notebook? No.
Under his books? On his chair?

Jim's friend found a paper.
It was Jim's homework!
Where?
In the wastebasket!

Story notes

Ask about the story:
Did Jim do the homework? Where did Jim look for his homework? Where was Jim's homework? Who found Jim's homework? Did Mr. Marino find Jim's homework? What was Zoe doing? Was Ting drawing? How did Jim's paper get into the wastebasket?

Ask about your students:
Do you read in school? What do you like to do in school? What do you think about when you draw? Are you reading a book? Do you have homework to do after school? Did you do your homework? Did you have homework yesterday?

Dialogue

Components: Cassette, Topic 13 Wall Chart, Picture Dictionary (pp. 26–27).

See page xix for techniques and strategies for presenting and practicing dialogues.

Mr. Marino:	It's 9:15! Hand in your homework, boys and girls!
Jim:	What homework, Zoe?
Zoe:	It's on the board, Jim. Mr. Marino wrote it there yesterday. See it?
Jim:	Oh yeah.
Paul:	Didn't you do the homework?
Jim:	Yes, I did it.
Paul:	Did you write the story?
Jim:	Yes, I wrote the story.
Zoe:	Did you draw the picture?
Jim:	Yes, I drew the picture, but I can't find it! I think I lost it.
Zoe:	Maybe you didn't lose it.
Paul:	Is it in your desk?
Jim:	No, I thought it was in my notebook.
Paul:	Maybe it fell on the floor. What's that?
Jim:	Where?
Paul:	Right there! In the wastebasket!
Jim:	It's my homework! Great! I found it!

Dialogue notes

Challenge the children to invent a new but similar dialogue, substitute their own names, vary the questions *(Did you look in your book? Did you look in the notebook?)*, and make up their own endings.

Beats!

Components: Cassette, Beats! (Topic 13).

See page xx for techniques and strategies for presenting and practicing Beats!

Look what I wrote!
    What did you write?
I wrote a story.
    So did I.

Look what I drew!
    What did you draw?
I drew a picture.
    So did I.

Look what I found!
    What did you find?
I found a paper.
    Hey! That's mine!

    That's my story!
    I was looking for that!
Here! Take it!
    Thanks! That's mine!

Beat notes

Once the children are familiar with the vocabulary and rhythm of this Beat, invite two volunteers to act out the story as the others recite.

Worksheets

Worksheet 1: Where's my homework? (p. 25)

This worksheet focuses on the use of the verbs. Ask the children to look at the first picture and describe what the girl is doing. Direct their attention to the words at the bottom of the page. Tell them that they will find the words needed to complete the sentences.

Where's my homework? Name ____

Write.

1. The girl likes to ____. She is reading a ____.
2. She likes to ____. She's drawing with ____.
3. The boy is ____. He's thinking about his ____.
4. The teacher is ____. He is writing on the ____.

book — thinking — board — writing — chalk — homework — read — draw

Topic 13 25

Worksheet 2: Where's my homework? (p. 26)

For the exercise at the top of the page, place a book on the floor. Ask the children to raise their hands when you say a true sentence, and to drop them when you say a false sentence. Then, pointing to the book, say one or two false sentences using topic vocabulary words *(The book is on the desk. The book is in the wastebasket).* Then say, *The book is on the floor.* Tell the children to circle the picture that correctly depicts what the sentences say. Then have the students write the missing words in the sentences at the bottom of the page.

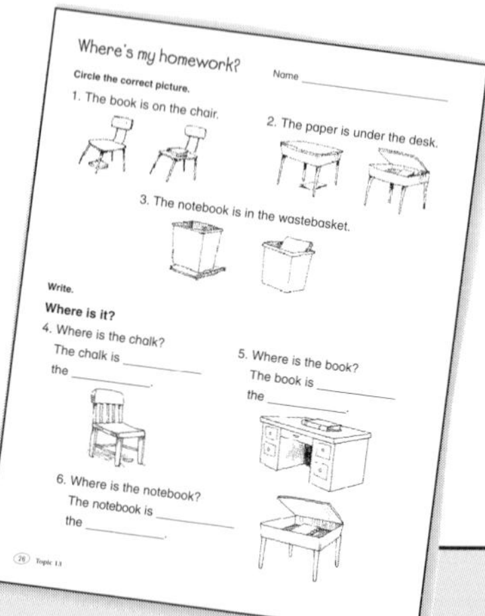

Where's my homework? Name ____

Circle the correct picture.

1. The book is on the chair.
2. The paper is under the desk.
3. The notebook is in the wastebasket.

Write.

Where is it?

4. Where is the chalk? The chalk is ____ the ____.
5. Where is the book? The book is ____ the ____.
6. Where is the notebook? The notebook is ____ the ____.

26 Topic 13

Activities

- Ask the children to list regular daily activities. If needed, prompt them with questions: *What's the first thing we do when we get to school? What do we do right after lunch?* Make a list, putting the items in sequential order. Have the children write each activity on a separate index card. Then tell them to mix the cards up and hand them to a neighbor. Each child puts the cards in the correct order, referring to the list if necessary.

- Make a skit. Have the children form small groups to discuss the topic of a short skit about school activities or events. You may suggest that they write down their ideas to keep track of them. Prompt the children to write a skit. Help them choose characters, and allow time for them to invent and practice dialogues. Allow nonspeaking parts so that everyone can be comfortably included. Then set aside a time when the groups can share their skits with the class.

- Help each child make a "My Day in School" book. Distribute pages for the children to write on. Then give them a partial sentence to complete, for example: *In school I like to …; In school I don't like to …; In school I always …; In school I sometimes …; In school I never …* Or ask the children to write or dictate their own captions. Have the children illustrate their books before binding the pages together.

Bodies and bones!

Content

- Parts of the body
- Body movements
- The skeleton

Language

- Identifying parts of the body: *This is his head. My fingers are part of my hand. She has two legs and two arms.*
- Relating skeletal structures to specific body parts: *I have bones in my body. My ribs are in my chest. Her spine is in her back.*
- Describing body movements: *He bends his legs. I can shake my head. She is stretching her back. He is moving his legs.*
- Following directions involving body parts and body movements: *Wave your hand. Stomp your feet. Bend your knees. Touch your toes.*

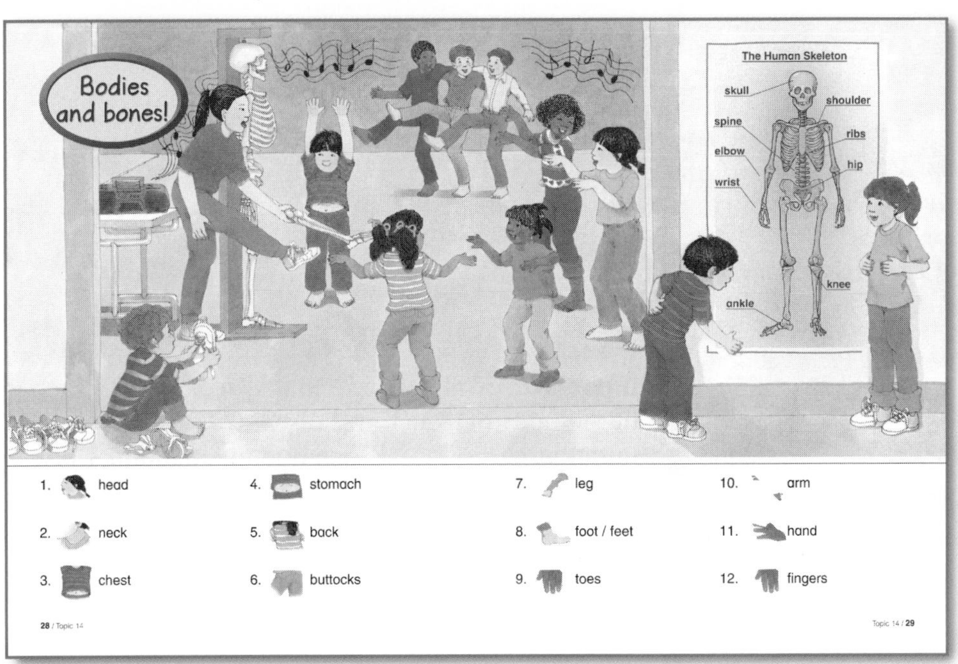

Music is playing, and Mrs. Lee is giving a dance lesson to teach her students how their bodies and skeletons interrelate. She is using the skeleton, "Mr. Bones," as a model and is urging the students to exercise all the parts of their bodies while dancing. The boys are kicking their legs up high. Ting and Zoe are trying to wave their arms gracefully. Jasmin and Samantha are having a great time wiggling their hips. Jackie stretches high, exposing his ribs and stomach. Tommy is hurrying to take off his sneakers in order to join the group. Outside the gym, an older student and Jo-Jo study the poster of the skeleton on the bulletin board. The student shows Jo-Jo where the ribs are, and Jo-Jo is delighted because he has just felt his spine in his back.

Words

1. head
2. neck
3. chest
4. stomach
5. back
6. buttocks
7. leg
8. foot/feet
9. toes
10. arm
11. hand
12. fingers

Labels

skull
spine
elbow
wrist
ankle
shoulder
ribs
hip
knee

Additional Words

thumb	wave
joint	kick
jaw	bend
move	wiggle
touch	twist
shake	

Components: Topic 14 Wall Chart, Picture Dictionary (pp. 28–29), Cassette, Word and Picture Cards (Topic 14).

See page xiv for techniques and strategies for presenting and practicing words.

The human skeleton

1. head	5. back	9. toes
2. neck	6. buttocks	10. arm
3. chest	7. leg	11. hand
4. stomach	8. foot/feet	12. fingers

Labels

skull	wrist	ribs
spine	ankle	hip
elbow	shoulder	knee

Notes

Introduce each part of the body by pointing to that part in the picture on the Wall Chart. Ask the children to point to the same part on their own bodies, and then to hold up the matching picture card. Model questions and answers about each part of the body: *What is this? This is the head. Point to your head. This is my head.*

Workbook page

Explain that on this page each word for a part of the body is missing some letters. Tell them that the missing letters are called *vowels (a, e, i, o, u).* Ask the children to follow the line from the word *ch_st* to the picture, and ask: *What part of the body is that? What letter is missing? Is it a vowel?* You may want to suggest that they refer to their word cards for help in filling in the missing letters.

Components: Picture Dictionary (pp. 28–29), Cassette, Story (Topic 14).

See page xviii for techniques and strategies for presenting and practicing stories.

Hey, Mr. Bones!
I can dance like you.
Inside my body
there's a skeleton, too.

The ribs in your chest
are just like mine.
And in my back
I can feel my spine.

My arms have elbows
and wrists like you.
My legs have knees
and ankles, too.

My hands have fingers.
My feet have toes.
I can wiggle my hips.
Get ready! Here goes!

Story notes

If possible, exhibit an articulated skeleton. As each part of the body or skeleton is discussed, ask the children to find that part on their own bodies, including those parts of the body mentioned in the story: *spine, ribs, wrists, ankles, elbows, hips.* Encourage the children to feel the bones under their flesh.

Ask about the story:
What are the boys doing? Who is stretching? What part of her body is Ting moving? What is the teacher doing? What part of his body did Jo-Jo feel?

Ask about your students:
What's inside your body? What is on the outside of your body? Can you feel your spine? Where are your ribs? Can you kick your legs way up high? How high can you stretch your arms? Where does your body bend? What parts of your body bend?

Components: Cassette, Topic 14 Wall Chart, Picture Dictionary (pp. 28–29).

See page xix for techniques and strategies for presenting and practicing dialogues.

Jo-Jo: Look at the skeleton! What a lot of bones!
Older girl: We have bones just like the skeleton. I can feel my ribs.
Jo-Jo: Where are my ribs?
Older girl: In your chest.
Jo-Jo: I can feel my ribs!
Older girl: I can feel my spine.
Jo-Jo: Where is my spine?
Older girl: In your back. Bend over.
Jo-Jo: I can feel my spine.

(music in background getting louder)
Mrs. Lee: Move your bodies to the music! Shake your head. Stretch your neck. Swing your arms and legs. Wave your hands. Kick your feet. Bend your back! Good, Jackie!
Marcus: Look at us, Mrs. Lee!
Mrs. Lee: Wow, Marcus! You're kicking those legs up high!
Ting: How's this, Mrs. Lee?
Mrs. Lee: Great, Ting! Bend your arms at the joints. Bend your elbows and wrists. Be graceful.
Zoe: Look at Samantha and Jasmin. They're wiggling their hips!
Samantha: Hurry up, Tommy! Dancing is fun!

Dialogue notes

Explain that the word *joint* means the connection point between parts of the body *(The leg bends at the knee joint)*. Have the children choose partners and create dialogues in which they take turns asking and answering questions about their bones and other parts of the body, using this format:

Where is your neck?
Here is my neck. Where is your leg?
Here is my leg. Where is your foot?

Components: Cassette, Beats! (Topic 14).

See page xx for techniques and strategies for presenting and practicing Beats!

Do we have bones?
Sure we do.
I have bones,
and so do you.

Do we have leg bones?
Sure we do.
Leg bones and arm bones,
and hip bones, too.

Bones in our necks?
Bones in our faces?
We have bones
in all kinds of places!

Backbones,
front bones,
and side bones, plus!
Put them all together and
that makes us!

Beat notes

Practice the Beat as a group, and then encourage the children to invent body motions to go with each stanza. They might, for example, pat themselves on the chest while saying, *I have bones,* and then open their hands wide while saying *and so do you.* (Remember that in some cultures pointing is considered very rude.) Continue through the Beat and indicate, by gesture or movement, the part of the body mentioned.

Worksheets

Worksheet 1: Bodies and bones! (p. 27)

Ask a series of questions to review the words: *Where is your head? Is this my foot? Are my fingers on my feet?* Then tell the children to use the words at the bottom of the page to label the parts of the body in the picture. Help the children cut out the words and glue them in the correct spaces. If you like, the children can use the words at the bottom for reference and instead write the words in the boxes.

Bodies and bones!

Name ____________

Cut out and glue.

head neck leg

foot arm toe hand

chest finger stomach

Topic 14 27

Worksheet 2: Bodies and bones! (p. 28)

Hold up your hands and model the question-and-answer pattern: *How many hands do I have? One, two. I have two hands.* Be sure the children can recognize the verbal form for the numbers *one, two,* and *ten.* You may want to write the numerals with the words as a reference. Allow beginning writers to dictate the description of the things they can do with their hands.

Bodies and bones!

Name ____________

Write

How many?

1. She has one ____________.
2. She has two ____________.
3. She has two ____________.
4. She has ten ____________.
5. She has ten ____________.

Draw and write.

1. How many hands do you have?
   I have ____________.

2. What can you do with your hands?
   I can ____________.

28 Topic 14

Activities

- To the tune of "This Is the Way We Wash Our Clothes," chant with the children as they move around in a circle:

  This is the way we point our toes,
  Point our toes,
  Point our toes,
  This is the way we point our toes,
  As we move along.

  Create verses using action words and parts of the body (for example, *This is the way we shake/bend our legs, wiggle our toes, wave our arms, nod our heads*). Invite the children to demonstrate motions and invent new verses.

- Make a child-size skeleton using cardboard with metal paper fasteners to connect the joints. Roll out a length of craft paper on the floor. Trace each child in a motion pose. Then place the cardboard skeleton inside the figure outline and allow the child to position and trace the skeleton. Encourage them to decorate their figures and label the body parts.

- Create a fitness center in a corner of your room. Put a mat on the floor and help the children make a chart that shows exercises, such as bicycling on their backs, jumping jacks, doing body twists, and touching toes. Set aside time for children to show each other exercises. Encourage the children to keep a record of their workouts.

- Play Simon Says. Tell the children that this is a game that requires them to listen closely and mimic the leader only when they hear the "magic words": *Simon says.* If the leader gives a direction and demonstrates an action without saying *Simon says,* they should not mimic the action. If they do, they have to sit out until only one child is left playing. That child becomes Simon, and the play begins again.

- Sing "Head, Shoulders, Knees, and Toes" (see Topic 3, Activities section).

What's new in the hall?

Content

- Emotions
- Resolving conflicts

Language

- Expressing and describing your own feelings and the feelings of others: *I am happy. I feel very tired. I'm worried. It made me angry. She felt so sad she cried.*
- Describing actions associated with emotions: *Why is she frowning? When I am very tired I yawn and yawn. I smile when I'm happy. The funny story made him laugh.*
- Using words to talk about and resolve conflicts: *Why are you angry? I'm angry because our picture is all spoiled! I'm sorry. I didn't see the paint. Did I spoil the picture? It's OK, Diego. Don't worry. I think we can fix it.*

There is a lot going on in the school hall. Mrs. Diaz's class is on its way to gym. Partners are holding hands. Most of the children look happy, but Jo-Jo looks tired and is yawning. Jackie is crying because he has ripped his cutout. Mrs. Diaz is offering soothing words and assuring him that it can be mended. Some students from Mr. Marino's class are sprawled on the floor, painting a big picture. Diego has just spilled paint all over the picture. He is horrified. Other students are displaying varying degrees of surprise, anger, worry, and humor.

Words

1. happy
2. sad
3. tired
4. surprised
5. angry
6. scared
7. worried

Verbs

8. smile
9. yawn
10. cry
11. frown
12. laugh

Additional Words

accident
spoiled
ripped
giggle
horrified
funny
worry
humor
frightening
scary
sleepy
cutout

Words

Components: Topic 15 Wall Chart, Picture Dictionary (pp. 30–31), Cassette, Word and Picture Cards (Topic 15).

See page xiv for techniques and strategies for presenting and practicing words.

What's new in the hall?

1. happy
2. sad
3. tired
4. surprised
5. angry
6. scared
7. worried

Verbs

8. smile
9. yawn
10. cry
11. frown
12. laugh

Notes

Once the students are familiar with the vocabulary words, play a game. Call out one of the emotions depicted in the illustration (for example, *angry*). Prompt the children to show that emotion with their facial expressions. Then reverse the procedure. Make a face, and ask the children to say what emotion they think you are showing with your expression. You may want to let each child make faces in a mirror for a while to allow him or her to become more familiar with his or her own range of expression.

Workbook page

Ask the children to show you an angry face. Then ask them to show you the picture card that shows an angry face. Tell them to look at the pictures on the page and to draw a line from each emotion word to the face that seems to show that feeling. Point out that the words missing from the sentences in the writing exercise can be found at the bottom of the page.

Stories

Components: Picture Dictionary (pp. 30–31), Cassette, Story (Topic 15).

See page xviii for techniques and strategies for presenting and practicing stories.

There's Mrs. Diaz's happy class!
Are they going to the gym? Yes!
That's why they are smiling.
But Jo-Jo is yawning. He's tired.

Oh, no. Jackie is crying.
His cutout ripped.
Don't be sad, Jackie.
It just needs some glue.

The first graders are painting.
Uh-oh! Diego spills the paint!
His friends are surprised.
Diego is scared. Is the picture spoiled?

One boy laughs. He thinks it's funny.
Alison frowns. She's angry!
Don't worry, it's OK.
Maybe it looks better that way!

Story notes

This is an opportunity to discuss common minor disasters (such as spills or rips) or lost belongings. Encourage the children to tell their own stories about things that have happened to them, or that they can imagine happening. Role-play what they might say and do when an accident happens in school or at home. Discuss apologies, and how they serve to ease tension when accidents happen.

Ask about the story:
Point to someone who is sad. Is Samantha smiling? Does Alison think the spilled paint is funny? How does Jackie's face show how he feels? Why do you think Alison is frowning? Who is yawning? Where were they making a painting?

Ask about your students:
Would it make you angry if someone ripped your picture? What would you say? How would you feel if you ripped your own cutout? What activity makes you feel happy? What makes you laugh? How do you feel at the end of the school day? How do you move when you're tired? How does your voice sound when you're sad?

Dialogue

Components: Cassette, Topic 15 Wall Chart, Picture Dictionary (pp. 30–31).

See page xix for techniques and strategies for presenting and practicing dialogues.

Vanessa:	Hi, Jasmin!
Jasmin:	Hi, Vanessa!
Vanessa:	Are you going to gym?
Jasmin:	Yes! I'm so happy! I love gym!
Vanessa:	What's the matter with Jackie? He looks sad.
Jasmin:	Mrs. Diaz! Jackie's crying!
Mrs. Diaz:	Oh, his cutout ripped. Jackie, it's all right. We can fix it with some glue.
Jasmin:	What are you doing, Vanessa?
Vanessa:	We're painting a big picture!
Alison:	Diego! Watch out! Oh, you spilled the paint all over our picture!
Kids:	Mr. Green! Come quick!
Mr. Green:	What happened?
Alison:	Diego spilled the paint! Our picture is all spoiled!
Diego:	I'm sorry. I didn't see the paint. Did I spoil the picture?
Mr. Green:	Don't worry, Diego. I think we can fix it.
Alison:	I'm so angry!
Mr. Green:	Alison, it was an accident.
Boy:	I think it looks funny.
Kid:	It looks better that way!
Other kids:	Yeah!

Dialogue notes

Repeat the opening phrase *I'm happy!* but vary your tone of voice. Use an angry voice, then a very sad voice, and a bouncy and cheerful voice. Ask the children which voice sounds as if it goes best with the sentence. Then listen to the tape and ask the children to raise their hands when they hear someone who sounds happy. Repeat this process, and each time ask them to indicate when they hear a voice that expresses a way someone could feel (and sound): sad, angry, worried, scared, surprised.

Beats!

Components: Cassette, Beats! (Topic 15).

See page xx for techniques and strategies for presenting and practicing Beats!

Why are you yawning?
Because I'm tired.
Why are you crying?
Because I'm sad.

Why are you frowning?
Because I'm angry.
Don't feel bad!
Don't feel bad!

Let's play together.
What'll we play?
Let's play tag.
OK.

Why are you laughing?
This is fun!
Now we're happy!
Run! Run! Run!

Beat notes

Encourage the children to act out the feelings mentioned in the Beat: *Show me with your face that you are really happy. Show me with your whole body that you are very, very angry. How do you move when you are very tired?* Practice the Beat in two groups until everyone is comfortable with the words. Then ask the children to take partners and repeat the Beat, using their bodies and voices to enhance the process.

Worksheets

Worksheet 1: What's new in the hall? (p. 29)

Direct the children's attention to the pictures on the worksheet. Ask what the child in the first picture is feeling. Tell them that the pictures are clues to help them remember the words for each kind of feeling. Ask them to write in the spaces provided the kinds of situations or things that set off those emotions.

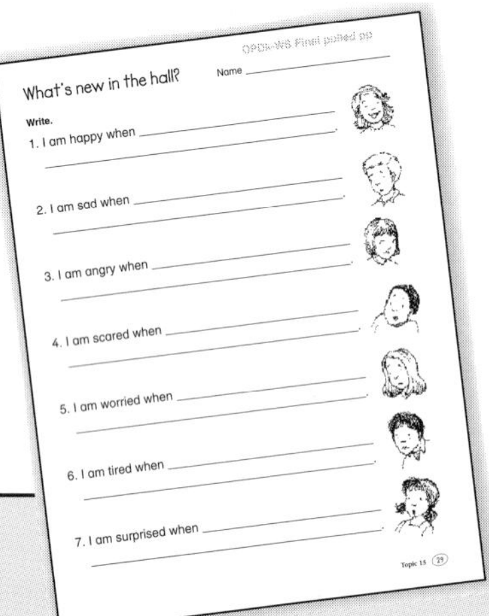

What's new in the hall? Name ____________

Write.

1. I am happy when ____________
2. I am sad when ____________
3. I am angry when ____________
4. I am scared when ____________
5. I am worried when ____________
6. I am tired when ____________
7. I am surprised when ____________

Topic 15 29

Worksheet 2: What's new in the hall? (p. 30)

Tell the children that each set of sentences has an arrow pointing to the picture that illustrates them, so there are clues for filling in the missing words. Review the use of the *-ing* form of the verbs: *She laughs. She is laughing. Jackie is crying.*

Tell the children to write the missing words in the spaces provided. You may write the words on the board for them to refer to, or suggest they use their word cards as a reference.

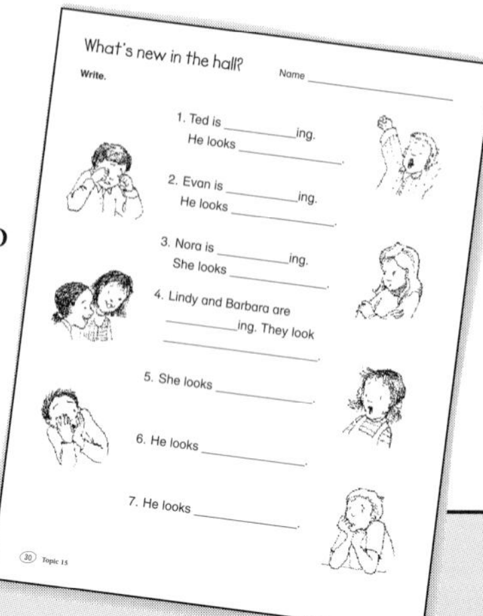

What's new in the hall? Name ____________

Write.

1. Ted is ________ing. He looks ________.
2. Evan is ________ing. He looks ________.
3. Nora is ________ing. She looks ________.
4. Lindy and Barbara are ________ing. They look ________.
5. She looks ________.
6. He looks ________.
7. He looks ________.

30 Topic 15

Activities

- Play emotion charades using the word and picture cards. Invite volunteers to pick a card and act out the emotion shown without using any words. Prompt the other children to guess the emotion. Vary the game by writing a situation on a piece of paper *(Your building block tower fell; It's time for recess),* and tell the child to act out how he or she would feel in that situation.

- Lead the class in singing this simple song:

  If you're happy and you know it, clap your hands.
  If you're happy and you know it, clap your hands.
  If you're happy and you know it,
  Then your face will surely show it.
  If you're happy and you know it, clap your hands.

  Add other verses:

  If you're sad and you know it, cry "Boo-hoo." …
  If you're surprised and you know it, shout "Oh, my!" …
  If you're angry and you know it, yell "I'm mad!" …
  If you're worried and you know it, say "Oh, dear!" …
  If you're tired and you know it, give a yawn. …

- Play a circle game. Invite the children to sit in a circle. Begin by saying: *I am happy when* _____. Turn to your neighbor and ask, *When are you happy?* Prompt the children to continue this pattern of question and response until everyone in the circle has had a chance to complete the sentence, giving his or her own reason for being happy. Repeat the process with other emotion words.

- Have a talk with a small group of children about tough emotions, such as sorrow, fear, anger, or anxiety. You may begin by asking, *What makes you cry?* Call on volunteers to tell about occasions when they cried, and encourage everyone to participate. Then discuss ways the class knows to find comfort or solace, from others and from inside themselves.

TOPIC 16 Gym time!

Content

- Gym activities and equipment
- Ways of moving

Language

- Asking and answering questions about gym activities: *Can you tumble? Can I jump on this mat? I can't skip, but I can hop. I can crawl through the hoop.*
- Using prepositions to indicate place and direction: *I hopped around the mat. She jumped over the hoop. He went around the hoop.*

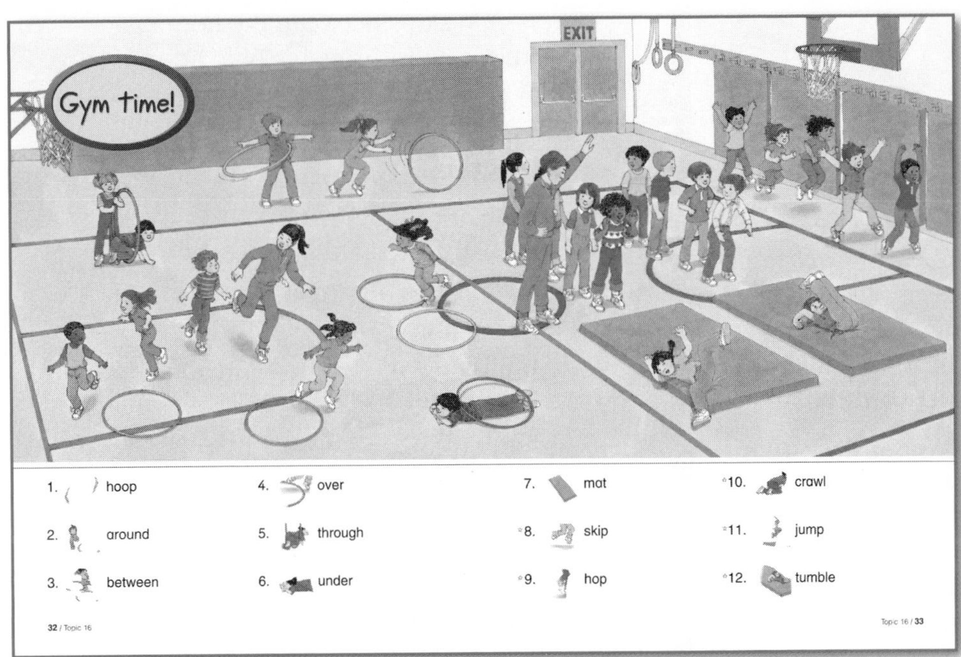

It's time for gym class. Two classes are exercising in the gym. Mrs. Lee's kindergartners are having fun skipping around the hoops. Jasmin is skipping between two hoops. Samantha is skipping over a hoop. Jo-Jo is crawling through a hoop. Jackie is lying under a hoop. How did he get there? Off to the side of this group, a boy is happily twirling a hoop around his hips while a girl chases after a rolling hoop that has gotten away from her. Tommy is hopping. Mrs. Lee is trying to teach him how to skip. The second graders in Mr. Ryan's class are doing warm-up exercises and tumbling on the mats. Ting and Jim have just had their turn. Jim's tumble is a good one, but Ting flops over. Zoe laughs. Mr. Ryan is not happy about that. It's Zoe's turn now!

Words

1. hoop
2. around
3. between
4. over
5. through
6. under
7. mat

Verbs

8. skip
9. hop
10. crawl
11. jump
12. tumble

Additional Words

exercise
warm-ups
pairs
jumping jacks
stretch
twirl
chase

Words

Components: Topic 16 Wall Chart, Picture Dictionary (pp. 32–33), Cassette, Word and Picture Cards (Topic 16).

See page xiv for techniques and strategies for presenting and practicing words.

Gym time!

1. hoop	4. over	6. under
2. around	5. through	7. mat
3. between		

Verbs

8. skip	10. crawl	12. tumble
9. hop	11. jump	

Notes

Clear an area where the children can move freely. Distribute the picture cards for *skip, hop, crawl, jump,* and *tumble.* Invite a volunteer to pick a card, look at it, and then, without revealing the card, demonstrate the action it shows. The other children say the word aloud. You may also use word cards.

Reinforce the meanings of the prepositions *around, between, over, through,* and *under* by playing a simple circle game. Provide a small hoop, a flat book, and a piece of string long enough to be placed in a circle around the hoop. Then place two (or all three) objects in relation to each other, and describe what you did. Prompt your neighbor to continue the game by asking, *Where will you put the book?*

Workbook page

Direct the students' attention to the picture clues for the missing words. Point out that all the missing words can be found in the middle of the page. For the pictures at the bottom, have students write the word that describes the relationship between the hoops and the mats.

16 Gym time!

Write.

1. He can ______ 2. She can ______ 3. She can ______

4. He can ______ 5. She can ______ 6. I can ______

jump skip crawl tumble hop

between over through under around

Stories

Components: Picture Dictionary (pp. 32–33), Cassette, Story (Topic 16).

See page xviii for techniques and strategies for presenting and practicing stories.

Kindergarten hoop game today!
Skip! Skip! Around the hoops!
Tommy can't skip. He hops.
Mrs. Lee shows him. Step, hop. See?

Samantha skips over the hoops.
Jasmin skips between the hoops.
Jo-Jo crawls through a blue hoop.
Who's under the red hoop? It's Jackie!

The second graders do warm-ups.
Good! Keep jumping!
Ready to tumble on the mats?
Line up in pairs! Jim and Ting first.

On your mark! Get set! Go!
Jim tumbles. Ting flops.
Ha! Ha! Don't laugh, Zoe.
Your turn next!

Story notes

This is an opportunity to talk about the concept of being a good sport. Help each child to express how they might feel in Zoe or Ting's position by asking questions: *Was it okay for Zoe to laugh at Ting for flopping? How do you think Ting felt? How do you feel if someone laughs at you?* Encourage the children to think of how Zoe could help Ting learn to tumble better.

Ask about the story:
Who was trying to learn to skip? What was Tommy doing? Who was exercising with a hoop? Who was under a hoop? Who was skipping over the hoops? Where was Jo-Jo?

Ask about your students:
Who can hop? Can you skip? Can you jump over the string? Who can jump over the moon? What do you like to do in gym? What would you like to learn to do?

Dialogue

Components: Cassette, Topic 16 Wall Chart, Picture Dictionary (pp. 32–33).

See page xix for techniques and strategies for presenting and practicing dialogues.

Jim:	What exercises are we going to do today, Mr. Ryan?
Mr. Ryan:	First we're going to run, jump, and tumble. First group start your jumping jacks! Second group line up in pairs!
Jim:	Are we going to tumble on the mats?
Mr. Ryan:	Yes, we are.
Ting:	Can you tumble, Zoe?
Zoe:	Sure, I know how to tumble.
Ting:	I don't.
Mr. Ryan:	Ready? Ting and Jim! On your mark! Get set! Go!
Zoe:	Ha! Ha! Ting looks funny!
Mr. Ryan:	Zoe, we're all learning!
Zoe:	I'm sorry.
Mr. Ryan:	You're next, Zoe and Paul!
Zoe:	Uh-oh.
Tommy:	Mrs. Lee, Mrs. Lee!
Mrs.Lee:	What is it, Tommy?
Tommy:	I can't skip.
Mrs.Lee:	Yes, you can. I know you can.
Tommy:	I can't skip, but I can hop.
Mrs.Lee:	Well, hopping is much harder than skipping.
Tommy:	It is?
Mrs. Lee:	Yes! Watch, I'll show you how to skip.
Tommy:	Thanks, Mrs. Lee.
Mrs. Lee:	Let's do it together. Step, hop! Step, hop! Good!
Mrs. Lee & Tommy:	Step, hop! Step, hop! Step, hop!

Dialogue notes

Divide the class into two groups, and model a variation of the dialogue for the children to practice:
Teacher: We're going to tumble on the mats.
Second speakers: I know how to tumble.
Third speakers: I don't. (*or:* I do, too.)

Practice this version, and then change the activity:
Teacher: We're going to hop across the room.
Second speakers: I know how to hop.
Third speakers: I don't. (*or:* I do, too.)

Once the children catch the pattern, invite volunteers to call for the next activity. Encourage children to change roles.

Beats!

Components: Cassette, Beats! (Topic 16).

See page xx for techniques and strategies for presenting and practicing Beats!

Can you run fast?
Sure I can.
Watch me run!
I can run faster.

Can you jump high?
Sure I can.
Watch me jump!
I can jump higher.

Can you make a muscle?
Sure I can.
Mine is big.
Mine is bigger.

Hey, you guys!
Hey, you guys!
Mine is the biggest!
I exercise!

Beat notes

Practice the Beat until all the children are comfortable with it. Then go to a gym or outdoor play area where there's room for running and jumping. Ask the children to form two or more lines across the space. Prompt them by saying to the first line, *Can you run fast?* Tell them to finish the stanza in chorus and then run to a designated finish line. Repeat this a few times, and then prompt them with, *Can you jump high?* or *Can you make a muscle?* For each stanza, remind them to finish the words before they go into action. Invite volunteers to take the prompter's role, and to vary the words (for example, *Can you hop fast? Can you crawl slowly?*).

Worksheets

Worksheet 1: Gym time! (p. 31)

Remind the children to look at the pictures for clues to the missing words. Point out that the word missing from the first sentence in each pair appears in the sentence below, and that all the missing words can be found at the bottom of the page.

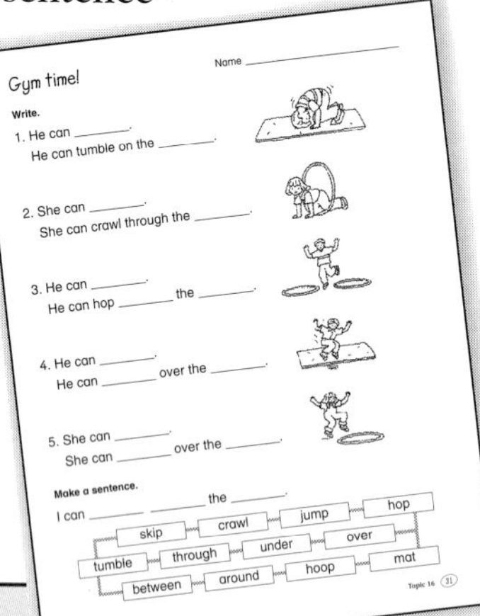

Gym time!

Name ____________

Write.

1. He can ______.
   He can tumble on the ______.
2. She can ______.
   She can crawl through the ______.
3. He can ______.
   He can hop ______ the ______.
4. He can ______.
   He can ______ over the ______.
5. She can ______.
   She can ______ over the ______.

Make a sentence.

I can ______ ______ the ______.

skip crawl jump hop tumble through under over between around hoop mat

Topic 16 31

Worksheet 2: Gym time! (p. 32)

Encourage the children to color the pictures as they follow the directions. You may want to review the prepositions. In the second exercise, remind them that the pictures are clues for the missing words *(through, around,* and *between).*

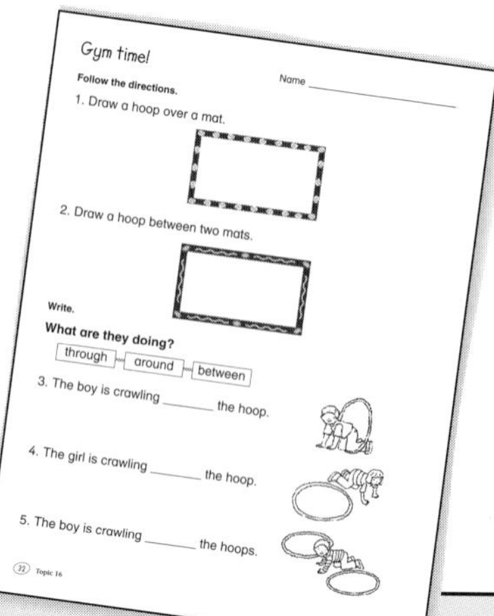

Gym time!

Name ____________

Follow the directions.

1. Draw a hoop over a mat.
2. Draw a hoop between two mats.

Write.

What are they doing?

through around between

3. The boy is crawling ______ the hoop.
4. The girl is crawling ______ the hoop.
5. The boy is crawling ______ the hoops.

32 Topic 16

Activities

- Sing the song "Skip to My Lou." Add verses such as, *I can hop now, how about you?* or *I can jump high, how about you?* Encourage the children to act out the words of the song. Extend this activity by elaborating on the actions described. For example, tape a piece of paper on the floor and lead the singing (demonstrating the action) with combinations of verbs and prepositions (for example, *I can jump over; I can hop around*). In another variation, invite a volunteer to demonstrate an action, and then ask the other children to make up a verse about it *(She can crawl around; They can jump up).*

- Play a jump-rope game. Help the children practice jumping *over, between, under, around,* and *through* a slowly swinging rope while they sing a jump-rope jingle.

- Introduce the children to the book *Wild Wild Sunflower Child Anna* by Nancy White Carlstrom (Macmillan) or other children's books that describe physical activities. After reading the book aloud, talk about it with the children. Encourage them to act out portions of the poem: running, jumping, climbing, spinning, or tumbling.

- Set up a simple obstacle course (with the children's help) in the gym, on the playground, or in a cleared space in your classroom. Then call out directions: *Run to the mat; Tumble on top of it; Hop to the hoop; Crawl through it; Skip to the table; Crawl under it; Walk to the chair; Jump around it; Touch your toes and go back to the start.* Changing both the course and the instructions provides endless possibilities for practice. Encourage children to design their own paths and work together to write them down for others to try. Another variation would be for one child to move through the obstacle course while another narrates (for example: *She's climbing over the chair. She's crawling under the table. She's hopping between the chair and the mat. ...*).

What's for lunch?

Content

- Lunchtime foods
- School cafeteria routines

Language

- Identifying and naming ethnic specialty foods: *She is eating sushi with chopsticks. They chose peanut butter sandwiches. The cafeteria has tacos for lunch today.*
- Asking and answering questions about foods and food preferences: *Do you like tomatoes or carrots better? I like carrots a lot.*
- Understanding the use of *bought* versus *brought*: *What did you bring for lunch? I brought a sandwich. What did you buy? I bought tacos.*

Words

1. tray
2. taco
3. apple
4. milk
5. can
6. carrot
7. egg roll
8. sushi
9. garbage can
10. sandwich
11. salad
12. cookie

Additional Words

straw
napkin
cafeteria
share
cash register
clean up
recycling bin
garbage
bring/brought
buy/bought
healthy
salty
sweet
dessert

It's lunchtime and the scene is the school cafeteria. A clock says 12:15. Ting, Alison, and Alison's friend Yuka are sitting at a table comparing lunches. Yuka has a Japanese lunch box with sushi and chopsticks in it. Ting shows them a plastic bag with egg rolls she has brought to share. Alison has a tuna fish sandwich and some raw carrot sticks. They all want to share. Alison holds up a see-through bag of her mother's cookies that she brought for everybody. Marcus and Jim are heading toward the table, carrying trays. They have just bought peanut butter sandwiches, bowls of salad, apples, and drinks. Marcus has a container of milk. Jim chose a can of juice. Diego and Zoe are at the counter. They have each taken trays, silverware, and an apple. A cafeteria lady is handing them each a taco on a plate. They will go next to the cash register to pay for their lunch and get napkins and straws.

Words

Components: Topic 17 Wall Chart, Picture Dictionary (pp. 34–35), Cassette, Word and Picture Cards (Topic 17).

See page xiv for techniques and strategies for presenting and practicing words.

What's for lunch?

1. tray	5. can	9. garbage can
2. taco	6. carrot	10. sandwich
3. apple	7. egg roll	11. salad
4. milk	8. sushi	12. cookie

Notes

Ask the class to arrange the picture cards on their desks to show a good lunch. Encourage the children to see how many different lunches they can make from the cards. Invite volunteers to show their choices. Say the words aloud and prompt the children to repeat them. Then distribute index cards on which the children can draw other foods they like to eat for lunch. Ask them to write (or dictate) the words for these foods on the reverse side of the index cards. Ask students to take turns placing a collection of cards in the center of the circle to represent a meal. Each time, ask the other children to look at the cards and describe the lunch.

Workbook page

Each of the food words in this unit has a place in the menu box, but only the first letters are printed; it's the children's job to fill in the missing letters. Offer some strategies for solving the puzzle. Students may check their word cards for foods that start with *a*. Only one food word on the list starts with *a: apple*. Just to make sure, suggest they count the number of letters in the word before they fill in the letters. Point out that more than one of the words starts with the letter *s*, and that two of those have five letters each. In the second exercise, students circle the foods they like to eat.

Stories

Components: Picture Dictionary (pp. 34–35), Cassette, Story (Topic 17).

See page xviii for techniques and strategies for presenting and practicing stories.

It's 12:15! Lunchtime!
Some people buy lunch.
Some people bring lunch.
Everyone is hungry.

Diego and Zoe take trays.
What's for lunch? Tacos! Yum!
What else? Apples? Milk? Juice?
Put the cans in the bin. Don't forget!

Alison brought a sandwich and carrots.
Ting brought noodles and egg rolls.
Alison's friend has a small lunch box.
What's inside? Sushi and chopsticks!

Move over! Here come Jim and Marcus!
They bought sandwiches and salad.
Alison brought a surprise.
Cookies for everyone!

Story notes

This is a good opportunity to engage the children in a discussion of lunchtime procedures in your classroom and school. Ask them to talk about how lunch in their school is similar to or different from what is shown in the illustration.

Ask about the story:
What time was lunchtime? Where did everyone go to eat lunch? What did Alison bring for lunch? Who brought egg rolls? What did Marcus eat for lunch? What did Diego and Zoe buy? Who wanted to share the cookies?

Ask about your students:
What is your favorite food? What did you eat for lunch yesterday? What will/did you have for lunch today? Who makes your lunch? Where do you eat lunch? When do you eat lunch? Do you like to share? Do you like to try new foods?

Components: Cassette, Topic 17 Wall Chart, Picture Dictionary (pp. 34–35).

See page xix for techniques and strategies for presenting and practicing dialogues.

Alison:	What did you bring, Ting?
Ting:	I brought egg rolls.
Alison:	M-m-m-m, good! I brought a tuna fish sandwich. Let's share.
Ting:	OK. What did you bring, Yuka?
Yuka:	Sushi.
Alison:	How do you eat it?
Yuka:	With my chopsticks.
Cafeteria lady:	Don't forget to clean off the table when you finish.
Alison:	We know. Put the cans in the recycle bin—
Ting:	—and the garbage in the garbage can.
Alison:	Look! I brought cookies!
Ting:	How many cookies did you bring?! We won't be able to eat all those cookies!
Alison:	Yes, we will. Here come Jim and Marcus!

Dialogue notes

Divide the class into groups of three. Practice the first six exchanges between Alison, Ting, and Yuka (beginning with *What did you bring, Ting?* and ending with *Sushi*). Then ask for volunteers to practice these exchanges, substituting other foods:

First speaker:	What did you bring to share?
Second speaker:	I brought _________.
First speaker:	M-m-m-m good! I brought ______.
Second speaker:	OK. I like ________. (to third speaker:) What did you bring?
Third speaker:	I brought ____________.
First and second speakers:	That sounds good.
All three:	Let's all share.

Components: Cassette, Beats! (Topic 17).

See page xx for techniques and strategies for presenting and practicing Beats!

M-m-m-m, I'm hungry.
What shall we eat?
　What do you want?
　Fish or meat?

I want spaghetti
with lots of cheese.
　I'll have soup
　and a sandwich, please.

M-m-m-m, I'm thirsty.
What shall we drink?
　Juice or milk?
　What do you think?

Chocolate milk.
　That's too sweet!
　I'll take tomato juice.
Let's eat!

Beat notes

Talk with the children about the contractions in this Beat. You can have them repeat some of the lines without the contractions, clapping the beat as they speak, and comparing the number of syllables: *M-m-m-m, I'm hungry* (four claps) *M-m-m-m, I am hungry* (five claps). Explain that the word *shall* means the same, in this context, as the word *will*.

Worksheets

Worksheet 1: What's for lunch? (p. 33)

Encourage children to set a clock with movable hands to the times they eat each meal mentioned on the worksheet. Point out that the images along the right side of the worksheet are clues to help them think of foods they eat. Remind them that they can draw and write about any other foods they choose.

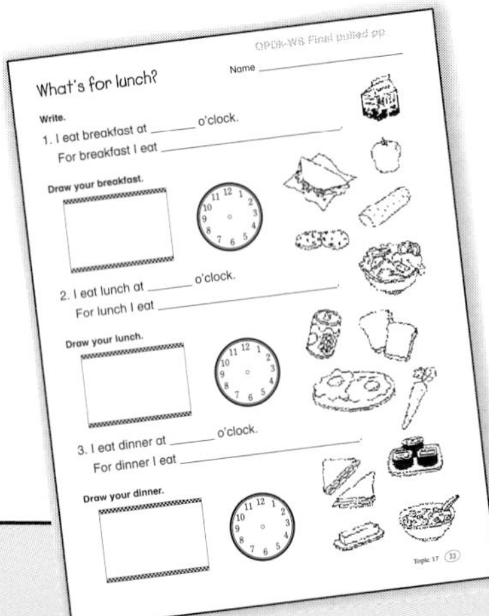

What's for lunch?

Name ____________

Write.

1. I eat breakfast at ______ o'clock.
   For breakfast I eat ______________.

Draw your breakfast.

2. I eat lunch at ______ o'clock.
   For lunch I eat ______________.

Draw your lunch.

3. I eat dinner at ______ o'clock.
   For dinner I eat ______________.

Draw your dinner.

Topic 17 33

Worksheet 2: What's for lunch? (p. 34)

Ask the children to look at all the pictures and say what they see happening in each one. After some discussion, tell them to think about going to eat in a cafeteria. Ask a volunteer to suggest which picture on the worksheet shows the first thing that happens. As soon as the picture labeled *We go to the cafeteria* (the first in the correct sequence) is identified, write the number 1 in the space provided. Tell the children to number the rest of the pictures, in order, from 2 to 8.

What's for lunch?

Name ____________

Number the pictures in order.

☐ We get trays.

☐ We put our food on our trays.

☐ We eat lunch.

☐ We sit down.

☐ We go outside.

☐ We wait in line.

1 We go to the cafeteria.

☐ We throw away our garbage.

34 Topic 17

Activities

- Ask children to keep a lunch log for a week. Give them five pieces of paper and tell them to record on each page, in words and pictures, what they eat for lunch that day. Then bind the pages together to make a book.

- Set up a classroom recycling center. Talk about why recycling is important. Invite volunteers to make labels for each container. You might want to prompt the children to collect aluminum cans for several weeks and turn them all in at once for the deposit.

- Make vegetable soup together. Invite children to cut vegetables and stir them as they cook. Add shaped pasta or alphabet noodles to the soup. As you work together, talk about the ingredients (where and how they grow, for example) and model questions and answers as you narrate the process: *I am cutting the beans in small pieces. Can you wash the potatoes?*

- Read the book *Everybody Cooks Rice* by Norah Dooley (Scholastic), a multicultural book about neighborhood families who all eat rice but prepare it in different ways. Then talk about rice and ask who eats it at home.

OPIC 18

Let's play!

Content

- Playground activities
- Playground equipment
- Playground safety

Language

- Describing activities incorporating the names for playground equipment: *She is climbing up the bars. He slides down the slide. The girls are on the swing. I will throw the ball to you.*
- Discussing playground safety rules: *Hold on to the swing with two hands. Look down before you slide. Where is it safe to throw the ball?*
- Expressing likes and dislikes: *I like to swing high. It's fun to slide feet first. I don't like to climb high.*

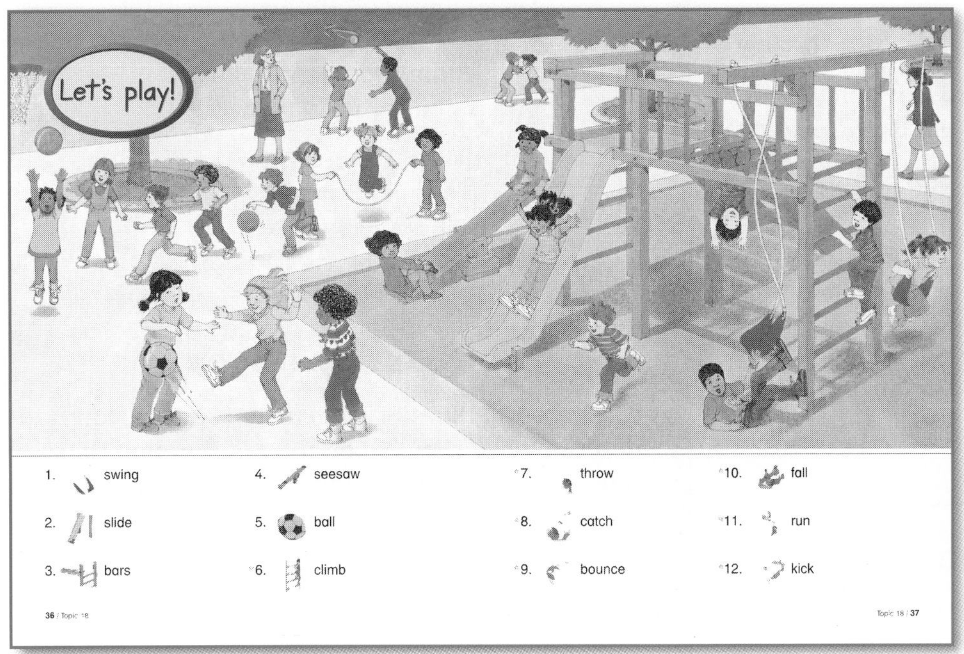

Words

1. swing
2. slide
3. bars
4. seesaw
5. ball

Verbs

6. climb
7. throw
8. catch
9. bounce
10. fall
11. run
12. kick

Additional Words

jump rope
whistle
ladder
basket
basketball
upside down
hang
jungle gym

Lunchtime is over and it's playground time. There are balls bouncing and children running everywhere. Marcus and Jim practice throwing a ball against a wall and catching it. Is that a fight going on over there? A teacher is ready to blow a whistle if anyone misbehaves. Some children are jumping rope and others are shooting baskets with a basketball. Jasmin is coming down the slide fast and loving it. Samantha goes up and down on the see-saw with Vanessa. Jo-Jo climbs on the bars while Jackie hangs upside down. Zoe and Ting are busy bouncing a big ball. Tommy is running toward them to get the ball. Diego falls off the swing in his hurry to go after the ball. Neither one gets to the ball in time, because Alison gets there first. She just kicks the ball right out of Ting's hand.

Words

Components: Topic 18 Wall Chart, Picture - Dictionary (pp. 36–37), Cassette, Word and Picture Cards (Topic 18).

See page xiv for techniques and strategies for presenting and practicing words.

Let's play!

1. swing
2. slide
3. bars
4. seesaw
5. ball

Verbs

6. climb
7. throw
8. catch
9. bounce
10. fall
11. run
12. kick

Notes

Talk to the class about nouns (words for things) and verbs (words for actions). Point out that *swing, seesaw,* and *slide* are both things (nouns) and actions (verbs). Model questions and answers to explore these words: *What is she doing? She is swinging. What is she swinging on? She's swinging on the swing.*

Invite the children to play a charades game. Spread the word cards on a table, with the words facedown. Ask a volunteer to choose one card and pantomime the word shown. The challenge is for the other children to say the word.

Workbook page

Tell the children that they can find the clues for filling in the puzzle by looking at the pictures toward the bottom of the page. Direct their attention to the first pair of words. Point out that the first and last letters of each word are already filled in.

Stories

Components: Picture Dictionary (pp. 36–37), Cassette, Story (Topic 18).

See page xviii for techniques and strategies for presenting and practicing stories.

Let's play!
Samantha loves the seesaw.
Jasmin loves the slide.
She's sliding down too fast!

Balls are bouncing everywhere!
Marcus throws a ball. Catch it, Jim!
Ting and Zoe are bouncing a big ball.
The boys want to play with the ball, too.

Diego jumps off the swing to get it.
Oops! He falls down.
Jo-Jo climbs down off the bars.
Tommy runs to get the ball.

Surprise! Alison runs, too.
She kicks the ball!
Pow! What a kick!
Too bad, boys!

Story notes

After reading this story together, ask the children to describe what they did on their playground the last time they were out playing. Ask the children if there are rules on their playground. Prompt them to talk about cooperation, sharing space, and safety issues. Encourage the class to make a chart of playground rules they think are important. Encourage them to make a list of dos as well as don'ts.

Ask about the story:
What are Jim and Marcus doing? Who is climbing? Did someone fall? What was Diego doing before he fell? Where is the teacher? What are the other children doing? Who kicked the ball?

Ask about your students:
What equipment do we have at our school? What playground do you like? Do you like to swing or to climb better? How do you play ball? Can you go down the slide headfirst?

Dialogue

Components: Cassette, Topic 18 Wall Chart, Picture Dictionary (pp. 36–37).

See page xix for techniques and strategies for presenting and practicing dialogues.

Jasmin:	I love the slide! I can go fast!
Samantha:	I love the seesaw. I can go up and down, and I can see everyone! See my sister? She's bouncing a big ball with Ting.
Jasmin:	I see Tommy. Where's he going?
Tommy:	Jo-Jo! C'mon! Let's get that ball!
Jo-Jo:	What ball?
Tommy:	Zoe and Ting's ball! C'mon, Diego!
Diego:	Okay, here I come! Ow!
Jo-Jo:	Are you OK, Diego?
Diego:	Yeah.
Zoe:	Bounce the ball to me, Ting. We gotta keep it away from the boys.
Ting:	Yeah! They can't have it!
Alison:	Hi, you two!!
Zoe and Ting:	Alison!!
Diego:	What happened?
Tommy:	Alison kicked the ball! We'll never get it now.
Everyone:	Wow! What a kick!

Dialogue notes

Divide the class into two parts and elaborate on the exchange between Jasmin and Samantha *(I love the slide! I can go fast. I love the seesaw. I can go up and down, and I can see everyone).*Then ask for suggestions for other sentences about playground equipment that follow a similar pattern (*I like the bars, I can climb high,* and so on). Write the children's suggestions on a chart, and encourage pairs of children to practice reciting as many exchanges as they can, referring to different activities or playground equipment in each exchange.

Beats!

Components: Cassette, Beats! (Topic 18).

See page xx for techniques and strategies for presenting and practicing Beats!

Throw that ball!
Throw it fast.
Catch it!
Catch it!
It went right past!

Throw that ball!
Throw it slow.
Catch it!
Catch it!
It went too low.

Roll that ball!
Not too fast!

You caught it!
You caught it!
Hooray!
At last!

Beat notes

Encourage the children to pantomime the Beat while they learn it. Have lines of children stand and face each other so they can pretend to throw, catch, and roll an imaginary ball as they speak. If possible, continue reciting the Beat outside on the playground while throwing, catching, and rolling a real ball.

Worksheets

Worksheet 1: Let's play! (p. 35)

Help the children read aloud the list of activities. Demonstrate that each phrase has a companion illustration among the surrounding pictures. Then tell them to use those ideas, and the words provided, to finish the sentences at the top of the page. Ask the children to work with partners to complete the final question at the bottom of the page by interviewing each other about favorite playground activities.

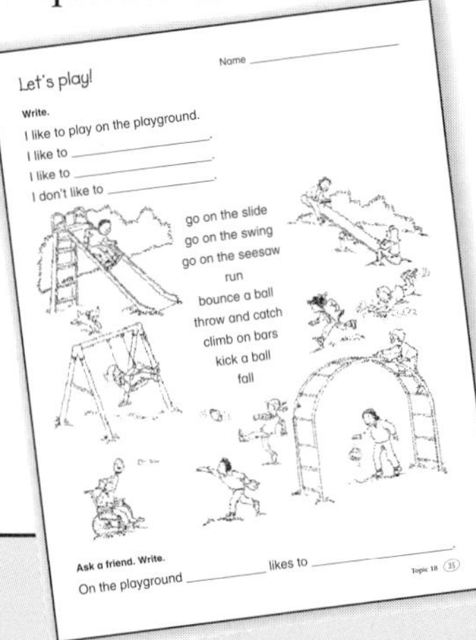

Let's play!

Name ____________

Write.

I like to play on the playground.
I like to ____________.
I like to ____________.
I don't like to ____________.

go on the slide
go on the swing
go on the seesaw
run
bounce a ball
throw and catch
climb on bars
kick a ball
fall

Ask a friend. Write.

On the playground ________ likes to ____________.

Topic 18 35

Worksheet 2: Let's play! (p. 36)

Tell the children that each set of unfinished sentences tells about the picture beneath it. Suggest that they look at the picture first and then read the sentences to themselves. Remind them that all the words they need are shown at the bottom of the page.

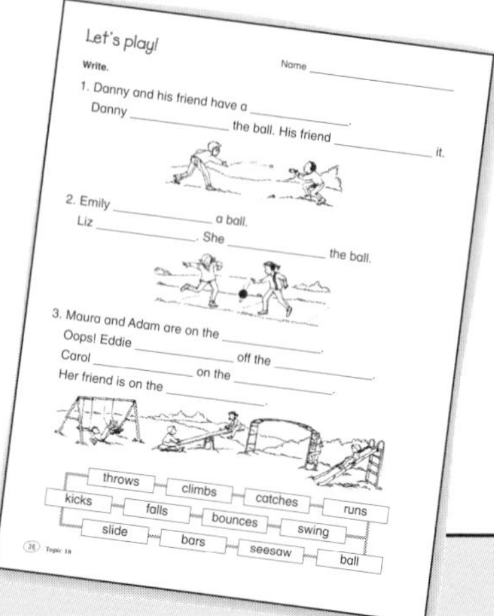

Let's play!

Write.

Name ____________

1. Danny and his friend have a ________.
Danny ________ the ball. His friend ________ it.

2. Emily ________ a ball.
Liz ________. She ________ the ball.

3. Maura and Adam are on the ________.
Oops! Eddie ________ off the ________.
Carol ________ on the ________.
Her friend is on the ________.

throws climbs catches
kicks falls bounces runs
slide bars seesaw swing ball

36 Topic 18

Activities

- Play Follow the Leader. Lots of good language practice can come out of this activity. Divide the class into several small groups and ask each group to choose a leader. Encourage the children to talk about what they are doing at or on each piece of playground equipment by asking occasional questions (for example: *What did you do? Did you slide down feet first?*). Tell the children that each time you yell the word *change*, a new person should become leader and lead the group to a new piece of equipment.

- Invite your class to join you in a safety inspection of the playground. Before you begin, ask them to talk about what they think is safe, and what they think would be dangerous in a playground. Then tour the playground to look for the specific things they mention. For instance, children can help spot broken toys, splinters on wooden climbing equipment, or jagged metal on the fence. If litter is a problem, you may suggest that the class take responsibility for checking for broken glass on a regular schedule. When you return to the classroom, ask the children to talk about what they noticed that they had expected, and what surprised them.

- Play an add-on circle game. Start by reciting *Out in the playground what do we do? I like to catch a ball. What about you?* Tell the person next to you to repeat the opening phrase. Then repeat that phrase, changing the pronoun appropriately, and add a new activity (that is: *Out in the playground what do we do? She likes to catch a ball. I like to bounce a ball. What about you?*). Continue in this way until everyone in the circle has had a chance. That leaves *you* having to repeat the complete list! Play a variation for a second round by replacing the words with a pantomime of the actions.

What's the matter?

Content

- Sickness and injuries
- Sympathy
- School nurse's office

Language

- Identifying minor illnesses and injuries: *I have a sore throat/a fever/a stomachache/a bump/a cut.*
- Recognizing and describing how we feel: *My stomach aches. My throat feels scratchy. I'm sneezing a lot. I fell down, and now my knee hurts. I bumped my head.*
- Expressing sympathy: *I'm sorry you feel sick. How can I help you?*

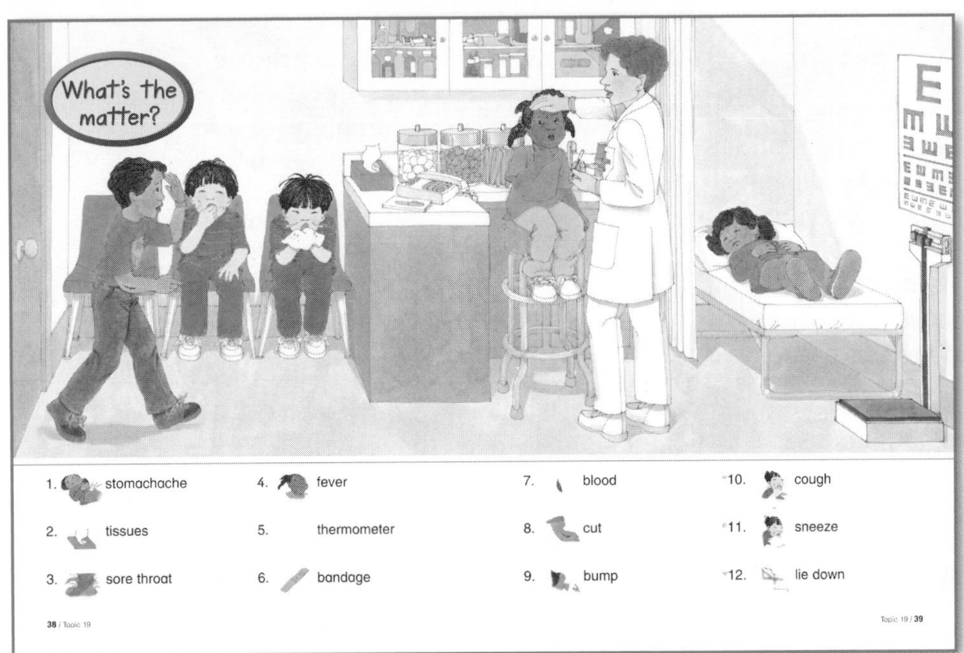

Who's in the nurse's office today? Miss White, the nurse, is taking care of Samantha. Samantha has a sore throat. Miss White has just taken her temperature, and the thermometer shows that she has a fever. Vanessa is lying down because she has a stomachache. Jackie and Jo-Jo are coughing and sneezing. They have colds. Jackie takes a tissue to sneeze into. Here comes Diego! He has a bump on his head and blood on his elbow. Something must have happened to him on the playground. He needs a bandage. Just another busy day for Miss White. Hope everyone feels better tomorrow!

Words

1. stomachache
2. tissues
3. sore throat
4. fever
5. thermometer
6. bandage
7. blood
8. cut
9. bump

Verbs

10. cough
11. sneeze
12. lie down

Additional Words

- cold
- temperature
- earache
- toothache
- headache
- dizzy
- nurse
- bruise
- scrape
- bleed
- sore

 **Components:** Topic 19 Wall Chart, Picture - Dictionary (pp. 38–39), Cassette, Word and Picture Cards (Topic 19).

See page xiv for techniques and strategies for presenting and practicing words.

What's the matter?

1. stomachache	4. fever	7. blood
2. tissues	5. thermometer	8. cut
3. sore throat	6. bandage	9. bump

Verbs

10. cough	11. sneeze	12. lie down

Notes

Shuffle the word and picture cards. Sort through the pile together. Name the cards as you select them, and ask the children to join you in acting out the ailments and injuries, and imagining the objects: *What's this? It's a tissue. What can we do with a tissue? Oh, I see ____ is wiping her nose.* After you've identified and discussed the cards, ask the children to make cards for other illnesses and injuries to add to this group.

Point out the use of some words, such as *bump, cough, sneeze, cut,* and *bandage,* as both nouns and verbs in this unit.

Workbook page

Tell the children that each sentence on the top half of the page describes one of the six pictures. Tell them to look at the pictures and draw the line from the picture to the sentence it matches. Then direct their attention to the three sentences at the bottom of the page. Explain that there are two pictures for each sentence, and tell them to circle the picture that shows what the sentence says.

19 What's the matter?

Match.

1. She has a stomachache.
2. She has a fever.
3. She has a cut.
4. She has a bump.
5. She has a sore throat.
6. She has a bandage.

Circle the correct picture.

7. He's coughing.
8. He's sneezing.
9. He's lying down.

Components: Picture Dictionary (pp. 38–39), Cassette, Story (Topic 19).

See page xviii for techniques and strategies for presenting and practicing stories.

What's the matter?
Is everybody sick?
Vanessa has a stomachache.
She's lying down.

Jackie and Jo-Jo have bad colds.
Jackie is coughing.
Jo-Jo is sneezing. Kachoo!
Here. Have a tissue.

Samantha has a sore throat.
She feels hot. Does she have a fever?
Check the thermometer.
Uh-oh! Better call her mother.

Here's Diego! What happened?
He has blood on his elbow
and a bump on his head.
Bring out the bandages!

Story notes

Invite volunteers to talk about times when they felt sick or got hurt. Ask them to describe their symptoms and explain what they, or someone else, did to make them feel better. Discuss the concept of sympathy. Ask questions: *What do you say when someone gets hurt? or if someone feels sick? How can you help someone who is hurt or feeling sick? What shouldn't you do or say to someone who is hurt or feeling sick?*

Ask about the story:

Who is sneezing and coughing? What's the matter with Jackie? Who has a bump on the head? Who is bleeding? What do you think happened to Diego? Does Diego need a bandage? How can the nurse help Jo-Jo?

Ask about your students:

How do you feel? What happens when you have a cold? What makes you feel better? Do you sleep more when you are sick? Did you take medicine?

Dialogue

Components: Cassette, Topic 19 Wall Chart, Picture Dictionary (pp. 38–39).

See page xix for techniques and strategies for presenting and practicing dialogues.

Nurse:	What's the matter, Samantha?
Samantha:	I don't know.
Nurse:	Do you have a cold?
Samantha:	I don't know.
Nurse:	You feel hot. Let me take your temperature. Oh, Jackie, listen to that cough! I'll look at you next. And you too, Jo-Jo. ... Samantha, you have a fever. Does your throat hurt?
Samantha:	Yes.
Nurse:	Open your mouth, and let me look at it. It's very red.
Samantha:	Do I have a sore throat?
Nurse:	Yes, I think you do. I'm going to call your mother.
Diego:	Miss White ...
Nurse:	Diego! What happened to you?
Diego:	I jumped off a swing and fell down. I have a cut on my elbow. Can I have a bandage?
Nurse:	Of course! But first I'll have to wash your elbow. And look at that bump on your head! How did that happen?
Diego:	The swing hit me!
Nurse:	Oh, dear. I hope you all feel much better tomorrow.

Dialogue notes

Elaborate the scene by asking a few students to role-play Jackie coughing and a few others to play Jo-Jo sneezing. Next, invite the children to reenact the dialogue between Miss White and the students. Encourage the children to substitute their own explanations for how someone may have gotten a bump and a cut: *I fell off the slide. I was running and I tripped.*

Beats!

Components: Cassette, Beats! (Topic 19).

See page xx for techniques and strategies for presenting and practicing Beats!

I don't want to go to school.
    What's the matter with you?
I have a headache.
    Oh? You do?

And I have a stomachache.
    My, that's sad.
And I have an earache.
    That's too bad.

And I have a sore throat.
    Let me see.
    Open your mouth.
    It looks fine to me.

    If you're so sick,
    You'd better not go.
    But you're going to miss the party.
Oh!
I'm not that sick!
I can go!

Beat notes

Divide the class into two groups. One says the parent's lines and the other says the child's lines. Encourage the children taking the child's role, holding their heads, their stomachs, their ears, and then their throats.

Once the Beat is familiar to the group and easy to recite, have them switch roles. Then ask the class to take a break to talk about the Beat. Ask the children if any of them have ever pretended to be sick so they wouldn't have to do something they didn't want to do, or if they have missed doing something because they really were sick.

Worksheets

Worksheet 1: What's the matter? (p. 37)

Direct the children's attention to the pictures under the questions. Tell them to look at each picture and then answer the question. Encourage full answers to questions when appropriate (for example: *Does she have a stomachache? No, she doesn't have a stomachache. She has a sore throat*).

What's the matter? Name

Write yes or no.

1. Does she have a stomachache?
2. Does he have a cut?
3. Does she need a bandage?
4. Does she need a tissue?
5. Is she lying down?
6. Is he coughing?

Topic 19 37

Worksheet 2: What's the matter? (p. 38)

Tell the children that the words in each sentence have been mixed up. Students must put the words in each sentence into the correct order. Suggest some strategies. For example, children can write each word on a separate piece of paper and move the pieces around to come up with a word order that makes sense.

What's the matter? Name

Unscramble the sentences.

1. a stomachache has She
2. fever a has He
3. sore has a throat He
4. bump head has She on her a
5. mouth her has thermometer She a in

38 Topic 19

Activities

- Play What's the Matter with Me? Ask a volunteer to act out an ailment while the other children try to guess what it is by asking questions: *Do you have a headache? Do you have a fever? Do you have a sore throat? Do you cough? Do you have a cut?* When the ailment is guessed correctly, the first patient can choose another child to take a turn feigning illness.

- Arrange a trip to visit your school nurse's office. Before the trip, brainstorm with the children and identify a few questions to ask during your visit. Ask the nurse to show the equipment in the office and explain its use. When you return to class, work together to write a thank-you note on chart paper to the nurse, including specifics about what you learned. Invite the children to illustrate the note.

- Sing the tune of "If You're Happy and You Know It," adding new verses that use the vocabulary words:

  If you cough and you know it, cover your mouth. . . .
  If you sneeze and you know it, get a tissue. . . .
  If you cut yourself and you know it, put on a bandage. . . .
  If you bump yourself and you know it, get some ice. . . .
  If your throat hurts and you know it, go see the nurse. . . .

  The children can make up more verses as they learn new words.

- Make a nurse's office in the classroom. Prompt pairs or groups of children to role-play visits to the school nurse. Suggest that they take turns being the nurse and the student patient. Model questions and answers to help them invent their own dialogues. For writers, make up a simple chart on which the "nurse" can fill in the "patient's" name, symptoms, and steps taken.

TOPIC 20

Music!

Content

- Musical instruments
- Musical sounds
- Movements to music

Language

- Talking about musical instruments and how they are played: *She is blowing on a trumpet. Those children are holding triangles. I want to beat my drum with my hand. She shakes the maracas.*
- Comparing the sounds of musical instruments: *The flute sounds soft. The trumpet makes a loud sound. The tuba makes the lowest sound. The piccolo makes the highest notes.*
- Describing responses to music: *We can clap our hands to the rhythm. Sing the words to the song while I play the tune. Can you dance to this tune?*

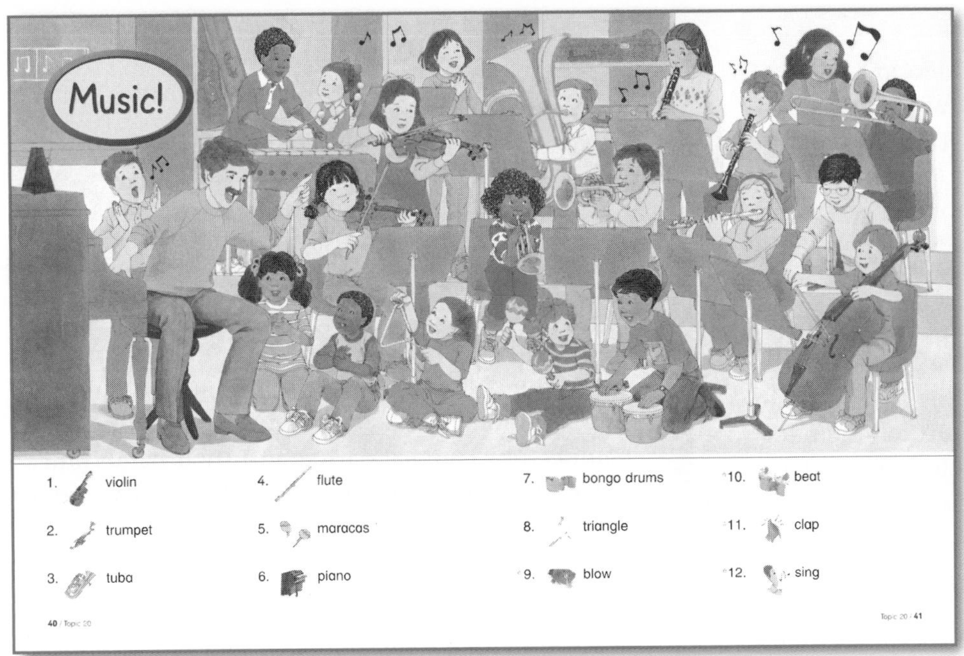

In the music room, the band and orchestra students are letting the younger students try out their instruments. Ting is trying the violin. Jim has the tuba, Zoe has the trumpet, and Alison has the flute. Marcus is playing a trombone. Diego is beating the bongo drums. Other students are having fun tapping the triangles and shaking the maracas. Some are singing and clapping in time to the music, while the teacher, Mr. Mooney, plays the piano. Everyone is having a great time!

Words

1. violin
2. trumpet
3. tuba
4. flute
5. maracas
6. piano
7. bongo drums
8. triangle

Verbs

9. blow
10. beat
11. clap
12. sing

Additional Words

music
tune
song
rhythm
strings
bow
clarinet
saxophone
trombone
bass drum
snare drum
drumsticks

Words

Stories

Components: Topic 20 Wall Chart, Picture Dictionary (pp. 40–41), Cassette, Word and Picture Cards (Topic 20).

See page xiv for techniques and strategies for presenting and practicing words.

Music!

1. violin
2. trumpet
3. tuba
4. flute
5. maracas
6. piano
7. bongo drums
8. triangle

Verbs

9. blow
10. beat
11. clap
12. sing

Notes

Spread the picture cards on the table. On a piece of chart paper draw three big circles. Write the word *play* on a piece of paper and hold it up. Model this sentence for them to repeat: *I play the piano.* Then ask them to repeat the sentence, holding up the picture card for each instrument as they say it in the sentence.

Hold up the card for the verb *blow.* Ask the children to find the cards for instruments that are played by blowing air through them. When they have located the cards for *trumpet, tuba,* and *flute,* tell them to place those cards in one of the circles on the chart. Repeat the process with the card for the verb *beat.*

Workbook page

Tell the children that in the first exercise, the first letter in the name of each instrument has been left off. Their task is to write it in. The pictures help tell them what the word should be. Remind them that they can use their word cards as referents. Then tell them that the four questions at the bottom of the page are missing the verbs.

20 Music!

Write the first letter.

1. _iano 2. _iolin 3. _rumpet 4. _lute

5. _uba 6. _aracas 7. _ongo _rum 8. _riangle

Write.

9. ________ the trumpet. 10. ________ the drum.

11. ________ your hands. 12. ________ with me.

Components: Picture Dictionary (pp. 40–41), Cassette, Story (Topic 20).

See page xviii for techniques and strategies for presenting and practicing stories.

Something fun happened today!
The band and orchestra played,
and then,
we tried their instruments!

Ting tried the violin. Squeak!
Jim tried the tuba. Oompah!
Zoe blew the trumpet. Blah-h-h!
Alison's flute was soft. Tweet!

The triangles went Ding! Ding!
The maracas went Cha! Cha! Cha!
Plinkety plank! went the piano.
Diego beat the bongos. Bippity bop!

We sang out loud, and we clapped.
Clap! Clap! Ding! Ding! Cha! Cha!
We made good music.
Mr. Mooney said so.

Story notes

Invite the children to make different rhythmic and musical sounds. Talk about the different kinds of sounds they can make using just their hands and voices. Find out if any of your students plays a musical instrument. Invite the child to bring his or her instrument to school and play it for the class.

Ask about the story:
What instrument did Jim play? Did Alison make a loud noise or a soft noise? How did Ting play the violin? Who was beating the bongo drums? Who was making music? What was the teacher doing?

Ask about your students:
Would you like to play a musical instrument? What instrument would you like to play? Which sound do you like best? How can you make music with no instrument?

Dialogue

Components: Cassette, Topic 20 Wall Chart, Picture Dictionary (pp. 40–41).

See page xix for techniques and strategies for presenting and practicing dialogues.

Ting:	Listen, Zoe! I can play the violin with the bow. It has a high sound. Or I can pluck the strings. That's easier!
Zoe:	Listen to the trumpet.
Older boy:	Blow harder.
Ting:	Wow! That's loud!
Zoe:	My brother plays the trombone. It's even louder!
Alison:	I like the flute. Listen!
(tuba sounds)	
Alison:	What's that?
Jim:	It's the tuba!
Teacher:	Play along, everybody. Shake the maracas! Tap the triangles! Clap your hands! Beat the bongos, Diego! Great music, kids!

Dialogue notes

Talk about the kinds of sound that the different instruments make. If possible, play a cassette with a variety of instrument sounds. Play (or make) an instrument sound, and have the children tell you whether it is a high or a low sound. Play or make another sound and compare it with the first: *Is it higher or lower?* Play or make a third instrument sound and compare it to the first two: *Which of the three sounds was highest? lowest?* Do the same with loud and soft instrument sounds.

Beats!

Components: Cassette, Beats! (Topic 20).

See page xx for techniques and strategies for presenting and practicing Beats!

Do you know how to play the flute?
Sure, you blow it.
Toot! Toot! Toot!

Do you know how to play the drum?
Sure, you beat it.
Bum! Bum! Bum!

How do you play the violin?
Play it with a bow.
How do you play the tuba?
Blow, blow, blow!

How about the triangle?
You tap it.
Ding! Ding! Ding!
Can you play all those instruments?
No, I just sing!

Beat notes

Play tape-recorded music with a strong rhythmic beat (or make up your own beat using a drum), and lead the class in a march around the room. The children pretend to play the flute by saying "Toot! Toot! Toot!", the drum by saying "Bum! Bum! Bum!", and the triangle with "Ding! Ding! Ding!"

Worksheets

Worksheet 1: Music! (p. 39)

Tell the children to look at the pictures for clues to fill in the missing words. At the bottom of the page, tell them they can check a box for *yes* or *no* to answer the questions.

Music!

Name ________

Write.

1. He plays the ________.
2. She plays the ________.
3. She plays the ________.
4. He plays the ________.
5. She plays the ________.

Check one.

6. Do you play an instrument?
   - ☐ No, I don't.
   - ☐ Yes, I do. I play the ________.
7. Do you like to sing?
   - ☐ No, I don't.
   - ☐ Yes, I do.

Worksheet 2: Music! (p. 40)

Point out that each person in the picture has a space nearby on which a number can be written. Help the children read each sentence. Tell them to find the person that sentence describes in the picture, then write the number of the sentence on that line. You may encourage children to work on this page in pairs or small groups.

Music!

Name ________

Number the picture.

1. He's singing a song.
2. He's clapping his hands.
3. She's beating the bongo drum.
4. She's playing the flute.
5. She's blowing the trumpet.
6. He's playing the violin.

Activities

- Use familiar words to reinforce the concept of rhythm, and show that words and language always have a beat and rhythm. Clap while giving directions or reciting each child's name. Vary your movement by patting your thighs, stamping your feet, or sitting on the floor and patting it in a simple rhythm. Lead the singing of a favorite classroom song that contains strong rhythm patterns, such as "Old McDonald" or "If You're Happy and You Know It." Both of these songs have repetitive phrases and encourage clapping, clicking, stamping, and self-made sounds while letting the children enjoy a song they know well.

- Play the game Musical Freeze. Play energetic, rhythmic band music and let the children move around the room. When you stop the music, they must freeze in place and not move until the music resumes. Vary the style of music, encouraging them to adjust their body movements to the feeling of the music.

- If possible, provide an opportunity for children to play real instruments, or to listen to them played live. Bring in some real instruments. Have the children close their eyes. Make a sound with one of the instruments and let the children guess which instrument made it.

- Play a clapping rhythm game. Begin by clapping a simple rhythm and having the children clap it back to you. Then let the children take turns clapping a rhythm for the class and having the class clap the same rhythm back to them afterward. Make simple rhythm instruments.

Theme 4: My Town

Topic 21 Can we cross now?
Topic 22 Look at the toys!
Topic 23 Can we have a pet?
Topic 24 Let's go to the library!
Topic 25 I'm sick!
Topic 26 Who's at the hospital?
Topic 27 Busy supermarket!
Topic 28 Errands in town
Topic 29 Dinner's ready!
Topic 30 Nice evening!

Theme Bibliography

Abuela
written by Arthur Dorros; illustrated by Elisa Kleven.
Puffin Books, 1997. ISBN 0140562257
This imaginative adventure, shared by a young girl and her grandmother, is written in simple yet vivid language. The text models the "If I could fly ... I would..." grammatical structure. The beautiful collage illustrations, packed with details of the urban environment, can be used to extend vocabulary and spark conversation. Spanish words and phrases scattered throughout the book provide an opportunity for talking about speaking more than one language. A glossary of Spanish terms is included at the end of the book.

A is for Africa
by Ifeoma Onyefulu.
Puffin Books, 1997. ISBN: 0140562222
This ABC book explores the family ties and traditional activities in a Nigerian community. The text itself may be difficult for beginning readers. However, the vivid photographs are rich in detail and draw in the reader. Use the illustrations to generate questions and prompt students' acquisition of new vocabulary.

And To Think That I Saw It On Mulberry Street
written and illustrated by Dr. Seuss.
Random House, 1997. ISBN 0679887946
A boy walking home from school, anticipating his father's question about what he saw as he walked, lets his imagination run wild. He embellishes the one sight he sees, a simple horse and cart, so he can have a good story to tell. Dr. Seuss's classic pictures, rhymes, and repetitions introduce a variety of grammatical structures and useful vocabulary. Students can use this book as a starting point to relate their own journeys (both real and imaginary) to and from school.

Be-Bop-A-Do-Walk!
written and illustrated by Sheila Hamanaka.
Simon and Schuster, 1995. ISBN 0689802889
Two girls, Emi and Martha, accompany Emi's father on a long walk from the Lower East Side of Manhattan all the way up to Central Park. Emi is Japanese-American, and her friend is African-American. This story covers a lot of urban ground. The girls see sights both real and imagined, shown through illustrations that bring the city's diversity to life. The book provides opportunities for talking about such diverse subjects as community life, jazz, art, and friendship.

Cloudy with a Chance of Meatballs
written by Judi Barrett; illustrated by Ron Barrett.
Aladdin Paperbacks, 1982. ISBN 0689707495
Imagine a country where food falls from the sky. That's the subject of this silly, delightful story of Chewandswallow, where the people eat whatever the weather provides. Children will find familiar words for such things as foods and cooking and eating implements. The unfamiliar setting will tickle them and inspire them to invent their own weather menus and tall tales.

Corduroy
written and illustrated by Don Freeman.
Puffin Books, 1976. ISBN 0140501738
Corduroy is a slightly shopworn teddy bear who lives in a department store. Lisa is the little African-American girl who falls in love with him. This warm story provides a vehicle for comparing simple past and present perfect tense, and exploring contractions. The simple, pleasing illustrations can generate vocabulary for shopping and stores, and for expressing emotions.

Doctor De Soto
written and illustrated by William Steig.
Demco Media, 1997. ISBN 0606126759
This Newberry Award–winning book tells the silly but wonderful story of how Doctor De Soto, a compassionate and clever mouse dentist, and his able assistant help a fox with a toothache, and later outwit the same fox when he returns to eat them. Use this clever book to introduce dialogue, and prompt discussions of dental and health care, and ethics.

On Market Street
written by Arnold Lobel; illustrated by Anita Lobel.
Mulberry Books, 1989. ISBN 0688087450
Using rhymes and repeated language patterns, this book invites readers to join in an alphabetical shopping trip along Market Street. Its shopping themes and sophisticated artwork make a creative point of entry for discussion and role play.

Our New Puppy
by Isabelle Harper and Barry Moser.
Scholastic Inc., 1996. ISBN 0590569260
An exuberant new puppy is brought into a home that already has a dog, two cats, and several people. The simple story is complemented by illustrations that are bright, vivid, and full of interest. Use them to prompt students to talk about animal behavior and pets they have or would like to have. The book can also spark a discussion about welcoming newcomers and adjusting to them.

Pearl Moscowitz's Last Stand
written by Arthur A. Levine; illustrated by Robert Roth.
William Morrow & Co., 1993. ISBN 0688107532
Pearl Moscowitz has welcomed many new neighbors into her multi-ethnic neighborhood since her mother convinced the city to plant trees. When the last ginkgo on the block is threatened, she digs in her heels and takes a stand. The bright pictures can generate vocabulary and discussion of different foods and traditions. The story can be a stepping-off point for an exploration of community change and cooperative action.

Roxaboxen
written by Alice McLerran;
illustrated by Barbara Cooney.
Puffin Books, 1992. ISBN 0140544755
To an outsider, Roxenboxen may appear to be a desolate hill in the desert. But a magical, spirited town blooms and grows there as the local children turn it into their own community of the imagination. The words and pictures will invite students to explore imaginative play. The book will also provide opportunities to discuss games, play, ideas, landscapes, and the concept of community.

Tar Beach
written and illustrated by Faith Ringold.
Dragonfly Books, 1996. ISBN 0517885441
This book, based on a story quilt that hangs in the Guggenheim Museum, tells of Cassie Louise Lightfoot, an eight-year-old who enjoys family outings on "Tar Beach"—actually the rooftop of her family's Harlem apartment building. Cassie imagines that she can fly over the city and lay claim to all she sees. Students can act out flying over their own neighborhoods and pointing out the things and places they might see.

To Market, To Market
written by Anne Miranda; illustrated by Janet Stevens.
Harcourt Brace Jovanovich, 1997. ISBN 0152000356
This flamboyant and wacky extension of the familiar nursery rhyme combines illustrations of black-and-white realism with brightly colored fantasy. Chaos erupts as the older shopper brings home a series of animals, until they all shop together for the ingredients for a good lunch. Invite the students to recite the repetitive language pattern and make up their own disastrous results. For all their hilarity, the illustrations can be used to generate vocabulary for animals, vegetables, and shopping.

Trucks
written and illustrated by Anne Rockwell.
E.P. Dutton, 1992. ISBN 0140547908
The pleasing illustrations in this book show many kinds of trucks, as well as a variety of activities and environments. Prompt students to learn new words as they identify elements in the pictures. The text describes the different kinds of trucks in simple, declarative sentences. It can be easily used as a basis for question-and-answer exercises.

Worksong
written by Gary Paulsen;
illustrated by Ruth Wright Paulsen.
Harcourt Brace, 1997. ISBN 0152009809
Beautiful illustrations depict people at work, from carpenters and farmers to nurses and street cleaners, in a celebration of everyday working life. There are only a few words on each page; many of them can also be found thoughout the Picture Dictionary. Use this book to prompt children to talk about their own lives, and the kinds of work they and other members of their family do.

Can we cross now?

Content

- Places in a community
- Traffic and vehicles
- Police officers and street safety

Language

- Describing a community scene: *There are many stores. There wasn't a lot of traffic. The man is coming out of the library.*
- Asking about and describing a location: *Where is the sports store? The sports store is across the street from the police station. The sports store is next to the library.*
- Discussing traffic and street safety: *Can we cross now? Yes, it's safe to cross now. The cars stop when the light turns red.*
- Identifying vehicles and describing their location: *The motorcycle is in front of the truck. The taxi is at the traffic light.*
- Describing police officers at work: *The police officer stops the cars so we can cross the street. We can ask the police officer how to get to the store.*

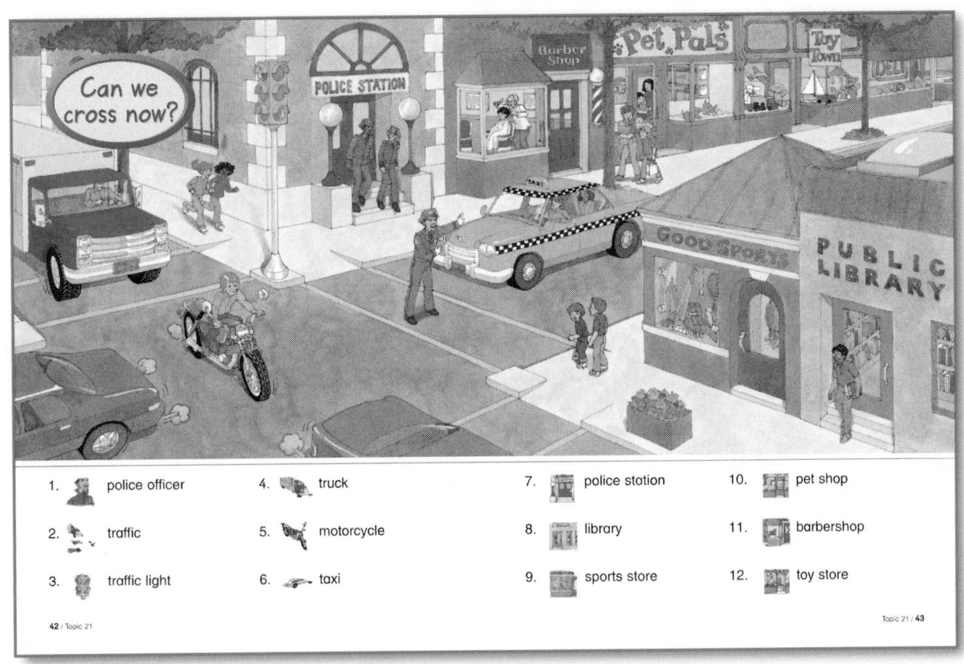

Words

1. police officer
2. traffic
3. traffic light
4. truck
5. motorcycle
6. taxi
7. police station
8. library
9. sports store
10. pet shop
11. barbershop
12. toy store

Additional Words

busy
honking
haircut
crosswalk
sidewalk
corner
bottom
top

Main Street is busy. There are a lot of stores. People are walking on the sidewalks. Tommy and Jim are waiting to cross the street. Police Officer O'Toole is stopping traffic so they can cross safely. There are a truck, a taxi, a motorcycle, and cars at the intersection. Jo-Jo is in the barbershop getting a haircut. He doesn't look very happy. Jackie and Mrs. Cheng are in the pet shop. The traffic light turns red and the traffic stops. The boys can cross now. Where are they going? To the toy store!

Words

Components: Topic 21 Wall Chart, Picture Dictionary (pp. 42–43), Cassette, Word and Picture Cards (Topic 21).

See page xiv for techniques and strategies for presenting and practicing words.

Can we cross now?

1. police officer
2. traffic
3. traffic light
4. truck
5. motorcycle
6. taxi
7. police station
8. library
9. sports store
10. pet shop
11. barbershop
12. toy store

Notes

Make a map of the intersection in the Dictionary illustration. Use a heavy marker to show the intersection of two perpendicular streets. Use a different color marker to indicate sidewalks. Narrate as you draw: *These are the streets in the town. These are the sidewalks.* Reinforce the vocabulary as you add each item to the map, modeling questions and answers about location: *Where is the sports store? The sports store is across the street from the police station.* Encourage children to play "traffic," using the map and the picture cards. Allow time for them to take turns being the police officer. Announce changes in the color of the traffic light.

Workbook page

Provide crayons or markers of the colors called for on this page. Review the color words if needed. If the children are unsure of a word, suggest they look in the Dictionary. Show them how to follow the lines from each person to the store where he or she is going, and ask them to write the name of the store in the sentence.

Stories

Components: Picture Dictionary (pp. 42–43), Cassette, Story (Topic 21).

See page xviii for techniques and strategies for presenting and practicing stories.

Main Street was busy.
The stores were busy.
The police officer was busy.
There was lots of traffic. Honk! Honk!

There were trucks and taxis,
and a motorcycle. Br-roo-o-om!
Tommy and Jim passed the library and
the sports store, and waited on the corner.

Were they going to the pet shop? No.
But Jackie was in the pet shop.
Were they going to the barbershop? No.
But look! Jo-Jo was getting a haircut!

The traffic light turned red. Stop, cars!
Police Officer O'Toole held up his hand.
Now it was safe to cross the street.
Have fun at the toy store, boys!

Story notes

Ask the children to compare their own community with the one depicted in the illustration. Focus on the topics addressed by the vocabulary: vehicles and stores. Ask the children if they see the same vehicles and stores where they live.

Ask about the story:
What was busy? Was there a lot of traffic? What is happening to Jo-Jo? Where are Mrs. Cheng and Jackie? Why did Tommy and Jim wait on the corner? Why did the cars stop? Who helped Jim and Tommy cross the street?

Ask about your students:
Use this opportunity to review street safety procedures. You may want to make a wall chart with the rules the children suggest.

Do you cross the street on your way to school? Where do you cross the street? How do you know it is safe to cross the street? What are good rules for crossing the street?

Dialogue

Components: Cassette, Topic 21 Wall Chart, Picture Dictionary (pp. 42–43).

See page xix for techniques and strategies for presenting and practicing dialogues.

Officer O'Toole:	Hello, boys! Where are you going today? Are you going to the pet shop?
Jim and Tommy:	No, Officer O'Toole.
Officer O'Toole:	Did your mom tell you to go to the barber for a haircut?
Jim and Tommy:	No, we're going to the toy store.
Officer O'Toole:	Oh, so that's where you're going. Do you know where it is?
Jim:	It's across the street, past the police station, and the barber-shop, and the pet shop.
Officer O'Toole:	Right! You know where you're going. Smart boys!
Tommy:	Can we cross now?
Officer O'Toole:	No, don't cross the street yet. Wait for the light to change.
Jim and Tommy:	OK.
Officer O'Toole:	It's green for the cars now. Wait till the light turns green for you and red for the cars.
Jim:	The light just changed, Officer O'Toole! Can we cross now?
Officer O'Toole:	Yes, come along! The cars have stopped. You can cross!
Jim and Tommy:	Thanks, Officer O'Toole!
Officer O'Toole:	Have a good time, and don't spend all your money!

Dialogue notes

When the children are comfortable with this dialogue, ask volunteers to invent new dialogues. They can decide where they are starting out on the map (or they can use the wall chart as a reference) and choose their destination. Then one volunteer should ask another for directions. Encourage them to take turns asking for and giving directions.

Beats!

Components: Cassette, Beats! (Topic 21).

See page xx for techniques and strategies for presenting and practicing Beats!

Can I cross now?
Can I cross now?
What are the rules?
Do you know how?

Stand on the corner,
Wait for the light.
Look to the left,
and look to the right.

Green's on the bottom.
Red's on the top.
Don't cross the street
till the cars all stop.

There are two lights
I can see.
Red for the cars,
and green for me!
Go on the green.
Stop on the red.
Can I cross now?
Of course. Go ahead!

Beat notes

Have the children make a traffic light. Show them how to draw three circles, one on top another, on both sides of a piece of stiff paper or cardboard. On one side children color the top circle red to show a red light. On the other side they color the bottom circle green to show a green light. As you teach the Beat, encourage the children to use hand and body motions (for example, to turn their heads right and left, and to point to the top and bottom of their traffic lights). Then have them recite the Beat in chorus at first, and then in two groups as question and response, holding up their red or green light every time they hear the corresponding color word.

Worksheets

Worksheet 1: Can we cross now? (p. 41)

The children should fill in the missing words in the sentences according to what the pictures show. Remind them that they can refer to the wall chart as well as the illustration to help them identify and spell the words.

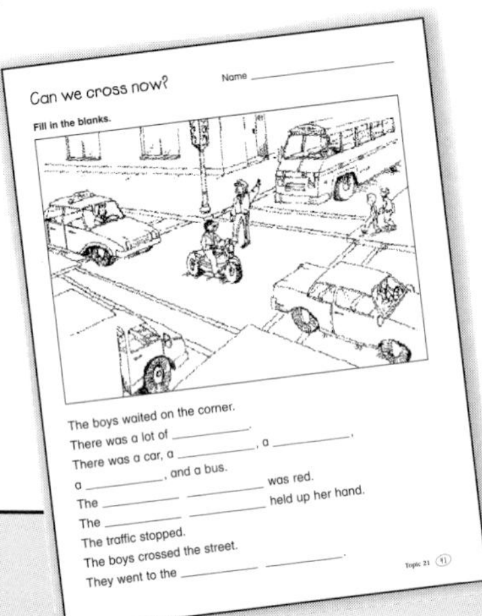

Can we cross now? Name ________

Fill in the blanks.

The boys waited on the corner.
There was a lot of ________.
There was a car, a ________, a ________,
a ________, and a bus.
The ________ ________ was red.
The ________ ________ held up her hand.
The traffic stopped.
The boys crossed the street.
They went to the ________ ________.

Topic 21 91

Worksheet 2: Can we cross now? (p. 42)

The missing words can all be found at the bottom of the page. Remind the children to use the pictures for clues. You may want to let pairs of children do this worksheet together so that they can help each other read the questions.

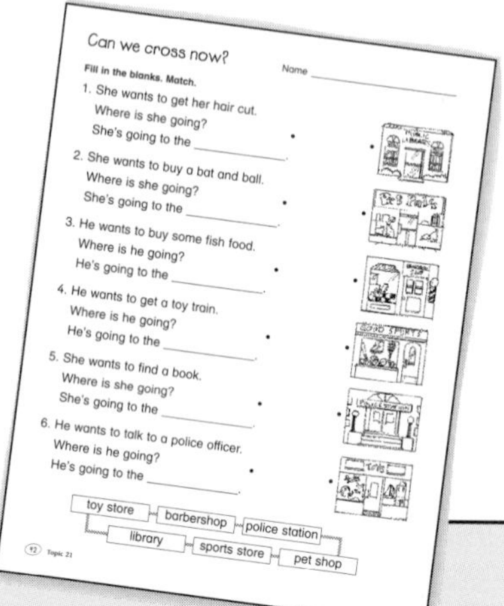

Can we cross now? Name ________

Fill in the blanks. Match.

1. She wants to get her hair cut.
   Where is she going?
   She's going to the ________.
2. She wants to buy a bat and ball.
   Where is she going?
   She's going to the ________.
3. He wants to buy some fish food.
   Where is he going?
   He's going to the ________.
4. He wants to get a toy train.
   Where is he going?
   He's going to the ________.
5. She wants to find a book.
   Where is she going?
   She's going to the ________.
6. He wants to talk to a police officer.
   Where is he going?
   He's going to the ________.

toy store · barbershop · police station · library · sports store · pet shop

92 Topic 21

Activities

- Play Red Light, Green Light. One child is the "traffic light"; she stands facing away from the others at the far end of the space and calls out, "Green light!" The other children then move toward her from the base line until the "traffic light" turns suddenly and calls out "Red light!" Then all movement has to stop, and any child caught moving (by the "traffic light") has to go back to the line. When a child approaches close enough to touch the "traffic light," that child takes her or his place and the game begins again.

- Teach the classic street safety song:
  Don't cross the street in the middle,
  in the middle,
  in the middle, in the middle, in the middle,
  in the middle of the block.
  Teach your eyes to look up.
  Teach your ears to hear.
  Walk up to the corner where the coast is clear,
  And wait, and wait, and wait
  until you see the light turn green!

- Take a walking field trip in your school neighborhood. As you walk along, provide language models by asking and answering questions about what you are doing and seeing: *We are crossing the street. There's a store. What kind of store is it? It's a shoe store.*

- Set up a street scene in the gym or on the playground. Help the children make cardboard traffic signs. Let some students use the signs to direct "traffic" as their classmates travel around the gym or playground in pretend vehicles.

- Use blocks, empty boxes, or clay to make a model community that can be changed or added to daily. Label each store with a sign that shows its name and a picture clue. Children can make people and vehicles out of clay, or paste pictures cut from magazines onto stiff cardboard.

Look at the toys!

Content

- Toys
- Money
- Making purchases

Language

- Asking about and identifying toys: *Look at the dolls. Are there any stuffed animals? What is this toy? It's a toy plane.*
- Expressing wants and likes: *I like the trains. She wants a game. Tommy wants to buy the kangaroo.*
- Asking and telling prices: *How much does this cost? How much is this game? This car is fifty cents.*
- Identifying money and adding up combinations to find sums: *Two nickels make one dime. I have two quarters, so I have fifty cents.*
- Discussing borrowing and lending: *Can I borrow a nickel? I will lend you seven cents.*

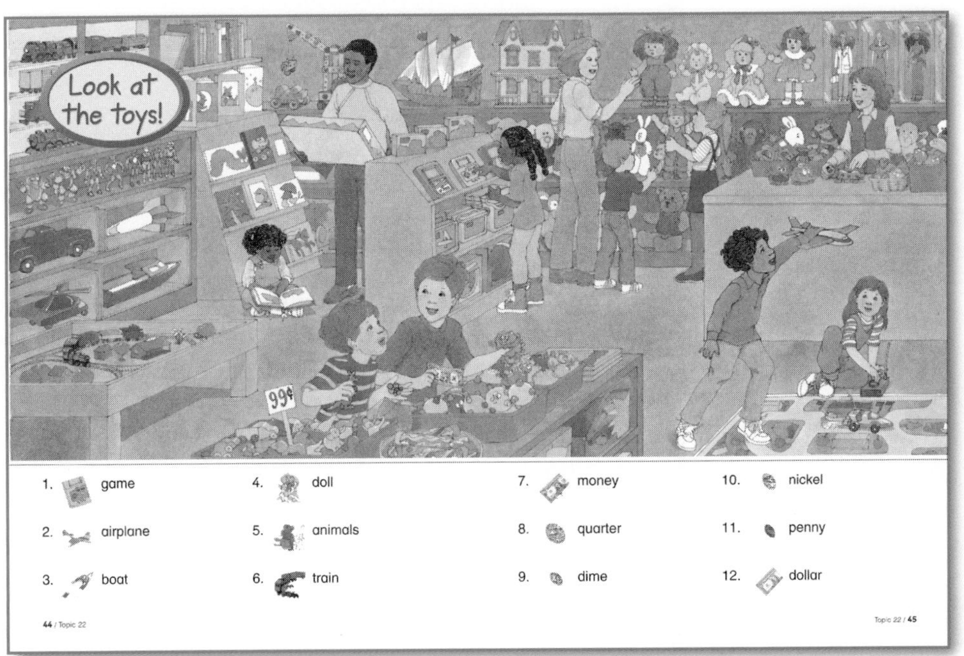

Tommy and Jim are at the toy store. What will they buy? There are all kinds of games, planes, boats, trains, dolls, animals, and sports gear. A boy is pretending to fly an airplane. One girl is playing with an electronic game, and another girl is playing with a car. Some parents are looking at the toys on the shelves. A girl is holding a doll, and a little boy is sitting on the floor looking at a picture book. The salesperson stands behind the counter surveying the whole scene. Tommy has just chosen what he wants: a bright orange kangaroo. The sign says it costs ninety-nine cents. Does he have enough money? He's showing Jim the money he has: three quarters, a dime, a nickel, and two pennies. Jim has a dollar bill in his hand. What are they going to do?

Words

1. game
2. airplane
3. boat
4. doll
5. animals
6. train
7. money
8. quarter
9. dime
10. nickel
11. penny
12. dollar

Additional Words

price
cost
change
coins
salesperson
lend
borrow
cash register
add

Words

Components: Topic 22 Wall Chart, Picture Dictionary (pp. 44–45), Cassette, Word and Picture Cards (Topic 22).

See page xiv for techniques and strategies for presenting and practicing words.

Look at the toys!

1. game	5. animals	9. dime
2. airplane	6. train	10. nickel
3. boat	7. money	11. penny
4. doll	8. quarter	12. dollar

Notes

Lay out the picture cards for toys, and have the children set a price for each toy. Make a price list on a chart. Invite a volunteer to be the salesperson. Let the children take turns playing customer and choosing a toy to buy. Model the language needed for a simple transaction: *How much is this? How much does this cost? Twenty-five cents. Here's twenty-five cents. Thank you. You're welcome.* Encourage children to make additional cards for other toys. The children can also make extra money cards, or you may want to provide some real or toy coins for them to use.

Workbook page

The children should write the name for each unit of money above its picture. Point out that the first letter(s) of each word has already been filled in as a clue. Next, demonstrate with a few coins how to add up totals. Then tell them to look at the two pictures of money, write the missing words, add up the totals, and write in the spaces provided. At the bottom of the page, the children may want to circle more than one toy among the choices. Ask them to be sure there is enough money shown to buy more than one choice. If not, they should choose just one toy.

Stories

Components: Picture Dictionary (pp. 44–45), Cassette, Story (Topic 22).

See page xviii for techniques and strategies for presenting and practicing stories.

Look at those games!
Try one. Buzz-z-z! Bonk! Bonk!
Here comes an airplane! Zoo-o-om-m!
And a boat! Arnh! Arnh! Arnh!

See those dolls with the long hair?
And the stuffed animals? They're cute!
Jim likes the little trains whizzing
around. And the helicopters!

What is Tommy holding in his hand?
It's a bright orange kangaroo!
He takes out his money.
The kangaroo costs ninety-nine cents.

Tommy has three quarters, a dime,
a nickel, and two pennies.
Does he have enough money?
He really wants that orange kangaroo!

Story notes

Invite volunteers to tell the group about their favorite toys. Prompt them to describe their toys and how they play with them. You may ask each child to make a picture of his or her favorite toy and write or dictate a sentence or two about it. Combine the pictures into a class book.

Ask about the story:
Who is playing with the plane? Which toy does Jim like? How much does the kangaroo cost? How much money does Tommy have? How much money does Jim have?

Ask about your students:
What toy do you like? Which toy would you buy? Did you ever buy a toy? Where did you buy a toy? How much did the toy cost? Who do you give the money to in a store?

Dialogue

Components: Cassette, Topic 22 Wall Chart, Picture Dictionary (pp. 44–45).

See page xix for techniques and strategies for presenting and practicing dialogues.

Tommy:	Jim! Do I have enough money to buy this animal?
Jim:	It's a kangaroo.
Tommy:	I know. We're learning about kangaroos in school.
Jim:	Don't you want a car or a plane? Or one of those neat action men?
Tommy:	No, I want this kangaroo.
Jim:	OK. Where's your money?
Tommy:	Here.
Jim:	Let's see. You have three quarters. That's seventy-five cents. And a dime. That's eighty-five cents.
Tommy:	And a nickel and two pennies.
Jim:	That's ninety cents with the nickel, and two more pennies. You have ninety-two cents, Tommy.
Tommy:	How much do I need?
Jim:	The sign says "99 cents." You need seven more cents.
Tommy:	I don't have any more money. Mom said if I don't have enough money I can't buy anything. I really like him, Jim.
Jim:	All right. I will lend you some money.
Tommy:	Will you lend me seven cents?
Jim:	Yes, but I only have a dollar. I'll have to get it changed. Come on over to the cash register.
Tommy:	Thanks, Jim. You're a good brother.
Jim:	I know.

Dialogue notes

Encourage the children to use the dialogue as a basis for inventing their own dialogues. Create a toy store activity center, and allow time for small groups to play in it. One child can pretend to be the salesperson, while the others can play customers. Encourage them to choose toys to purchase, discuss their cost and the amount of money they have, and the concept of lending money or helping friends make a purchase.

Beats!

Components: Cassette, Beats! (Topic 22).

See page xx for techniques and strategies for presenting and practicing Beats!

Can I get this plane?
    How much is it?
Ninety-nine cents.
    Sure, why not?

    It's a very nice plane.
    What's the matter?
I only have a nickel.
That's all I've got.

What about this plane?
    How much is it?
Thirty cents.
I like it a lot.

But I only have a nickel.
    I have a quarter.
    You can borrow it.
Thanks a lot!

Beat notes

Divide the class into two groups, and practice the Beat as question and response. Then have the groups switch and practice the other voice. Provide the children with props and play money so they can act out the Beat as they recite it.

Worksheets

Worksheet 1: Look at the toys! (p. 43)

Talk with the children about price tags. You may want to write a price on a small piece of paper and attach it with a string to a classroom toy to demonstrate how price tags work. Explain that they should look at the pictures on the page for clues as they fill in the missing words. Suggest that they count up the coins to find out how much money they have for each question. They can write *yes* or *no* on the space given.

Look at the toys! Name ____________

Fill in the blanks.

What do you want to buy? How much money do you have?

1. I want to buy this ____________.
   I have four ____________.
   Do I have enough money? ____________.
2. I want to buy this ____________.
   I have two ____________, two ____________
   and one ____________.
   Do I have enough money? ____________.

Topic 22 43

Worksheet 2: Look at the toys! (p. 44)

Help the children cut out the toys with their price tags from the bottom section of the page. You may suggest that they arrange the toys from least to most expensive. Then explain that the coins at the top of the page show how many cents there are in each kind of coin, for example, a quarter is "25¢." As the children find a toy that costs the same as the amount shown, help them paste it into the space provided. The numerical equivalent of each vocabulary word (*quarter* = 25¢) can be found in each blank space.

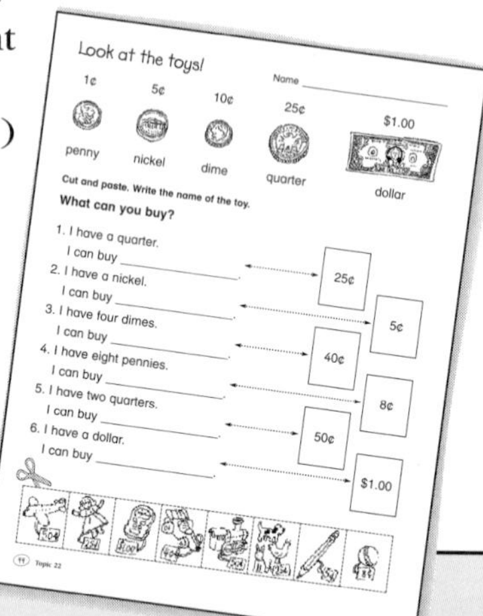

Look at the toys! Name ____________

1¢	5¢	10¢	25¢	$1.00
penny	nickel	dime	quarter	dollar

Cut and paste. Write the name of the toy.

What can you buy?

1. I have a quarter.
   I can buy ____________. 25¢
2. I have a nickel.
   I can buy ____________. 5¢
3. I have four dimes.
   I can buy ____________. 40¢
4. I have eight pennies.
   I can buy ____________. 8¢
5. I have two quarters.
   I can buy ____________. 50¢
6. I have a dollar.
   I can buy ____________. $1.00

44 Topic 22

Activities

- Make a toy store activity center, where children can practice making purchases and using the topic vocabulary. Have the children help you put price tags on small toys. If possible, include toys that correspond to the vocabulary words. Provide them with a collection of toy or real coins to use.
- Share with your children some of the many children's books that are about toys, for example, *Corduroy* and *A Pocket for Corduroy* by Don Freeman (Scholastic). Then help them write their own stories about their favorite toys.
- Start a classroom foreign-coin collection. If possible, bring in coins and bills from other countries and ask children if they have any foreign money they can show. Compare the different types of money.
- Host an International Toy Day. Look in encyclopedias and the library for information about popular toys in other countries. Invite the children to bring in special toys from other countries to share and display in your classroom or in a school display case. Label each toy and invite families and friends to come to school and see the exhibit.

Can we have a pet?

Content

- Pets and pet care
- Names of adult and baby animals
- Animal sounds

Language

- Identifying animals that people keep as pets: *I have a pet dog. She has a new kitten. We have fish in the classroom.*
- Identifying and describing things pets need: *Cats need food and water every day. You have to feed pets. Dogs need to be taken on walks.*
- Describing ways to take care of pets: *I brush my puppy. He feeds his turtle. She changes the water in the fish tank.*
- Identifying and describing animal sounds: *My kitten meows. The bird is squawking. The puppies go "woof, woof."*

Words

1. bird
2. fish
3. fish tank
4. turtle
5. mouse
6. cage
7. dog
8. cat
9. kitten
10. puppy
11. collar
12. leash

Additional Words

pet
bark
meow
curl up
wag

The animals in the pet shop are making a lot of strange noises. The bird is squawking, the kitten is meowing, the dogs say "ruff!", and the fish are making glub-glub sounds. The Chengs are getting a new pet, a cute little tan puppy. Jackie is holding him and patting him gently. Jo-Jo is attaching a leash to his collar. The puppy is wagging his tail. The pet shop man is giving instructions for the care of the puppy: Feed him, brush his coat, keep him clean and healthy, and give him exercise and lots of love. Good luck!

Words

Components: Topic 23 Wall Chart, Picture Dictionary (pp. 46–47), Cassette, Word and Picture Cards (Topic 23).

See page xiv for techniques and strategies for presenting and practicing words.

Can we have a pet?

1. bird	5. mouse	9. kitten
2. fish	6. cage	10. puppy
3. fish tank	7. dog	11. collar
4. turtle	8. cat	12. leash

Notes

Ask the children to make a circle, bringing picture cards with them. Then tell them they can choose any animal picture card from the collection and hold it up. Show them the picture of the fish, and begin a question-and-answer round-robin. Start by modeling the language: *What pet do I have? I have a fish.* Then turn to the child on your right and ask: *What pet do you have?* Prompt him or her first to answer according to the animal picture card he or she is holding up, and then to turn to the next child to carry on with the game. Continue until all of the children have had a chance to ask and answer the question. Then, if appropriate, repeat the process, adding a sentence that tells about something that each pet needs or uses: *What pet do I have? I have a cat. My cat needs cat food. What pet do you have?*

Workbook page

The children should write the word for each pet shown in the picture at the top of the page. Then, for each of the empty pet homes shown at the bottom of the page, tell them to draw the missing pet and write the missing words. Remind them to look at the top of the page for the missing words.

23 Can we have a pet?

Fill in the blanks.

meow, meow | ruff, ruff | squeak, squeak | purr, purr

cat | mouse | kitten | turtle | dog | fish | bird

Draw the pet. Fill in the blanks.

Who lives here?

1. A ________ lives here.

2. A ________ lives here.

3. A ________ lives here.

Stories

Components: Picture Dictionary (pp. 46–47), Cassette, Story (Topic 23).

See page xviii for techniques and strategies for presenting and practicing stories.

The Cheng twins are getting a new pet!
Squawk! goes a big green and red bird.
Glub! Glub! go the blue and yellow fish
swimming in the fish tank.

Big dogs, little dogs! Ruff! Ruff! Yowl!
Listen to them barking in their cages.
The cats are curled up sleeping.
Meow! Oh, one little kitten is awake.

See that little tan puppy? That's the one!
The pet shop man lets Jo-Jo hold him.
Pat him gently. He loves that!
Give him food, and exercise, and love.

Put on his collar. Put on his leash.
His tail is wagging. He's ready to go.
Mrs. Cheng has his dog food and brush.
Good luck! Take good care of him!

Story notes

Take this opportunity to invite the children to describe pets they have and pets they might like to have. Ask focused questions (such as *What did you feed your pet? How did you take care of your pet?*) to help the children clarify their descriptions.

Ask about the story:

What animals do Jo-Jo and Jackie see in the pet shop? Does Jo-Jo want a turtle? What kind of pet does Jackie want? Where do the fish live? What does Jo-Jo put on the puppy? Who pats the puppy? Who tells the boys how to take care of the puppy? What does the pet shop man tell the boys?

Ask about your students:

Who has a pet? What is your pet's name? Is your pet big or little? What do you do for your pet? Can you pat a fish? Would you like to pat a kitten? What does a turtle eat?

Dialogue

Components: Cassette, Topic 23 Wall Chart, Picture Dictionary (pp. 46–47).

See page xix for techniques and strategies for presenting and practicing dialogues.

Jo-Jo:	We want this puppy, Mama.
Mrs. Cheng:	A puppy is a lot of work, boys. Don't you want a turtle or a mouse?
Jo-Jo:	No, we want this puppy! We love this puppy!
Mrs. Cheng:	Will you two take care of him?
Jo-Jo:	Yes, we will!
Mrs. Cheng:	But look at all these things he needs! Food, a brush, a leash, a collar! Someone has to feed him, and brush him, and keep him clean, and walk him so he gets exercise.
Jo-Jo:	We're going to take turns. First I'm going to feed him, and Jackie's going to brush him. Then Jackie's going to feed him, and I'm going to brush him.
Mrs. Cheng:	Who's going to walk him?
Jo-Jo:	We'll walk him together.
Mrs. Cheng:	And where's he going to sleep?
Pet shop man:	Maybe you can find him a nice old blanket to sleep on. And be sure you keep his collar on him, so people will know he belongs to you. He'll be your responsibility. Keep him healthy and happy!
Mrs. Cheng:	All right, boys, he's yours!
Twins:	Yeah-h-h!

Dialogue notes

Encourage the children to make up short dialogues in which one child plays a pet shop clerk and the others play family members discussing acquiring a new pet. Encourage the children to vary the kind of pet they are discussing, and prompt them to add details referring to what each kind of pet needs.

Beats!

Components: Cassette, Beats! (Topic 23).

See page xx for techniques and strategies for presenting and practicing Beats!

I wish I had a puppy.
Would you take good care of him?
Yes, I'd walk him, and I'd feed him,
and I'd teach him how to swim.

I wish I had a kitten.
Would you take good care of her?
Yes, I'd pat her very gently,
and I'd listen to her purr.

I wish I had a little bird.
I wish I had a mouse.

I'd let my pet fly way up high.
I'd keep mine in my house.

Beat notes

Help the children to invent gestures and actions to accompany the Beat as they recite it, by asking questions and eliciting narration: *How could you show us that you're walking a puppy? What do you do when you feed a dog?* Prompt them to pantomime the basic actions described by the Beat, and use the opportunity for extending their vocabulary usage by encouraging elaboration, for example: *Do you put your puppy on a leash? Does your puppy have a collar?*

Worksheets

Worksheet 1: Can we have a pet? (p. 45)

Each pet shown in the column on the right can be matched with an item used to take care of it (shown in the column on the left). The children can draw lines to show which pictures go together. For the questions, explain that they check only one of the boxes *(Yes, I do* or *No, I don't).*

Can we have a pet? Name ____________

Match.

Answer the questions.

Do you have a pet? Put an X in the box for your answer.

☐ Yes, I do. I have a ____________.

How do you take care of your pet?

☐ No, I don't.

What kind of pet would you like to have?

What would your pet need?

Topic 23 45

Worksheet 2: Can we have a pet? (p. 46)

The pictures are clues to completing the sentences. Point out that each missing word is one of the unit vocabulary words. Children may want to use the Dictionary or Wall Chart as references for identifying and spelling the words.

Can we have a pet? Name ____________

Fill in the blanks.

1. The ________ is in the ________.
2. The ________ is in the ________.
3. The ________ is barking.
4. The ________ is wearing a ________ and a ________.
5. The ________ is sleeping.
6. The ________ is awake.
7. The ________ is eating.
8. The ________ is in its cage.

46 Topic 23

Activities

- By far, the best way to introduce children to the idea of pets and pet care is to have a classroom pet that they can observe and help care for. If this isn't possible, you can arrange for your children to visit a pet store. A student or a visitor can bring in a pet.

- Play a guessing game with animal sounds. Make a sound (for example, meow like a cat) and ask the children to identify which animal makes that sound. Then call for volunteers to make a sound for the other children to identify. Start with the sounds and animals depicted in the Dictionary illustration and described in the story. As the children become more comfortable, encourage them to expand their animal sound repertoire.

- Make a bulletin board display. Ask the children to draw a picture of themselves with their pet. Help the child label the picture with the pet's name, the kind of animal it is, and the child's own name. Ask him or her to write or dictate a short story about the pet. Children who have no pets can contribute a section about a pet they would like to have.

- Make pet masks. Provide paper bags or paper plates, markers, yarn, glue, construction paper, or other materials for children to use in making masks of imaginary pets. When all the masks are finished, hold a "pet parade."

Let's go to the library!

Content

- Library procedures
- Library materials

Language

- Identifying library materials and their use: *I can look up a word in the dictionary. The atlas has maps.*
- Asking for help: *Can you help me? How do you use this dictionary? How can I find a book? Where's the call number on this book? Do you have a book about dogs?*
- Asking and answering questions about library procedures: *How long can I keep this book? You can keep that book for two weeks. How many books can I check out? You can check out two books at a time.*

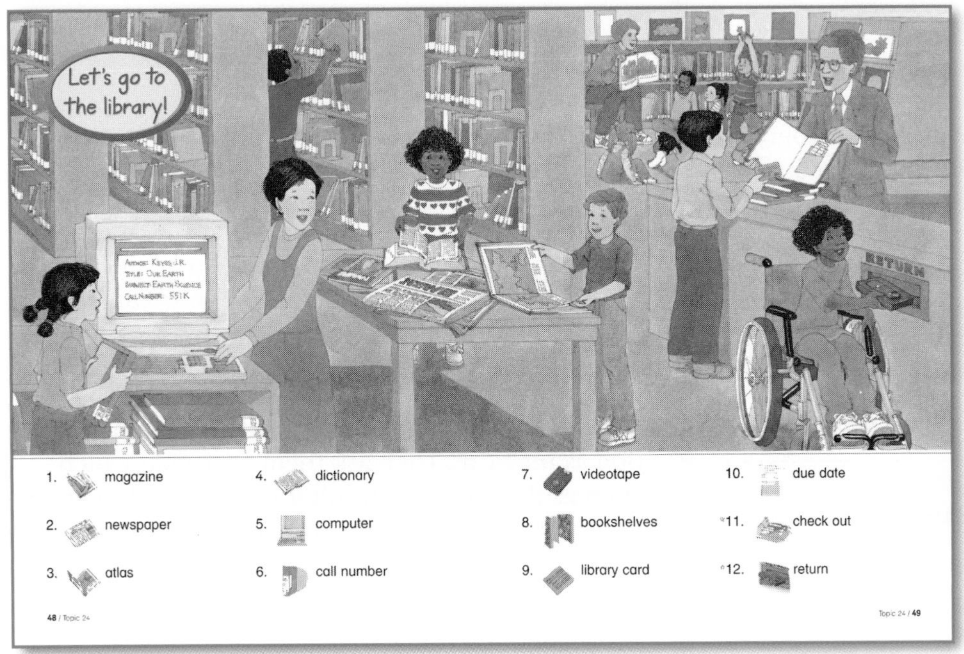

Ting, Zoe, and Jim have come to the public library to do some research about the earth for their homework. Zoe and Jim have spread out newspapers and magazines on the table. Ting is trying to locate books using the computer catalog with the librarian's help. She is learning how to locate books by their call numbers. The librarian is also helping Jim find a map in the atlas and Zoe find a word in the dictionary. Jim's brother, Tommy, is listening to a story in the far corner. Marcus is in the bookshelves, looking for a book for Samantha. Marcus's sister Mariah is returning some videotapes. Ting's brother, Henry, is checking out three books. He is giving the librarian at the checkout desk his library card. The librarian cautions him to be sure to return the books on time!

Words

1. magazine
2. newspaper
3. atlas
4. dictionary
5. computer
6. call number
7. videotape
8. bookshelves
9. library card
10. due date

Verbs

11. check out
12. return

Additional Words

reference book
map
card catalog
quiet
research
locate
homework

Words

Components: Topic 24 Wall Chart, Picture Dictionary (pp. 48–49), Cassette, Word and Picture Cards (Topic 24).

See page xiv for techniques and strategies for presenting and practicing words.

Let's go to the library!

1. magazine
2. newspaper
3. atlas
4. dictionary
5. computer
6. call number
7. videotape
8. bookshelves
9. library card
10. due date

Verbs

11. check out
12. return

Notes

Gather the children around a table where you have spread out some magazines and newspapers, an atlas, a dictionary, a videotape, and a library card. Encourage them to examine the dictionary and volunteer any information they have about it. Model questions and answers: *Does the dictionary have pictures and words? Yes, there are a lot of words and some little pictures.* Repeat this process with each item illustrating a vocabulary word, and give the children time to become familiar with the different learning tools in the illustration.

Workbook page

For the first set of exercises, tell the children to draw a line from each word to the picture that shows it. Then, tell them to fill in the missing words on the rest of the page. Remind them that the illustrations are clues.

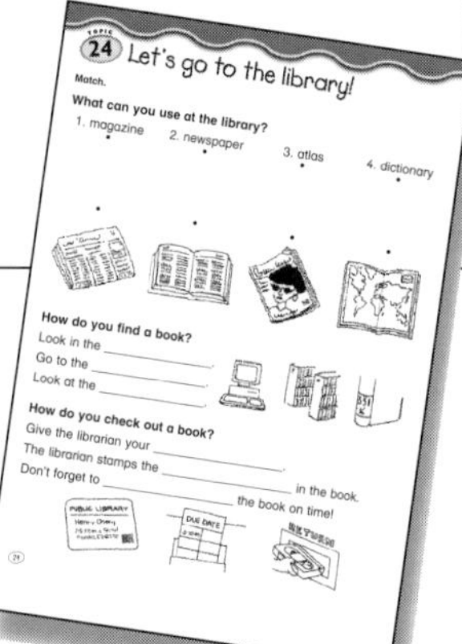

TOPIC 24 Let's go to the library!

Match.

What can you use at the library?

1. magazine 2. newspaper 3. atlas 4. dictionary

How do you find a book?

Look in the ______.
Go to the ______.
Look at the ______.

How do you check out a book?

Give the librarian your ______.
The librarian stamps the ______ in the book.
Don't forget to ______ the book on time!

Stories

Components: Picture Dictionary (pp. 48–49), Cassette, Story (Topic 24).

See page xviii for techniques and strategies for presenting and practicing stories.

Who spread those magazines and
newspapers all over the table?
Zoe and Jim and Ting.
This homework looks hard!

Jim has an atlas, Zoe has a dictionary,
and Ting is at the computer
finding books.
A librarian is helping all of them.

There's Mariah returning videotapes.
Marcus is in the bookshelves looking
for a picture book for Samantha.
He just found one.

Guess who's checking out three books?
It's Henry.
He gives the librarian his library card.
She puts the due date in the books.
Return them on time! Please!

Story notes

Ask the children to name as many sources of information as they can. Then ask them to decide which sources they would consult if they wanted to know how to spell a word, how to build a model car, or what the weather will be tomorrow. Use the discussion to reinforce the children's understanding of the variety of information resources.

Ask about the story:
Why do Zoe, Ting, and Jim go to the library? What is Ting looking for? Can she find books with the computer? Who is helping the children in the library? What is Henry checking out? Does Henry use a library card? Can he keep the book? What does Mariah return?

Ask about your students:
If possible, schedule a trip to the school or public library. After the trip, engage the children in a discussion of the experience: *Was it noisy or quiet in the library? Why is it quiet in the library? Were there many people? What were they doing? When you take a book home from the library, do you keep it?*

Dialogue

Components: Cassette, Topic 24 Wall Chart, Picture Dictionary (pp. 46–47).

See page xix for techniques and strategies for presenting and practicing dialogues.

Ting:	Thanks for helping me use the computer.
Librarian:	You're welcome, Ting. I'm glad you found the books.
Ting:	Now I understand about call numbers.
Zoe:	What are call numbers?
Ting:	The numbers on the books. Then you know where to find the books. All the bookshelves have numbers on them, too.
Zoe:	Oh.
Jim:	I think I need some help. This is hard. I don't know how to use this atlas.
Librarian:	I'll show you.
Zoe:	Can you help me, too? How do you use this dictionary?
Librarian:	I'll show all of you.
Zoe and Jim:	Great!
Ting:	Can we take some of the magazines home?
Librarian:	Yes, you can. Do you know how to check them out?
Ting:	Do we just show our library cards?
Librarian:	That's right, and be sure to return everything by the due date.
Ting, Zoe, and Jim:	We will.
Zoe:	See? This isn't so hard. It's going to be easy.
Ting:	I think it's fun!

Dialogue notes

Encourage children to role-play a trip to the library. They can take turns playing the librarians, help each other find books, and check books in and out. Prompt them to ask and answer questions about the uses of library materials and library procedures.

Beats!

Components: Cassette, Beats! (Topic 24).

See page xx for techniques and strategies for presenting and practicing Beats!

I was looking for a book
at the library.
He was looking for a book
at the library.

I was pulling one out,
but it fell on the floor.
He was pulling one out,
but it fell on the floor.

I was picking it up
when guess what I saw!
He was picking it up
when guess what he saw!

That was the book
I was looking for!
That was the book he was
looking for.

Beat notes

This Beat has a statement-echo structure, with the statement voice in the first person *(I)* and the echoing voice in the third person *(he)*. To begin practice, speak the first couplet of each stanza and prompt the children to respond with the second. Clap along with the beat. Once the children are familiar with the pattern, invite volunteers to be the first speaker, as the rest of the class echoes. For the final stanza, have the second group change the *I* to *he* as they say the line in unison.

Worksheets

Worksheet 1: Let's go to the library! (p. 47)

The children should look at the pictures and write each word. Suggest that they think about the libraries they have visited. Ask them to follow directions by circling the things they would expect to find in a library. They may like to color the pictures.

Let's go to the library! Name ______

Circle the things you can find in a library. Write the words.

Topic 24

Worksheet 2: Let's go to the library! (p. 48)

The pictures are clues to help the children identify the missing words. When they have filled in all of the blanks, you can help them to read the page aloud.

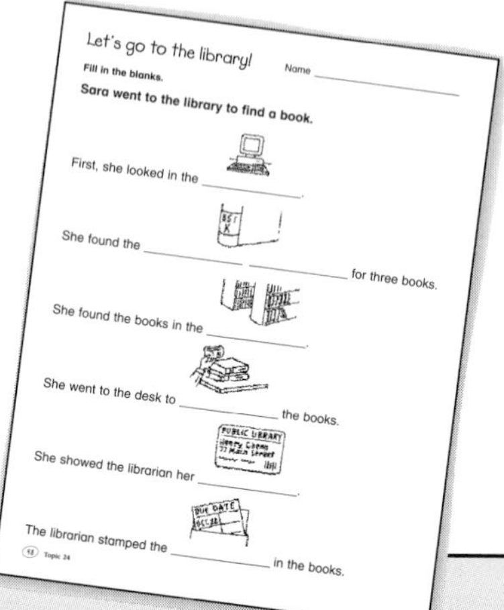

Let's go to the library! Name ______

Fill in the blanks.

Sara went to the library to find a book.

First, she looked in the ______.

She found the ______ ______ for three books.

She found the books in the ______.

She went to the desk to ______ the books.

She showed the librarian her ______.

The librarian stamped the ______ in the books.

Topic 24

Activities

- Turn a bookshelf in your classroom into a small lending library. Ask the children what you will need, and then help them make library cards, due date cards (self-stick notes work well), and some kind of catalog. Let two children each day sign up to be classroom librarians, and provide time for the group to play at checking out and returning books.

- Make special bookmarks using recycled paper. Encourage children to decorate strips of discarded paper (you can laminate or cover them with clear contact paper to make them more durable). Children may like to make special bookmarks to give as gifts.

- Make a class atlas of countries that your children's families came from or have visited. Discuss the idea while referring to a large world map. Then make a list of the countries you want to include. Let every child choose a country he or she wants to represent. Then, give each individual or small group an outline map of their country to color and label and put into the book.

- Ask the children to think of a word they want to find in the dictionary, and then narrate as you look for that word (for example: *We want to find the word* skunk. *The first letter of* skunk *is* s, *so I go to the part of the dictionary where the words start with* s).

TOPIC 25 I'm sick!

Content

- Visit to a doctor's office
- Checkup procedures
- Sickness and medical care

Language

- Expressing physical states: *I have a cold. My throat feels sore. My head hurts. My stomach doesn't hurt.*
- Describing procedures: *She used the stethoscope to hear my heart. The girl stood on the scale. The doctor wrote things on her chart.*
- Describing medical care and instructions: *She had to get a shot. He will take tablets for his sore throat. The doctor gave my mother a prescription for drops. She put the drops in my ears.*

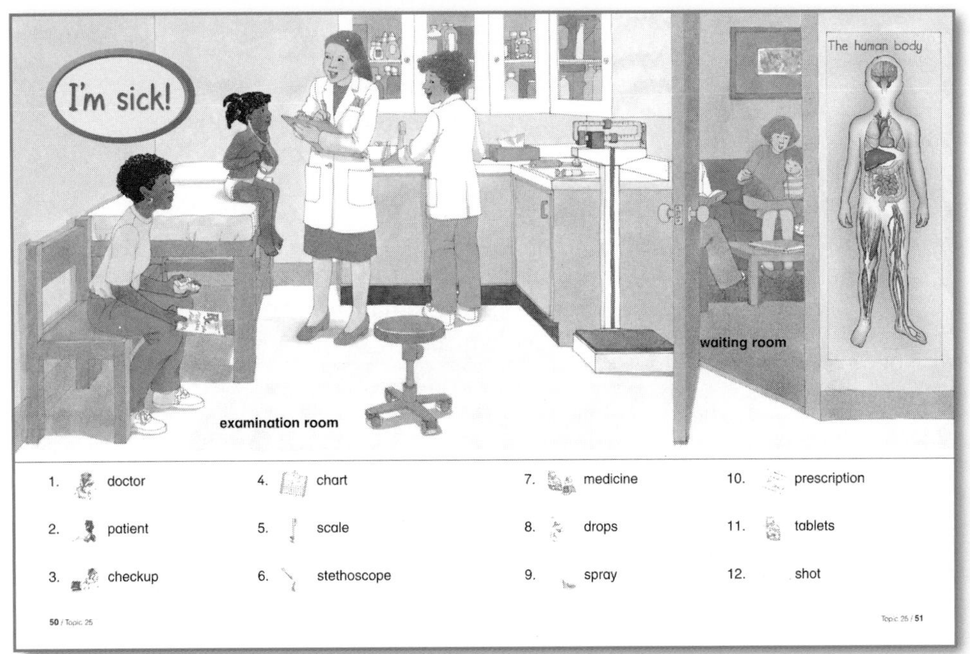

Words

1. doctor
2. patient
3. checkup
4. chart
5. scale
6. stethoscope
7. medicine
8. drops
9. spray
10. prescription
11. tablets
12. shot

Labels

examination room
waiting room

Additional Words

examine
virus
weigh
temperature
thermometer
nurse

Samantha is at the doctor's office. The waiting room is filled with sick patients and their parents. Samantha is in the examining room with her mother, Dr. Mack, and a nurse. Dr. Mack has weighed Samantha on the scale and taken her temperature. The doctor has also listened to her heart and lungs with the stethoscope. She has given Mrs. Jackson a prescription and medicines for Samantha: nose spray and ear drops, with instructions on how to use them. Samantha does not need a shot. Dr. Mack is writing on Samantha's chart and smiling at her. Samantha is using the stethoscope to listen to her very own heart beating!

Words

Components: Topic 25 Wall Chart, Picture Dictionary (pp. 50–51), Cassette, Word and Picture Cards (Topic 25).

See page xiv for techniques and strategies for presenting and practicing words.

I'm sick!

1. doctor	5. scale	9. spray
2. patient	6. stethoscope	10. prescription
3. checkup	7. medicine	11. tablets
4. chart	8. drops	12. shot

Labels

examination room
waiting room

Notes

Invite volunteers to describe visits they have made to a doctor when they were sick, or when they were just getting a regular checkup. Ask them to describe what happened when they first got to the doctor's office. Help the children compare their experiences.

Invite the children to play What Do I Need? Model the game by describing and pantomiming a symptom (for example, put your hands to your throat and say, *I have a sore throat; what do I need?*). Prompt the students to respond in words or by holding up one of their word cards. Then ask each child to pick a partner. Partners take turns playing the roles of doctor and patient.

Workbook page

Each line points to a picture depicting one of the topic words. At the bottom of the page are all the missing words. The children should write the words on the lines provided. Suggest that they cross out each word as they use it to label a part of the picture.

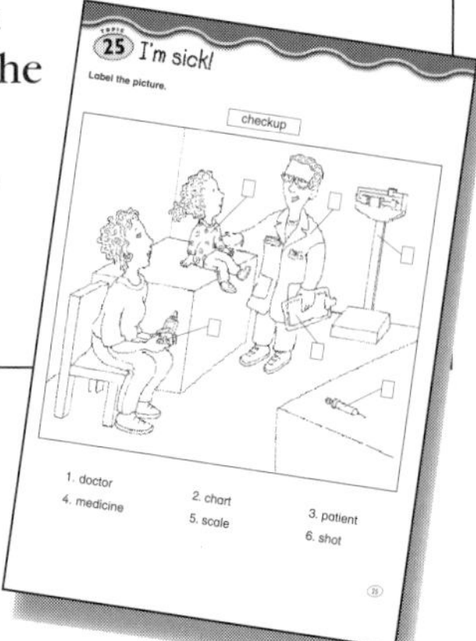

Stories

Components: Picture Dictionary (pp. 50–51), Cassette, Story (Topic 25).

See page xviii for techniques and strategies for presenting and practicing stories.

The waiting room was crowded.
The patients were sick.
Samantha was having her checkup.
Dr. Mack wrote everything on her chart.

Samantha's temperature was 101°.
She weighed 63 pounds on the scale.
Dr. Mack looked in her ears, nose,
and throat. They all looked red.
She needed medicine!

Dr. Mack listened to her heart with the
stethoscope. Bum-bum, bum-bum!
Then she listened to her lungs.
Breathe in. Breathe out. Good!
Could Samantha listen, too? What fun!

Dr. Mack gave Mrs. Jackson eardrops,
nose spray, and a prescription for tablets.
No shot, Samantha!
Samantha felt better already!

Story notes

Talk with the children about reasons for going to a doctor. Ask them to suggest different reasons as you list their ideas on a piece of chart paper. You may also want to review the words in Topic 19 (What's the Matter?) and encourage the children to use those words as well as the ones they are learning in this topic.

Ask about the story:
Who was sick? What are these people waiting for? Why do they have to wait? What is this [point at an item]*? What is the doctor doing? How can Samantha hear her heart beat? What do they use the scale for?*

Ask about your students:
Did you get a checkup? Who went to the doctor with you? Did the doctor weigh you on the scale? Did the doctor give you a shot? Do you like to get a shot? Did the doctor she give you medicine? Did the medicine help you feel better?

Dialogue

Components: Cassette, Topic 25 Wall Chart, Picture Dictionary (pp. 50–51).

See page xix for techniques and strategies for presenting and practicing dialogues.

Doctor:	Well, young lady, you have a fever.
Samantha:	My throat hurts.
Doctor:	It's very red. Do your ears hurt?
Samantha:	Yep.
Doctor:	Her ears look a little red, too, Mrs. Jackson.
Samantha:	And my nose.
Doctor:	Do you have a stuffy nose?
Samantha:	Yep. I can't breathe.
Doctor:	Her lungs are fine, Mrs. Jackson. She's just got a virus. She should be better in a few days.
Samantha:	Can I listen with that?
Doctor:	With my stethoscope? Sure. Here you are! You can hear your heart beat.
Samantha:	I can?
Doctor:	Try it and see. Mrs. Jackson, I'm giving you some nose spray, eardrops, and a prescription for some tablets. Give Samantha one tablet twice a day, with meals.
Mrs. Jackson:	Oh, thank you, Doctor.
Doctor:	Call me and let me know how she's doing.
Samantha:	My heart sounds funny!
Doctor:	It sounds nice and strong!
Mrs. Jackson:	I think she feels better already.
Samantha:	Yes! I feel better! Thanks, Dr. Mack!
Doctor:	You're welcome! Get well soon!
Samantha:	OK. Good-bye!

Dialogue notes

Encourage the children to invent their own dialogues after listening to this one a few times. They can take turns role-playing a patient, a parent, and a doctor during a visit to the doctor's office. Prompt them to ask and answer questions similar to those in the dialogue.

Beats!

Components: Cassette, Beats! (Topic 25).

See page xx for techniques and strategies for presenting and practicing Beats!

I went to the doctor.
He gave me a shot.

Ouch! It hurt!
But guess what I got!

Did you get some tablets?
Did you get some drops?

I didn't get any medicine.
I got a lollipop!

Beat notes

Have the children practice the Beat together until they are comfortable with the words and rhythm. Then invite individuals or small groups to take turns volunteering to ask the questions in the second stanza: *Did you get some tablets? Did you get some drops?* Encourage the children to add actions as they say the lines.

Worksheets

Worksheet 1: I'm sick! (p. 49)

The pictures are clues to the missing words the children should write in each sentence. Point out that all the missing words can be found at the bottom of the page.

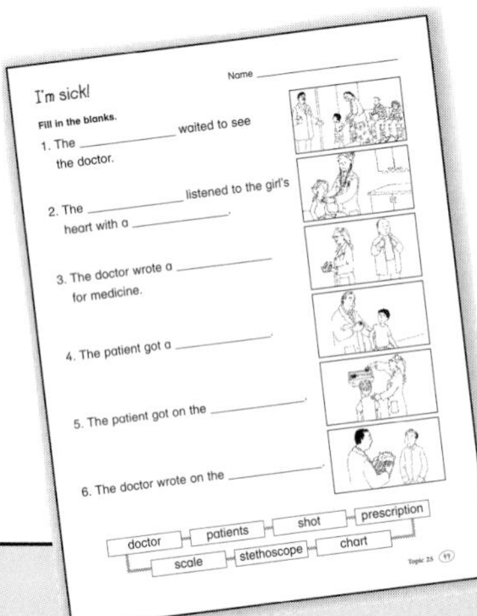

I'm sick! Name ____________

Fill in the blanks.

1. The ____________ waited to see the doctor.
2. The ____________ listened to the girl's heart with a ____________.
3. The doctor wrote a ____________ for medicine.
4. The patient got a ____________.
5. The patient got on the ____________.
6. The doctor wrote on the ____________.

doctor | patients | shot | prescription | scale | stethoscope | chart

Topic 25 49

Worksheet 2: I'm sick! (p. 50)

Ask the children to look at each picture and write about what they see. If they are just beginning to write, you can suggest that they simply write the vocabulary words for things they see in the picture.

I'm sick! Name ____________

Write about each picture.

50 Topic 25

Activities

- Investigate germs. Read aloud the delightful book *Those Mean, Nasty, Dirty, Downright Disgusting But ... Invisible Germs* by Judith Rice (Redleaf Press). It gives you and your class a common vocabulary of delightfully nasty things to say about germs.
- Make a book. Ask the children to suggest things people can do to stay healthy. Write down their ideas, and prompt them by asking questions *(What kinds of food keep us healthy? Does washing keep us healthy? When should we wash our hands?)*. Have the children work with partners or in small groups to draw a picture illustrating one of the ideas. Help them write or dictate a sentence about it. Combine the pages into a class book.
- Set up an activity center. Provide props (such as a stethoscope, measuring tape to measure height, a chart clipboard, and a small flashlight), and provide time and space for small groups of children to make their own plays about getting sick, going to the doctor, and taking treatment.
- If possible, invite a doctor or other health-care worker to visit the class and talk about his or her job. Prepare the children in advance by asking them to come up with some questions they would like to ask. After the visit, ask the children to collaborate on a large thank-you note, decorated with the children's illustrations and comments.

Who's at the hospital?

Content

- Places in a hospital
- People who work in a hospital
- Activities that take place in the hospital
- Medical equipment

Language

- Identifying people and places in a hospital: *The nurse is pushing the wheelchair. The doctor is looking at the X ray. They took him to the emergency room. The babies are in the nursery.*
- Describing what people are doing: *The paramedics push the stretcher into the hospital. The people are waiting to see a doctor. The mother is resting in the hospital bed.*
- Using *why* and *because: Why is the girl in the emergency room? Because she got cut on some broken glass. Why is the man in a wheelchair? Because he fell down and broke his leg.*

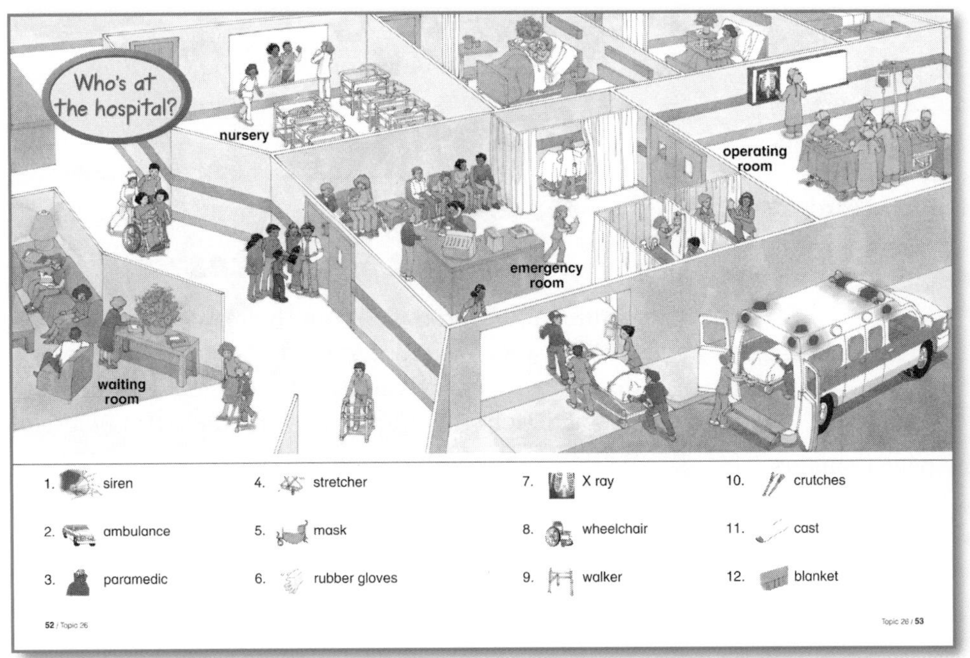

Words

1. siren
2. ambulance
3. paramedic
4. stretcher
5. mask
6. rubber gloves
7. X ray
8. wheelchair
9. walker
10. crutches
11. cast
12. blanket

Labels

waiting room
nursery
emergency room
operating room

Additional Words

flashing
broken
operation
hug

Flashing lights and sirens announce the arrival of an ambulance at the emergency entrance of the hospital. Paramedics are pushing patients in on stretchers. The emergency room is crowded with patients, busy doctors, and nurses. In the operating room, a patient is lying anesthetized on the table. The doctors are wearing scrubs, caps, masks, and rubber gloves. One doctor is consulting an X ray. New babies are in the nursery. One mother has her baby in bed with her. In the hall patients are walking up and down. A man is using a walker, and a girl is on crutches.

Jasmin, Diego, and their grandmother have been waiting for their grandfather. He fell down and has his broken arm in a cast. Everybody is happy to see Grandpa. He is laughing and hugging Jasmin. And here comes Yuka's family! Her mother is in a wheelchair, holding a new baby wrapped in a pink blanket. Yuka's family is happy, too.

Words

Components: Topic 26 Wall Chart, Picture Dictionary (pp. 52–53), Cassette, Word and Picture Cards (Topic 26).

See page xiv for techniques and strategies for presenting and practicing words.

Who's at the hospital?

1. siren
2. ambulance
3. paramedic
4. stretcher
5. mask
6. rubber gloves
7. X ray
8. wheelchair
9. walker
10. crutches
11. cast
12. blanket

Labels

waiting room
emergency room
nursery
operating room

Notes

Lay out the picture cards. If possible, provide some props, such as a small blanket, a pair of rubber gloves, or a mask for the children to handle. Invite each child to take a card. Model a question-and-answer pattern (for example, hold up one card, turn to a child, and say: *I have a mask. What do you have?*). Give each child the opportunity to ask and answer the question.

Workbook page

Each of the three illustrations on the page contains pictures of some of the topic words. Tell the children to write the words. Point out that the first letter of each word has already been written in as a clue. For example, the first letter of the first word is *p*, and there are two *paramedics* pushing the stretcher in the top picture.

Stories

Components: Picture Dictionary (pp. 52–53), Cassette, Story (Topic 26).

See page xviii for techniques and strategies for presenting and practicing stories.

Sirens blowing! Lights flashing!
Here comes an ambulance!
Paramedics carry patients on stretchers.
The emergency room is full.

In the operating room, doctors wear masks
and rubber gloves, and look at X rays.
In the nursery, the babies are sleeping.
One mother has her baby in bed with her.

Jasmin and Diego are in the waiting room.
Grandpa broke his arm. Where is he?
Who's that coming in the wheelchair?
It's Yuka's mother with a new baby!

Where's Grandpa? Here comes a man
with a walker and a girl with crutches.
And here's Grandpa! He has a cast!
His arm is all fixed! He can even hug!

Story notes

Invite children to talk about their own experiences with hospitals and emergency rooms. Ask them to discuss why people go to the emergency room of a hospital. Help them to understand the word *emergency*, with its connotation of urgent need.

Ask about the story:
Why were Jasmin and Diego in the waiting room? What was wrong with Grandpa? How did the doctors help him? What did they put on Grandpa's arm? Who was in the wheelchair? What did Yuka's mother have?

Ask about your students:
Have you seen an ambulance? Why does it have flashing lights? Why does it have a siren? Were you ever a patient? Did you ever visit someone in the hospital?

Dialogue

Components: Cassette, Topic 26 Wall Chart, Picture Dictionary (pp. 52–53).

See page xix for techniques and strategies for presenting and practicing dialogues.

Jasmin:	*Abuelita*, what happened to Grandpa?
Grandma:	He broke his arm.
Jasmin:	How did he break his arm?
Grandma:	He fell down.
Jasmin:	Where is Grandpa?
Grandma:	He'll be here soon.
Diego:	Here comes someone in a wheelchair!
Jasmin:	Is it Grandpa?
Diego:	No, it's Yuka's mother.
Jasmin:	Why is she in a wheelchair?
Grandma:	So many questions, Jasmin!
Diego:	So she won't drop the baby.
Jasmin:	Who's the baby?
Grandma:	It's Yuka's new little sister, Jasmin. She looks like Yuka. See her?
Jasmin:	Uh-huh. What's the matter with that man?
Grandma:	He has a walker because he needs help to walk. Oh! Here's Grandpa!
Jasmin, Diego, and Grandma:	Hello, Grandpa!
Grandpa:	Hello! Hello! Here I am. Good as new!
Jasmin:	Grandpa! What's that on your arm?
Grandpa:	It's a cast, to make it better.
Jasmin:	Does it hurt?
Grandpa:	No, it feels fine.
Jasmin:	Will your arm still hug?
Grandpa:	Of course it will. Here, I'll show you. I'll give you a big hug.
Jasmin:	I love you, Grandpa!

Dialogue notes

Explain that *Abuelita* is an affectionate word for *grandma* in Spanish. Ask your students if they know any other words for *grandma*. On the board, list the words for *grandmother* and the languages they come from. Invite the child who suggests a word to teach you and the whole class how to pronounce it in that language.

Beats!

Components: Cassette, Beats! (Topic 26).

See page xx for techniques and strategies for presenting and practicing Beats!

Hear that siren?
Move along fast!
    Here comes an ambulance
    rushing past.

Get to the hospital!
Get there quick!
    Someone had an accident!
    Someone is sick!

Someone needs an operation.
Right away!
    Someone had a baby.
    What a day!

Doctors at the hospital
are busy as can be.
    If I ever go there,
    they'll take good care of me!

Beat notes

Let the children listen to the Beat several times, adding as many actions as they can: *Hear that siren?* (cupping their ears), *rushing past* (sweeping their arms across their bodies), *Someone had an accident!* (putting their hands up to their heads), *Someone is sick!* (holding their heads), *Someone had a baby* (holding a pretend baby and rocking), and *If I ever go there* (pointing to themselves).

Worksheets

Worksheet 1: Who's at the hospital? (p. 51)

The pictures are clues to help the children fill in the missing words in the sentences. They can use the Wall Chart or the Dictionary illustration as a reference in spelling the words.

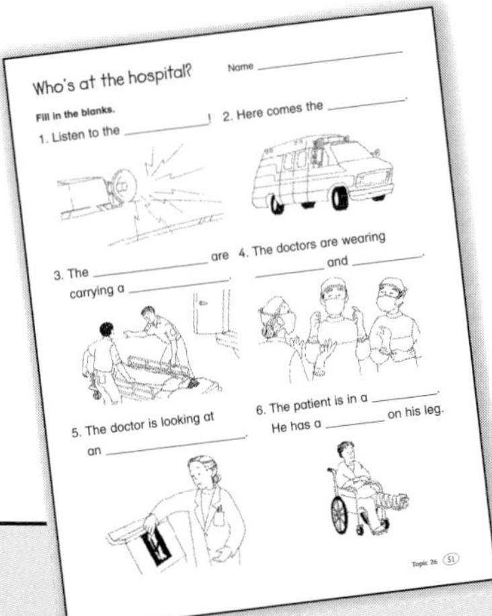

Who's at the hospital? Name ___

Fill in the blanks.

1. Listen to the ___!
2. Here comes the ___.
3. The ___ are carrying a ___.
4. The doctors are wearing ___ and ___.
5. The doctor is looking at an ___.
6. The patient is in a ___. He has a ___ on his leg.

Topic 26 51

Worksheet 2: Who's at the hospital? (p. 52)

Help the children read the questions. If needed, give them some guidance in writing their own answers. This exercise is intended to be open-ended, and some children may draw on words from other topics, or from their own basic knowledge.

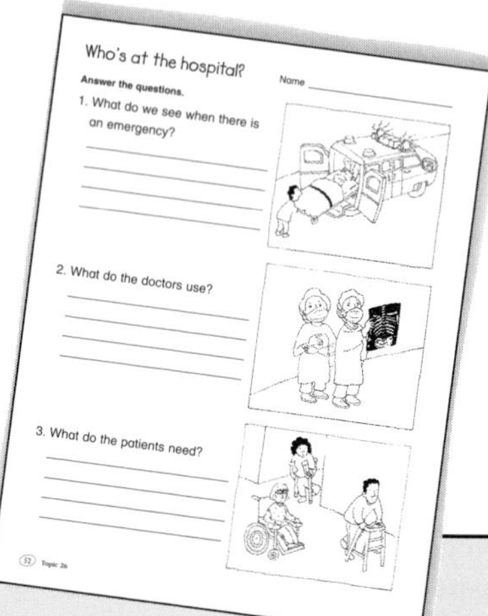

Who's at the hospital? Name ___

Answer the questions.

1. What do we see when there is an emergency?
2. What do the doctors use?
3. What do the patients need?

52 Topic 26

Activities

- Use this opportunity to review and practice the procedure for calling 911 in an emergency. Remind the children to give their names, addresses, and phone numbers, and to try to explain what type of emergency they have. Do they need an ambulance? Is someone hurt? Is someone sick? Urge the children to stay on the line and to listen for instructions on what to do in the emergency situation. Invent several pretend situations and let the children practice making 911 calls.
- Schedule a class visit to your local hospital. If this is not possible, invite a hospital worker to your classroom to talk about his or her job.
- Make cards. Provide paper, markers, and other materials, and help the children make get-well cards for people who are in the hospital, congratulations cards for new mothers and their babies, or decorations for the children's ward. Ask your local hospital for appropriate recipients.
- Set up a pretend emergency room in your classroom. A wagon or cart with wheels can be an ambulance. Children pretending to be paramedics can make siren sounds and turn flashlights on and off as they rush their doll or stuffed-animal patients to the emergency room, where other children pretend to be doctors and nurses who put pretend casts or bandages on the "patients."

Busy supermarket!

Content

- Foods and food categories
- Grocery shopping procedure
- Containers

Language

- Identifying categories of food according to the sections of a supermarket: *The bananas are in the fruit section. She got fish in the seafood section.*
- Identifying quantities and containers: *Mom chose two pounds of beef. Buy a bag of rice. The chips are in a bag. Put the food in the cart. The boy got a box of cookies.*
- Describing actions: *We bought bananas. I put the box of cookies in the cart. She got the milk in the dairy aisle.*
- Asking and answering questions using different tenses: *Did you get a pineapple? I got three bananas. Will you buy some seafood? I will buy meat. Have you written a list?*

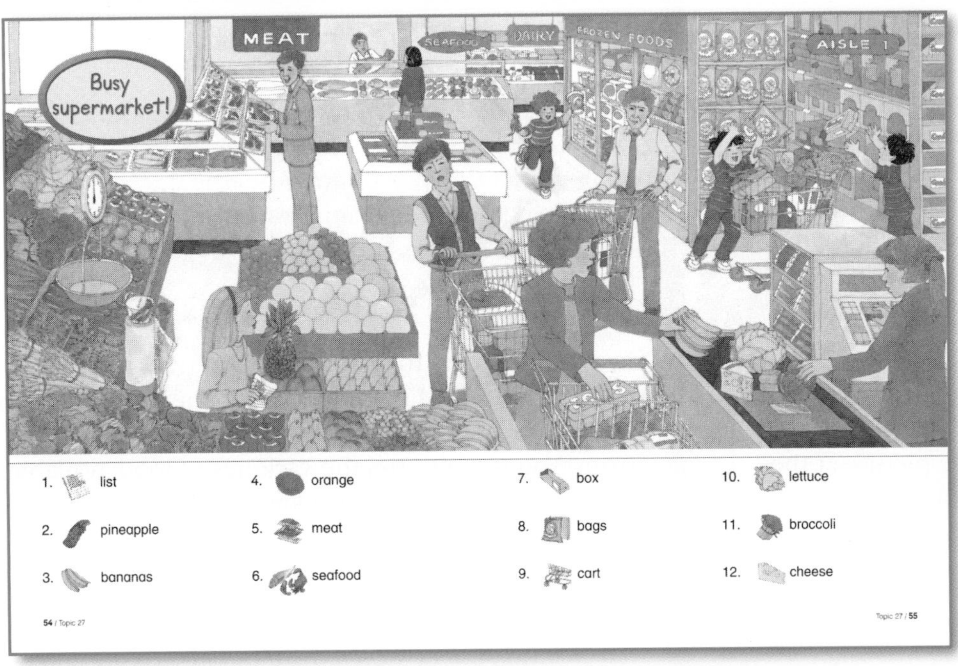

The supermarket is busy! The aisles are crowded. Alison is helping her father with the grocery shopping. She is in the fruit and vegetable section and has her mother's grocery list. She has found a big, beautiful pineapple. Mr. Matthews is in the meat section, holding up a package of chopped beef that looks good. Where is Mrs. Cheng? The twins are throwing all kinds of things into her shopping cart. There she is, at the seafood counter buying fish. Mrs. Young is ready to check out, but where is Tommy? Some unhappy customers are waiting in the checkout line behind her. Tommy emerges triumphantly from the frozen food section carrying ice cream for his kangaroo!

Words

1. list
2. pineapple
3. bananas
4. orange
5. meat
6. seafood
7. box
8. bags
9. cart
10. lettuce
11. broccoli
12. cheese

Additional Words

aisle
dairy
frozen foods
fruits
vegetables
clerk
groceries
customer
fresh
chicken
ice cream
chips
cookies

 **Components:** Topic 27 Wall Chart, Picture Dictionary (pp. 54–55), Cassette, Word and Picture Cards (Topic 27).

See page xiv for techniques and strategies for presenting and practicing words.

Busy supermarket!

1. list	5. meat	9. cart
2. pineapple	6. seafood	10. lettuce
3. bananas	7. box	11. broccoli
4. orange	8. bags	12. cheese

Notes

Bring in a paper bag and a cardboard box as props. Ask the children to hold up a word card for each word, and prompt them to identify the two containers (you might ask: *Is this a bag? Is this a box or a bag?*). Then model a pattern of phrases that allows the children to practice the vocabulary. Hold up a word or picture card for one of the foods, and say: *I will buy this meat. I'll put it in the bag.* Then turn to a child and ask, *What will you buy?* Once the children have caught on to the pattern, let them ask each other to identify the foods and announce that they will put them in either the box or the bag.

Workbook page

The children may want to color the picture at the top of the page before they mark the items. Help them read the directions. You can model different ways to frame questions: *Where is the banana? Show me the broccoli. Which one is the lettuce? Is this cheese? Is the pineapple next to the oranges?*

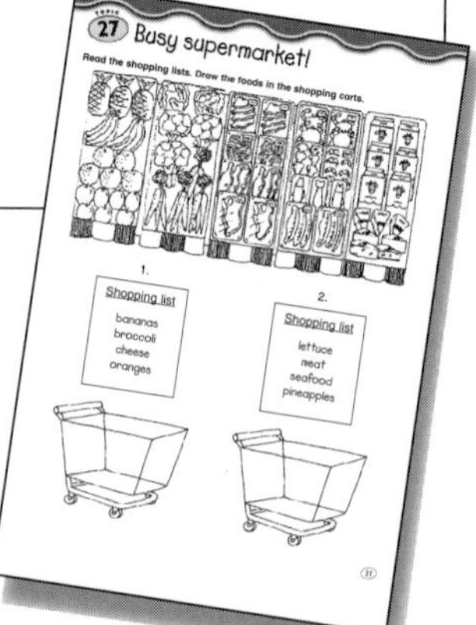

 **Components:** Picture Dictionary (pp. 54–55), Cassette, Story (Topic 27).

See page xviii for techniques and strategies for presenting and practicing stories.

Alison is by the fruits and vegetables.
What does Mom's list say?
Let's see. A pineapple. A big one!
Got it! Now where's Dad?

Mr. Matthews is looking at meats.
Beef looks good.
He finds a nice steak.
Too expensive! OK, chopped beef.

Mrs. Cheng is in the seafood section
buying fish. Uh-oh! The twins are
throwing boxes and bags into her cart.
Chips, cookies, cheese,
and a bunch of bananas!

Hello! Mrs. Young is at the checkout.
Lettuce? Broccoli? She has everything.
But where's Tommy? In aisle 2,
getting ice cream for his kangaroo!

Story notes

Invite volunteers to describe shopping for food. If appropriate, ask them if food shopping is different in the United States than it is in the country they came from. You may discuss the varieties of food available, and how it is displayed, packaged, and sold.

Ask about the story:
Who has a grocery list? What does Alison want to buy? What is Mrs. Young going to buy? What kind of meat was too expensive? Which meat did Mr. Young choose? Where was Tommy? Who is buying seafood? What was Tommy looking for?

Ask about your students:
Where does your family buy food? Who shops for food in your family? Do you go to the supermarket? Did you buy food at the grocery store? Is the store close to your home? Do you bring a list? What do you like to buy at the market?

Dialogue

Components: Cassette, Topic 27 Wall Chart, Picture Dictionary (pp. 54–55).

See page xix for techniques and strategies for presenting and practicing dialogues.

Alison:	Dad! I got the pineapple!
Mr. Matthews:	Good, Alison! And I got the beef!
Alison:	Hello, Mrs. Young!
Mrs. Young:	Hello, Alison. Are you doing the shopping for your family?
Alison:	No, my dad's here. He's over there getting the meat.
Mrs. Young:	Hello, Mr. Matthews! I see you have a good helper.
Mr. Matthews:	Yes, I do!
Mrs. Young:	Oh my, Alison! Are those the Cheng twins I see?
Alison:	Yes! Look what they're doing!
Mr. Matthews:	I wonder where Mrs. Cheng is.
Alison:	She's getting fish.
Mrs. Young:	I hope she comes back soon. I guess the twins made their own shopping list! Have you seen Tommy, Alison?
Alison:	I think he's over there by the ice cream.
Mrs. Young:	Ice cream? Oh dear, I'm ready to check out. My bags are almost filled!
Alison:	I'll get him for you, Mrs. Young.
Mrs. Young:	Thank you, Alison.
Tommy:	Mom! Wait! My kangaroo wants ice cream! I got a gallon!

Dialogue notes

Ask the children to choose partners and invent a dialogue between Alison and her dad, modeled on this one. Suggest they begin by writing a shopping list together. Then, have them replace the words *Dad* and *Alison* with their own names, and "shop" for the items on their list:

First child:	I got the _________!
Second child:	Good, _____. And I got the _______!
First child:	Good, and I got the __________!

Continue through their list of words.

Beats!

Components: Cassette, Beats! (Topic 27).

See page xx for techniques and strategies for presenting and practicing Beats!

Where's the bread?
I can't find the bread.
    It's right over there, in aisle 1.

Where are the eggs?
I can't find the eggs.
    They're right over there, in aisle 2.

Where's the checkout?
I can't find the checkout.
    Here it is! Right here!

Oh dear, that's funny.
    What's the matter?
I can't find my money!

Beat notes

Put the children into small groups to practice the Beat. Once they have the words and rhythm down, encourage them to add new stanzas by substituting other vocabulary words and locations in the questions, for example:

Where is the fish?
I can't find the fish.
    It's right over there,
    in aisle 5.

Where are the oranges?
I can't find the oranges.
    They're right over there,
    in aisle 7.

Worksheets

Worksheet 1: Busy supermarket! (p. 53)

Have the children look at the food sections illustrated at the top of the page. Tell them to follow directions 1-6 very carefully. Then direct their attention to the small pictures at the bottom of the page. Have them identify each item and color it as directed.

Busy supermarket! Name

Fruit | Vegetables | Dairy

Follow the directions.

1. Draw a red circle around the bananas.
2. Draw a green circle around the pineapples.
3. Draw a square around the oranges.
4. Put an X through the broccoli.
5. Draw a triangle around the cheese.
6. Draw a blue circle around the lettuce.
7. Color the list yellow.
8. Color the cart blue.
9. Color the bags orange.
10. Color the boxes green.

Topic 27 53

Worksheet 2: Busy supermarket! (p. 54)

Tell the children to look at the foods at the bottom of the page. Ask them to write the words on the shopping list for the things they would like to buy. Help the children cut out the squares at the bottom of the page. You may want to review the words as they work by holding up each piece and asking, *What is this?* Then have them glue the items they have chosen in the shopping cart.

Busy supermarket! Name

Write a shopping list.
Cut and paste to fill your cart with the food on your list.

Shopping list

54 Topic 27

Activities

- Make a chart with columns labeled by the name of a section of a supermarket: *seafood, meat, dairy, frozen foods, produce, bakery, cereals and grains.* Ask the children to think of foods they would find in each section. Begin with the vocabulary words, and then expand to other foods. Provide magazines or newspapers with pictures of food for the children to cut and paste in each section.

- Create a supermarket learning center in the classroom. Help the children glue pictures on cardboard to represent different foods and to organize the store in sections. Set up a check-out area with a toy cash register and play money. Provide boxes and bags. Encourage the children to practice dialogues as they role-play buying and selling food. Once the center is set up, it can be used for many projects.

- Give small groups of children a cardboard box and a shopping list. Send them to the supermarket learning center in the classroom. Tell them to put each item in a bag as they find it and cross it off the list.

- Play Twenty Questions with vegetables and fruits. One child thinks of a fruit or vegetable, and the other children ask questions that have *yes/no* answers *(Is it bigger than my hand? Is it green inside?)* and try to guess what it is.

Errands in town

Content

- Stores and services in town
- Errands
- Postal service

Language

- Identifying the role of stores and services in a community: *You can get the medicine at the drugstore. Dad went to the post office for stamps.*
- Describing routines: *We go to sleep early and get up early every morning. I get out of school in the afternoon. My father does the laundry on Saturday.*
- Describing actions: *Mom will buy a cake at the bakery. I need to go to the pet store for fish food. They went to the bank, the library, and the toy store.*

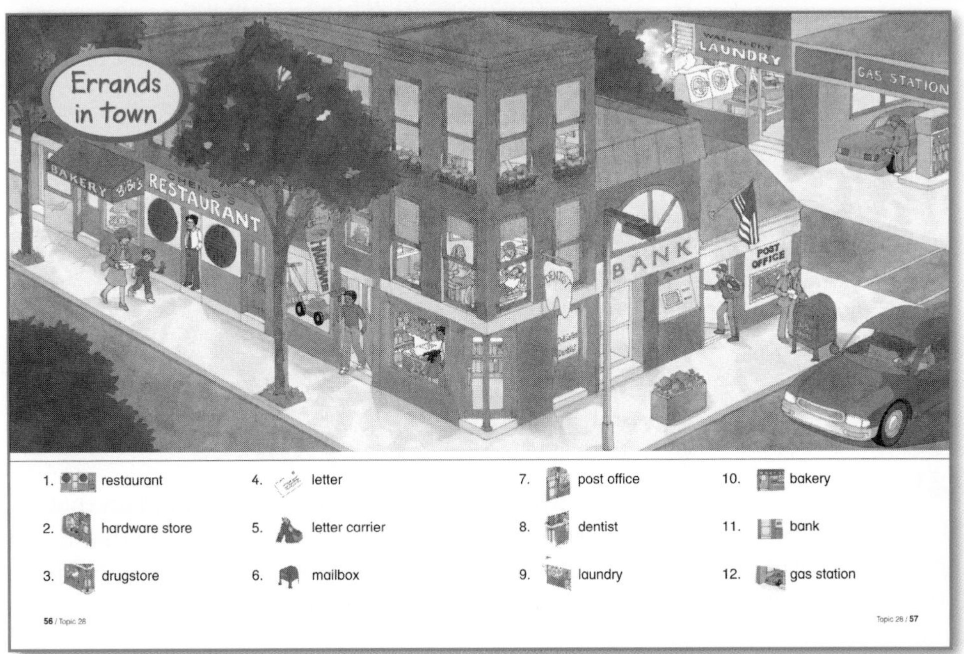

It's the end of the day, just before dinner, and it's getting a little dark. Good smells are coming from the Chengs' restaurant and from the bakery! Steam is coming from a vent in the roof of the laundry. Somebody's clothes are getting nice and clean! Lots of people are doing errands. Mrs. Jackson and Samantha are in the drugstore getting Samantha's prescription filled. Mr. Jackson has gone to the bank and to the hardware store to buy a rake. Mr. Matthews is mailing a letter in the mailbox in front of the post office, as a letter carrier goes inside. Alison and her mother are in the dentist's office, where the dentist is checking Alison's teeth. The gas station is busy. Here come Tommy and Mrs. Young from the bakery with something in a box.

Words

1. restaurant
2. hardware store
3. drugstore
4. letter
5. letter carrier
6. mailbox
7. post office
8. dentist
9. laundry
10. bakery
11. bank
12. gas station

Additional Words

- errands
- druggist
- stamp
- take-out food
- gas
- smell

Words

Components: Topic 28 Wall Chart, Picture Dictionary (pp. 56–57), Cassette, Word and Picture Cards (Topic 28).

See page xiv for techniques and strategies for presenting and practicing words.

Errands in town

1. restaurant
2. hardware store
3. drugstore
4. letter
5. letter carrier
6. mailbox
7. post office
8. dentist
9. laundry
10. bakery
11. bank
12. gas station

Notes

Choose one of the word cards and describe the place without revealing the word (for example: *This place smells good. We can buy food and eat it there, or we can take the food home to eat. What do we call this place?*). Review each word in the same manner. Then invite a volunteer to choose a word card and describe or act out the word for his or her classmates to guess. You may add the words from Topic 21.

Workbook page

Tell the children to look at line 1. Tell them to guess the name of the business by checking for vocabulary items that start with the letter *b*. Tell them that another clue is in the list of items to the right of each word. Two of the three items are things found in that type of business, but one is not. Once they have completed the name of the business, tell them to color (or mark) the two items they would find at that business. (The remaining item should be left blank.)

Topic 28 Errands in town

Fill in the blanks. Color the things you will see in each place.

1. b___ cake bread hammer
2. d___ medicine tablets cat
3. l___ pencil clothes stove
4. g___ s___ scale car gas
5. h___ s___ nail hammer melon

Stories

Components: Picture Dictionary (pp. 56–57), Cassette, Story (Topic 28).

See page xviii for techniques and strategies for presenting and practicing stories.

It's the end of the day, getting dark.
Smell that good food?
That's the Chengs' restaurant!
Everyone is doing errands.

The Jacksons hurry down the street.
Mr. Jackson goes to the hardware store.
Mrs. Jackson takes Samantha to the drugstore to get her medicine.

A letter carrier is going into the post office.
There's Mr. Matthews
mailing a letter in the mailbox.
Where's Alison? She's at the dentist.

Steam is coming from the laundry.
Clean clothes!
And smell those pies in the bakery!
What's in that box, Mrs. Young?
Time to hurry home for dinner!

Story notes

Talk with the children about errands. Explain that *errand* is just another word for something that needs to be done, a task or small job. Invite volunteers to describe errands they do with their families.

Ask about the story:
What time of day do you think it is? Where did Mr. Jackson go? Where is Alison? What is Mr. Matthews putting in the mailbox? What do you think Mrs. Young has in the box? Who is standing by the restaurant? Why are Mrs. Jackson and Samantha in the drugstore?

Ask about your students:
Who does errands in your family? Can you help run errands for your family? Where would you go to buy a hammer and some nails? What can you get at a bakery? Does the letter carrier come to your home? Where do you mail a letter?

Dialogue

Components: Cassette, Topic 28 Wall Chart, Picture Dictionary (pp. 56–57).

See page xix for techniques and strategies for presenting and practicing dialogues.

Samantha:	Can we eat at the Chengs' restaurant, Mommy? That food smelled so good.
Mrs. Jackson:	It would be nice, Samantha, but we have to do errands.
Samantha:	What does Daddy have to do?
Mrs. Jackson:	Daddy has to go to the bank.
Samantha:	Why?
Mrs. Jackson:	He has to get some money. And then he has to go to the hardware store.
Samantha:	What do we have to do?
Mrs. Jackson:	We have to get your medicine.
Samantha:	Is it going to take long here?
Mrs. Jackson:	A few minutes. We have to wait for the druggist to fill your prescription.
Samantha:	Are we going anywhere else?
Mrs. Jackson:	Just to the post office. I need stamps. And then we have to take you home.
Samantha:	Because I'm sick.
Mrs. Jackson:	That's right. And on the way home, we have to get gas at the gas station.
Samantha:	Mommy! Let's get takeout from the Chengs' restaurant.
Mrs. Jackson:	Samantha, that's a great idea!
Samantha:	Will Daddy like that?
Mrs. Jackson:	I'm sure he will.

Dialogue notes

Once the children are comfortable with the words and phrases, have them choose partners and make up their own dialogues, using questions such as *What do we have to do? Where do we have to go? Where are you going? Where did you go?*

Beats!

Components: Cassette, Beats! (Topic 28).

See page xx for techniques and strategies for presenting and practicing Beats!

I have to go to the bank because
I need some money.
I have to go to the bakery.
I want some rolls with honey.

I have to go to the drugstore.
I need tissues for my nose.
I have to go to the laundry
to wash my clothes.

Are you going to the post office?
Please get some stamps.
Are you going to the cleaners?
Please pick up my pants.

I'm getting really tired.
These errands are so slow.
Let's go to the movies
and see a show!

Beat notes

Explain that *the cleaners* is like *the laundry,* but it is a short name for *the dry cleaners.* Both places clean your clothes. Divide the class into two groups to practice the Beat. Ask the first group to say the first two lines of each stanza, and ask the second group to say the third and fourth lines. Have the children suggest hand and body movements that can be added to the Beat. Then let the groups switch parts and say the Beat again.

Worksheets

Worksheet 1: Errands in town (p. 55)

Help the children read the first question*: Where do we go to mail a letter?* (Point out that all the questions in this exercise begin with the same word.) Tell them that the pictures are clues and that all the missing words can be found at the bottom of the page.

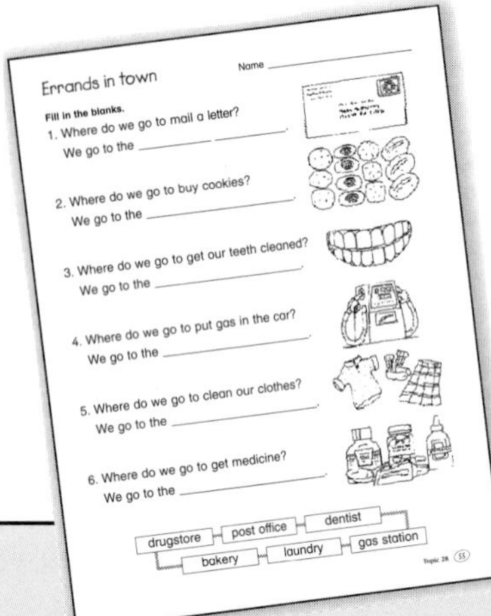

Errands in town   Name ________

Fill in the blanks.

1. Where do we go to mail a letter?
   We go to the ______ ______.
2. Where do we go to buy cookies?
   We go to the ________.
3. Where do we go to get our teeth cleaned?
   We go to the ________.
4. Where do we go to put gas in the car?
   We go to the ________.
5. Where do we go to clean our clothes?
   We go to the ________.
6. Where do we go to get medicine?
   We go to the ________.

drugstore | post office | dentist | bakery | laundry | gas station

Topic 28 55

Worksheet 2: Errands in town (p. 56)

Children use the boxed words to label each picture at the top of the page. Help the children read the sentences at the bottom of the page. Direct their attention to the underlined word in the first sentence, and ask: *Do you get your teeth cleaned at the post office? Where do you get your teeth cleaned?* Then tell them to cross out the incorrect word, and write the correct word on the line provided.

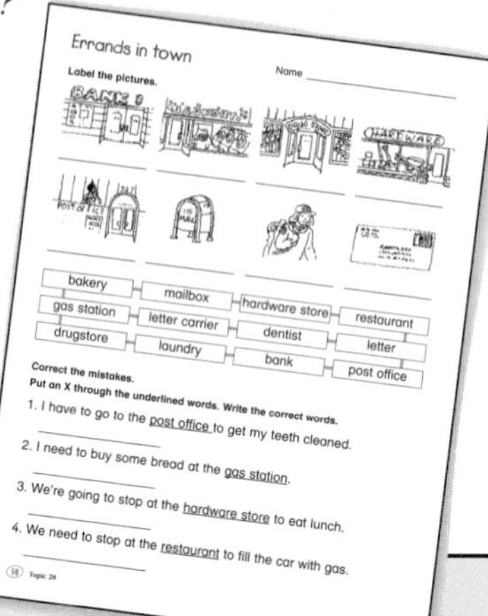

Errands in town   Name ________

Label the pictures.

bakery | mailbox | hardware store | restaurant | gas station | letter carrier | dentist | letter | drugstore | laundry | bank | post office

Correct the mistakes.
Put an X through the underlined words. Write the correct words.

1. I have to go to the <u>post office</u> to get my teeth cleaned.
   ____
2. I need to buy some bread at the <u>gas station</u>.
   ____
3. We're going to stop at the <u>hardware store</u> to eat lunch.
   ____
4. We need to stop at the <u>restaurant</u> to fill the car with gas.
   ____

56 Topic 28

Activities

- Make up a series of errands and write them on index cards *(I need stamps; I want to buy some cookies; I have to wash my clothes).* Let children take turns drawing an errand card and saying what they would do (for example, *I need stamps, so I will go to the post office to buy stamps*). As the children become more skillful, suggest that they pick up two or three cards at a time.

- Have children work together in pairs or small groups to draw pictures and dictate one or two sentences about a store or business in their neighborhood. When they have finished, prepare a bulletin board display or assemble the pages into a book and add it to your classroom library.

- Set up a classroom post office. Encourage the children to write notes (or draw pictures) and place them in an envelope. Each child can write the name and address of his or her correspondent, write his or her return address, and draw a stamp. Then have them mail their letter in a classroom mailbox. Have children take turns sorting and delivering the mail.

- Play a round-robin game. Start by describing an errand *(I need to buy stamps)* and asking, *Where can I go?* Let a volunteer answer: *You can go to the post office.* Then prompt that child to describe a different errand and ask another child to answer. Continue in this manner until all the children have had a chance to ask and answer the questions.

Dinner's ready!

Content

- Dinners from different cultures
- Family mealtime

Language

- Describing meals: *We eat roast beef and potatoes for dinner. I eat rice and beans with chicken for my dinner.*
- Expressing likes and dislikes: *I like to eat vegetables. She doesn't like chicken.*
- Expressing preferences: *I like tomatoes better than corn. I like meat more than vegetables.*
- Asking for or offering something: *May I help you? Do you want more? Help yourself! Please pass the potatoes. May I have dessert now?*

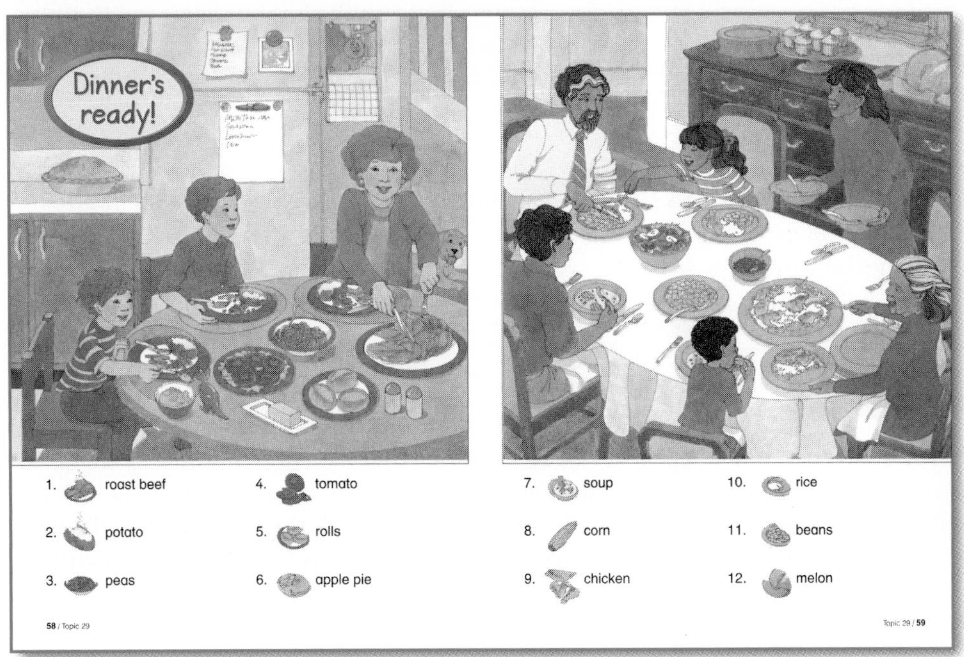

Words

1. roast beef
2. potato
3. peas
4. tomato
5. rolls
6. apple pie
7. soup
8. corn
9. chicken
10. rice
11. beans
12. melon

Additional Words

dessert
baked
ice cream
cake
dish
good
better
best

Two dinners are represented here—the Youngs' dinner and the Lopez's dinner. The Youngs are having roast beef, baked potatoes, peas, lettuce and tomato salad, and rolls. The Lopezes are having a Peruvian soup with *choclo* (pieces of corn on the cob), chicken, rice and beans, melon, and little cakes for dessert. Tommy has put a dish of ice cream on the table for his kangaroo and is trying to feed him. Mrs. Young is helping Jim to more roast beef. She tells Tommy to stop playing with his kangaroo and eat while his dinner is hot. There's apple pie waiting for dessert!

Words

Components: Topic 29 Wall Chart, Picture Dictionary (pp. 58–59), Cassette, Word and Picture Cards (Topic 29).

See page xiv for techniques and strategies for presenting and practicing words.

Dinner's ready!

1. roast beef	5. rolls	9. chicken
2. potato	6. apple pie	10. rice
3. peas	7. soup	11. beans
4. tomato	8. corn	12. melon

Notes

Introduce the words to the children one at a time. Hold up two cards and express a preference (for example, *I like tomatoes better than peas*). Ask the children to take turns picking up two cards and expressing a preference for one item over the other. You can extend this activity by having them pick up three cards and say which food they like least, which food they like better than another, and which food they like best.

Workbook page

Tell the children that all the foods shown on the dinner plate are written backwards in the row below (with the last letter first). Tell them to rewrite the words on the lines provided. In the second exercise, some letters are missing from each word. Suggest that they use their word cards as reference.

Stories

Components: Picture Dictionary (pp. 58–59), Cassette, Story (Topic 29).

See page xviii for techniques and strategies for presenting and practicing stories.

Something smells good in Tommy's kitchen.
It's roast beef with baked potatoes,
peas, lettuce and tomato salad,
and rolls. Nice hot rolls! M-m-m-m.

Tommy has a little dish on the table
for his kangaroo. It's ice cream!
Eat up your dinner, Tommy.
Guess what's for dessert? Apple pie!

Something smells good in Diego's kitchen.
It's soup with corn. What else?
Chicken with rice, and beans.
Hot and steaming!

Diego likes the corn best.
Jasmin helps Grandpa with his chicken.
What's for dessert?
Melon and little cakes. Yum!

Story notes

Invite volunteers to describe dinnertime at their homes. Remember that for some families the big meal is eaten at midday, and the evening meal is a lighter, less substantial supper. Ask the children to talk about who prepares the dinner and who cleans up afterwards.

Ask about the story:
What smelled good in Tommy's kitchen? Does Diego's dinner smell good? Can Tommy's toy kangaroo eat ice cream? What did Diego like to eat best? What was Diego's favorite food for dinner?

Ask about your students:
What smells good in your kitchen? Who cooks at your house? What do you like to have for dinner? Which vegetable do you like best? Do you like chicken? Does your family eat special foods from your country?

Dialogue

Components: Cassette, Topic 29 Wall Chart, Picture Dictionary (pp. 58–59).

See page xix for techniques and strategies for presenting and practicing dialogues.

Jim:	Mom, you're the best cook in the whole world!
Mrs. Young:	Thank you, Jim. Do you want some more roast beef?
Jim:	Sure!
Mrs. Young:	How about some more peas? And help yourself to lettuce and tomatoes.
Jim:	OK. Tommy, kangaroos don't eat ice cream.
Tommy:	Mine does.
Mrs. Young:	Eat your dinner while it's hot, Tommy. You like roast beef and baked potatoes. You can play with your kangaroo later.
Tommy:	I want to show him to Diego. He likes animals. I wonder what Diego is having for dinner.
Grandma:	Diego, please pass this plate to your papa. Haven't you finished your soup yet?
Diego:	Yes, but I want to eat all the corn. It's so good!
Jasmin:	I love chicken and rice and beans.
Grandpa:	That's why you're so healthy, Jasmin!
Jasmin:	Grandpa, can you eat your chicken?
Grandpa:	I think so.
Jasmin:	But you broke your arm. Can I help you?
Grandpa:	All right. You hold the chicken with your fork so I can cut it with my knife.
Jasmin:	This is fun, Grandpa!
Grandpa:	Yes, it is! And there's melon and cakes for dessert!
Jasmin:	Goody! Diego, hurry up! Mama made little cakes for dessert!

Dialogue notes

Have two groups practice this exchange:

Mrs. Young:	Do you want some more roast beef?
Jim:	Sure!
Mrs. Young:	How about some more peas? And help yourself to lettuce and tomatoes.

Then substitute different foods.

Beats!

Components: Cassette, Beats! (Topic 29).

See page xx for techniques and strategies for presenting and practicing Beats!

I don't like stew.
    Sure you do.
    Of course you like it.
No, I don't.

I don't like stew.
    Try a little bit.
    I know you'll like it.
No, I won't.

    Here's a taste.
    It's good for you.

    How do you like it?
I don't like stew!

Beat notes

Divide the class into two groups to practice the Beat. Have pairs to practice it together, switching roles from time to time. Then encourage the children to recite the Beat in pairs, substituting other foods for *stew*.

Worksheets

Worksheet 1: Dinner's ready! (p. 57)

Ask the children to draw the foods they like to eat for dinner on the empty plate at the top of the worksheet. The foods shown can be used as clues, but children can draw any food they like and should not feel limited to those presented in the topic. Ask them to write or dictate the names for the foods they like to eat for dinner.

Dinner's ready! Name

Draw.
What do you like to eat for dinner?

Write.
For dinner I like to eat

Topic 29 57

Worksheet 2: Dinner's ready! (p. 58)

Explain that the worksheet is a questionnaire form. You can have the children work in groups of three. Each child can interview the other two. The pictures at the bottom of the page are just clues; the children can include any foods they wish.

Activities

- Make place mats to use for snacktime and class parties. Give each child a large sheet of construction paper to decorate with crayons, markers, paint, and stickers. Laminate them or cover them with clear self-adhesive paper.

- Provide dishes, flatware, napkins, and other appropriate items for the children to use in a housekeeping corner. Encourage play in which children pretend to serve and share meals. Model phrases they can practice as they play: *May I have some ______, please? Would you like some _______? Thank you. No, thank you.*

- Choose a country and do research to learn more about the different kinds of food that are eaten there. Compare the foods eaten there to those eaten at school and in the children's homes. If possible, get a recipe for a food from the country you have chosen, make it, and let the class sample it at snack time.

- Ask the children to plan a menu for a special dinner they would like to serve to a friend or family member. Have them describe the meal and draw a picture. Then display the pictures on a class bulletin board or combine them to make a classroom book.

Nice evening!

Content

- Leisure activities at home
- Evening routines
- Electronic devices

Language

- Describing leisure activities: *I'm watching TV. Dad is listening to music on the stereo. My brother is doing his homework. We played a game.*
- Identifying and describing the uses of electronic devices: *We have earphones for our CD player. I can use the remote to turn off the television.*
- Describing simultaneous actions using *while: I'm listening to music while my sister is doing homework. He was practicing the piano while we were playing a board game.*

It's evening at the Jacksons'. Mrs. Jackson is in the kitchen, helping Mariah with her homework. The radio is on. Zoe and Samantha are playing a game on the living room floor in front of the television. Zoe is looking at the TV, and Samantha is poking her because it is her turn at the game. Marcus is practicing his trombone loudly. The cat is startled. Mr. Jackson is resting in his chair with his headphones on. He has just put on his favorite CD and clicked the remote to turn up the stereo, and is smiling contentedly. What a nice evening!

Words

1. stereo
2. television
3. remote
4. CD
5. headphones
6. radio

Verbs

7. rest
8. play
9. watch
10. help
11. talk
12. practice

Additional Words

TV
click
volume
turn up
music
trombone
noisy
quiet

Words

Components: Topic 30 Wall Chart, Picture Dictionary (pp. 60–61), Cassette, Word and Picture Cards (Topic 30).

See page xiv for techniques and strategies for presenting and practicing words.

Nice evening!

1. stereo	3. remote	5. headphones
2. television	4. CD	6. radio

Verbs

7. rest	9. watch	11. talk
8. play	10. help	12. practice

Notes

Refer to the Dictionary illustration or the Wall Chart as you model language for asking and talking about each verb: *What is Marcus practicing? Marcus is practicing the trombone.* Ask the children to suggest other activities that people practice. You may want to say that *CD* stands for *compact disc* and that *remote* stands for *remote control.*

Workbook page

Help the children write the correct verb beneath each picture. Then ask them to color the pictures of things they like to do (at the top of the page) or that they like to use (at the bottom of the page). You can suggest that they simply draw a circle around the things they like to do or use. You may also want to engage the children in a discussion about things they don't like to do during their evenings at home.

Stories

Components: Picture Dictionary (pp. 60–61), Cassette, Story (Topic 30).

See page xviii for techniques and strategies for presenting and practicing stories.

Dinner is over, dishes all done.
Mrs. Jackson helps Mariah with
her homework.
Got it!
Thanks, Mom.

Mr. Jackson rests in his chair.
What beautiful music on the stereo!
Zoe and Samantha are playing
a game while they watch television.

Blaaam! Blaaaat! What's that?
Marcus is practicing his trombone!
Can't hear the TV! Turn it up!
Talk a little louder!

Mr. Jackson puts on his headphones,
slides in a favorite CD,
and clicks the remote.
That's better! What a nice evening!

Story notes

Invite children to compare the evening activities described in the story to their own evening activities. Write on a chart all the things the children mention that they do at home in an evening.

Ask about the story:
How can Mrs. Jackson help Mariah? Is Mariah watching television? What are Zoe and Samantha doing? What does Mr. Jackson listen to? Why does Mr. Jackson put on headphones? Is Marcus making a lot of noise? Is Marcus very quiet?

Ask about your students:
Does anyone in your home play a musical instrument? What do you do while that person practices? What do you like to do at night? Do you do your homework while you watch TV? What games do you like to play? What kind of music do you like to listen to? Do you use headphones? Why do people use headphones?

Dialogue

 **Components:** Cassette, Topic 30 Wall Chart, Picture Dictionary (pp. 60–61).

See page xix for techniques and strategies for presenting and practicing dialogues.

Samantha:	Zoe! Zoe! It's your turn to play! Come on!
Zoe:	Wait a minute, Samantha! I want to watch what happens on the TV.
Mr. Jackson:	Keep the TV nice and low so I can hear the stereo.
Samantha:	We will. Are you resting, Daddy?
Mr. Jackson:	Well, I was resting!
Marcus:	Sorry, Dad. I have to practice my trombone now.
Mr. Jackson:	That's all right, Marcus. When you're finished practicing, I want you to play something for us.
Marcus:	OK, Dad.
Mr. Jackson:	Wynona! Marcus is going to give us a concert later.
Mrs. Jackson:	Oh, I'd just love it!
Mr. Jackson:	Are you almost finished helping Mariah?
Mrs. Jackson:	Almost. Mariah and I are talking about the last question in her homework.
Mr. Jackson:	Good. I'm just going to rest a little while longer and listen to my music. Where's the remote so I can turn it on and off from my chair?
Samantha:	It's on top of the stereo. And put your headphones on, Daddy!
Mr. Jackson:	Good idea!

Dialogue notes

Suggest that the children use the model from the dialogue *(When you're finished practicing, ...)*, adding on their own endings, for example: *When you're finished practicing, play a game with me.* You may want to prompt them to respond, positively or negatively: *Okay, when I'm finished I will play* or *No, sorry, when I'm finished I want to watch TV.*

Beats!

 **Components:** Cassette, Beats! (Topic 30).

See page xx for techniques and strategies for presenting and practicing Beats!

Finish up your dinner!
Finish, everyone!
We finished our dinner.
Now let's have fun!

Who's going to do the dishes?
Let's get them done.
We finished the dishes.
Now let's have fun!

What about your homework?
Is it all done?
We finished our homework.
Now let's have fun!

We can watch TV,
or play a game instead.
Tell us a story,
and then we'll go to bed!

Beat notes

Say the Beat as a whole class several times. Then let a small group of volunteers say the first two lines of each set of four, while the whole class says the third and fourth lines of each set. Encourage the children to pantomime as many actions in the Beat as they can.

Worksheets

Worksheet 1: Nice evening! (p. 59)

Help the children read the sentences. The missing words can be found at the bottom of the page.

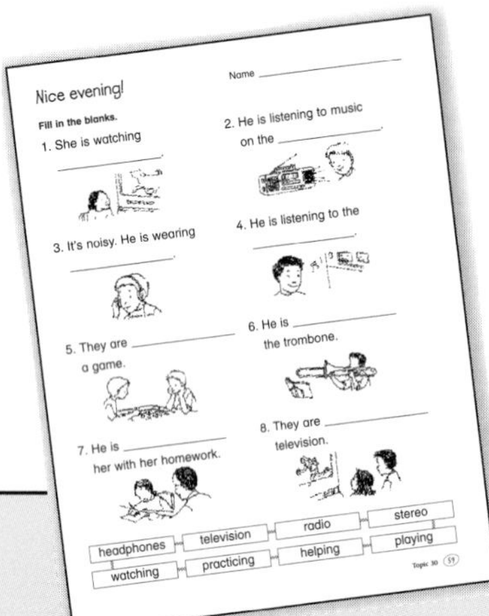

Nice evening! Name ____

Fill in the blanks.

1. She is watching ____.
2. He is listening to music on the ____.
3. It's noisy. He is wearing ____.
4. He is listening to the ____.
5. They are ____ a game.
6. He is ____ the trombone.
7. He is ____ her with her homework.
8. They are ____ television.

headphones | television | radio | stereo | watching | practicing | helping | playing

Topic 30

Worksheet 2: Nice evening! (p. 60)

Tell the children that the words at the top of the page are there to stimulate their imaginations, not to limit their responses. In the spaces provided, they must draw pictures of activities they do at home, then write the word for each activity.

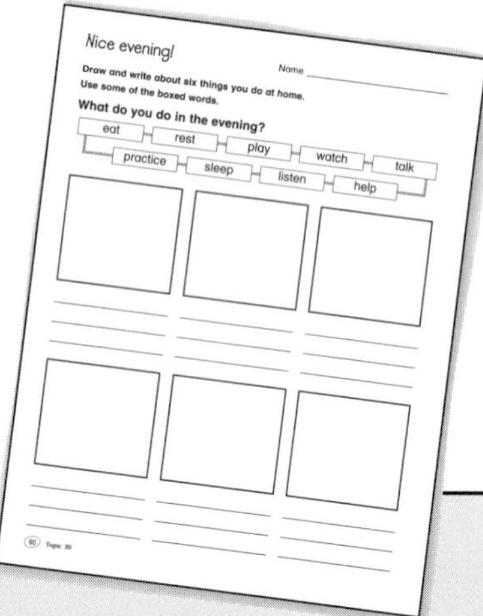

Nice evening! Name ____

Draw and write about six things you do at home. Use some of the boxed words.

What do you do in the evening?

eat | rest | play | watch | talk | practice | sleep | listen | help

Topic 30

Activities

- Let the children teach each other games that their families play together. Your students may know games that their classmates have never played. Invite volunteers to teach the class how to play their favorite games. Encourage the children to teach these new games to their families.
- Help the children make a chart showing the average number of hours that all the students in the class spend watching TV, eating, reading, being at school, and sleeping every day.
- Make a puppet theater. Have the children make ice-cream-stick or paper-bag puppets. Act out the stories in the Picture Dictionary and on the cassettes.
- Bring in a tape recorder or portable radio and play a variety of music for the children. Ask them to try to describe each genre. Prompt them to express their preferences and bring in music they especially like to share.

Theme 5: The Weekend

Topic 31 Saturday at the mall
Topic 32 Happy birthday!
Topic 33 Sunday in the city
Topic 34 Street scene
Topic 35 New building going up!
Topic 36 Fire!
Topic 37 Big harbor!
Topic 38 Carnival!
Topic 39 Great restaurant!

Theme Bibliography

Big City Port
written by Betsy Maestro and Ellen DelVecchio; illustrated by Guilio Maestro.
Scholastic Inc., 1987. ISBN 0590415778
This book is an excellent extension for Topic 37. The descriptive pictures and simple, clear text bring the busy world of the city dockyards to life. Students will find words they have learned from the Dictionary in the illustrations, and can expand their vocabulary by identifying other elements in the pictures.

Carousel
by Brian Wildsmith.
Oxford University Press, 1996. ISBN 0192723189
Like Brian Wildsmith's other books (see the Theme 7 Bibliography, page 201), *Carousel* is an inviting colorful display with few words, making it an ideal book for English-language learners. On each page, the words can easily be covered so that children can imitate the animals and re-create other carousel sights and sounds.

Country Fair
written and illustrated by Elisha Cooper.
Greenwillow Books, 1997. ISBN 0688155316
A barren field outside of town is transformed into a whirl of activity the day of the country fair. Tents are erected, and people and animals fill the field. The text loops around the pages, giving a sense of the fair's activities and general commotion. This may be difficult for emerging readers to follow, but with repetitive readings it can become an enjoyable challenge. The many illustrations provide reinforcement of the vocabulary items from Themes 4–6.

Emergency!
by Gail Gibbons.
Holiday House, 1994. ISBN 0823412016
This book, like many of the author's books, communicates practical information in a simple, readable style with descriptive illustrations. The brightly colored illustrations depict emergency situations with a focus on vehicles and specialized equipment. They convey a general sense that everything is under control as the experts get to work. The final pages offer illustrated notes on policing, firefighting, and past rescue operations.

"Fire! Fire!" said Mrs. McGuire
written by Bill Martin, Jr.; illustrated by Richard Egielski.
Harcourt Brace, 1996. ISBN 0152275622
The strong, detailed pictures add humor and interest to this modern retelling of an old nursery rhyme. The text is full of action and humor, and features women in a number of unexpected roles. It is formatted in a series of questions and answers set as a rhyming dialogue. This book can be a starting point for students to invent their own rhyming interchanges.

Good Morning, City
written by Elaine Moore; illustrated by William Low.
Bridgewater Books, 1995. ISBN 0816736545
This lovely book invites children to witness dawn breaking over the city. It shows working people either ending their long night shifts or preparing to start the new day. The language is lyrical, but not overly complex. The illustrations can provide opportunities to discuss feelings as well as actions.

Happy Birthday, Jesse Bear!

written by Nancy W. Carlstrom; illustrated by Bruce Degan. Simon & Schuster Children's Books, 1994. ISBN 0027172775

This book, part of the *Jesse Bear* series, tells the story of Jesse's birthday party. In bouncy rhyme and bright pictures it covers all of the traditional birthday activities: mailing the invitations, decorating the house, and throwing the party itself, complete with presents, games, and cake. This story makes a good extension to Topic 32. Students can locate words they've already learned and add new words to a word bank.

I Like the Music

written by Leah Komaiko; illustrated by Barbara Westman. HarperTrophy Books, 1989. ISBN 0064431894

A child prefers the music of street musicians and the spontaneous beat of everyday life to the austerity of the symphony hall. Then one night, her grandmother takes her to a concert in the park. Rhythm and rhyme enliven the text of this bright celebration of music. The language is colloquial and inventive, and the cartoon-style pictures provide opportunities for expanding vocabulary.

The Little House

by Virginia Lee Burton. Houghton Mifflin Co., 1998. ISBN 0395891124

This story of a little country house that is gradually enveloped by a growing city has been a classic since it won the Caldecott Medal in 1943. In simple yet vivid language, the author describes the coming of the road, the shift from rural to suburban to urban, and the ever-passing seasons. The illustrations enable students to talk about feelings and identify objects.

The Night I Followed the Dog

written and illustrated by Nina Laden. Chronicle Books, 1994. ISBN 0811806472

This is a zany story about a curious boy who wants to find out what dogs do at night. So he follows his seemingly ordinary dog to a doggy nightclub aptly named The Dog House. The expressive illustrations depict many kinds of dogs in fancy clothes. The text is handwritten, and words are highlighted by different styles and clever visual imagery. Encourage your students to look closely at the words and use similar techniques to write their own words.

Sky Scrape/City Scape: Poems of City Life

edited by Jane Yolen; illustrated by Ken Condon. Boyds Mills Press, 1996. ISBN 1563971798

A selection of poems that evoke the feelings and exuberant energy of a city, from Langston Hughes, Carl Sandberg, Lilian Moore, and others. You can use such poems as "The Streetcleaner's Lament," and a quartet of skyscraper poems, to extend the contextualization of words from Topics 33–35.

Today is Monday

written and illustrated by Eric Carle. Paper Star Publishing, 1997. ISBN 0698115635

From Monday to Sunday, each day of the week is introduced with one of Carle's distinctive, bold, tissue-paper collages. Each collage introduces a different animal eating a different food. The story builds up to a cumulative song that young children will enjoy singing and acting out. The music is provided at the back of the book.

Tool Book

written and illustrated by Gail Gibbons. Holiday House, 1982. ISBN 0823406946

This book identifies carpenter's tools with clear illustrations. The tools are categorized by function: tools that measure, tools that cut, and so forth. Use this text in conjunction with Topic 35 to expand the children's understanding of the words and to add new, related words.

Tools

written by Ann Morris; photographs by Ken Heyman. Lothrop Lee & Shepard, 1992. ISBN 0688101704

Clear, descriptive photos show people all around the world at work using different tools. The text is simple and straightforward. It does not name the tools or the actions. This allows you to have students identify the people and their tools. Many of the content words presented in the Dictionary are depicted here. The picture index in the back of the book names each tool and identifies where it was photographed.

Town and Country

by Alice and Martin Provensen. Brown Deer Publications, 1994. ISBN 0152001824

A journey of discovery and comparison of life in a bustling city and in the busy countryside. Much of the detailed text is presented in the second person. It provides opportunities for expanding vocabulary, as well as modeling and building on grammatical structures. The illustrations can be related to numerous Dictionary topics. The visuals can be especially useful in prompting discussion of different kinds of work.

Saturday at the mall

Content

- Stores and shopping
- Signs
- Snack foods

Language

- Asking about and describing the location of a person: *Where is Mr. Cheng? He's on the escalator. Where is Henry? He's in the arcade.*
- Asking about and describing places: *Where can you buy snacks? You can buy snacks in the snack bar. Where is the arcade? It's on the lower level.*
- Recognizing and reading signs: *The exit sign is on the door. This rest room is for men.*
- Describing activities: *They bought shoes at the shoe store. The girls were eating a snack. They went down on the escalator.*

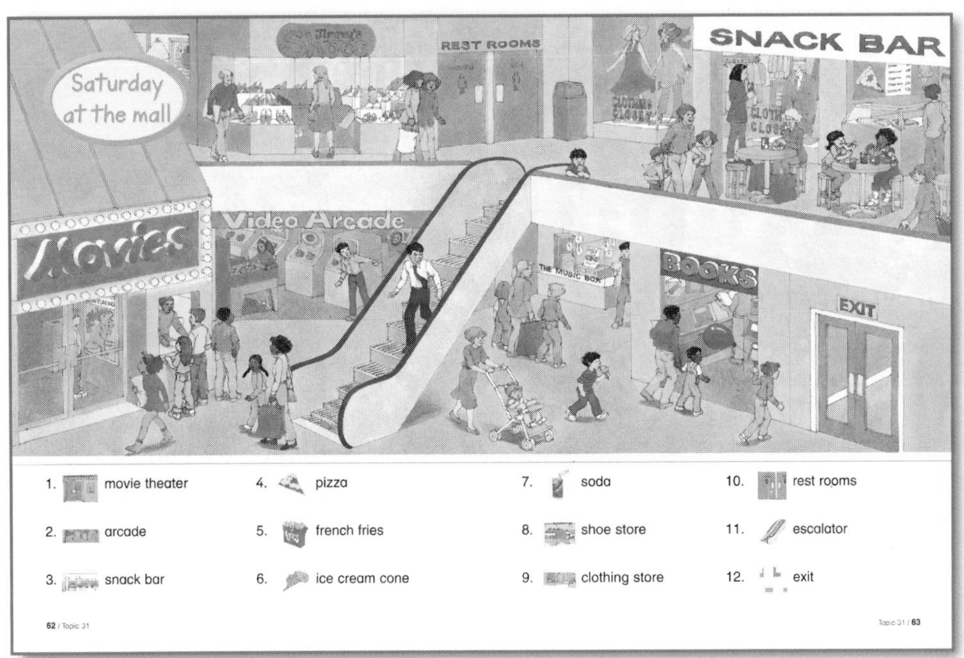

Words

1. movie theater
2. arcade
3. snack bar
4. pizza
5. french fries
6. ice cream cone
7. soda
8. shoe store
9. clothing store
10. rest rooms
11. escalator
12. exit

Additional Words

window-shop
upper level
lower level
ticket booth
slice

It's Saturday morning and the Cheng family and Ting's friend Zoe are at the shopping mall. There are two levels of stores, with an escalator connecting them. Zoe and Ting are on the upper level at the snack bar. Ting is eating pizza; Zoe has french fries. Both girls have cans of orange soda. Mrs. Cheng is admiring the clothes she sees in the window of the clothing store. Henry is in the arcade on the lower level. Jackie is at the top of the escalator. But where is Jo-Jo? Henry sees him and calls up to his father. He points to Jo-Jo, who is eating an ice cream cone and excitedly following a boy with a big red balloon toward the exit. Mr. Cheng has seen him, too. He is halfway down the escalator, glaring at Jo-Jo and yelling, "Jo-Jo! Come back here!"

Words

Components: Topic 31 Wall Chart, Picture Dictionary (pp. 62–63), Cassette, Word and Picture Cards (Topic 31).

See page xiv for techniques and strategies for presenting and practicing words.

Saturday at the mall

1. movie theater
2. arcade
3. snack bar
4. pizza
5. french fries
6. ice cream cone
7. soda
8. shoe store
9. clothing store
10. rest rooms
11. escalator
12. exit

Notes

Hold up the picture card for one of the stores—for example, *movie theater*—and say: *Here is the movie theater. We can go to the movie theater to see movies.* Continue in this manner, talking a bit about each location as you review the words. Then prompt the children to say the word or hold up their word cards in response to such questions as: *Where can I buy shoes? If I want to play a video game, where should I go?* Respond by modeling answers *(Yes, I can play video games in the arcade.)*.

Workbook page

This is a puzzle page with a coded message. First, children should write the words (the pictures are clues), writing one letter on each short line. Point out that some letters are enclosed in boxes. When all the missing words are filled in, tell them to copy the boxed letter from word number 1 into the box numbered 1 at the bottom of the page. Do the same for the boxed letter number 2, and so on. Then help them to read the secret message *("time to shop")*.

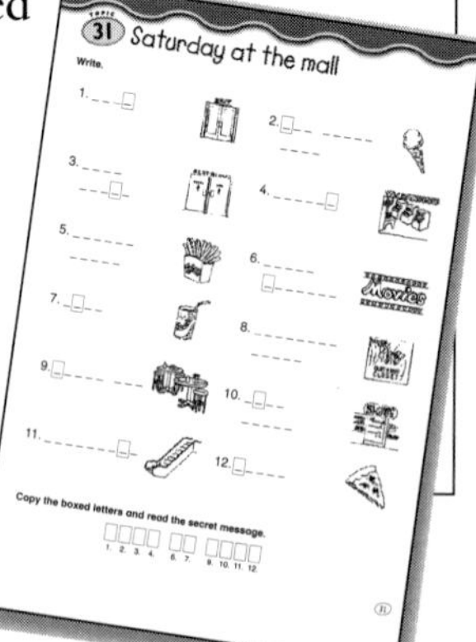

Stories

Components: Picture Dictionary (pp. 62–63), Cassette, Story (Topic 31).

See page xviii for techniques and strategies for presenting and practicing stories.

It's Saturday at the shopping mall.
Let's go to the movies!
Let's go to the arcade!
Let's go to the snack bar!

Who wants pizza? Ting and Henry.
Who wants french fries? Zoe.
Who wants an ice cream cone?
Jackie and Jo-Jo. Sodas, anyone?

Mr. and Mrs. Cheng window-shop.
Such nice shoes and clothing!
Henry is playing games in the arcade.
Jo-Jo? Where's Jo-Jo?

Is he in the rest room? No.
Is he on the escalator? No.
He's following a boy with a big red balloon out the exit!
Jo-Jo! Come back here!

Story notes

Invite volunteers to describe their experiences in shopping malls. Ask the children to name the kinds of stores (or the things that can be bought) in a mall, and write their contributions on a large chart.

Ask about the story:
Which stores are on the lower level? Who was on the upper level? Who was in the arcade? What were Ting and Zoe eating? Was Mr. Cheng eating something? What was Mrs. Cheng looking at? Did Henry see Jo-Jo? Where is Mr. Cheng? Why is Henry pointing? Where was Jo-Jo going?

Ask about your students:
Who has been to a mall? Do you like to go to the mall? Why? What do you like best about the mall? What don't you like? Who has been on an escalator? What did you do at the mall? What snacks do you like to eat? Where would you go to buy shoes? Is there a movie theater in the mall you go to?

Dialogue

Components: Cassette, Topic 31 Wall Chart, Picture Dictionary (pp. 62–63).

See page xix for techniques and strategies for presenting and practicing dialogues.

Mr. Cheng:	How's the pizza, Ting?
Ting and Zoe:	It's good!
Zoe:	The french fries are good too!
Mr. Cheng:	What kind of soda did you get?
Ting:	Orange.
Mr. Cheng:	Jackie, be careful with that ice cream cone. It's dripping! Where's Jo-Jo? Did he go into the rest room?
Ting:	I don't know. I think he went with Henry.
Mr. Cheng:	Where's Henry?
Ting:	He's down there in the arcade.
Mr. Cheng:	Henry! Have you seen Jo-Jo? Is he in the arcade?
Henry:	No. There he goes.
Mr. Cheng:	Where?
Henry:	Out the exit!
Mr. Cheng:	I see him! Jo-Jo! Where do you think you're going? Come back here!

Dialogue notes

Take this opportunity to talk with the children about getting lost or separated from the people they are with in a crowded place like a mall. Ask them to say what they would do if they got lost, or if a younger sibling or friend were lost, and ask them to describe how they could avoid getting lost. Encourage them to make up dialogues about trying to find someone who is missing.

Beats!

Components: Cassette, Beats! (Topic 31).

See page xx for techniques and strategies for presenting and practicing Beats!

Here we are at the shopping mall!
Where shall we go?
    Let's go up on the escalator
    and look down below.

I see the music store.
    I see the games.
What's at the movies?
    I can't read the names.

I wish I had that baseball cap,
hanging on the rack.

    I wish I had a pizza.
    Let's get a snack!

Beat notes

Practice the Beat as a group. Then put the children into two groups to recite the lines alternately as written. You can ask them to stand near the Wall Chart and point to the stores mentioned or referred to as they recite the Beat.

Worksheets

Worksheet 1: Saturday at the mall (p. 61)

The pictures are clues to help the children fill in the missing words. Help them read the instructions at the bottom of the page, then help them write or dictate a full-sentence answer as indicated.

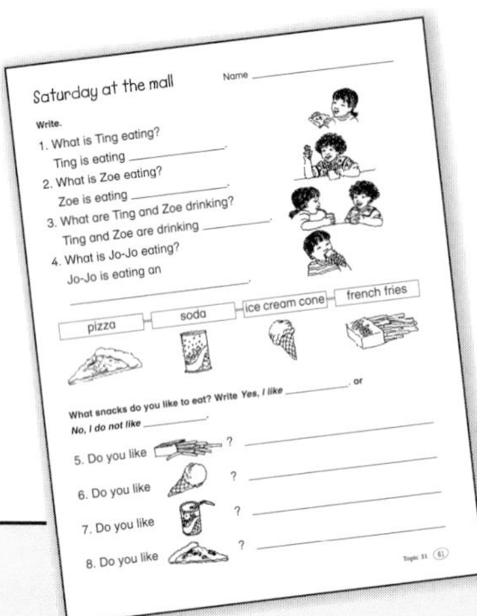

Saturday at the mall Name ________

Write.

1. What is Ting eating?
   Ting is eating ________.
2. What is Zoe eating?
   Zoe is eating ________.
3. What are Ting and Zoe drinking?
   Ting and Zoe are drinking ________.
4. What is Jo-Jo eating?
   Jo-Jo is eating an ________.

pizza — soda — ice cream cone — french fries

What snacks do you like to eat? Write *Yes, I like* ________, or *No, I do not like* ________.

5. Do you like ? ________
6. Do you like ? ________
7. Do you like ? ________
8. Do you like ? ________

Topic 31 61

Worksheet 2: Saturday at the mall (p. 62)

The map and the items for sale surrounding it are clues, but the children don't have to limit their answers to the items shown. Ask them to write or dictate three things they would like to buy in a shopping mall, and the kind of store where they could buy such things.

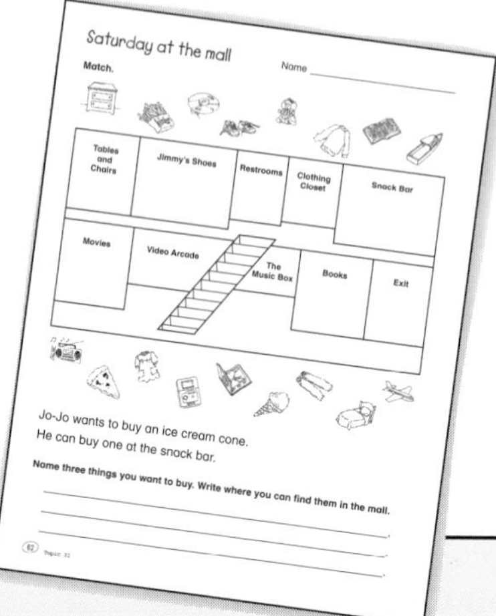

Saturday at the mall Name ________

Match.

Jo-Jo wants to buy an ice cream cone.
He can buy one at the snack bar.

Name three things you want to buy. Write where you can find them in the mall.

________.
________.
________.

62 Topic 31

Activities

- Play I'm Lost! Have the children role-play being lost at a mall. Have one child pretend to be lost, while others pretend to be the missing child's family members, salesclerks, or security guards. Prompt them to think about and then practice ways to get help. This is an opportunity for reinforcing the children's ability to say their names, addresses, and phone numbers clearly.

- Make a map of a mall on mural paper, with large segments to represent the stores in this topic and any other stores students suggest. Ask the children to help you label the stores. Then provide old magazines or catalogs for the children to look through so they can cut out items to paste in each store (for example, shoes in the shoe store, a dress in the clothing store, a movie ad in the movie theater).

- Play Word Finder. Give each child a list (triple-spaced for ease of use) of six of the twelve vocabulary words. Then give each child one word card hidden inside a piece of folded paper, so that no one else sees the card. Tell the children to look at their cards and cover them again. Then tell them to circulate around the room and ask each other if they have the card for one of the words on their list. Model the question: *Do you have the card for* ice cream cone*?* If the answer is *yes*, they can check off the word on their list; if the answer is *no*, they move on to ask again.

Happy birthday!

Content

- Birthdays and birthday parties
- Giving and receiving presents
- Age

Language

- Using birthday greetings and polite expressions: *Happy birthday! Thank you for coming to my party. Thank you for inviting me.*
- Talking about birthday traditions and decorations: *Here is the birthday cake, with one candle for every year, and one to grow on! Blow out the candles and make a wish. Let's sing the birthday song.*
- Asking and talking about age and birthdays: *When is your birthday? My birthday is in September. I was born on January 18. I will be eight years old in August.*
- Using expressions for giving and receiving presents: *This present is for you. I hope you like it. Thank you for the gift. Thanks. I like this a lot! You're welcome.*

Words

1. balloon
2. present
3. card
4. ribbon
5. wrapping paper
6. baseball bat
7. jewelry
8. puzzle
9. helicopter
10. candy
11. cake
12. candles

Additional Words

gift
earrings
ring
bracelet
necklace
piñata
wish
icing
matches
streamers
bow
blowers
polite

It's Alison's birthday. There are pink and green balloons all around. The table is decorated with colorful plates, cups, and napkins. There are streamers, blowers, and candies at each place. A side table is cluttered with wrapping paper, ribbon, birthday cards, and Alison's presents. A broken piñata hangs from above. Alison is seated at the head of the table, waiting for her birthday cake. She is wearing two of her new presents: a baseball cap and the new earrings that Zoe gave her. Ting, Diego, Yuka, and two other classmates are also seated. Zoe and a boy are heading toward the table, but the two other boys are still playing with the toys. Mrs. Matthews is ready with the cake. It has pink icing, seven candles, and a big number seven. Mr. Matthews has lit the candles and is still holding the matches. Everyone is looking at the cake and singing "Happy Birthday."

Words

Components: Topic 32 Wall Chart, Picture Dictionary (pp. 64–65), Cassette, Word and Picture Cards (Topic 32).

See page xiv for techniques and strategies for presenting and practicing words.

Happy birthday!

1. balloon
2. present
3. card
4. ribbon
5. wrapping paper
6. baseball bat
7. jewelry
8. puzzle
9. helicopter
10. candy
11. cake
12. candles

Notes

Place the word and picture cards in a bag or box decorated to look like a birthday present. Invite a volunteer to come up and reach in to pick a card. Help that child say the word, and then present it to the other children. Then ask the children to return to their places with the cards they picked. When all the words have been presented, ask the children to talk about which cards could be grouped together—for example, the presents *(baseball bat, jewelry, puzzle, helicopter)* or the foods *(cake, candy)*. Help them define the categories. Then bring the children back together to present their words again. Prompt them to explain the category: *We have decorations. I have balloons. And I have candles.*

Workbook page

Help the children read the instructions for coloring the picture. Point out that the wrapped present should be colored green, along with the paper and ribbon. Encourage the children to talk about the things shown in the picture as they color them.

Stories

Components: Picture Dictionary (pp. 64–65), Cassette, Story (Topic 32).

See page xviii for techniques and strategies for presenting and practicing stories.

It's October 2nd, Alison's birthday!
She's having a party. She's seven!
Mr. Matthews put pink and green
balloons all around the house.

Presents and cards are everywhere!
Quick! Rip off the ribbon and
wrapping paper. What's inside?
A baseball bat! Jewelry!
A puzzle! A helicopter!

Diego gave Alison a piñata.
Surprise! There's candy inside!
Mrs. Matthews baked a beautiful cake
with pink icing and candles on top.

Time to light the candles and sing!
Make a wish, Alison, and
blow out the candles!
Happy birthday!

Story notes

Invite volunteers to describe a birthday party of their own, or a birthday party they went to. Some children may not have experienced birthday parties like the one depicted here. Encourage them to talk about how birthdays (or name days) are recognized in their families.

Ask about the story:
What did Alison get for her birthday? What was in the piñata? How did the piñata get broken? What colors are the balloons? Who gave Alison earrings? How many candles are on Alison's cake? How old is she? Is everyone sitting at the table? What is the boy playing with?

Ask about your students:
Did you ever go to a birthday party? What would you like to give a friend for his or her birthday? What present would you like to get for your birthday? Do you like balloons? What do you say when someone gives you a gift? What do you say when you give someone a gift? When is your birthday? How old will you be on your next birthday?

Dialogue

Components: Cassette, Topic 32 Wall Chart, Picture Dictionary (pp. 64–65).

See page xix for techniques and strategies for presenting and practicing dialogues.

Alison:	Zoe! Thank you for these earrings! I love them!
Zoe:	You're welcome.
Alison:	And that's a great birthday card!
Zoe:	I made it just for you!
Diego:	Do you like my piñata?
Alison:	I love it, Diego, it's great!
Ting:	Do you like my present? It's a puzzle.
Alison:	Yes, I love puzzles. You can help me do it. And Dad, you're going to have to play baseball with me now that I have a new baseball bat.
Mr. Matthews:	That'll be fun, honey.
Diego:	Let's have the birthday cake! I'm hungry.
Mr. Matthews:	I'm lighting the candles now! Are you all ready to sing?
Kids:	Yeah.
Mrs. Matthews:	Here comes the birthday cake! Now, Alison, make a wish and blow out the candles.
Everyone:	Yay!!! Happy birthday, Alison!

Dialogue notes

Explain birthday party traditions such as placing a specific number of candles on a cake (one for each year and one to grow on) and making a wish when blowing out the candles. Then, working with two or three children at a time, model exchanges such as: *Happy birthday. Is it your birthday today? Yes, it's my birthday today. How old are you? I'm six years old. Here's a present. Thank you. You're welcome.*

Beats!

Components: Cassette, Beats! (Topic 32).

See page xx for techniques and strategies for presenting and practicing Beats!

Is that for me?
    Yes, it is!
What's in the box?
Let me see!

    First take the card.
    Read it! Read it!
What's in the box?
Let me see!

    Take off the paper.
    Open it! Open it!
What's in the box?
Now I see!

It's a car!
    A big red car!
A great big red car
just for me!
    Happy birthday!!!
Thank you!
    You're welcome!

Beat notes

Ask the children to take turns acting out the Beat (with real objects, if possible). Be sure to use this opportunity to practice mannerly expressions, such as saying *Thank you* and *You're welcome*. The children may like to make up other verses with other presents to take out of the box. As an example:

It's a doll
a little doll, a cute little doll.
just for me.

Worksheets

Worksheet 1: Happy birthday! (p. 63)

Help the children read the coloring instructions and count the number of identified objects. For the last question, tell them they can use the pictures as clues, but their list of things they would like to get should not be not limited to the words in this topic.

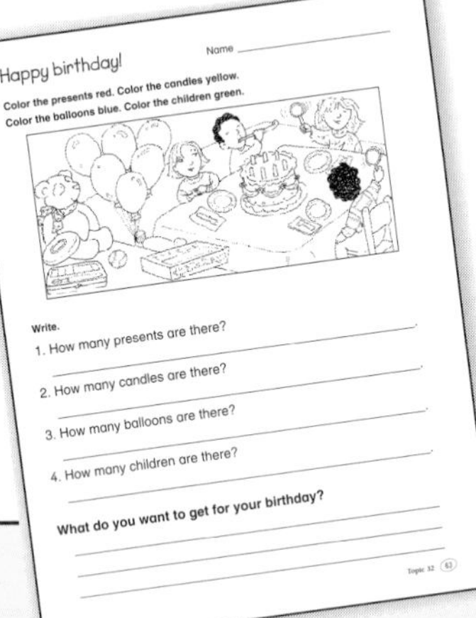

Happy birthday! Name

Color the presents red. Color the candles yellow. Color the balloons blue. Color the children green.

Write.

1. How many presents are there?
2. How many candles are there?
3. How many balloons are there?
4. How many children are there?

What do you want to get for your birthday?

Topic 32 63

Worksheet 2: Happy birthday! (p. 64)

Help the children use their skills of logical sequencing to fill in the missing words. Tell them that each missing word can be found among the pictures and words around the margins of the page.

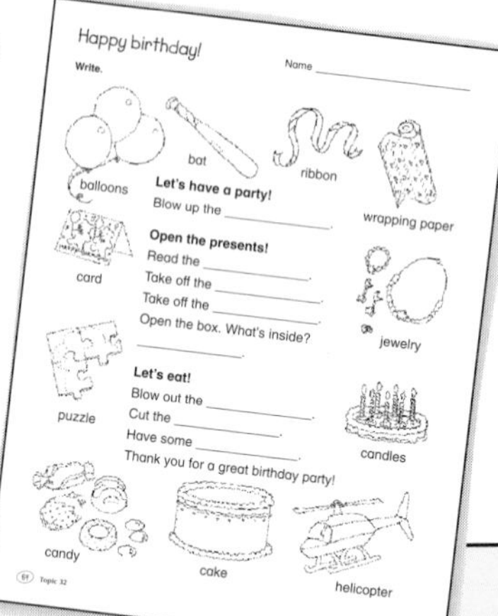

Happy birthday! Name

Write.

balloons bat ribbon wrapping paper

Let's have a party!
Blow up the ____.

card

Open the presents!
Read the ____.
Take off the ____.
Take off the ____.
Open the box. What's inside?
____.

jewelry

puzzle

Let's eat!
Blow out the ____.
Cut the ____.
Have some ____.
Thank you for a great birthday party!

candles

candy cake helicopter

64 Topic 32

Activities

- Explain that piñatas are a Mexican custom. Mention other birthday traditions. In China, noodles are served to wish the birthday child a long life. In the Philippines, the outside of the birthday child's house is adorned with blinking colored lights. In Russia, children might receive a birthday pie with greetings carved into the crust. Invite the children to share what they know about birthday celebrations in other cultures and to teach their classmates birthday songs they know.

- Make a large, colorful chart showing the month and day of each child's birthday. Hang it on the wall and let the children take turns being the "birthday checker," the one who informs the rest of the class that a birthday is coming soon. Be sure to sing the "Happy Birthday" song as each special day arrives.

- Celebrate each child's birthday with the activity poem, "Somebody's Birthday":

  Today is _____'s birthday,
  Let's make her/him a cake.
  (Put hands together, palms up.)
  On it ____ (raise five, six, or seven fingers)
  candles we'll place.
  Then each make a secret wish,
  Blow all of them out: *s-s-s-swish!*
  (Blow a deep breath and fold up fingers.)

- Teach the children how to play some traditional American party games that are still popular: Musical Chairs, Pin the Tail on the Donkey, and Duck Duck Goose. Then let children from other cultures teach the class whatever games they may know.

- As a class, plan a surprise birthday party for someone special in the school, such as the principal, nurse, or custodian. Let the children help make and hang decorations in your room. Encourage them to offer suggestions for party games and snacks. Have each child make a birthday card for the special person. On the day of the party, invite the birthday person to come to your room. Prompt the children to use the vocabulary and language structures related to the topic.

Sunday in the city

Content

- Modes of transportation
- City sights
- Urban sanitation

Language

- Asking about and describing modes of transportation: *Where will the plane land? It will land at the airport. Let's take the bus. Can we go there on a subway? The highway is crowded with cars and trucks.*
- Describing city sights: *There are flowers on the roof of that apartment house. Look at the smokestacks on the factory. The buildings are very tall.*
- Describing activities to keep the city clean: *Don't litter. The street cleaner is picking up the trash. Please, put your gum wrapper in the trash can.*

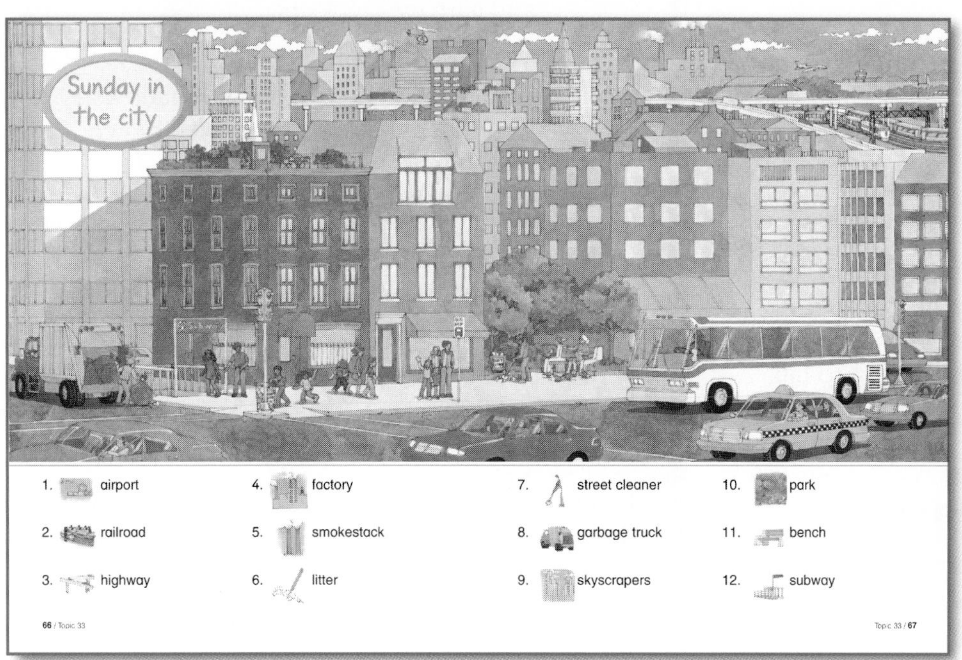

Words

1. airport
2. railroad
3. highway
4. factory
5. smokestack
6. litter
7. street cleaner
8. garbage truck
9. skyscrapers
10. park
11. bench
12. subway

Additional Words

parking space
transportation
gum
shadows
trash
bus stop

The Young, Matthews, and Lopez families are in the city. A street cleaner is picking up litter and putting it in a trash can with a sign that says, "Don't litter!" A garbage truck is picking up bags of garbage from the curb. Jasmin sees bright red flowers in a roof garden. In a little park with a bench between two buildings, an old woman is sitting on a bench feeding the birds. In the distance, there's a factory with plumes of smoke coming from the smokestacks, railroad tracks with trains passing under a crowded highway, and an airport with planes and a circling helicopter. Mrs. Lopez has started down the stairs into the subway, and Mr. Lopez is motioning to Diego and Jasmin to come along. Jasmin waves to Alison, while Diego throws his gum wrapper into the trash can. Mr. and Mrs. Matthews and Alison stand at the bus stop. Mrs. Young, Jim, and Tommy join them. Mrs. Young has Tommy by the hand. He is looking up at the tall skyscrapers.

Words

Components: Topic 33 Wall Chart, Picture Dictionary (pp. 66–67), Cassette, Word and Picture Cards (Topic 33).

See page xiv for techniques and strategies for presenting and practicing words.

Sunday in the city

1. airport
2. railroad
3. highway
4. factory
5. smokestack
6. litter
7. street cleaner
8. garbage truck
9. skyscrapers
10. park
11. bench
12. subway

Notes

Ask the children to hold up their picture cards as you point to items on the Wall Chart. Then prompt them to talk about places and things in your community that are similar to those shown in the illustration. For example, you can ask: *Is there a highway close to here? What does the highway look like? Have you been to an airport? What can you see at an airport? What happens to litter in our park?* Ask the children to compare the environment they live in with the one depicted in the dictionary. Encourage them to talk about their own experiences.

Workbook page

The pictures on the page are clues for the children to use in finishing the sentences. You may want to have a group discussion focusing on sensory response to a city before starting this page. If they live near or in a city, encourage the children to use their own experiences to complete the exercises.

Stories

Components: Picture Dictionary (pp. 66–67), Cassette, Story (Topic 33).

See page xviii for techniques and strategies for presenting and practicing stories.

It's Sunday in the city!
People are coming from the airport,
on the railroad, in buses and cars.
The highway is crowded!

The city is noisy.
It has factories and smokestacks.
It's dirty with litter.
Street cleaners pick it up,
and garbage trucks take it away.

The city is beautiful.
Tall, tall skyscrapers, purple shadows.
And there's a little park with a bench
and flowers on a rooftop!
Look up! Where is the sky?

Let's walk!
Let's take a bus! Let's take a taxi!
Let's take a subway under the ground!
Let's see the city!

Story notes

Using as many of the vocabulary words as possible, describe a city to the children. If you are in a big city, ask the children to compare the illustration with the city around them.

Ask about the story:
Could you get to this city by airplane? train? car? Do you think the city is noisy or quiet? Why? What was the street cleaner doing? Why was there garbage for him to pick up? What kinds of things do you think the street cleaner finds?

Ask about your students:
Have you been in a city? Did you ride a city bus? How did you get to the city? What did you see there? Was it noisy or quiet in the city? How is the city in the picture the same as your neighborhood? How is it different?

Dialogue

Components: Cassette, Topic 33 Wall Chart, Picture Dictionary (pp. 66–67).

See page xix for techniques and strategies for presenting and practicing dialogues.

Mr. Matthews:	There's so much traffic. I'm glad we came into the city on the railroad.
Mr. Lopez:	It would be hard to find a parking space today.
Diego:	Look at those skyscrapers! Wow! Are they tall!
Tommy:	I can't see the sky.
Jasmin:	Look! I see flowers way up on a roof!
Alison:	It's a roof garden.
Tommy:	Why did they make a garden way up there?
Jasmin:	Because it's pretty!
Diego:	Dad, can I have some gum?
Mr. Lopez:	All right. Give everybody a piece, but put your gum wrappers in the garbage can.
Diego:	What does the sign say?
Mr. Lopez:	It says, "Don't litter." That means don't just drop your wrappers in the street. Put them in the can and keep the street clean.
Alison:	I see the street cleaner, cleaning up the litter.
Jasmin:	I see the garbage truck, picking up the garbage.
Diego:	I see the subway. Are we going to take the subway?
Mr. Lopez:	Yes. We're going to take the subway because we're going to the carnival later.
Mr. Matthews:	And we're going to take the bus. We're going to the museum. So, have a good time everyone!
Everyone:	You, too. Have a good time in the city!

Dialogue notes

Encourage the children to invent their own dialogues based on this one. Model a pattern in which one child points out a sight and another child describes it.

First child: Look! I can see the highway.
Second child: There are lots of cars and trucks. I can see the railroad line.
Third child: It goes under the highway. I can see ...

Beats!

Components: Cassette, Beats! (Topic 33).

See page xx for techniques and strategies for presenting and practicing Beats!

I love the city!
The cars go whizzing by.
Let's go up a skyscraper,
way up high!

Up to the top we go!
This skyscraper is tall!
When we look down from the top,
everything looks small!

Let's take a subway train!
A subway train goes fast!
It's dark inside the tunnel.
Here's our station! At last!

I love the city!
Nothing's ever slow.
People hurry everywhere!
I wonder where they go.

Beat notes

Ask if any of the children have ever been up high in a big building. Did they climb stairs all the way up? If not, how did they get up high? Did they go to the very top? Did they go outside? Did they look outside from a window? Let each child share something from his or her experiences. Ask the whole class to repeat the first two verses of the Beat. Discuss the size of objects seen from far away. Then, if you wish, you could ask similar questions about riding a subway underground.

Worksheets

Worksheet 1: Sunday in the city (p. 65)

To complete the missing words in the story, help the children read the sentences and then look for the words at the bottom of the page. In the "Unscramble" section, you may offer the clue that the syllables are scrambled. Help them say the scrambled version, clapping the syllables and marking the breaks in the word, and then tell them to rewrite the word with the syllables in order.

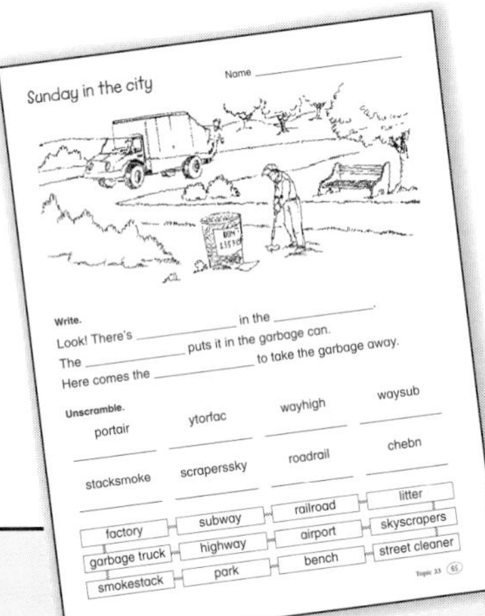

Sunday in the city　Name ____________

Write.

Look! There's ____________ in the ____________.

The ____________ puts it in the garbage can.

Here comes the ____________ to take the garbage away.

Unscramble.

portair　ytorfac　wayhigh　waysub

stacksmoke　scrapersky　roadrail　chebn

factory　subway　railroad　litter

garbage truck　highway　airport　skyscrapers

smokestack　park　bench　street cleaner

Topic 33　65

Worksheet 2: Sunday in the city (p. 66)

Help the children read each sentence and find the picture at the bottom of the page that fits the description. Then have them write the correct word on the line provided at the right. You may suggest that they cross out each picture and word clue as they use it.

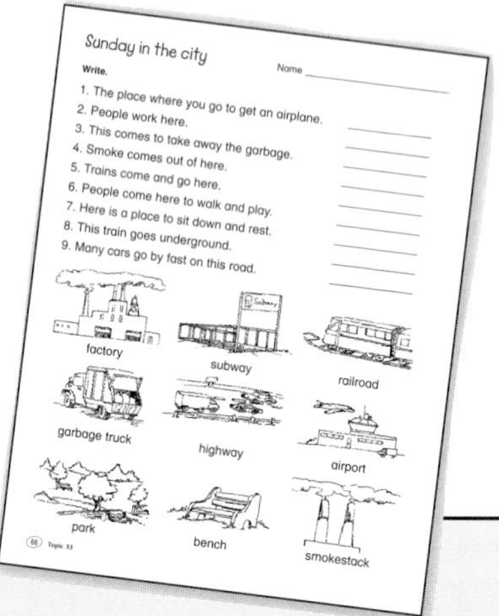

Sunday in the city　Name ____________

Write.

1. The place where you go to get an airplane.
2. People work here.
3. This comes to take away the garbage.
4. Smoke comes out of here.
5. Trains come and go here.
6. People come here to walk and play.
7. Here is a place to sit down and rest.
8. This train goes underground.
9. Many cars go by fast on this road.

factory　subway　railroad

garbage truck　highway　airport

park　bench　smokestack

66　Topic 33

Activities

- Create a City Soundscape. Begin by reading aloud the book *City Sounds* by Craig Brown (Greenwillow Books). After reading, ask the children to name and imitate something in the city that makes a noise. Write down each suggestion. Once various sounds have been identified, assign two or three children to imitate each noisemaker. Then start the soundscape by calling out a noisemaker. Add sounds, one at a time, until the whole class is involved. Use your hands to signal changes in volume. Let the children take turns being the conductor. If you can, record the soundscape.

- Set up chairs to represent some mode of transportation. Slight variations, and the children's imaginations, can create an airplane, a train, or a bus. Let the children create the setting as you offer language models for paying fares, boarding, being seated, finding a destination, and disembarking.

- Encourage your class to initiate a Don't Litter campaign at your school. Have them make posters and signs to hang in the halls, cafeteria, and playground. Join with other classrooms and assign areas to help keep clean. Use this opportunity to talk about recycling.

- Make a neighborhood map. On a large piece of mural paper, draw the square block where your school is located. Then draw in the structures on the block, labeling them with the children's help. Encourage the children to make pictures of their school and other buildings on the block to display with the map. If interest is high, expand to include the opposite side of each street around your square block.

TOPIC 34 Street scene

Content	Language
Sounds and sights of the city	Describing a place: *There are many music, dance, and theater programs in the city. This museum shows photography.*
Cultural activities	Asking about and describing professions: *What is the man doing? He is a musician. He is playing a guitar. What are those boys? Those boys are dancers.*
	Describing locations of people in relation to other people or places: *Alison is on the steps to the museum. The mime is behind Alison on the steps. The dancers are in front of the musicians.*
	Expressing wishes: *I wish I knew how to dance. He wishes he had a guitar. I wish we could see a play.*

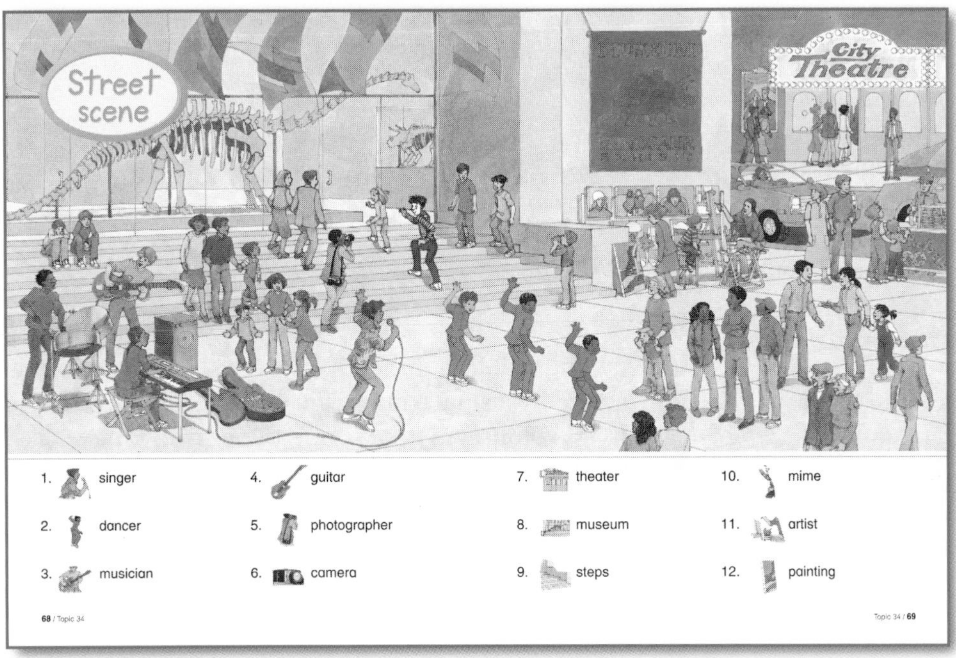

Words

1. singer
2. dancer
3. musician
4. guitar
5. photographer
6. camera
7. theater
8. museum
9. steps
10. mime
11. artist
12. painting

Additional Words

statue
steel drum
keyboard
microphone
horns
dinosaur
pretzel vendor
perform
performance

The Youngs and the Matthewses have come to a cultural area of the city. There are a museum, a theater, and lots of street activity: street musicians, boys dancing, a photographer with two cameras taking pictures, an artist displaying his paintings, and a mime. People are gathered around watching and smiling. Mrs. Young is admiring the artist's paintings while the artist is busy doing a portrait of Tommy. Meanwhile, Alison climbs the steps to the museum, where a big banner advertises a dinosaur exhibit. A mime is mimicking her walk. People are laughing. Jim shouts up to her from the bottom of the steps, but Alison knows the mime is there and she's laughing, too.

Words

Components: Topic 34 Wall Chart, Picture Dictionary (pp. 68–69), Cassette, Word and Picture Cards (Topic 34).

See page xiv for techniques and strategies for presenting and practicing words.

Street scene

1. singer	5. photographer	9. steps
2. dancer	6. camera	10. mime
3. musician	7. theater	11. artist
4. guitar	8. museum	12. painting

Notes

Describe different types of museums, and the things people see there. Point to the museum on the Wall Chart. Ask the children to hold up their *museum* picture card. Invite them to suggest some things that might be in the museum that is on their cards. Repeat this process with the *theater* picture card, describing different types of plays or programs that might be put on there. Then start to explore the "street scene" together by introducing one word at a time, talking about it, and letting the children identify the illustration. Prompt the children to talk about the pictures by asking questions: *Here is the photographer. What could he be taking a picture of? Where would the singer stand?* Continue until the children understand and can use the words comfortably.

Workbook page

Tell the children to look at the two rows of pictures. The people in the top row use the things in the row below. Tell them to draw a line to show which things are used by which people. For example, the camera is used by the photographer. Then ask them to label the last row of pictures on the page. Tell them the words can be found at the bottom.

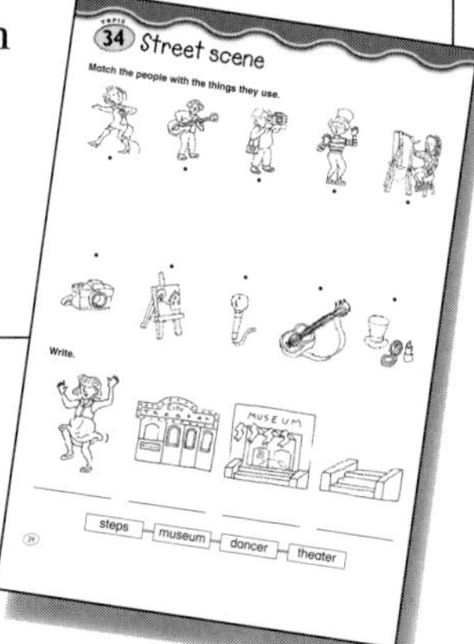

Stories

Components: Picture Dictionary (pp. 68–69), Cassette, Story (Topic 34).

See page xviii for techniques and strategies for presenting and practicing stories.

City streets! Horns honking,
singers singing, dancers dancing,
musicians playing guitar, keyboard,
and steel drums on the corner.

Jim watches a photographer with
two cameras taking pictures of
someone in front of the museum.
Wait a minute! It's Alison!

She's walking up the museum steps.
A mime is imitating Alison!
He's walking the same way she does.
It's funny! Everyone is laughing!

Tommy sees an artist leaning
his paintings against a wall.
They're beautiful! Sit down, Tommy.
He wants to paint you!

Story notes

Ask the children if they have ever seen a live performance by a singer, musician, mime, or other performer. Invite volunteers to describe the performance. Ask questions, such as: *Where was the performer? Where were you? How did the audience react?*

Ask about the story:

Vary the tense of your questions to prompt children to practice using other tenses. *Who is taking pictures of Alison? What was the photographer taking a picture of? Where was Alison going? What instruments are the musicians playing? What does the painter use to make pictures? How were the boys dancing? How does the photographer make a picture? What had the artist painted? Who is the mime imitating? Why is everyone laughing?*

Ask about your students:

Do you like to sing? Did you ever perform for an audience? Have you been to a museum? What did you see there? Have you ever seen a play? How can you make a picture?

Dialogue

 **Components:** Cassette, Topic 34 Wall Chart, Picture Dictionary (pp. 68–69).

See page xix for techniques and strategies for presenting and practicing dialogues.

Alison:	Look at those boys dancing, Dad!
Mr. Matthews:	They're really good dancers.
Alison:	I wish I knew how to dance.
Mr. Matthews:	I'll teach you!
Alison:	And look at the musicians.
Mr. Matthews:	They're good, too.
Alison:	I like the guitar. I wish I had a guitar.
Mrs. Matthews:	Look! There's the theater!
Alison:	I like plays. I wish we could go to the theater.
Mrs. Matthews:	Too many wishes, Alison. Maybe next time we come to the city we can go to a play. But today we're going to the museum.
Alison:	Oh! I'm glad we're going to the museum. Can we see the dinosaurs?
Mr. Matthews:	Of course we can. I like the dinosaurs the best!
Alison:	I love the dinosaurs!
Mrs. Matthews:	You go on ahead up the steps, Alison.
Alison:	OK!
Jim:	Hey, Alison! Turn around! Someone's following you!
Alison:	Oh! It's a mime!
Jim:	Yes! And a photographer is taking pictures of you! O-o-o! Maybe you'll be in the newspapers.
Alison:	Sure! I'll be famous!

Dialogue notes

After the children have listened to the dialogue a few times, encourage them to invent dialogues in which they make their own wishes. Prompt them by asking: *Where do you wish you could go in the city? What do you wish you could see? What do you wish you could do?*

Beats!

 **Components:** Cassette, Beats! (Topic 34).

See page xx for techniques and strategies for presenting and practicing Beats!

Who's that singing
over on the corner?
    Girls are singing!
    It's a busy street!

    Who's that dancing
    over on the corner?
Boys are dancing!
It's a busy street!

Someone's painting!
    Someone's taking pictures!
Someone's selling pretzels!
    Let's go eat!

Singing sweet!
Dancing feet!
Pretzels to eat!
What a busy street!

Beat notes

Separate the children into two groups to practice the Beat. You may want to have them say the final stanza in unison. Have the children pantomime the last stanza; they may pretend to hold a microphone for *singing sweet,* or kick up their heels for *dancing feet,* and munch on an imaginary pretzel for *pretzels to eat.*

Worksheets

Worksheet 1: Street scene (p. 67)

Each unfinished sentence describes a person and some kind of work he or she does. The pictures give the children a clue to the missing words; all the words can be found at the bottom of the page.

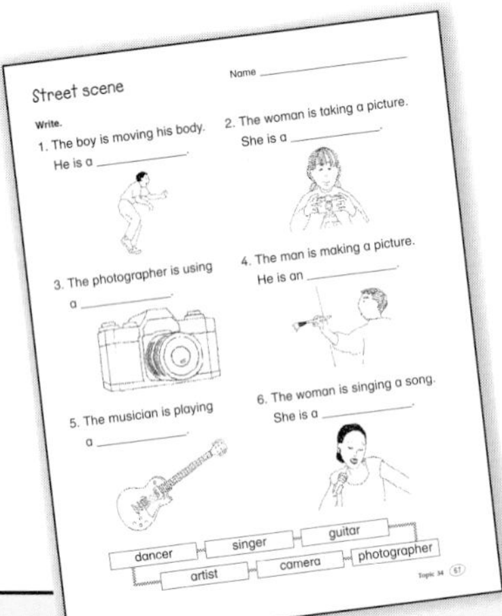

Street scene

Name ____________

Write.

1. The boy is moving his body. He is a ____________.
2. The woman is taking a picture. She is a ____________.
3. The photographer is using a ____________.
4. The man is making a picture. He is an ____________.
5. The musician is playing a ____________.
6. The woman is singing a song. She is a ____________.

dancer singer guitar artist camera photographer

Topic 34 67

Worksheet 2: Street scene (p. 68)

Ask the children to think about the different artists and performers shown in the Dictionary topic. The pictures are clues; students should label each picture by writing the missing word in the sentence *If I were a/an ...* Then have them write or dictate their ideas of what they would do if they did that kind of work.

Street scene

Name ____________

Write.

1. If I were an ____________ I would ____________
2. If I were a ____________ I would ____________
3. If I were a ____________ I would ____________
4. If I were a ____________ I would ____________
5. If I were a ____________ I would ____________
6. If I were a ____________ I would ____________

68 Topic 34

Activities

- If possible, visit a local museum with your class. As you walk through the museum, provide the class with language models and narrate what you and they are seeing. After returning to school, write experience charts or stories with lots of illustrations, and bind them into a class book.
- Be a mime! Explain briefly that mimes act out roles without ever speaking. Invite the children, one at a time, to act out a role found in the topic (*musician, singer, artist,* and so forth). Whisper a word in the child's ear, or let him or her pick an appropriate word card. Then ask the other children to guess what word is being represented.
- Teach the children the activity poem "I Wish ..." Encourage them to act out the lines as you recite them. Then take turns, with some children reciting the poem as others act it out:

I wish I were a jumping jack;
I'd jump up from a box.
I wish I were a rocking horse;
I'd rock and rock and rock.
I wish I were a spinning top;
I'd spin around and 'round.
I wish I were a quiet child;
I'd sit right down.

- Have a talent show. Discuss the different types of artists depicted in the topic. Then invite children individually or in small groups to sign up for a class talent show. Allow each child or group a few minutes to perform. Help them by announcing their performance (saying who they are, what they will be doing, and where they learned how to do it: *Judy and Tom are going to do a hip-hop dance. They didn't make up this dance. They learned it from the TV*).

New building going up!

Content

- Building construction
- Machines and vehicles
- Construction workers

Language

- Asking about and describing professions: *What do the plumbers do? Plumbers put water pipes in buildings. What is the plumber doing? The plumber is connecting two pipes.*
- Identifying and describing the function of construction vehicles: *There is a cement mixer. The dump truck is carrying a load of rocks. The crane is lifting a beam.*
- Describing activities: *The backhoe digs a deep hole. The dump truck takes the dirt away.*

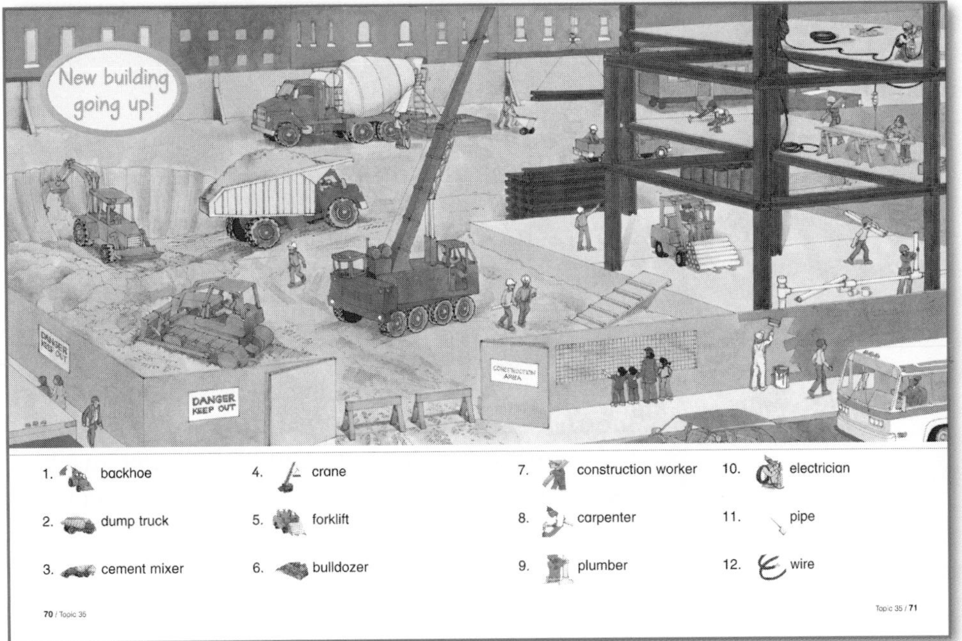

Mrs. Cheng, Ting, Jo-Jo, and Jackie are standing behind the guard fence looking at a construction site in the city and excitedly asking their mother all kinds of questions. Jo-Jo and Jackie want to be construction workers! There is a guard fence around the area. There are many construction workers on the site. They all wear hard hats. A backhoe is digging, and a bulldozer is pushing the dirt around. A fully loaded dump truck is driving away. A cement mixer is revolving and pouring cement. One section of a new building is already up. A crane is lifting steel beams into place. Down below, a forklift is bringing pipes to the plumber, who is fitting pipes together to install the water lines. Carpenters are cutting and carrying wood and nailing down a floor, an electrician is working with wires, and a painter is painting the fence around the site.

Words

1. backhoe
2. dump truck
3. cement mixer
4. crane
5. forklift
6. bulldozer
7. construction worker
8. carpenter
9. plumber
10. electrician
11. pipe
12. wire

Additional Words

hard hat
electricity
beam
hole
machine
wood
dirt
supplies
hammer
saw
nails

Components: Topic 35 Wall Chart, Picture Dictionary (pp. 70–71), Cassette, Word and Picture Cards (Topic 35).

See page xiv for techniques and strategies for presenting and practicing words.

New building going up!

1. backhoe
2. dump truck
3. cement mixer
4. crane
5. forklift
6. bulldozer
7. construction worker
8. carpenter
9. plumber
10. electrician
11. pipe
12. wire

Notes

Spread out the word and picture cards for construction site vehicles and machines, so that your students can examine them. Then tell them that they are planning to make a big building. Model questions and answers: *First we need a deep hole. How can we dig a deep hole?* Direct their attention to the construction vehicles, and ask them to choose the one that can dig a hole. Help them identify the backhoe, provide the word for them to repeat, and explain how it works. Repeat this process with each word for a construction site vehicle. Then lay out the cards for the different kinds of construction worker. Again, model questions and answers: *Who drives the backhoe to dig the hole? The construction worker can drive the backhoe.*

Workbook page

Help the children follow the directions for coloring the pictures. Tell them that the words for each picture can be found at the bottom of the page. Point out that the pictures have been grouped in three categories: machines, workers, and materials.

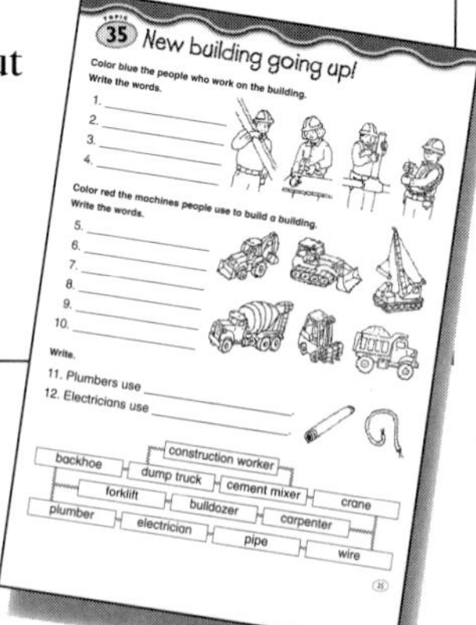

Components: Picture Dictionary (pp. 70–71), Cassette, Story (Topic 35).

See page xviii for techniques and strategies for presenting and practicing stories.

Dig! Dig! Dig!
A backhoe digs a deep hole.
Ting watches. Down, down.
How far down can it go?

Dump trucks take the dirt away.
Cement mixers roll and pour cement.
Cranes swing. Bulldozers push.
Construction workers work hard!

One side of the building is up.
Painters are painting walls.
Carpenters are cutting wood.
A forklift brings supplies.

Plumbers fix pipes for water.
Electricians fix wires for electricity.
Hey, city!
Here comes a new skyscraper!

Story notes

Invite volunteers to describe construction projects they have seen. Tell them that the Dictionary depicts a big construction site, but many of the same machines, materials, and workers can be found (in smaller quantities) at any work site. Ask them if they know anyone who has helped build something.

Ask about the story:
What digs a big hole? Which vehicle takes dirt away? How do they get the heavy beams to the top of the building? Does the cement mixer carry the dirt away? What do the plumbers put in? Who puts in the wires for lights? Where was the Cheng family? What are the workers building?

Ask about your students:
Have you seen a construction site? What did you see? Who was working on the building? Were they using machines? What kinds of vehicles did you see? What kinds of tools were the workers using? Did the workers wear hard hats? Where do you think the trucks take the dirt?

Dialogue

Components: Cassette, Topic 35 Wall Chart, Picture Dictionary (pp. 70–71).

See page xix for techniques and strategies for presenting and practicing dialogues.

Ting:	Mama, how far down can construction workers dig?
Mrs. Cheng:	They can dig pretty deep.
Ting:	Can they dig to China?
Mrs. Cheng:	What? Dig down to China?
Ting:	Our teacher told us that China is on the other side of the earth. Maybe they can dig to China.
Mrs. Cheng:	I don't think that backhoe is strong enough, Ting.
Jo-Jo:	Mama, why do they wear those hats?
Mrs. Cheng:	The construction workers wear those hats so their heads won't get hurt. Something might fall on them. They're called hard hats.
Ting:	What do the plumbers do?
Mrs. Cheng:	They put the pipes together so water can go through them. That's why we have water in our house.
Ting:	Oh. Who fixes the lights?
Mrs. Cheng:	Electricians. See? They're putting the wires in the rooms so electricity can go through them.
Ting:	And turn on the lights!
Mrs. Cheng:	And the TV and the computer ...
Ting:	Oh, yes!
Jo-Jo:	That big dump truck looks just like my dump truck. Can I get a bulldozer, Mama?
Mrs. Cheng:	And I suppose Jackie wants a cement mixer, too.
Jo-Jo:	Yeah, we want to be construction workers, and we're going to build a skyscraper!

Dialogue notes

Encourage the children to invent their own dialogues, using this exchange as a model:

Student A:	What do the plumbers do?
Student B:	They put the pipes together so water can go through them.

Beats!

Components: Cassette, Beats! (Topic 35).

See page xx for techniques and strategies for presenting and practicing Beats!

I see a backhoe
digging a big hole.
I see a cement mixer
roll, roll, roll.

Look, there's a bulldozer
pushing up the ground.
Look, there's a big crane
swinging all around.

Dig, dig!
Bang, smack!
Push, pull!
Whizzz, whack!

What are they building?
Those machines look like my toys.
I don't know what they're building,
but they make a lot of noise!

Beat notes

Have all the children practice the Beat until they are comfortable with the words and phrasing. Explain that you want them to control the volume of their voices, to speak softly when your hands are open flat and low, and to let their voices rise as you raise your hands. Then have them recite the Beat again, conducting the volume with hand motions. At first, it may be easiest if you let them raise their voices only for the third stanza, but as they become more skillful with volume control you can invent new patterns and invite volunteers to take over the role of conductor.

Worksheets

Worksheet 1: New building going up! (p. 69)

Explain that this puzzle page has several parts to it. Tell the children to fill in the missing letters in the labels for each picture. They can use their word cards as reference. Then (for more experienced readers) ask them to follow the trail of the pipes and figure out why the words are in the order they are in (it's alphabetical order).

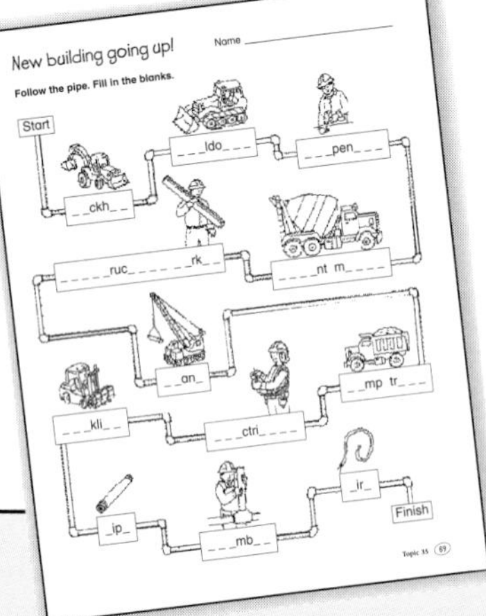

New building going up!   Name ____________

Follow the pipe. Fill in the blanks.

Start

__ckh__

___ldo___

___pen___

_____ruc_____rk__

____nt m____

__an_

___kli__

___ctri____

__mp tr___

_ip_

___mb__

_ir_

Finish

Topic 35 69

Worksheet 2: New building going up! (p. 70)

Help the children read the short verses that describe each vocabulary word. Then tell them to draw a line from the description to the picture matching the word.

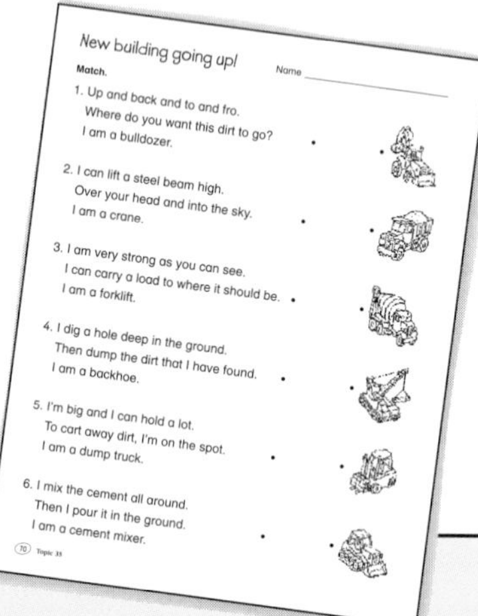

New building going up!   Name ____________

Match.

1. Up and back and to and fro.
   Where do you want this dirt to go?
   I am a bulldozer.
2. I can lift a steel beam high.
   Over your head and into the sky.
   I am a crane.
3. I am very strong as you can see.
   I can carry a load to where it should be.
   I am a forklift.
4. I dig a hole deep in the ground.
   Then dump the dirt that I have found.
   I am a backhoe.
5. I'm big and I can hold a lot.
   To cart away dirt, I'm on the spot.
   I am a dump truck.
6. I mix the cement all around.
   Then I pour it in the ground.
   I am a cement mixer.

70 Topic 35

Activities

- If possible, visit a real construction site. Before going, ask the children to make a list of the things and people they expect to see. After the trip, have them list the things and people they saw. Ask them to compare the two lists. Then encourage them to draw pictures or write or dictate short stories about the site, to be combined in a class book or bulletin board display.

- Play an identification game. Invite a group of children to sit in a circle. Explain that you ask a question and then roll the ball to someone, who answers the question. If that child can't think of the answer, he or she can roll the ball to another person. The child who answers the question then gets to ask the next question. Model a few questions and answers: *What digs a hole? A backhoe digs a hole.* (Alternatively: *What does a backhoe do? A backhoe digs a hole.*) Encourage variety in question-and-answer format, tense, and content.

- Give a small group of children a series of sentence strips that you have prepared in advance. Explain that to add information you can add words to simple sentences. Each series should have a simple sentence (for example: *Tonya drives a backhoe*) and several longer sentences, each with an added word that acts as a modifier *(Tonya drives a big backhoe; Tonya drives a big yellow backhoe; Tiny Tonya drives a big yellow backhoe).* Challenge the children to put the sentences in order, from shortest to longest.

TOPIC 36 Fire!

Content

- Fire and fire-fighting
- Fire-fighting equipment
- Fire safety and emergency procedures

Language

- Asking about and describing a situation: *There's smoke coming out of the windows. Where is the fire? People are on the street looking at the building. The fire trucks are coming down the street.*
- Explaining processes: *The firefighters climb ladders to help people get out of the burning building. The hose sprays water up high to put out the fire. The mask and air tank helps the firefighter breathe.*
- Discussing safety precautions and emergency procedures: *Never play with matches. Check the batteries in your smoke alarms. Call 911 if you see a fire.*
- Describing what people are wearing and the equipment they are using: *The firefighters have coats and hats on. They are wearing big rubber boots. They have radios and air tanks.*

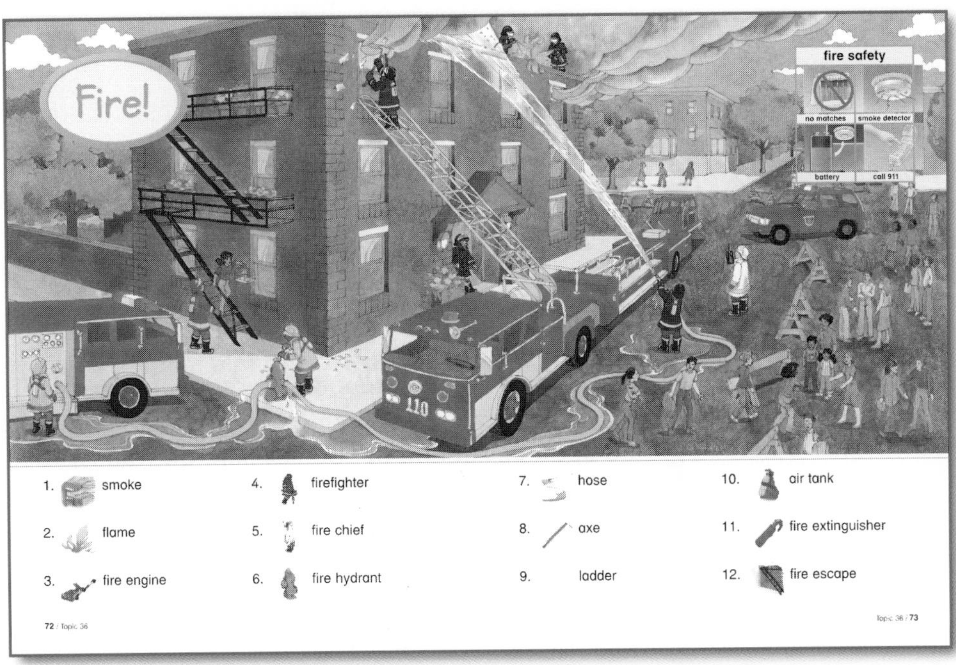

Words

1. smoke
2. flame
3. fire engine
4. firefighter
5. fire chief
6. fire hydrant
7. hose
8. axe
9. ladder
10. air tank
11. fire extinguisher
12. fire escape

Labels

fire safety
no matches
smoke detector
battery
call 911

Additional Words

flashlight
batteries
incinerator
helmet
orders
barricade
shield
pump
emergency

The Lopez family is watching a fire from behind a barricade on a city street. Smoke and flames are billowing up from the roof of a building, and from some of the windows. There are two fire engines, one ladder truck and one pump truck. The fire chief is shouting orders into his radio. Firefighters with helmets, masks, and air tanks on their backs are following those orders. Some firefighters are climbing up the ladder. One is breaking a window with an axe, and others have attached a hose to the fire hydrant and are directing the water at the fire. Others on the roof are using their fire extinguishers against the flames. People have been evacuated from the building and are standing and watching the firefighters. A woman is coming down the fire escape, holding a birdcage with a parakeet inside. An inset shows safety precautions.

Words

Components: Topic 36 Wall Chart, Picture Dictionary (pp. 72–73), Cassette, Word and Picture Cards (Topic 36).

See page xiv for techniques and strategies for presenting and practicing words.

Fire!

1. smoke	6. fire hydrant	10. air tank
2. flame	7. hose	11. fire extin-guisher
3. fire engine	8. axe	12. fire escape
4. firefighter	9. ladder	
5. fire chief		

Labels

fire safety	smoke detector	call 911
no matches	battery	

Notes

On a tall sheet of paper, draw a building on a street. Provide language models as you draw in details; for example, as you draw a cloud of black smoke coming out of a window, you can say: *Uh-oh! There's a problem here! What's coming out of the window?* Then make a sound like a siren, and ask, *What's happening now?* As this goes on, invite a volunteer to tape the appropriate picture card next to the building. Continue asking questions to elicit the other topic words, and have children tape the cards in position. When the picture is complete, review the words one by one, pointing to each item or person. Tape the scene on the wall, and ask volunteers to tell the story in their own words.

Workbook page

Ask children to tell you what is happening in the picture. Then point out the boxed numbers near specific objects and people in the picture. Tell the children to write a word from the bottom of the page in each numbered blank line corresponding to the boxed number in the picture.

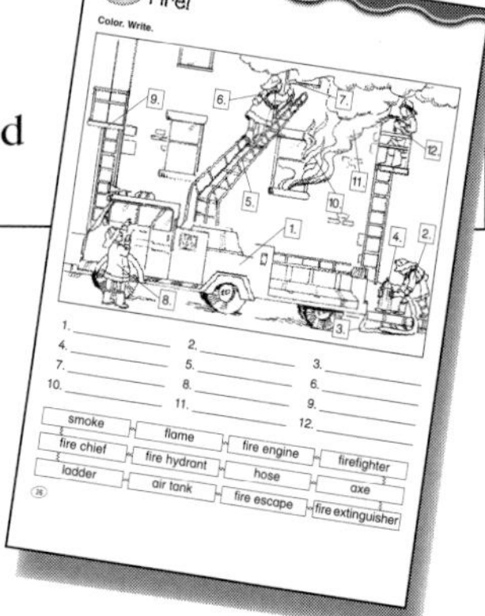

Stories

Components: Picture Dictionary (pp. 72–73), Cassette, Story (Topic 36).

See page xviii for techniques and strategies for presenting and practicing stories.

Fire! Fire! Call 911!
Smoke on the roof! Flames, too!
Here come the fire engines!
Firefighters pull on their helmets
and air tanks, ready to go!

The fire chief shouts orders.
Climb up the ladder! Quick!
Grab an axe! Break that window!
Turn on the fire hydrant!

Water shoots out of the hose!
The firefighters aim their fire
extinguishers at the crackling fire.
The flames get smaller.

Is everyone safe? Yes!
Someone's coming down the
fire escape with a birdcage!
The fire's out!

Story notes

Review fire safety measures and emergency procedures. Model—and then have children practice—making a 911 call to report a fire. Remind the children to tell the operator the address if possible so that the firefighters can find the fire. Be sure they know that they should first get out of the building and then find a safe place to call from.

Ask about the story:
Who is watching the fire? Where is the fire? How do they know there is a fire? Why did the police put up barricades? How did the firefighters get to the fire? What are they wearing? Where do the firefighters get water to put out fires? Why do they need ladders? Why do tall buildings need fire escapes?

Ask about your students:
Have you ever seen a fire? What would you do if you heard a fire alarm? Does your home have a fire escape? Why do you check the batteries in a smoke detector? How does a fire start? What can you do to keep your home safe from fire?

Dialogue

Components: Cassette, Topic 36 Wall Chart, Picture Dictionary (pp. 72–73).

See page xix for techniques and strategies for presenting and practicing dialogues.

Mr. Lopez: Here are the fire engines!
Jasmin: Where's the fire?
Diego: Up on the roof! I see smoke! And flames!
Fire chief: Stand back everyone, please! Stand back!
Mr. Lopez: That's the fire chief!
Jasmin: The firefighters are climbing up the ladder.
Diego: They have air tanks on their backs.
Jasmin: Why?
Mr. Lopez: So they can breathe when they go into the smoke.
Bystander: There's a lot of smoke in there!
Mr. Lopez: Were you inside?
Bystander: Yes, but the smoke alarms went off, so we all got out fast! I came down the fire escape.
Mr. Lopez: That's good! Look! They're putting out the flames with their fire extinguishers!
Diego: This is exciting! I want to be a firefighter!
Jasmin: Me, too!
Diego: Can girls be firefighters, Daddy?
Mr. Lopez: Sure they can.
Jasmin: See, Diego?
Mr. Lopez: Now children, tell me. What should you do if we ever have a fire in our house?
Diego: Call 911 on the telephone!
Mr. Lopez: That's right! And what else should you remember?
Diego and Jasmin: Never play with matches!
Diego: And Dad, you have to check the smoke alarms and put in new batteries!
Fire chief: The fire's out, folks!

Dialogue notes

Listen to the dialogue a few times. Set up a role-playing situation in which the children pretend to be watching firefighters respond to an emergency call. Encourage them to invent their own conversations about a fire.

Beats!

Components: Cassette, Beats! (Topic 36).

See page xx for techniques and strategies for presenting and practicing Beats!

Here comes a fire engine!
Hear the siren blast!
Hurry to the fire!
Get there fast!

Here comes another.
with a ladder and a hose.
Hook it up! Turn it on!
Up the water goes!

In through the windows!
In through the doors!
Firefighters climb up high,
checking all the floors.

Firefighters sure are brave!
"Hooray!" the people shout!
Everyone is happy!
The fire's out!

Beat notes

Practice the Beat with the entire class, and then set up a scene with some chairs and simple props. Separate the children into two groups. Have half the class pretend to be firefighters hurrying to the fire, hooking up the water, holding the hose, climbing through the windows and doors, and so forth, as the other half repeats the Beat. Then switch roles, and let the other group of children act out the Beat.

Worksheets

Worksheet 1: Fire! (p. 71)

Direct the children's attention to the picture. Then help them read the sentences, which provide a narrative for the illustration. Tell them to write in the box next to each sentence the letter from the correct part of the picture.

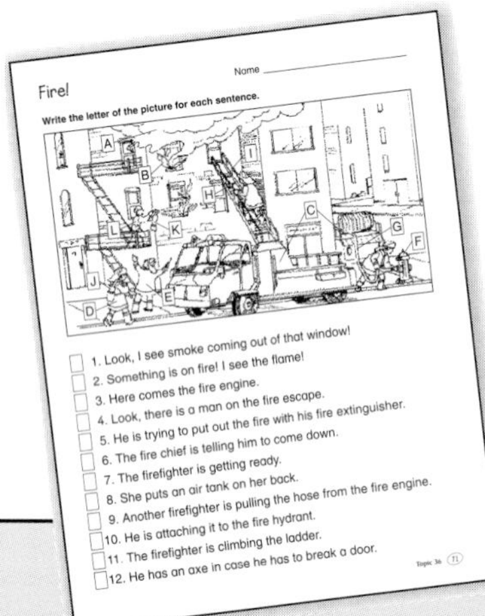

Fire!

Name

Write the letter of the picture for each sentence.

1. Look, I see smoke coming out of that window!
2. Something is on fire! I see the flame!
3. Here comes the fire engine.
4. Look, there is a man on the fire escape.
5. He is trying to put out the fire with his fire extinguisher.
6. The fire chief is telling him to come down.
7. The firefighter is getting ready.
8. She puts an air tank on her back.
9. Another firefighter is pulling the hose from the fire engine.
10. He is attaching it to the fire hydrant.
11. The firefighter is climbing the ladder.
12. He has an axe in case he has to break a door.

Topic 36 71

Worksheet 2: Fire! (p. 72)

Explain to the children that each picture on this page illustrates an emergency situation. Have children write or dictate a short description of how they would respond. You may want to have them complete this worksheet in pairs or small groups.

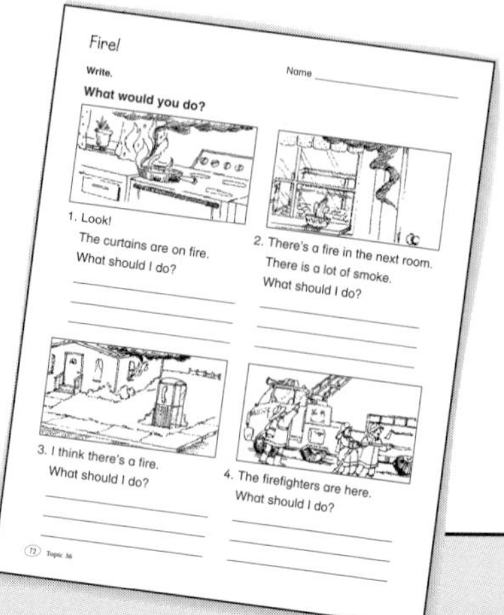

Fire!

Write.

Name

What would you do?

1. Look!
   The curtains are on fire.
   What should I do?
2. There's a fire in the next room.
   There is a lot of smoke.
   What should I do?
3. I think there's a fire.
   What should I do?
4. The firefighters are here.
   What should I do?

72 Topic 36

Activities

- Read *Fire! Fire!* by Gail Gibbon (HarperCollins) to show the children the different kinds of equipment used to help fight fires on land and water.
- Take a class trip to your local fire department or volunteer fire station. Assist the children in asking as many questions as they can about the equipment, the people, and fire safety. Have the children draw pictures and write or dictate short stories, and make a class book or bulletin board display. Write a class thank-you note to your hosts.
- This is a good opportunity to practice for a school fire drill. Explain the procedure in your school and, if possible, schedule a real fire drill (complete with sirens or bells) while you are covering this topic.
- Have the children work in groups to make fire safety posters. Brainstorm ideas for topics: *Use smoke detectors, Keep fire extinguishers handy, Call 911,* and *Stop, Drop, and Roll!* Encourage the children to combine words and pictures to make their point. Display the posters.

TOPIC 37 Big harbor

Content

- Boats
- Harbor sights and sounds
- Time of day

Language

- Describing a scene, including sounds: *The harbor is a very busy place. There are a lot of different boats. The tugboat bell goes clang! clang! The foghorn makes a deep sound: whooo! The sun is setting. Soon it will be dark.*
- Asking and answering questions about objects: *Is that a barge? No that's a tugboat. What is the forklift doing? It's moving a crate to the warehouse.*
- Asking about and describing locations: *Is the warehouse by the water? Yes, the warehouse is on the dock. Is the sailboat next to the lighthouse? No, the sailboat is under the bridge.*

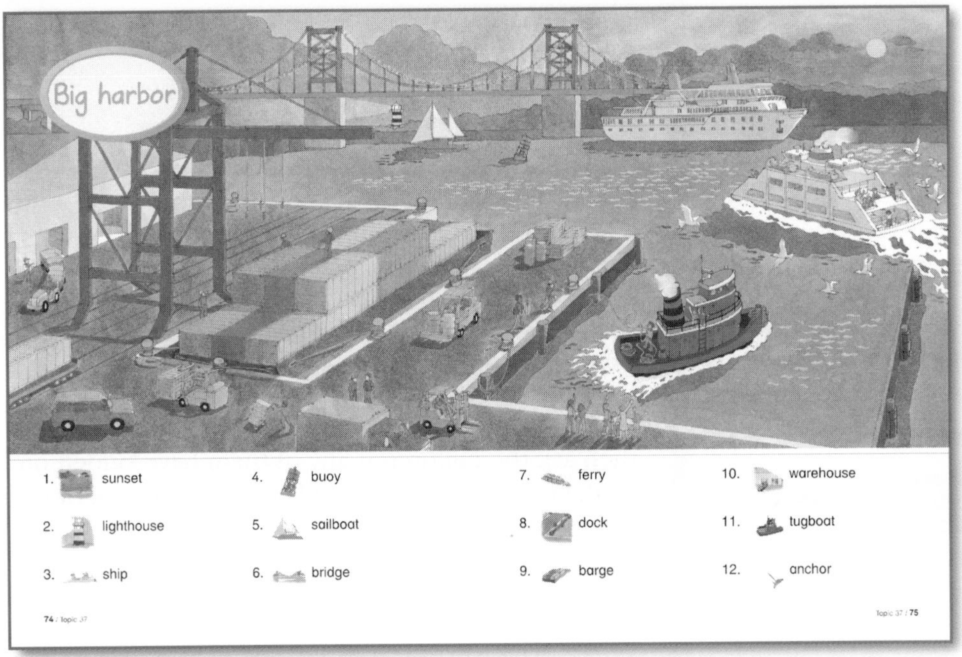

A city harbor at sunset is a busy place. A lighthouse stands at the entrance to the harbor. The fog is rolling in, and the foghorn is blowing. A sailboat is sailing under the bridge, and a big white ship is entering the harbor. It's going to anchor, and its anchor is hanging halfway down the hull. A buoy rocks nearby. Its bell is ringing. A ferry passes, and people wave from the decks. On the dock, dockworkers are busy unloading a barge. They are using forklifts to carry containers to the warehouse. There's a little red tugboat! It's taking Tommy, Jim, and their mother for a ride. Their uncle is the tugboat captain. They are having a wonderful time!

Words

1. sunset
2. lighthouse
3. ship
4. buoy
5. sailboat
6. bridge
7. ferry
8. dock
9. barge
10. warehouse
11. tugboat
12. anchor

Additional Words

fog
foghorn
container
crate
dockworker
bell
rock
sail
wave
unload
forklift

Words

Components: Topic 37 Wall Chart, Picture Dictionary (pp. 74–75), Cassette, Word and Picture Cards (Topic 37).

See page xiv for techniques and strategies for presenting and practicing words.

Big harbor

1. sunset	5. sailboat	9. barge
2. lighthouse	6. bridge	10. warehouse
3. ship	7. ferry	11. tugboat
4. buoy	8. dock	12. anchor

Notes

Point out that some of these words share a syllable. For example, the words *lighthouse* and *warehouse* both contain the word *house*, and *sailboat* and *tugboat* both contain the word *boat*. You may want to ask them what they think a *houseboat* might be, and what a *boathouse* might be.

Workbook page

Tell the children that the fog has covered parts of the words at the top of the page. Their task is to fill in the missing letters in the spaces provided. Point out that all the words are at the bottom of the page. After they have completed the second set of exercises and labeled the pictures, point out that the word *house* is part of both *warehouse* and *lighthouse*, just as the word *boat* is part of both *sailboat* and *tugboat*.

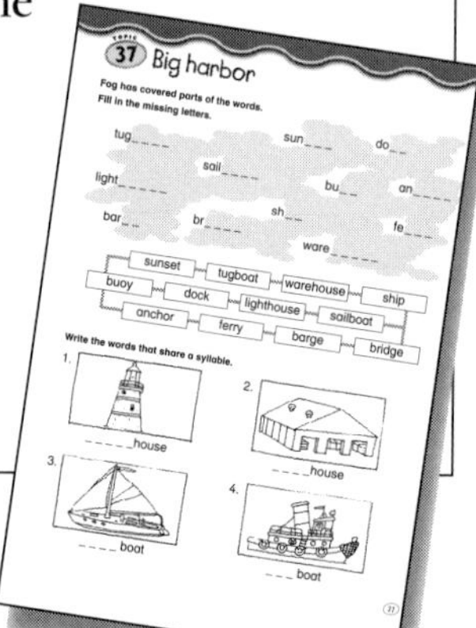

Topic 37 Big harbor

Fog has covered parts of the words. Fill in the missing letters.

tug____ sun___ do__ sail____ light_____ bu__ an____ bar__ br____ sh__ fe___ ware_____

sunset, tugboat, warehouse, ship, buoy, dock, lighthouse, sailboat, anchor, ferry, barge, bridge

Write the words that share a syllable.

1. _____house
2. ____house
3. ____boat
4. ___boat

Stories

Components: Picture Dictionary (pp. 74–75), Cassette, Story (Topic 37).

See page xviii for techniques and strategies for presenting and practicing stories.

It's almost sunset.
The lighthouse stands guard,
and the foghorn is blowing.
Who-o-o! Who-o-o!

A big white ship enters the harbor.
It's ready to drop its anchor.
The buoy rocks. Clang! Clang!
A sailboat is sailing under the bridge.
There goes a ferry! Wave, everyone!

Dockworkers rush up and down
the noisy dock, unloading a big
barge. Forklifts pick up containers
and carry them to the warehouse.

A little red tugboat just passed by.
Toot! Toot!
Tommy and Jim are on the tugboat!
They're going for a ride!

Story notes

Describe an experience you have had in a boat, and then ask the children if any of them have ridden on a boat. Encourage them to talk about their experiences.

Ask about the story:

Who was riding on the tugboat? What can they see at the entrance of the harbor? Where was the tugboat going? Why do they blow the foghorn? Where is the lighthouse? Which of the boats in the picture do you think would go fast? Which boat would be the noisiest when it is moving? What kind of boat would hold the most people?

Ask about your students:

Who has seen a harbor? Did you ever ride on a boat? What kind of boat was it? What was it like? How long was the boat trip? Who has seen a lighthouse? Where?

Dialogue

Components: Cassette, Topic 37 Wall Chart, Picture Dictionary (pp. 74–75).

See page xix for techniques and strategies for presenting and practicing dialogues.

Tommy:	I'm glad you're the captain of this tugboat, Uncle Pete.
Uncle:	So am I, Tommy! And it's fun to take you for a ride.
Jim:	There's the lighthouse at the entrance to the harbor!
Uncle:	Yep, there it is.
Jim:	Is that a foghorn, Uncle Pete?
Uncle:	Yes, the fog is coming in.
Tommy:	Is that why it's blowing?
Uncle:	Yes, Tommy. It's telling ships that the harbor is here. The ships can't see when it's foggy.
Jim:	What's that bell?
Uncle:	That's a buoy. There are rocks there.
Tommy:	Why is the bell ringing?
Uncle:	The rocks are dangerous. The bell is warning ships to stay away.
Tommy:	What's that big white ship doing?
Uncle:	It's going to anchor in the harbor. See? They're letting down the anchor.
Jim:	Uncle Pete, can this tugboat push a big barge like the one at the dock?
Uncle:	Sure it can. Tugboats are strong.
Jim:	Is it fun to work on a tugboat, Uncle Pete?
Uncle:	It's hard work, Jim, but it's a lot of fun.
Tommy:	Let's be tugboat captains, Jim!
Jim:	That's OK with me!

Dialogue notes

Encourage the children to pretend they are on the tugboat with Uncle Pete, and prompt them to invent their own dialogues based on the model of questions and answers about the sights of the harbor. You may encourage them to practice this exchange: *Is it fun to work on a tugboat? It's hard work, but it's a lot of fun.* Have them vary the kind of work mentioned (for example: *Is it fun to work in a warehouse?*). Remind the children that they can respond either positively or negatively.

Beats!

Components: Cassette, Beats! (Topic 37).

See page xx for techniques and strategies for presenting and practicing Beats!

Toot! Toot! Toot!
Here comes a tugboat!
  Push that big ship
  into the docks!

Clang! Clang!
Listen to the bell buoy!
  Danger! Danger!
  Stay off the rocks!

There goes a tanker
leaving the harbor.
  There goes a big barge
  out of the bay.

Hoo-oo! Hoo-oo!
  Listen to the foghorn!
  Boats go safely
  on your way!

Beat notes

Put the children into two groups to practice the Beat as written. Once the children are comfortable with the words and phrases, suggest adding sound effects. You can offer them kazoos or hollow cardboard tubes to amplify the *toot! toot!* sounds in the first stanza and the *hoo-oo! hoo-oo!* sound of the foghorns in the last stanza. They can accompany the *clang! clang!* of the bell buoy with cowbells or by banging metal lids together. Have them recite the last three lines in unison.

Worksheets

Worksheet 1: Big harbor (p. 73)

Encourage the children to use their picture cards to identify the different kinds of boats shown on the page. Have them write or dictate anything they wish about the boats. Depending on the child's level of language development, you might prompt him or her to describe the boat, using the words for colors or for comparing size. Or you may focus on what the boats do: carry passengers on long trips, make short trips across the harbor, and so on.

Big harbor

Name

Name each kind of boat and write something about it.

1.

2.

3.

4.

5.

ferry tugboat ship barge sailboat

Topic 37 73

Worksheet 2: Big harbor (p. 74)

Direct the children's attention to the picture on the page. Tell them they will be choosing between two possible endings of a sentence that answers a question. You can suggest that they read the question and the response with both endings before deciding which words to circle as the correct ending, according to the picture on the page.

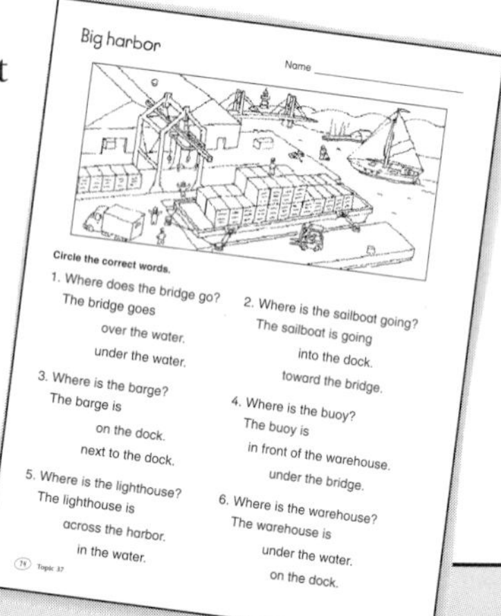

Big harbor

Name

Circle the correct words.

1. Where does the bridge go?
The bridge goes
over the water.
under the water.

2. Where is the sailboat going?
The sailboat is going
into the dock.
toward the bridge.

3. Where is the barge?
The barge is
on the dock.
next to the dock.

4. Where is the buoy?
The buoy is
in front of the warehouse.
under the bridge.

5. Where is the lighthouse?
The lighthouse is
across the harbor.
in the water.

6. Where is the warehouse?
The warehouse is
under the water.
on the dock.

74 Topic 37

Activities

- Teach the song "Row, Row, Row Your Boat":

  Row, row, row your boat
  gently down the stream,
  merrily, merrily, merrily,
  life is but a dream.

  The children may like to act it out, rowing an imaginary boat as they sing. They can also try singing it as a round.

- Provide materials for each child to make a simple model boat. Then help the children draw a harbor on a large piece of craft paper, including a bridge, buoys, rocks, docks, warehouses, a lighthouse, and beaches. Encourage them to take turns giving each other directions to move their boats around the harbor. This activity provides an opportunity to introduce or practice direction words *(left, right, forward, backward, straight ahead).*

- Play Harbor Tag (a version of Red Light Green Light). As in regular tag, one person is "it"; he or she is designated to be the *lighthouse.* "It" stands at one end of the playing area, in front of the base, which is designated the *dock.* The rest of the children are "boats"; they line up at the other end of the playing area. The "boats" creep forward, chanting: *Lighthouse, shine on the cold gray sea / What do you see, will you please tell me?* To which the lighthouse responds: *I see a _____!* If he or she does not name a boat, the children freeze, and anyone caught moving is sent back to the starting line. If the lighthouse calls out any of the names for boats, they race for the dock. If a "boat" is tagged, he or she becomes the new lighthouse.

- Make up an add-on story. With a harbor picture before the class, begin the story by saying something like *I went down to the harbor and I saw a tugboat.* Prompt the child nearest you to repeat your sentence and add on *(I went down to the harbor and I saw a tugboat and a dock).* Once everyone has had a chance to add something, repeat the entire string.

TOPIC

38 Carnival!

Content

- Carnival performers
- Carnival activities

Language

- Identifying carnival performers: *The clowns have funny faces! I saw an acrobat swing from a trapeze!*
- Describing carnival activities: *The Ferris wheel goes around slowly. The man sold me a ticket for the carousel.*
- Talking about tastes, aromas, sounds, and sights: *This cotton candy tastes very sweet! I heard a man announce a puppet show. I see fireworks. They're bright and loud! I smell popcorn!*
- Logical sequencing: *Diego and Grandpa bought a ticket before they went on the Ferris wheel. The carnival is over when the fireworks start.*

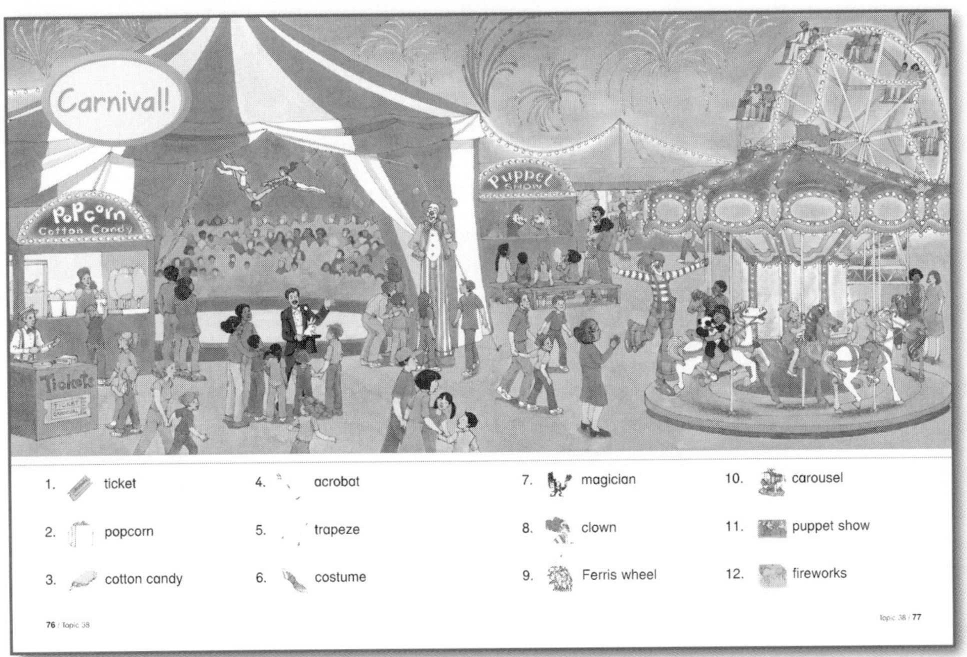

The whole Lopez family has gone to the carnival. There is a show going on inside the tent. Mr. and Mrs. Lopez are watching acrobats in sparkling costumes swinging from trapezes and twirling in the air. Jasmin is going round and round on the carousel outside, hugging a big stuffed panda she has won. She looks very proud of herself. Grandma is waving to her. Grandpa is high up in the Ferris wheel with Diego, looking down on everyone. There is a magician doing tricks, and red-nosed clowns with baggy pants are running around. One clown gets on the carousel with Jasmin. Vanessa, her mother and father, and Baby Rosa are watching the puppet show. Vanessa laughs and gets sticky pink cotton candy all over her clothes. The fireworks have begun! What a carnival!

Words

1. ticket
2. popcorn
3. cotton candy
4. acrobat
5. trapeze
6. costume
7. magician
8. clown
9. Ferris wheel
10. carousel
11. puppet show
12. fireworks

Additional Words

tent
show
tricks
twirl
waving
sparkle
loud
sweet

Words

Components: Topic 38 Wall Chart, Picture Dictionary (pp. 76–77), Cassette, Word and Picture Cards (Topic 38).

See page xiv for techniques and strategies for presenting and practicing words.

Carnival!

1. ticket
2. popcorn
3. cotton candy
4. acrobat
5. trapeze
6. costume
7. magician
8. clown
9. Ferris wheel
10. carousel
11. puppet show
12. fireworks

Notes

Draw an eye, an ear, a nose, and a mouth each on large pieces of paper, and lay them on a table or the floor where the children can reach them. Explain that the eye suggests seeing, the ear hearing, the nose smelling, and the mouth tasting. Then invite volunteers to choose one of the vocabulary words and decide in which of these categories to place it (*cotton candy,* for instance, can be tasted). Have them show their classmates by placing the word card on the "mouth" paper, or saying a sentence such as *At the carnival I can taste cotton candy.* Many of the words fit into more than one category (for example, *At the carnival I saw and heard a puppet show*). Encourage the children to help each other decide which categories each item can belong to.

Workbook page

Each picture contains clues for ways to finish its sentence. The children do not have to write all the words. Tell them to write or dictate the things about a carnival that are personal favorites (whether they've actually been to one or simply read about it) on the lines in number five. Tell them that all the topic words can be found at the bottom of the page.

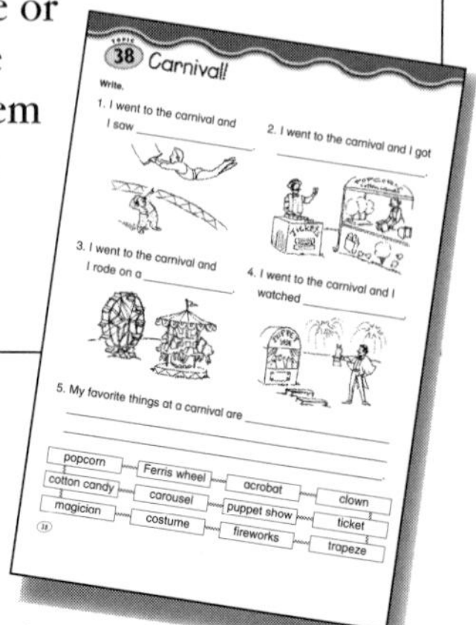

TOPIC 38 Carnival!

Write.

1. I went to the carnival and I saw
2. I went to the carnival and I got
3. I went to the carnival and I rode on a
4. I went to the carnival and I watched
5. My favorite things at a carnival are

popcorn | Ferris wheel | acrobat | clown | cotton candy | carousel | puppet show | ticket | magician | costume | fireworks | trapeze

Stories

Components: Picture Dictionary (pp. 76–77), Cassette, Story (Topic 38).

See page xviii for techniques and strategies for presenting and practicing stories.

Come get your tickets and popcorn!
Inside the tent, acrobats
twirl in the air, ooooh!
And swing from trapezes, aaaah!
Their costumes sparkle.

Outside, a magician does tricks,
and clowns with big red noses run
around in baggy pants. Ha! Ha!
Look! There's Diego high up
in the Ferris wheel!

Jasmin is riding round and round
on the carousel, hugging a big
stuffed panda. Grandma waves.
Vanessa watches the puppet show.
She has pink cotton candy! Sticky!

Whiz! Crack! Bang! What's that?
It's fireworks! Red! Green! Gold!
Shooting way up into the sky.
This carnival is the best!

Story notes

Ask the children to share whatever experiences they have had at a carnival, street festival, or other activity where rides were a feature. Encourage them to describe the things they heard, saw, smelled, and tasted. Ask if any of them have seen a magic show, a puppet show, or a trapeze act.

Ask about the story:
What is Jasmin riding? Who is watching her ride? Where is Diego? How did Diego get so high up? How many clowns do you see? What color is the clown's nose? What are the acrobats wearing? What does Vanessa eat? What colors were the fireworks?

Ask about your students:
Do you like to eat popcorn? Did you ever try cotton candy? What sounds did you hear at the carnival? Did you go on a ride? Do you like fast rides? What kind of show did you see? Were there clowns where you were?

Dialogue

Components: Cassette, Topic 38 Wall Chart, Picture Dictionary (pp. 76–77).

See page xix for techniques and strategies for presenting and practicing dialogues.

Diego:	This Ferris wheel is great, Grandpa. Gosh! We can look down and see the whole carnival.
Grandpa:	Yup, we can see the tent and the carousel. I think I can even see Grandma. Maybe Jasmin is on the carousel.
Jasmin:	Watch me, Grandma!
Grandma:	I see you, honey. Be careful! Hang on tight!
Jasmin:	I will. Here comes a clown, Grandma! He's gonna ride the carousel, too!
Grandma:	Yes, I see. Hang on!
Vanessa:	I love cotton candy! It's sticky!
Vanessa's mother:	Don't get it on your clothes!
Vanessa:	I won't. The puppets are funny. Can we get popcorn?
Vanessa's mother:	Maybe. Don't you want to see the acrobats?
Vanessa:	What's that?
Vanessa's father:	Look up, Vanessa!
Vanessa:	Ooooh! What is it?
Vanessa's father:	It's fireworks!
Everyone:	Fireworks! Fireworks! O-o-o-o! Ah-h-h-h! Beautiful! WOW!

Dialogue notes

Encourage the children to invent their own dialogues based on asking and answering questions about the Lopez family's evening at the carnival. Prompt them to ask *where, what,* and *who* questions.

Beats!

Components: Cassette, Beats! (Topic 38).

See page xx for techniques and strategies for presenting and practicing Beats!

Here! Get your tickets!
Get your popcorn and candy!
Shows! Games! Lots to do!
Have your tickets handy!

Can I go on the carousel?
I like to go round and round.
Can I go on the Ferris wheel?
Be sure you come back down!

I want to see the acrobats,
swinging on the trapeze.
I want to see the magician
doing tricks. Oh, please!

Let's watch the puppet show!
The clowns are coming now!
The fireworks are starting!
Pow!
Pow!
Pow!

Beat notes

Discuss the various rides and entertainment events at carnivals, and help the children act out the different things you can see and do at a carnival.

Worksheets

Worksheet 1: Carnival! (p. 75)

Review the concept of sequencing with the children. You may want to offer a simple example, acting out your words as you speak: *First I pick up the chalk. The next thing I do is write a word on the blackboard, and the last thing I do is erase the word.* Have the children write or dictate their own version of a visit to a carnival.

Carnival!

Name ______

Write. Draw.

What will you do at the carnival?

1. The first thing I will do at the carnival is ______.
2. The next thing I will do at the carnival is ______.
3. The last thing I will do at the carnival is ______.
4. When I am at the carnival I will not ______.

Topic 38 75

Worksheet 2: Carnival! (p. 76)

Children use the boxed words to label the pictures. You may want to encourage those children with fewer verbal skills to draw a picture to answer the cues.

Carnival!

Name ______

Label the pictures.

carousel, popcorn, puppet show, fireworks, clown, ticket, cotton candy, Ferris wheel

Write or draw.

What can you find at a carnival?

I can see ______.
I can hear ______.
I can smell ______.
I can taste ______.

76 Topic 38

Activities

- Make a puppet theater. The children can use the theater with puppets you provide as well as others they make themselves. Encourage them to use the theater for both role-playing games and small performances for friends.

- Make clown dolls out of recycled materials. Help the children decorate cardboard tubes. String the tubes together to make floppy legs and arms, and attach them to a plastic jug or cardboard box. Attach a balloon head on which they have drawn a face. Use yarn or paper strips for hair and other decorative features.

- Make a Ferris wheel. Cut a large circle of stiff paper and center it on a second, larger sheet lying on the floor. Attach it with a pin in the center, so that the wheel on top can be turned. Divide the circle into twelve wedges, continuing the line onto the paper beneath so that it too has twelve corresponding segments. Write each topic word in a wedge of the circle. Prompt the children to tell you a word that describes each of the topic words (for example, ask, *What does the clown look like?*). Write their answers in the outer segment that corresponds with clown *(funny, silly)*. When all the words have been described, attach the wheel to the wall. Turn the wheel to scramble the descriptions. Then ask, for instance, *Is the clown sweet and sticky?* Keep asking, moving the wheel wedge-by-wedge back into place, until the children agree that the descriptive words match the topic word.

- Talk with the children about the sounds they may hear at a carnival. Make a list of things, such as the clown honking a horn, the carousel playing music, the cotton candy seller yelling "Cotton candy!", the bang of the fireworks, the applause of the audience. Have children in pairs or small groups choose a sound to make, and invent with them a series of simple hand signs that indicate when a sound should begin and end, and its volume level. Then "conduct" the sounds of the carnival. Invite children to take turns being the conductor.

Great restaurant!

Content

- Restaurant etiquette
- Restaurant work and workers
- Restaurant procedures

Language

- Identifying people by their activities: *The chef is stirring the food in the pot. The cook is chopping vegetables. The waiter is pouring the tea.*
- Making and accepting suggestions: *The egg rolls here are very good. You might like the soup. Thank you, I'll try it.*
- Expressing likes and dislikes: *I like your kitchen, Mr. Cheng. I like to eat with chopsticks. I don't like tea. My favorite thing is the noodles.*
- Dining-out manners: *Give me a menu, please. May I have a napkin? The waiter will serve the food.*

Words

1. tablecloth
2. napkin
3. apron
4. pots
5. chef
6. menu
7. chopsticks
8. waiter

Verbs

9. pour
10. stir
11. chop
12. serve

Additional Words

pans
wok
tea
teapot
paddle
cleaver
carving knife
hostess
order
noodles

What fun to be at the Chengs' restaurant and see the busy kitchen at dinnertime! Mr. and Mrs. Jackson, Mariah, and Samantha sit in the dining room at the table with the pretty white tablecloth and napkins. Mrs. Cheng gives them menus and chopsticks and then pours tea. Ting shows Marcus and Zoe the kitchen. Mr. Cheng and his two cooks are busy preparing the food. One of them stirs soup with a paddle in a huge pot. Mr. Cheng, the chef, chops vegetables with a cleaver. He wears a big white chef's hat. The cooks wear white aprons. A waiter in the dining room is serving the Jacksons' food. It all smells delicious!

Words

Components: Topic 39 Wall Chart, Picture Dictionary (pp. 78–79), Cassette, Word and Picture Cards (Topic 39).

See page xiv for techniques and strategies for presenting and practicing words.

Great restaurant!

1. tablecloth	4. pots	7. chopsticks
2. napkin	5. chef	8. waiter
3. apron	6. menu	

Verbs

9. pour	11. chop
10. stir	12. serve

Notes

Introduce the verbs by pantomiming each action: *chop, stir, pour, serve.* Let the children take turns role-playing customers, waiters, chefs, and cashiers as they repeat the vocabulary, handle the objects, do the actions, and become comfortable with the words.

Workbook page

Explain to the children that some of the pictures on this page are labeled wrong. They should look at the picture and then the word. If the word is the correct label for the picture, they can leave it alone; but if it is the wrong word, they should cross it out and write the correct word in the space provided. Tell them that the words at the bottom of the page are wrong, too. The first syllable was written last and the last syllable first; they need to be unscrambled.

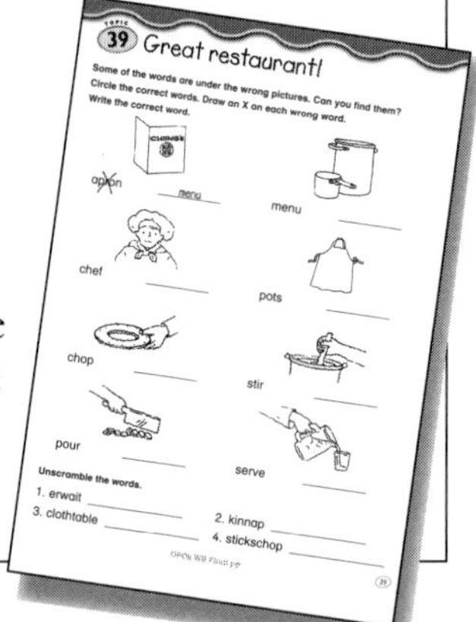
TOPIC 39 Great restaurant!

Some of the words are under the wrong pictures. Can you find them? Circle the correct words. Draw an X on each wrong word. Write the correct word.

apron menu

menu

chef

pots

chop

stir

pour

serve

Unscramble the words.

1. erwait

2. kinnap

3. clothtable

4. stickschop

Stories

Components: Picture Dictionary (pp. 78–79), Cassette, Story (Topic 39).

See page xviii for techniques and strategies for presenting and practicing stories.

Everyone loves the Chengs' restaurant. Crisp white tablecloths, napkins, little cups, and teapots. The tables look so pretty.

The Jacksons are here! Ting shows Zoe the big kitchen. Busy cooks in white aprons, and so many pots and pans!

A cook stirs rice in a huge pot. A chef with a big hat chops vegetables. Wow! He chops fast! It's Mr. Cheng!

Mrs. Cheng gives out menus and chopsticks, and pours tea. Here comes the waiter to serve the food! Come sit down! It smells delicious!

Story notes

Invite volunteers to describe occasions when they have eaten in a restaurant. If possible, have them say what kind of restaurant it was, and make a list to which everyone can add different kinds of restaurants.

Ask about the story:
Why did the tables look pretty? Who poured the tea? What did Mrs. Cheng give everyone? What did the cooks wear? What did the cook stir? How do you think Ting feels about her family's restaurant? How do you think Zoe and Marcus felt going into the kitchen?

Ask about your students:
What do you do when you come into a restaurant? Who tells you where to sit? How do you know what there is to eat at the restaurant? How do you know how much it costs? What do you say to the waiter? What happens after you give your order? Who serves the food?

Dialogue

 **Components:** Cassette, Topic 39 Wall Chart, Picture Dictionary (pp. 78–79).

See page xix for techniques and strategies for presenting and practicing dialogues.

Ting:	This is the kitchen. How do you like it?
Zoe:	Wow! Everything is so huge! Look at those pots and pans and those knives!
Marcus:	Is that man with the big hat the chef?
Ting:	Yes! That's my father, Marcus. Don't you recognize him?
Mr. Cheng:	Hello, Marcus and Zoe! Welcome!
Marcus:	Hello, Mr. Cheng.
Zoe:	I like your kitchen.
Mr. Cheng:	Thank you.
Zoe:	How can you chop vegetables so fast? You'll cut yourself.
Ting:	No he won't. He knows how to chop.
Zoe:	Look at that pot! I've never seen a pot that big! What's in it?
Ting:	Rice.
Zoe:	It's an awful lot of rice!
Marcus:	What's the big round pan with the handles, Ting?
Ting:	It's a wok. We'd better go back inside now. Your food's ready. The waiter is serving it.
Marcus:	OK. Thanks, Ting.
Zoe:	I love your restaurant.
Ting:	I'm glad you came!
Marcus and Zoe:	So are we!

Dialogue notes

Listen to the dialogue a few times and then ask the children to take on roles in a make-believe restaurant. Some children can be kitchen workers, some can be servers, and some can be customers. Prompt them to invent their own dialogues using the vocabulary words, in the context of either working in or visiting a restaurant.

Beats!

 **Components:** Cassette, Beats! (Topic 39).

See page xx for techniques and strategies for presenting and practicing Beats!

Pots and pans go "clang!" in the kitchen.
　Big knives go chop, chop!

Bubble, bubble goes the soup
　in a big enormous pot.

People in the dining room, hungry, hungry!
　What's on the menu today?

The food looks great!
Put your napkin in your lap.
　Here comes the waiter with the tray!

Beat notes

Encourage the children to pantomime the actions as they repeat the Beat. Play pots, pans, and silverware will add to the fun of acting out the Beat.

Worksheets

Worksheet 1: Great restaurant! (p. 77)

Tell the children that they are going to invent their own restaurants. Then review the questions and have them write or dictate their responses. Tell them that they can add to the pictures to illustrate their descriptions.

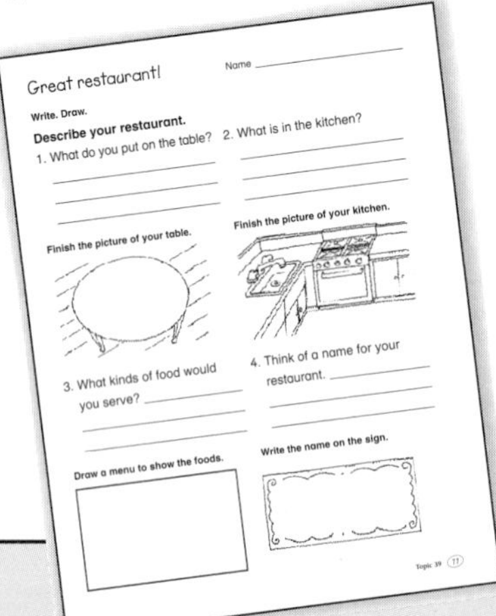

Great restaurant! Name ____

Write. Draw.

Describe your restaurant.

1. What do you put on the table?
2. What is in the kitchen?

Finish the picture of your table.

Finish the picture of your kitchen.

3. What kinds of food would you serve?
4. Think of a name for your restaurant.

Draw a menu to show the foods.

Write the name on the sign.

Topic 39 77

Worksheet 2: Great restaurant! (p. 78)

Explain that the children must fill in the missing words to describe what's happening at the restaurant. The pictures can be used as clues. Point out that all the missing words can be found at the bottom of the page.

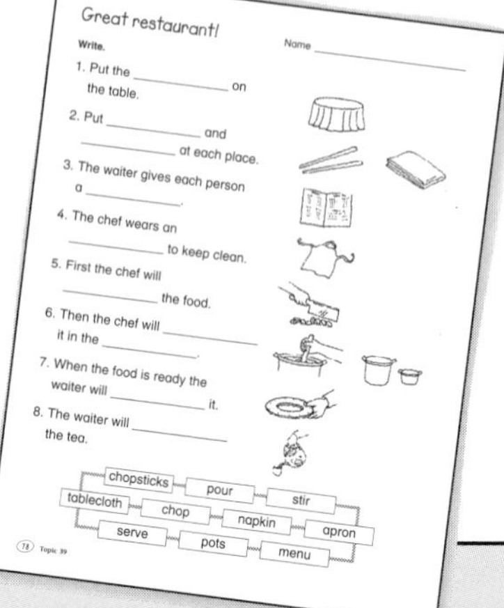

Great restaurant! Name ____

Write.

1. Put the ____ on the table.
2. Put ____ and ____ at each place.
3. The waiter gives each person a ____.
4. The chef wears an ____ to keep clean.
5. First the chef will ____ the food.
6. Then the chef will ____ it in the ____.
7. When the food is ready the waiter will ____ it.
8. The waiter will ____ the tea.

chopsticks pour stir tablecloth chop napkin apron serve pots menu

78 Topic 39

Activities

- Set up a restaurant in a corner of the classroom. There, the children can role-play to reinforce the vocabulary. Help them make a list of work done in a restaurant: cleaning the tables, taking money and making change, welcoming customers, washing the dishes, buying food to cook. You can extend this activity and explore many other topics: nutrition, good manners, money and transactions, food vocabulary, table setting, and cooking.

- Practice restaurant math. Have children take turns playing waiter and customer, setting prices, accepting payment, and giving change. If possible, bring in menus from a variety of restaurants, and have children choose meals and figure out the cost of each meal. Give each child some play money to spend. For example, say: *You have three dollars. What can you buy? How much change will you get?*

- Design menus. Each menu should include a variety of choices, descriptions of each dish, and a price. You can extend the basic activity by challenging the children to create theme menus: a menu for a restaurant for monsters, for example, that includes such things as slug soup and millipede sandwiches. Encourage the children to use their imaginations.

- Make a bulletin board display of photographs that show restaurants in different countries: a Chinese restaurant, a French sidewalk cafe, a Japanese restaurant with people seated on the floor, and so on. Encourage the children to talk about what they see, to find similarities and differences, and to share what they know about restaurants in other countries.

Theme 6: Vacation

Topic 40	Let's see the USA!	**Topic 44**	Working on the farm
Topic 41	Beach day	**Topic 45**	Camping out
Topic 42	We found a tide pool!	**Topic 46**	Bugs!
Topic 43	What's under the sea?	**Topic 47**	Ranch in the desert

Theme Bibliography

Ali, Child of the Desert

written by Jonathan London; illustrated by Ted Lewin.
Lothrop Lee & Shepherd, 1997. ISBN 0688125603

This is one of only a handful of current children's books that deal with Arab culture. While traveling across the Sahara to sell their herd of camels at the Moroccan market, Ali and his father are separated during a sandstorm. This book tells of Ali's adventure alone in the desert waiting for his father's return. Ali is rewarded for his persistence and hope when his father finds him the next day. This is a mature story and may require some teacher direction. A short glossary of important Arabic words and greetings is provided at the end of the book. The story can be read aloud or retold in the teacher's own words to ensure understanding.

Clams All Year

written and illustrated by Maryann Cocca-Leffler.
Bantam Doubleday Dell Books for Young Readers, 1998. ISBN 0440414474

Vivid illustrations of the author's childhood experiences show a typical vacation digging clams at the shore. The story follows the times of day and the days of the week, and ends with the holidays when the family enjoyed their clams. The story's structure provides additional vocabulary for integrated language acquisition. Use of the simple present and past tenses, plus a limited number of words per pages, make this an excellent book to read aloud. Follow up by using this as a story-starter for children to talk about their own summer vacations or visits with relatives.

The Day the Sheep Showed Up

written and illustrated by David M. McPhail.
Scholastic Inc., 1998. ISBN 0590849107

The day the sheep shows up is a confusing one for the rest of the barnyard animals. "What is this strange animal?" they ask. Finally the sheep introduces himself. The pictures and sounds of barnyard animals are well-suited for reading along. The text models dialogue that children can use in their own language as they talk about the story and act it out.

Have You Seen Bugs?

written by Joanne Oppenheim;
illustrated by Ron Broda.
Scholastic Inc., 1999. ISBN 0590059637

This book celebrates the natural world of insects in rhyme and pictures: "Bugs with stripes/or speckle/or spots,/shiny like metal/or covered with dots." The repeated word patterns and the rhymes are especially good for intermediate students. The book also works as a science connection: ESL students can read along in small groups with their mainstream classmates. The kinesthetic language is appropriate for TPR activities. The illustrations provide a great reference for students creating their own bug books.

I'm In Charge of Celebrations

written by Byrd Baylor; illustrated by Peter Parnall.
Simon & Schuster Children's Books, 1996.
ISBN 0689806205

"Celebrations" are frequently an important part of first- and second-grade learning. In this book the author celebrates the sand, sun, rocks, and plants of the desert. For ESL students this is an excellent read-along story to accompany the study of desert places. You may wish to create breaks in the reading, so students acquiring English can comment on the pictures and use TPR to act out what is going on. The reading can be further enhanced by creating a word bank of desert words appearing in the book.

Into the Sea

written by Brenda Z. Guiberson; illustrated by Alix Berenzy. Henry Holt & Co., 1996. ISBN 0805022635

This dramatic and powerful story of nature follows the periodic journey of a sea turtle, from the moment it crawls out of its egg to its full maturity. The story is told in the present tense. Each illustration tells what the turtle sees, hears, and smells. The straightforward text and exquisite illustrations reinforce vocabulary from Topics 41–43. The text for each picture can be read separately, acted out, and drawn by the students to further comprehension.

Let's Go Rock Collecting

written by Roma Gans; illustrated by Holly Keller. HarperCollins Children's Books, 1997. ISBN 0064451704

English-language learners are sure to enjoy this very basic introduction to geology. The text presents rock collecting as an interesting exploration of many types of rocks, showing different colors, structures, and origins. For the classroom, the diagrams and photographs provide a clear presentation of what kinds of rocks children may find on vacation, at home, in their own schoolyard, or anywhere.

Little Rabbit and the Sea

written and illustrated by Gavin Bishop. North-South Books, 1997. ISBN 1558588094

Little Rabbit desperately wants to see the sea. He persistently questions all of his acquaintances about the sea, and gets many different answers. Finally, a friendly seagull brings the sea to him inside a seashell. Each page has only one or two sentences, accompanied by an illustration that helps explain to Little Rabbit what the sea is like. The use of simile ("The sea is like...") is a useful addition to children's language. Children can enjoy this simple sweet story while learning about the sea.

The Milk Makers

written and illustrated by Gail Gibbons. Simon & Schuster Children's Books, 1996. ISBN 0689711166

This book tours the milk-making process from the milking machines that extract the cow's milk to the process of pasteurization, and ends with its packaging in cartons. It is an excellent supplement to Topic 44. You may want to use this for a science connection, as well. The amount of reading can be varied from page to page depending on the level of students. The adverbs of time featured in the narrative are also helpful for language learning.

On the Go

written by Ann Morris; photographs by Ken Heyman. William Morrow & Co., 1994. ISBN 0688136370

On the Go introduces the many forms of transportation used by people all around the globe. Ann Morris describes the ways people travel across land, over water, and through the air. Ken Heyman's photographs are taken from locations around the world. A picture index at the back of the book identifies the location of each photo and a world map places them in a geographical context. This book's rhyming structure and clear photography can be easily read aloud and followed by independent or paired reading.

The Town Mouse & the Country Mouse

an Aesop Fable adapted and illustrated by Janet Stevens. Holiday House, 1989. ISBN 0823407330

This is an adaptation of a classic Aesop fable about the city mouse visiting her country cousin and vice versa. For one, the country is too quiet. For the other, the city is too hectic. At the end, the country mouse returns to the farm and concludes, "It's better to have beans and bacon in peace than cakes and pies in fear." This book provides an excellent opportunity to use comparisons and contrasts to show the difference between communities and lifestyles. You can set up a Venn diagram at the beginning of this reading to chart the comparisons and contrasts you find as students follow the text.

The Water's Journey

written and illustrated by Eleanor Schmid. North-South Books, 1994. ISBN 1558580131

This illustrated account of the water cycle explains the water's journey from mountain snow all the way to the ocean. Each full-page illustration can be a point of entry to discuss aspects of Topics 41, 42, and 43. The simple text for each illustration can be broken down into questions for the class such as "What is happening in the picture?" and "Where is this happening?"

Let's see the USA!

Content

- Map of the United States
- Environmental regions
- Map symbols

Language

- Recognizing and interpreting features of a map: *The big line shows the Mississippi River. The blue areas are big lakes.*
- Asking and answering questions about environments of the United States: *Where is it hot most of the time? This area is desert. It is hot and dry there.*
- Asking and answering questions about geographical location: *Where is the desert? Is the lake in the forest area? The wetlands are by the coast.*
- Talking about destinations: *Where will she go on her vacation? Alison may go to the desert. Will you go to the desert? No, I will go to the wetlands.*
- Describing wants of others: *Diego would like to go to the Northwest. Ting wants to go to the beach.*

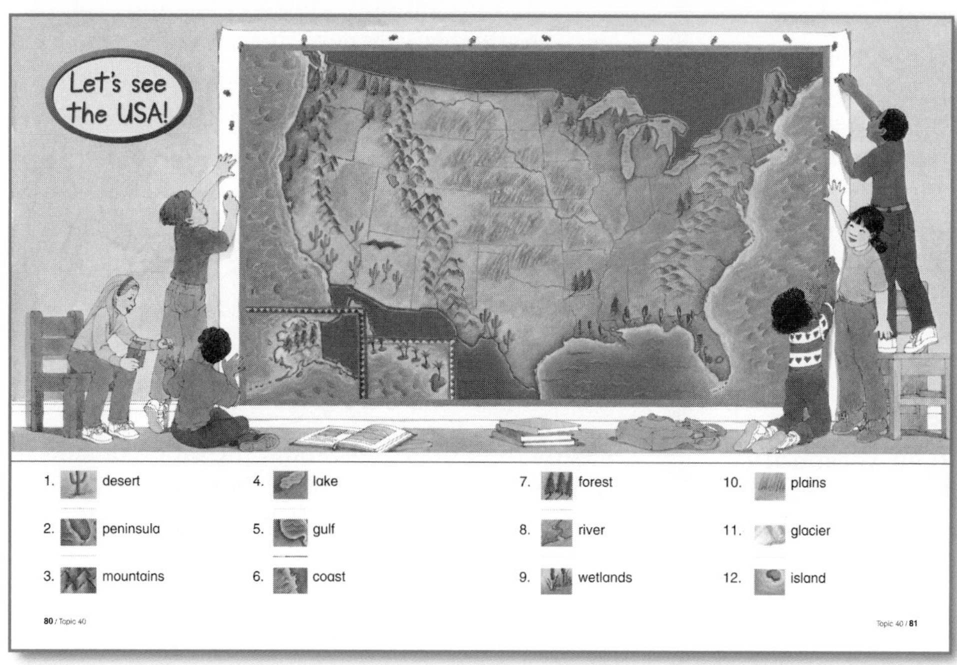

The children are hanging up a map of the United States, marked by symbols that show the variety of environments in the country. Among them are the southwest Sonora Desert, marked by a cactus symbol; the midwest Great Plains, marked by a symbol of waving grasses; wetland areas of the Florida Everglades and the Gulf Coast, marked by a symbol of cattails and rushes; small mountain symbols marking the Rockies and California mountain ranges of the west and the Appalachians of the east; forests marked by tiny tree symbols of the Northwest, the Northeast, and Alaska. In addition, the map shows the Mississippi, Missouri, Pecos, and the Rio Grande as blue lines; the Great Lakes and the Great Salt Lake; east and west coastal areas; the Gulf of Mexico; and the peninsula of Florida. Insets show the Hawaiian Islands and the mountains, forests, and glaciers of Alaska. Diego, Jim, Alison, Marcus, Zoe, and Ting are talking about places they would like to go on vacation.

Words

1. desert
2. peninsula
3. mountains
4. lake
5. gulf
6. coast
7. forest
8. river
9. wetlands
10. plains
11. glacier
12. island

Additional Words

Northeast
Northwest
Southeast
Southwest
Midwest
iceberg
canyon
prairies
swamp
marsh
beach
mountain range
peak

Words

Components: Topic 40 Wall Chart, Picture Dictionary (pp. 80–81), Cassette, Word and Picture Cards (Topic 40).

See page xiv for techniques and strategies for presenting and practicing words.

Let's see the USA!

1. desert	5. gulf	9. wetlands
2. peninsula	6. coast	10. plains
3. mountains	7. forest	11. glacier
4. lake	8. river	12. island

Notes

Narrate an imaginary cross-country trip, using the Wall Chart as a visual cue. Choose a destination that is far from your location. Point to the place where you are on the map, and explain that you will start there. Then point to the destination. As you move your finger across the face of the map, say each vocabulary word that comes up: *We are in the desert here. Now we cross the mountains. We drive through the wetlands and down onto the peninsula of Florida.* Ask the children to show you their matching word or picture cards for each feature you mention.

Workbook page

The pictures that can be matched to the vocabulary words are in two columns, one to the right of the words and one to the left. After the children have matched the pictures to the words, ask them to draw a place in the space provided below, and write or dictate something about the place they draw.

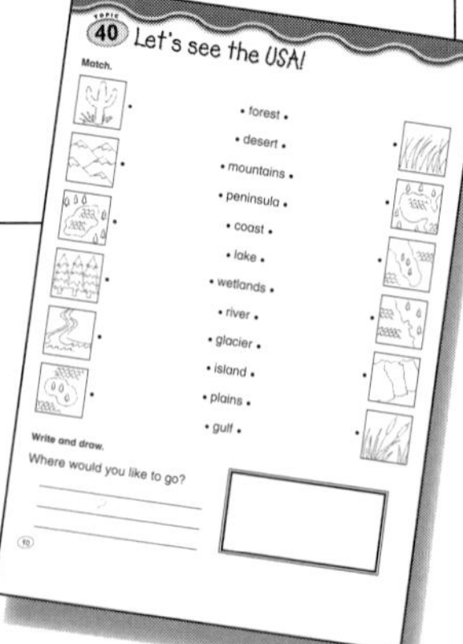

Stories

Components: Picture Dictionary (pp. 80–81), Cassette, Story (Topic 40).

See page xviii for techniques and strategies for presenting and practicing stories.

Where shall we go on vacation?
Alison may go to the Southwest desert
to see the canyon country and purple
mountains. Zoe might go boating
on a lake, or a gulf on the coast.

Diego would like to go to the Northwest
to see the big forests, or maybe camp by
a river in the Northeast. Ting might go
someplace in the Southeast. She loves
the beaches and wetlands.

Tommy and Jim will go to the Midwest,
to the plains where their grandparents live.
The United States is a great big country.
There are so many kinds of places to go!

Wouldn't it be fun to go way up north
to Alaska? And see icebergs and glaciers?
Or maybe we could go south to Hawaii,
the islands way out in the Pacific Ocean.
Let's go see it all!

Story notes

Using the Wall Chart, talk about the different land forms and climates. If possible, show photos of some regions. Help the children understand that other parts of the country look different from where they live.

Ask about the story:
Why would Alison like to go to the desert? What would Alison see there? Where does Zoe want to go? What kinds of places does Ting like? What part of the United States does Ting want to visit? Who is going to visit the plains? Is it true that the USA is a very small country?

Ask about your students:
Where in the United States would you like to go?

This question can serve as a springboard for conversation about climates, geographical features, and locations. Use stick-on dots for the destination, and together pore over the map and develop an itinerary. Jot down interesting landmarks, cities, or geographical features on the travel route. Supply books and travel brochures to find out more about the places on this imaginary trip.

Dialogue

Components: Cassette, Topic 40 Wall Chart, Picture Dictionary (pp. 80–81).

See page xix for techniques and strategies for presenting and practicing dialogues.

Marcus: Where are you going on vacation, Diego?
Diego: We might go camping somewhere by a river.
Marcus: We might go to a lake or maybe the ocean. My dad likes to go boating. Where will you go, Jim?
Jim: To visit my grandparents. They live on a farm way out on the plains in Kansas.
Alison: We may go to the mountains in Arizona and ride horses in the desert.
Zoe: Can you ride a horse?
Alison: No, but I could learn.
Ting: Maybe we'll go to Florida.
Zoe: Florida has lots of coast and wetlands.
Ting: And beaches. We love the beach!
Zoe: You know what we should do?
Ting: What?
Zoe: We should go all over the United States and see everything!

Dialogue notes

After listening to the dialogue and discussing possible destinations, ask the children to take part in similar dialogues, beginning with the question, *Where would you like to go on vacation?* Encourage the children to use the vocabulary words and respond with as much detail as possible. Here is an exchange for the children to practice as a jumping-off point for new dialogues:

Q: You know what we should do?
A: What?

Beats!

Components: Cassette, Beats! (Topic 40).

See page xx for techniques and strategies for presenting and practicing Beats!

I like to look at maps.
What are they all about?
Countries and oceans.
Are they hard to figure out?

Some maps have pictures
of mountains like these.
What's this?
A forest with big tall trees.

Look! These are rivers.
They run all across the land.
And is this a desert?
Yes!
Now I understand!

Here's a gulf, and here's a coast,
and an island and a lake.
I bet this is a peninsula!
Right!
This is great!

Beat notes

Recite the Beat in front of the Wall Chart or a large map of the United States that shows physical features, so that you can point to each feature as you talk about it. When the children are comfortable with the words and phrasing, let them take turns reciting the Beat in pairs or small groups, using the Wall Chart as a prop.

Worksheets

Worksheet 1: Let's see the USA! (p. 79)

Provide maps for children to use as models as they draw their own maps. Encourage them to use the words at the bottom of the page as they write or dictate something about their map.

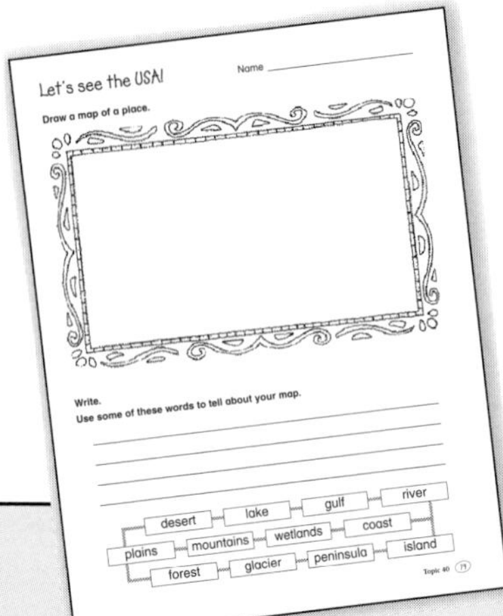

Let's see the USA! Name

Draw a map of a place.

Write.
Use some of these words to tell about your map.

desert lake gulf river plains mountains wetlands coast forest glacier peninsula island

Topic 40 79

Worksheet 2: Let's see the USA! (p. 80)

You might review the map symbols and the words in the word box. On the map of Alaska, the children find mountains, forests, glacier, peninsula, coast, river, lake, island, and gulf. They won't find desert, plains, or wetlands.

Let's see the USA! Name

Write the things that are on the map.

Circle the things that are not on the map.

desert lake gulf river plains mountains wetlands coast forest glacier peninsula island

80 Topic 40

Activities

- Make puzzles of the United States by helping the children glue a map onto heavy cardboard, then cut it along state lines. An alternative puzzle would leave the map whole and have the children place on the map geographical features (such as mountains, plains, wetlands, and deserts) that are drawn on pieces of translucent plastic. Have the children use the Dictionary illustration as a guide.

- Make a felt board with a girl and boy, and a variety of clothes: T-shirts, shorts, jeans, short-sleeved and long-sleeved shirts, sweaters, warm jackets, mittens, sun hats, warm hats, scarves. Have the children choose one card from a stack of shuffled word and picture cards. Invite them to discuss the weather conditions they think they would find in the region they chose, and have them dress the figures appropriately.

- Let's take an airplane trip! Divide the class into four groups: forest, wetlands, plains, and desert. Using resources from the library and personal experience, have each group create a mural, and make or gather artifacts that might be found in each location. In one corner of the room, make an "airplane" with seats (this can be as simple or as elaborate as you like). Take one trip a day by plane to each of the areas. The children representing the destination can be hosts to the other children.

- Play a circle game. Teach the refrain, to be said in unison: *We're going on a journey, we're going far away.* Then say: *I'm going to pack* __________, and name an item you would take on the trip. Begin again with the refrain in unison, and prompt your neighbor to repeat the item you said and add another. When everyone has a turn, say: *We've been on a journey, and now we're far from home. Let's unpack.* Help the children name all of the items. If you can, provide props and a bag or suitcase the children can pack and unpack.

Beach day

Content

- Beach environment
- Safety precautions for sea and sun
- Beach activities

Language

- Describing the beach environment: *The seagulls screech and circle in the sky. Here comes a wave! Wow, it's a big one!*
- Talking about safety precautions for sea and sun: *Don't get sunburned! Put on the sunblock. Don't swim out too far.*
- Describing activities at the beach: *Henry rides the waves on his surfboard. The lifeguard blows his whistle. Ting is building a sand castle.*
- Asking and answering negative questions: *Don't you want to go swimming? I will when I finish. Don't you need more sunblock? No, I'm fine.*

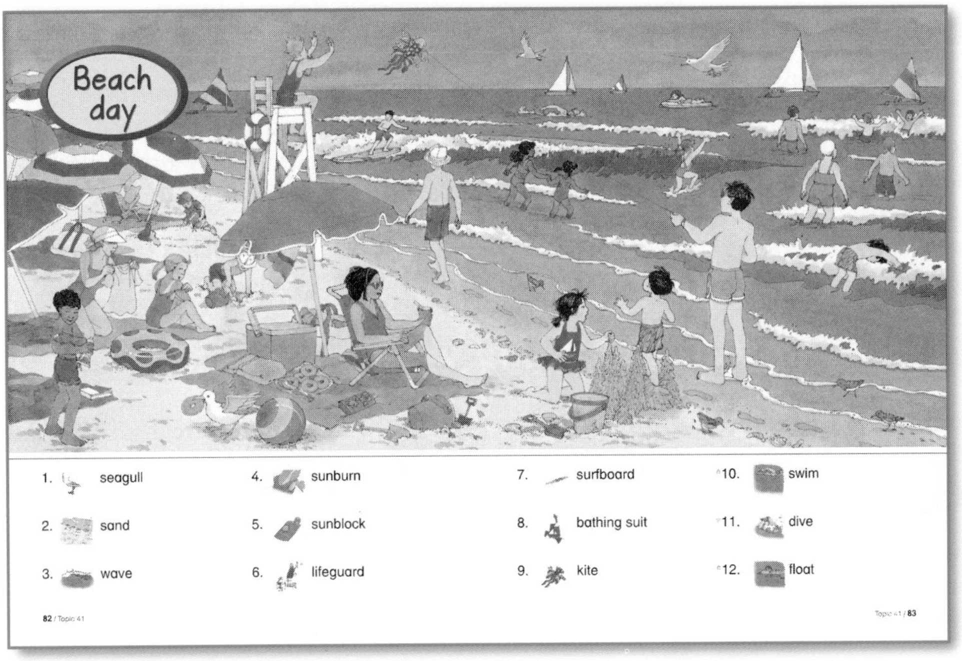

The Chengs are at a crowded beach. Seagulls are circling, and little sandpipers are running along the edge of the water. People are spread over the sand, with bright-colored beach umbrellas, blankets, and towels. The sand and sun are hot. One child has a sunburn. A boy is putting sunblock on himself. The lifeguard is standing up in his chair, blowing his whistle and waving at a girl on a rubber raft who's out too far. Henry is riding the waves on his surfboard. Jo-Jo is diving into a little wave. Mrs. Cheng watches them from under an umbrella. She has sunglasses on because the sun is bright. She doesn't know that a seagull has just stolen one of the bagels from the open bag beside her. Ting, in her new red bathing suit, is building a sand castle, dribbling some wet sand on top and looking at Jackie, surprised. Jackie is so busy watching Mr. Cheng fly a kite that he has just stepped backward onto the sand castle and smashed part of it.

Words

1. seagull
2. sand
3. wave
4. sunburn
5. sunblock
6. lifeguard
7. surfboard
8. bathing suit
9. kite

Verbs

10. swim
11. dive
12. float

Additional Words

umbrella
shade
pail
shovel
whistle
sunglasses
cooler
sea
footprints
sandpiper
sand castle
rubber raft
flying
riding
blowing

Words

Components: Topic 41 Wall Chart, Picture Dictionary (pp. 82–83), Cassette, Word and Picture Cards (Topic 41).

See page xiv for techniques and strategies for presenting and practicing words.

Beach day

1. seagull	4. sunburn	7. surfboard
2. sand	5. sunblock	8. bathing suit
3. wave	6. lifeguard	9. kite

Verbs

10. swim	11. dive	12. float

Notes

Familiarize the children with the words and then invite them to play a game like charades. Demonstrate by choosing a card from a shuffled deck of word cards and then doing a pantomime to help the children guess which word you picked. This is an opportunity to introduce verbs that are used with some of these nouns: *I am* flying *a kite. I'm a seagull, and I can* fly*. I'm* building *a sand castle or* digging *in the sand. I'm* riding *a surfboard,* wearing *a bathing suit,* rubbing *on sunblock. The lifeguard is* blowing *his whistle.*

Workbook page

The first three pictures show the vocabulary words that are verbs. The words at the bottom of the page can be used to help students write or dictate something about the things they see in the pictures.

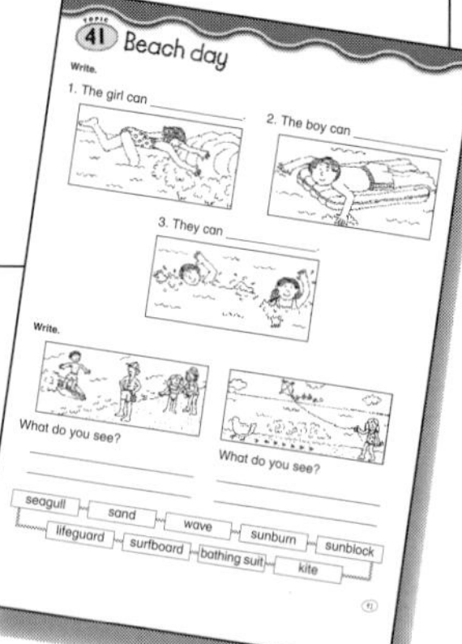
TOPIC 41 Beach day

Write.

1. The girl can ___

2. The boy can ___

3. They can ___

Write.

What do you see?

What do you see?

seagull | sand | wave | sunburn | sunblock | lifeguard | surfboard | bathing suit | kite

Stories

Components: Picture Dictionary (pp. 82–83), Cassette, Story (Topic 41).

See page xviii for techniques and strategies for presenting and practicing stories.

Seagulls screech and circle in the sky.
Sandpipers run back and forth along
the edge of the waves.
Bright sun, hot sand! Ouch!
Let's go swimming!

Don't get sunburned!
Put on the sunblock!
Ready, Jo-Jo? Dive in!
Mrs. Cheng watches from the umbrella.
Watch that seagull, Mrs. Cheng!
There goes your bagel!

Henry rides the waves on his surfboard.
The lifeguard blows his whistle loud!
Someone is out too far! It's a girl floating
on a rubber raft. Come back in!

Mr. Cheng and Jackie are flying their kite.
Where's Ting? There she is in her red
bathing suit, building a sand castle.
Watch out, Jackie! Don't step on it!
Oh, well. Let's go for a walk!

Story notes

Invite children to talk about their experiences at a beach. Some children may have never seen the ocean. Use the Wall Chart and encourage the children to talk about what they would see, hear, smell, and feel.

Ask about the story:
Is the beach crowded? Where do people keep their things at the beach? Who is diving into the waves? Why do you think the lifeguard has such a high chair? Why is the lifeguard blowing his whistle? What does the seagull have? Where did he get it? What did Jackie do? Was it an accident or on purpose? What was he watching?

Ask about your students:
Have you ever been to a beach? What did you see there? Was it far away? How did you get to the beach? Could you go swimming? Were there many people there? What do you like about the beach? What don't you like?

Dialogue

Components: Cassette, Topic 41 Wall Chart, Picture Dictionary (pp. 82–83).

See page xix for techniques and strategies for presenting and practicing dialogues.

Mrs. Cheng:	Be careful diving, Jo-Jo! That's a big wave!
Ting:	Mom! Look! How do you like my sand castle?
Mrs. Cheng:	It's beautiful, Ting! Don't you want to go swimming?
Ting:	I will when I finish. I'm putting some wet sand on top of the towers.
Mrs. Cheng:	Oh my! That's the lifeguard blowing his whistle. I hope Henry isn't out too far.
Ting:	Don't worry. He can ride back in on his surfboard.
Mrs. Cheng:	Do you need some more sunblock, Ting? I don't want you to get a sunburn.
Ting:	I'm fine, Mom.
Mrs. Cheng:	Your father and Jackie are coming back now with the kite. It's flying very high.
Ting:	Jackie! Watch where you're going! Dad! Jackie just stepped on my sand castle! It's all smashed!
Mr. Cheng:	Oh, my. Jackie, look at Ting's sand castle. We're sorry, Ting. We'll help you build another sand castle later.
Ting:	OK. Can we go for a walk?
Mr. Cheng:	Good idea! Let's go!

Dialogue notes

This dialogue provides models for asking and answering negative questions, such as *Don't you want to go swimming? I will when I finish. Don't you need more sunblock? I'm fine.* Encourage the children to make up their own questions and answers similar to these models, and to invent their own dialogues using the words in this unit.

Beats!

Components: Cassette, Beats! (Topic 41).

See page xx for techniques and strategies for presenting and practicing Beats!

Get ready to dive.
Here comes a wave!
    Wow! It's a big one!
Be brave!

    That was fun!
    Here's one more!
Let's ride this one
in to shore.

    What next?
Dig a tunnel in the sand.
We can meet underneath.
    I can feel your hand!

My mother is calling!
We have to go home.
    Good-bye, seagulls!
    Now you're all alone!

Beat notes

Separate the children into two groups to practice the Beat. You may want to have them say the lines as written and repeat them in unison. Have the children pantomime playing in the surf and digging in the sand.

Worksheets

Worksheet 1: Beach day (p. 81)

The pictures include images of all the vocabulary words in the topic. Prompt the children to sort the words into the three categories identified.

Beach day

Name

Write.

1. What did they take to the beach?

2. What does he see?

3. What can they do?

Topic 41 81

Worksheet 2: Beach day (p. 82)

Provide strategies for unscrambling words. You can point out that the first example ("thingba istu") is made of two words; if they unscramble the shorter word *(suit),* they can probably guess the longer word.

Beach day

Name

Unscramble. Write.

thingba istu, ikte, dvei, ardsburfo

tofla, awve, sbuumn, agsulle

wims, fegiuarld, ndsa, sockblun

82 Topic 41

Activities

- Have the children plan a day at the beach, including packing a bag with supplies. You can use the picture cards to represent some of the items *(bathing suit, kite, sunblock, surfboard).* You can also use the picture cards for words from other topics, such as *shirt, pants, towel,* and *umbrella.* If there's time, encourage children to act out their conception of a day at the ocean.
- Hunt for buried treasure. Set up a sand table and bury a specific number of small plastic toys, rocks, and seashells in the sand. Tell the children to use their fingers to find the hidden treasures. Encourage them to talk about what they are doing. Have them count the recovered treasure and check it against the original number of objects buried.
- Make sand words. Write the vocabulary words in block letters on cardboard. Have the children trace the letters with their fingers and outline them with marker or crayon. Then help them spread glue on each letter and sprinkle on sand. When the glue dries, shake off the excess sand. Use the sand letters for a variety of activities (for example, ask the children to close their eyes while you spell out a word, and then challenge them to guess the word by feeling the letters).
- Make waves. Prop one end of a plastic tub on a block so that the tub is slanted. Pour five or six cups of sand at the upper end of the tub, thus representing the slope of a sandy beach into the ocean. Add enough water to reach the edge of the sand. Invite the children to stir the water gently, and watch the sand. Talk with them about tides and storms. Ask what they think happens to the sand at the beach as the waves wash in and out.

We found a tide pool!

Content

- Tide pool ecology
- Marsh ecology
- Sea wrack and spawn
- Tides

Language

- Identifying and describing components of tide pool and marsh environments: *The little fish are trapped in the tide pool. Snails crawl along the bottom of the pool. The marsh grass waves in the breeze.*
- Describing tide changes: *A wave washed his footprints away because the tide was coming in. The minnows were trapped in the tide pool when the tide went out.*
- Expressing empathy with wildlife: *Let's catch some minnows. OK, but throw them back again. Be careful of the hermit crab. Put him back in the water.*

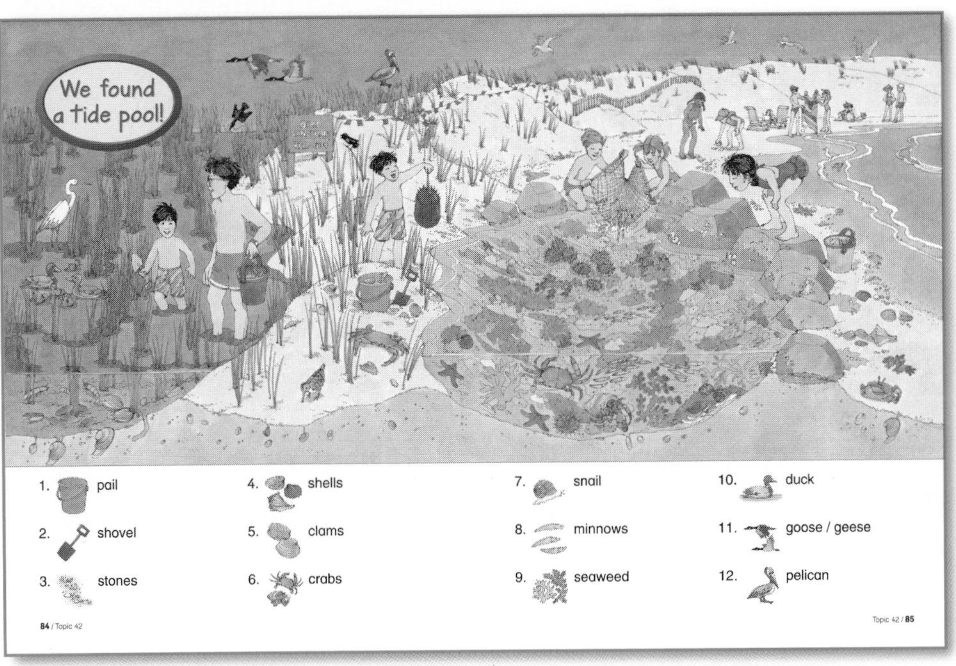

Words

1. pail
2. shovel
3. stones
4. shells
5. clams
6. crabs
7. snail
8. minnows
9. seaweed
10. duck
11. goose/geese
12. pelican

Additional Words

- sand dunes
- net
- high tide
- low tide
- horseshoe crab
- hermit crab
- crawl
- trap
- dart

Ting and Jo-Jo have crossed the sand dunes to a wilder part of the beach. Mr. Cheng and Jackie are farther along, in the marsh. The tide is coming in, and a young man and woman at the water's edge are holding up a dripping wet blanket. Ting has discovered a tide pool. There are snails at the bottom. One empty snail shell has a tiny hermit crab half inside it. A school of silver minnows swims through the seaweed. Two children have caught some of them in a net, but they are letting them go free, back into the pool. Ting and Jo-Jo's pails are filled with treasures, such as shells, clams, parts of dead crabs, and stones. Jo-Jo is holding a big horseshoe crab. In the marsh there are geese, ducks, and baby ducklings. A black cormorant dives into the water for fish. There are shrimp, mussels, clams, and oysters. A white pelican is sitting on a post looking toward the sea.

Words

Components: Topic 42 Wall Chart, Picture Dictionary (pp. 84–85), Cassette, Word and Picture Cards (Topic 42).

See page xiv for techniques and strategies for presenting and practicing words.

We found a tide pool!

1. pail
2. shovel
3. stones
4. shells
5. clams
6. crabs
7. snail
8. minnows
9. seaweed
10. duck
11. goose/geese
12. pelican

Notes

Once the children are comfortable with the words, invite volunteers to choose a card from a shuffled deck of picture cards and point to the item on the Wall Chart. Then, if appropriate, ask them to talk about the image on the card. You may want to prompt them with questions: *Is that a crab or a clam? Does the crab fly or crawl?* Continue until the children have identified and described each vocabulary word. You may want to talk about the use of the word *waves* as a verb *(the marsh grass waves in the wind)* in the story that follows.

Workbook page

Provide crayons or markers. Help the children read the instructions and use the pictures for reference points. Some vocabulary words can fit into more than one category. You can use this opportunity to discuss categorizing.

Stories

Components: Picture Dictionary (pp. 84–85), Cassette, Story (Topic 42).

See page xviii for techniques and strategies for presenting and practicing stories.

Let's climb over the sand dunes!
Bring your pails and shovels.
We can collect stones and shells and
dig for clams. Wow! A horseshoe crab!

And a tide pool! The tide's out, and
all the little fish are trapped.
Snails crawl along the bottom of the pool.
Who's in that snail shell? A hermit crab!

Silver minnows dart through the seaweed.
Let's catch some in the net.
OK, but throw them back again.
Look! The tide's coming back in!
Someone's blanket got all wet.

In the marsh, there are ducks and geese
and a blackbird sings "Ocalee, ocalee."
Mr. Cheng and Jackie look for turtles.
The green marsh grass waves in the wind,
and a white pelican waits for a fish.
Nice day!

Story notes

Most freshwater fish, one third of the birds, and one half of the shellfish in North America are born and live in wetlands, because the constant decay of plants and animals makes the soil and water good for growing things. Introduce environmental issues by pointing out that wetlands and the water around them have to be kept clean and free from pollution so that the wild fish, birds, and animals who live there are safe and protected.

Ask about the story:
Where are Mr. Cheng and Jackie? Who held up a horseshoe crab? How did the little fish get trapped? What was in the tide pool? What birds live in a marsh?

Ask about your students:
Who has been to the beach? Did you find any tide pools? What was in the tide pools? Did you see a marsh? What animals or birds were there?

If no one in the class has ever seen a tide pool, refer to the picture. Encourage the children to come up with their own descriptions of what they see.

Dialogue

 **Components:** Cassette, Topic 42 Wall Chart, Picture Dictionary (pp. 84–85).

See page xix for techniques and strategies for presenting and practicing dialogues.

Jo-Jo:	My pail is too heavy.
Ting:	That's because you picked up so many stones. I just picked up shells. I have a really big clam shell.
Jo-Jo:	What's this big thing, Ting?
Ting:	It's a horseshoe crab.
Jo-Jo:	Wow! It has a sharp tail!
Ting:	Put him back in the water, Jo-Jo.
Jo-Jo:	I will.
Ting:	O-o-o! There's a tide pool! Look at all the minnows swimming around!
Jo-Jo:	Why is that shell moving?
Ting:	There's a hermit crab inside it. That's his new house.
Jo-Jo:	Where did he get it?
Ting:	From a snail. It's a snail shell.
Jo-Jo:	Where did the snail go?
Ting:	I don't know.
Jo-Jo:	Where did Dad and Jackie go?
Ting:	Into the marsh. Look, Jo-Jo! There's a big white pelican in the marsh.
Jo-Jo:	He has a big mouth.
Ting:	That's his beak. He can hold lots of fish in his beak.
Jo-Jo:	Poor fish.
Ting:	Let's go get Dad and Jackie.
Jo-Jo:	OK.

Dialogue notes

Separate the children into two groups and have them repeat this exchange: *Where did my footprints go? A wave came in and washed them away.* Then prompt them to repeat the question, changing the person each time: *Where did his footprints go? Where did their footprints go?* Encourage the children to invent their own exchanges, based on this dialogue, using *where* questions as the first line.

Beats!

 **Components:** Cassette, Beats! (Topic 42).

See page xx for techniques and strategies for presenting and practicing Beats!

I like to fill my pail with shells
I find along the beach.
I like to pop the seaweed,
and hear the seagulls screech.

I like to walk in my bare feet.
I like to feel the wind.
I leave my footprints in the sand ...
until a wave comes in!

I like to watch the minnows
the waves have left behind.
Will we see snails? Or little crabs?
We don't know what we'll find.

And just beyond the sand dunes
there's a marsh we can explore.
The pelican waits for a fish.
The red-winged blackbirds soar.

Beat notes

Put the children into two groups to recite this Beat. Once they are familiar with the words and phrases, invite volunteers to add sound effects, such as the swishing of waves coming to shore, the "sh-shing" of the wind through the marsh grass, and the blackbird's cry. Then let each group have a chance to do all three roles.

Worksheets

Worksheet 1: We found a tide pool! (p. 83)

Provide markers or crayons for the children to use to add elements to the tide pool. Help the children understand that some of the things they can find are animals or plants that live in water, so those can be placed in both categories.

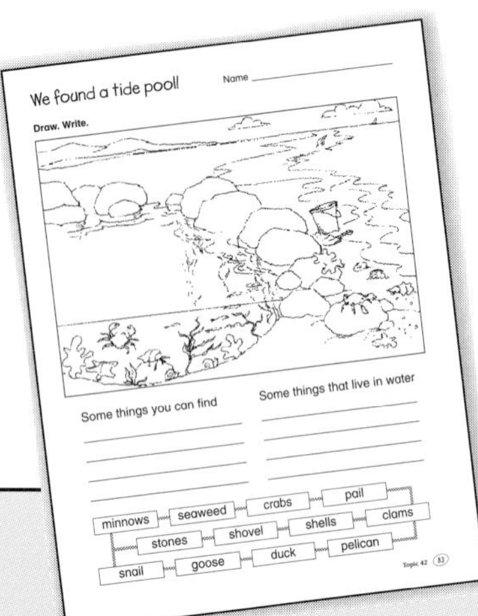

We found a tide pool! Name

Draw. Write.

Some things you can find

Some things that live in water

minnows seaweed crabs pail stones shovel shells clams snail goose duck pelican

Topic 42 83

Worksheet 2: We found a tide pool! (p. 84)

Help the children cut out the puzzle pieces along the dotted lines. You may want to have them glue the puzzle onto a file folder or piece of cardboard before cutting.

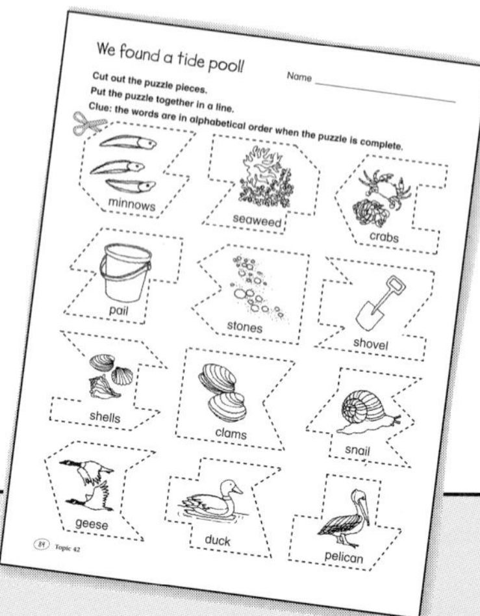

We found a tide pool! Name

Cut out the puzzle pieces.
Put the puzzle together in a line.
Clue: the words are in alphabetical order when the puzzle is complete.

minnows seaweed crabs pail stones shovel shells clams snail geese duck pelican

84 Topic 42

Activities

- Create a classroom tide pool. Provide blank index cards on which the children can draw or glue magazine pictures of tide pool plants and animals. Encourage them to take friends on tours of their tide pool. This is a good opportunity for prompting children to elaborate their language. You can prompt them by asking such questions as *What color is your shell? Is it hard or soft? Is the fish big or small?*
- Play a category game. Ask the children to find things that match a category you describe, on the Wall Chart or in the Dictionary illustration: *Show us something that is alive (or soft, or shiny, or something that might be warm during the day).* Encourage the children to invent categories of their own.
- Read the book *Moving Day* by Robert Kalan (Greenwillow) in which Hermit Crab takes a long, interesting walk to find a new home. In addition to exploring beach wildlife, this book reviews size and measurement concepts.
- Look for the birds. Have the children search for other birds in the Picture Dictionary. When a bird has been found, have them write the name or draw a picture and note the page on which it can be found. You may ask the children to write or dictate directions for finding the birds on the page, for example, *On page (84), the robin is sitting on a branch of a tree.*
- Make a shell puzzle. Make two photocopies of a page in a field guide or encyclopedia that shows seashells. Glue both copies to pieces of cardboard. Cut the shells out of one page. Challenge the children to match the shells. Or, make a second set of cutout shells and turn both sets facedown to play a concentration game. As each pair is found, they can be placed on the uncut page of shells.

What's under the sea?

Content

- The ocean
- Plants and animals of the ocean
- Snorkeling

Language

- Identifying and describing life in the ocean: *The dolphins are jumping! See that waterspout? That's a whale coming up for air. There are lots of fish swimming around the coral reef.*
- Describing the sport of snorkeling and its equipment: *Can you help me with my snorkel? Put on your fins and mask. Let's go! There's so much to see under the water!*
- Expressing conjectures: *Imagine what's out where it's deep!*

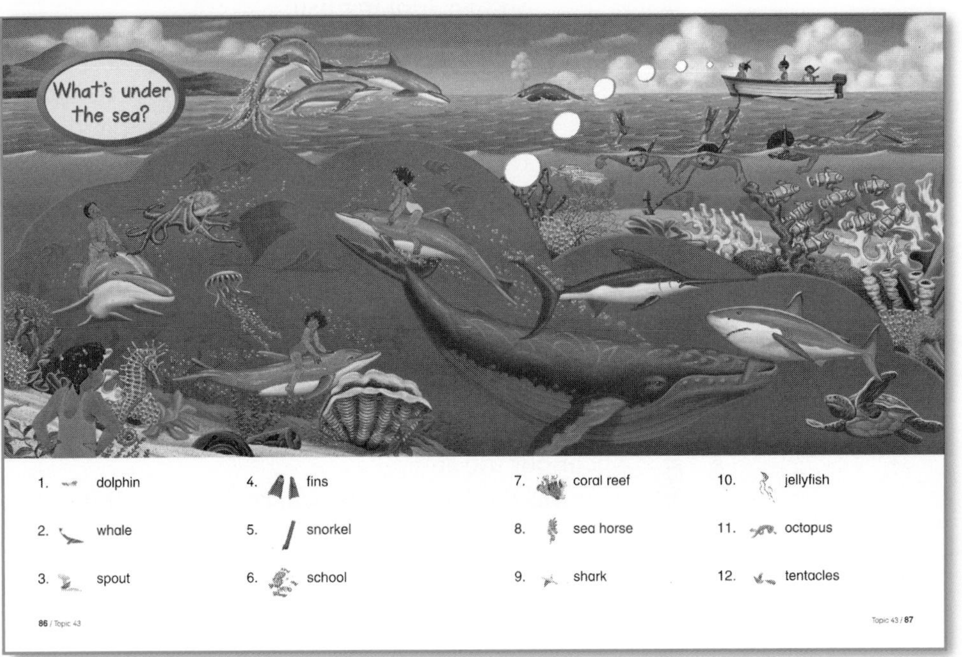

The Jacksons are going snorkeling. Their small motorboat is anchored in a shallow area close to shore. They see a whale's waterspout in the distance and three dolphins leaping nearby. Mr. Jackson, Marcus, and Zoe are face-down in the water, breathing through their snorkels, paddling with their fins, and peering into the depths below through their masks. They are looking at a coral reef and a school of brilliant multicolored fish. Mrs. Jackson, Samantha, and Mariah are in the boat, getting ready. Samantha excitedly imagines what is under the water. The deep ocean that exists in Samantha's imagination is inhabited by a whale, a shark, a sea horse, jellyfish, an octopus, a big sea turtle, and three dolphins. There's some debris on the ocean floor. Samantha imagines Zoe, Marcus, and Mariah ecstatically riding dolphins. She imagines herself standing on the ocean floor looking at a sea horse. It is too small to ride.

Words

1. dolphin
2. whale
3. spout
4. fins
5. snorkel
6. school
7. coral reef
8. sea horse
9. shark
10. jellyfish
11. octopus
12. tentacles

Additional Words

shallow
deep
surface
bottom
equipment
breathe

Words

Components: Topic 43 Wall Chart, Picture Dictionary (pp. 86–87), Cassette, Word and Picture Cards (Topic 43).

See page xiv for techniques and strategies for presenting and practicing words.

What's under the sea?

1. dolphin	5. snorkel	9. shark
2. whale	6. school	10. jellyfish
3. spout	7. coral reef	11. octopus
4. fins	8. sea horse	12. tentacles

Notes

You may want to compare the manufactured fins with the fins and tails of the fish, dolphins, and whale in the illustration. Ask the children to tell in their own words how the fins help make swimming easier and faster. Provide language models as necessary.

Workbook page

Help the children read all the words in the coloring pattern before beginning. You may need to help them understand the categories. When colored in, the first picture reveals a (brown) sea horse, and the second reveals a (purple) dolphin.

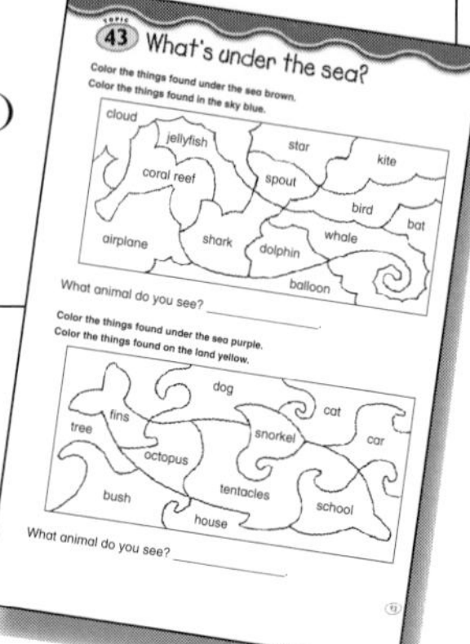

TOPIC 43 What's under the sea?

Color the things found under the sea brown.
Color the things found in the sky blue.

cloud, jellyfish, star, kite, coral reef, spout, bird, bat, whale, airplane, shark, dolphin, balloon

What animal do you see? ____________.

Color the things found under the sea purple.
Color the things found on the land yellow.

dog, cat, fins, tree, snorkel, car, octopus, tentacles, bush, school, house

What animal do you see? ____________.

Stories

Components: Picture Dictionary (pp. 84–85), Cassette, Story (Topic 43).

See page xviii for techniques and strategies for presenting and practicing stories.

Look! The dolphins are jumping!
Bet there's a whale out there, too.
See that waterspout? That's a whale
coming up for air. Ready with your fins
and masks and snorkels? Let's go!

Splash! See anything?
Pink fish, purple fish, a whole school.
Where? By the coral reef.
Strange-looking fish!

Imagine what's out where it's deep!
Maybe a sea horse we could ride. Too small!
Hope we don't see a whale or a shark!
Hope they don't see us!

Don't get stung by the jellyfish!
Don't let the octopus hug you
with its long tentacles. You'll be squished!
Know what's best? Ride the dolphins!

Story notes

Ask about the story:

How did the Jacksons get where they are? What made the waterspout? What kind of fish do they see under the water? What equipment do they use? How do they see under the water? How do they breathe? What animals do the Jacksons see? What animals does Samantha imagine? Why can't she ride the sea horse?

Ask about your students:

Have you ever seen a live whale or dolphin? Who has seen a whale or dolphin in a movie or TV show? Has anyone been to an aquarium? Would you like to be hugged by an octopus? Do you think the underwater world is really as Samantha imagined it? Why or why not?

Dialogue

Components: Cassette, Topic 43 Wall Chart, Picture Dictionary (pp. 86–87).

See page xix for techniques and strategies for presenting and practicing dialogues.

Mrs. Jackson:	I see a whale spout! Look, Samantha! The whale is blowing water way up in the air!
Samantha:	I see it, too! I wonder what the whale looks like.
Mrs. Jackson:	I bet it's big! And there are some dolphins jumping!
Zoe:	Come on in, Samantha! There are lots of fish swimming around the coral reef. A whole school!
Samantha:	Huh? A school? Do fish go to school, Mommy?
Mrs. Jackson:	No, Samantha. A school of fish is like a family. They swim together.
Samantha:	Oh. Can you help me with my snorkel?
Mrs. Jackson:	Sure.
Samantha:	Mommy, what's under the sea?
Mrs. Jackson:	Well, there are whales, and there might be a big shark or a little sea horse, but they're down where it's deep. We're going to stay here in the shallow water.
Samantha:	I want to see them. Maybe I can pretend. ... I think I see a whale. I think I see a shark.
Marcus:	Watch us, Samantha! These dolphins can go fast. What a ride!
Zoe:	Look out, Marcus! There's an octopus waving its tentacles at you. Don't let it catch you!
Marcus:	And you'd better watch out, Zoe! There's a big jellyfish after you!
Samantha:	I see a sea horse! Why is this sea horse so small? I can't ride it, but it's cute.
Marcus:	Ride the dolphins with us, Samantha! The dolphins are the best!

Dialogue notes

Tell one child to pretend that she or he is snorkeling and another child to pretend to be in a boat. Model a basic question-and-answer pattern: *What can you see under the water? I can see ...* Have the children take turns asking questions and giving answers.

Beats!

Components: Cassette, Beats! (Topic 43).

See page xx for techniques and strategies for presenting and practicing Beats!

How would you like to live
under the sea?
    Under the sea?
    Who? Me?

If you were a whale,
you could blow a big spout.
    A big spout?
    I might pass out!

If you were an octopus,
you could squirt ink.
    Squirt ink?
    I might sink!

If you were a shark,
you could swim deep down.
    Deep down?
    I might drown!

Wouldn't you like to live under the sea?
    Under the sea?
    Not me!

Beat notes

Make sure the children understand the phrase *pass out.* Explain that octopi can excrete (squirt out) an inky substance that clouds the water to confuse their prey and their enemies. Encourage the children to invent their own stanzas following the model presented here: *If you were a sea horse ...*

Worksheets

Worksheet 1: What's under the sea? (p. 85)

Provide markers or crayons for children to draw their own under-the-sea picture. Then prompt them to dictate or write a few sentences about their picture.

Worksheet 2: What's under the sea? (p. 86)

Pictures of some of the vocabulary words *(jelly-fish, dolphin, whale, shark, octopus, sea horse)* are hidden in the scene. Tell the children to find and circle the hidden images, and then write the words on the lines provided.

Activities

- Play a comparison game. Have the children look at the Picture Dictionary illustration and discuss together which animal shown is the smallest (in real life, not in the picture). Ask them to place the word/picture card for this animal to the left. Then assign the children to pairs and have them place the rest of the cards from left to right, going from smallest to largest. Then ask each pair to compare the order of their cards with that of another pair. Having done smallest-to-largest, the children can then be encouraged to come up with their own categories.

- Explore suction. Provide a variety of suction cups and surfaces for the children to try them on, including such things as a desk or tabletop, a piece of crumpled paper, a large smooth rock, a rough and uneven rock, a mirror or pane of glass, and a piece of fabric. Encourage students to experiment. Help them make predictions and test them, and report their findings to their classmates.

- Have each child (or a small group of children) choose one of the animals in the unit. Provide more pictures, preferably photographs as well as other art of the chosen animal; if possible, talk to the children (or help them read) about the way each animal moves, what it eats, and so forth. Then provide paper for the children to draw a picture of the animal, and help them write a sentence or two about it. Use the drawings for a bulletin board display, or make a class book with them.

- Tell an add-on story. Provide a seashell, which you pass to the next person to signify that you are passing on the story. Start by describing a scene like that in the illustration: *I went snorkeling and I anchored my boat near a coral reef. I put on my equipment and jumped into the water. I floated on the surface and looked down, and I saw a school of tiny fish swimming away from me toward a—* Pass the shell on to signal that the next person should add to the story.

Working on the farm

Content

- Farm environment and buildings
- Farm work and activities
- Farm animals

Language

- Describing a farm environment: *From the farmhouse you can see the cow pasture. The big barn is by the cornfield. The cherry orchard is next to the field.*
- Identifying and naming farm animals: *The goats and sheep are grazing in the green meadow. The bull bellows in his pen.*
- Asking and answering questions about farm routines and chores: *Who feeds the pigs? The farmhand feeds the pigs. Did somebody collect the eggs? Yes, Grandma collected the eggs.*

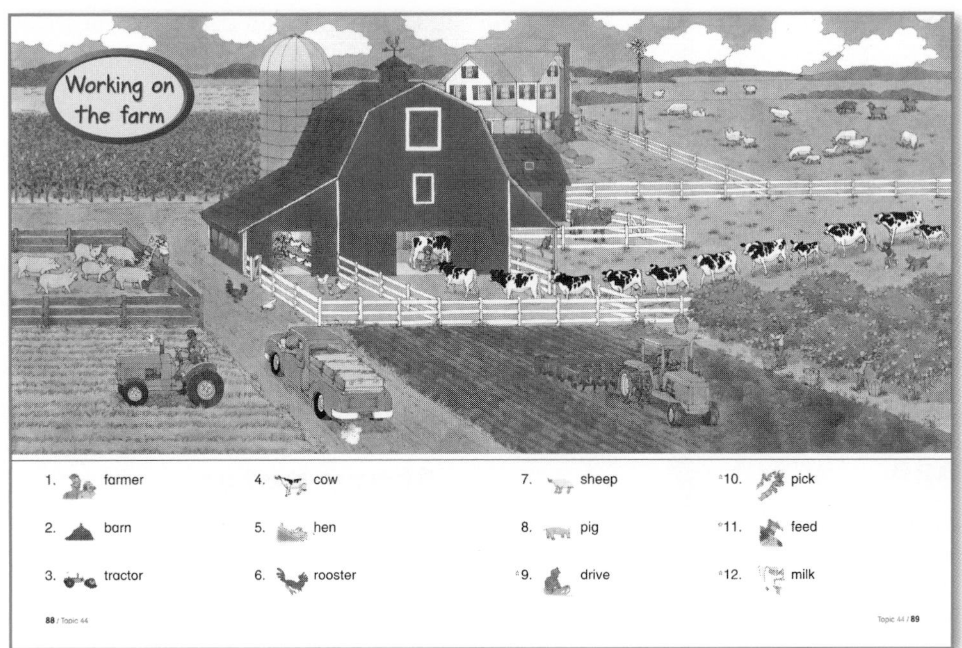

The Youngs are visiting their grandparents. They live in the Midwest on a farm with a farmhouse, barn, silo, fields, a peach orchard, a cow pasture, a meadow, and a view of the distant prairie. Sheep and goats are grazing in the meadow. The bull is bellowing in the pen. There are many chores to be done. A farmhand is feeding the pigs. Grandma is collecting eggs in the henhouse. The rooster is strutting along the road, and chickens and chicks are pecking along the path. Jim is driving a tractor with Grandpa sitting beside him. A boy and girl are picking peaches and putting them in baskets. A noisy old truck filled with bales of hay has just arrived. Tommy, smiling and looking very proud of himself, is bringing in a long line of cows from the pasture. He directs them to the barn, where Mrs. Young is milking one of them and smiling at Tommy.

Words

1. farmer
2. barn
3. tractor
4. cow
5. hen
6. rooster
7. sheep
8. pig

Verbs

9. drive
10. pick
11. feed
12. milk

Additional Words

farmhand
chores
hay
peaches
meadow
prairie
field
crop
pasture
farmhouse
lamb
goat
calf/calves
bull
wool
graze
plow
shear

Words

Components: Topic 44 Wall Chart, Picture Dictionary (pp. 88–89), Cassette, Words and Picture Cards (Topic 44).

See page xiv for techniques and strategies for presenting and practicing words.

Working on the farm

1. farmer	4. cow	7. sheep
2. barn	5. hen	8. pig
3. tractor	6. rooster	

Verbs

9. drive	11. feed	12. milk
10. pick		

Notes

If possible, bring in a child's play farm set and display it on a table. Reinforce the words by pointing to an item and asking questions: *Is this a sheep or a cow? Is this a farmer or a pig? Point to the barn.* Hold up the model tractor and ask, *What can you do with this?* Then introduce the verbs by pantomiming their actions *(milking the cow, throwing feed to chickens, driving a vehicle).* Let the children do the actions with you as they say the word.

Workbook page

Provide strategies for unscrambling the words. You may want to use this opportunity to discuss how verbs change when the subject is plural. The pictures provide the clues for writing the missing words in the sentences.

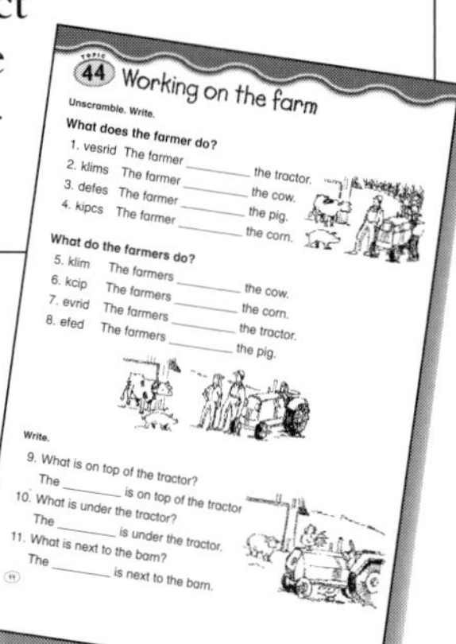

TOPIC 44 Working on the farm

Unscramble. Write.

What does the farmer do?

1. vesrid The farmer ________ the tractor.
2. klims The farmer ________ the cow.
3. defes The farmer ________ the pig.
4. kipcs The farmer ________ the corn.

What do the farmers do?

5. klim The farmers ________ the cow.
6. kcip The farmers ________ the corn.
7. evrid The farmers ________ the tractor.
8. efed The farmers ________ the pig.

Write.

9. What is on top of the tractor?
The ________ is on top of the tractor
10. What is under the tractor?
The ________ is under the tractor.
11. What is next to the barn?
The ________ is next to the barn.

Stories

Components: Picture Dictionary (pp. 88–89), Cassette, Story (Topic 44).

See page xviii for techniques and strategies for presenting and practicing stories.

It's great to be back on the farm!
Lots of chores to do. Plowing fields,
planting crops. The rooster struts,
and the chickens peck along the path.
Oink! Oink! Feed those pigs!

Grandma collects eggs from under
the hens. Jim drives the tractor with
Grandpa beside him. Here comes the hay!
Jake drives the old truck. Clackety bang!

From the farmhouse you can see clear
across the prairie. The goats and sheep
are grazing in the meadow.
Three new lambs!
Corn's ready for picking!
Peaches are ripe! Let's go pick some!

The bull bellows in his pen. Time for
Tommy to bring the cows and calves
from the pasture and put them in the barn.
Moo! Moo! Someone better milk them.
Not Tommy!

Story notes

Ask the children what things that they use come from a farm. Talk about different kinds of farms such as dairy farms, cattle ranches, organic farms, vegetable farms, and fruit orchards. Remind the children that almost everything they eat comes from a farm.

Ask about the story:
Which animals were being fed? Who was collecting eggs? Where did Grandma find the eggs? Did the rooster or the hen lay the eggs? Where were the sheep and the goats? Who was driving the tractor? What was Tommy's mother doing?

Ask about your students:
Have you ever been on a farm? What do farmers have to do every day? Do you think farmers work hard? What did you eat today? Where did that food come from? How do you think food gets from the farm to the store? Would you like to milk a cow? Which farm job would you like to do?

Dialogue

Components: Cassette, Topic 44 Wall Chart, Picture Dictionary (pp. 88–89).

See page xix for techniques and strategies for presenting and practicing dialogues.

Jim:	I like to drive the tractor, Grandpa.
Grandpa:	You're a good driver, Jim. Here comes Jake with the hay.
Jim:	Hi, Jake!
Jake:	Hi, Jim! Do you want to pick corn with me?
Jim:	Sure.
Jake:	And the peaches are ripe. We can pick them, too.
Jim:	Great! I love peaches!
Grandpa:	Did anyone feed the pigs?
Jake:	Yep. They were fed, and the eggs were collected.
Jim:	I know Grandma collected the eggs from the hens this morning. That old rooster got us up early.
Jake:	He loves to crow and wake everyone up.
Grandpa:	Tommy's doing a good job bringing the cows into the barn. Good job, Tommy!
Tommy:	Thanks, Grandpa. But I can't milk them, Mom.
Mrs. Young:	I'll teach you, Tommy, whenever you want.
Tommy:	OK. When are they going to take the wool from the sheep?
Mrs. Young:	It's not time to shear the sheep yet. Pretty soon, though.
Tommy:	You and Grandma and Grandpa are good farmers!
Grandpa:	Thank you, Tommy. And you and Jim are good helpers.

Dialogue notes

Have the children use the following question-and-answer pattern as a basis for inventing their own dialogues about farm chores:

Q: Did anyone feed the pigs?
A: Yes, the farmhand fed the pigs.

Once they are comfortable with the words and phrases, encourage them to vary the pattern. For example, they could answer with a negative *(No, the pigs haven't been fed yet)* or ask a question about work yet to be done *(Who will feed the pigs?)*.

Beats!

Components: Cassette, Beats! (Topic 44).

See page xx for techniques and strategies for presenting and practicing Beats!

Farmers must have lots of fun
milking all the cows.
    If you had to milk a cow,
    would you know how?

Farmers must have lots of fun
shearing sheep to get the wool.
    If I had to shear a sheep,
    would it push and pull?

Maybe I could feed the pigs,
waiting in their pens.
    Maybe I'd collect the eggs
    under all the hens.

Plant the crops!
    Pick the corn!
Always on the run.
    Farmers must have lots of fun
    when all the chores are done!

Beat notes

Separate the children into two groups to practice the Beat as written, saying the last line in unison. Then you can encourage them to add to the list of chores in the last stanza *(Milk the cows! Plow the field!)*. Challenge them to add as many chores in that format as they can think of.

Worksheets

Worksheet 1: Working on the farm (p. 87)

Help the children cut out the small pictures along the dotted lines and then place them on the large picture according to the instructions. You can have children work in pairs to help each other place the animals in different positions before gluing them in place.

Working on the farm   Name ____________

Cut and glue.
Put the rooster on the fence. Put the tractor by the corn.
Put the cow in the barn. Put the pig in the mud puddle.
Put the sheep on the grass. Put the farmer in the tree.

Topic 44 87

Worksheet 2: Working on the farm (p. 88)

Help the children read the sentences and figure out which word or words are wrong. You can ask them to tell you what is going on in the picture before they read the sentences. Or you can ask: *Is the rooster going to milk the cow? Who is going to milk the cow?*

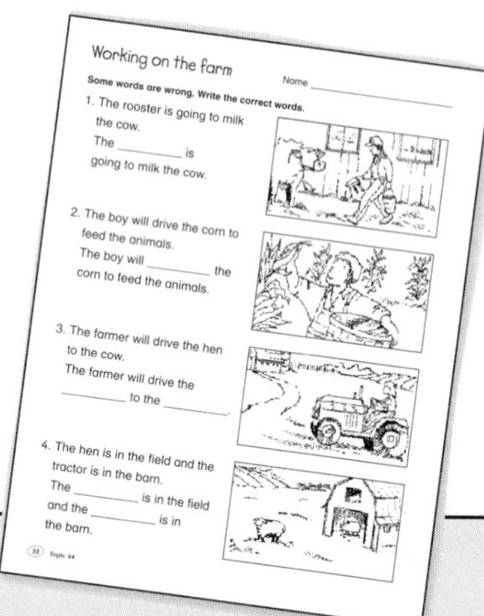

Working on the farm   Name ____________

Some words are wrong. Write the correct words.

1. The rooster is going to milk the cow.
   The __________ is going to milk the cow.
2. The boy will drive the corn to feed the animals.
   The boy will __________ the corn to feed the animals.
3. The farmer will drive the hen to the cow.
   The farmer will drive the __________ to the __________.
4. The hen is in the field and the tractor is in the barn.
   The __________ is in the field and the __________ is in the barn.

88 Topic 44

Activities

- Teach the song "Old McDonald":

  Old McDonald had a farm, ee-aye-ee-aye-oh!
  And on his farm he had a cow, ee-aye-ee-aye-oh!
  With a moo-moo here, and a moo-moo there,
  Here a moo, there a moo, everywhere a moo-moo.
  Old McDonald had a farm, ee-aye-ee-aye-oh!

- Make farm animals. Provide clay or play dough for children to use to make farm animals. As they work, ask questions to focus their attention: *How many legs does a cow have? Does a cow have a tail?*

- Set up a farm. Provide buckets for sorting and storing plastic farm animals, machinery, and buildings, and a large flat green board for setting up the farm. Or help the children build their own farm models with recyclables such as milk cartons, toilet paper rolls, and their animal models. Encourage the children to talk about what they are doing as they play.

- Teach the song "Farmer in the Dell":

  The farmer in the dell,
  The farmer in the dell,
  hi-ho the dairy, oh,
  The farmer in the dell.

  Modify the words of the song to reflect the nouns and verbs found in this unit (for example, *The farmer feeds the pigs*). Encourage the children to come up with new verses.

- Make a felt board harvest scene. Use different colors of felt to make bushes, stalks, and trees; and apples, berries, tomatoes, peaches, and corn. Show the class the board with the fruits and vegetables in place. Discuss where food comes from as they set up and harvest the fruits and vegetables from their felt board farm into different containers. Ask them for ideas for other crops they could add to the scene.

Camping out

Content

- Woodland environment
- Camping equipment
- Camping activities

Language

- Describing a woodland environment: *The river is cold. The deer is nibbling in the bushes. There is poison ivy by the river.*
- Describing camping equipment: *We sleep in a tent. We cook on a grill over a wood fire. Vanessa is still in her sleeping bag. Jasmin will ride in the canoe.*
- Talking about camping activities: *Did he catch a fish? He caught a big fish. Who's been eating the garbage? Must be a bear. Who's going boating?*
- Discussing outdoor safety: *Careful! That's poison ivy! Don't leave garbage where bears can find it. Wear your life jacket when you go in the boat.*
- Expressing wonder: *Listen to the frogs croaking! Look at that sunrise!*

Words

1. sunrise
2. waterfall
3. tent
4. sleeping bag
5. life jacket
6. rowboat
7. fishing rod
8. poison ivy
9. frog
10. deer
11. bear
12. woods

Additional Words

campsite
grill
canoe
bushes
fox
nibble
dump
r-r-ribbit

The Lopez family is camping in three tents at the edge of the woods next to a river with a waterfall. The sun is rising. Diego has jumped into the river with three other campers to take a shower under the waterfall. They are having a wonderful time. Jasmin is at the edge of the river watching a frog. Mrs. Lopez points to some poison ivy and cautions her not to step in it. Jasmin calls to a fisherman in a rowboat who is holding up a big fish for her to see. A fox runs stealthily across a corner of the campsite, and a deer nibbles on a bush. Vanessa is still in her sleeping bag in the tent with her mother and Baby Rosa. Her father is stretching and yawning. Mr. Lopez is cooking breakfast on the grill. Grandma was helping, but she is busy slapping some bugs away from the food. Grandpa is picking up garbage that was strewn on the ground. Who spilled it? A big bear, hiding in the woods!

Words

Components: Topic 45 Wall Chart, Picture Dictionary (pp. 90–91), Cassette, Word and Picture Cards (Topic 45).

See page xiv for techniques and strategies for presenting and practicing words.

Camping out

1. sunrise
2. waterfall
3. tent
4. sleeping bag
5. life jacket
6. rowboat
7. fishing rod
8. poison ivy
9. frog
10. deer
11. bear
12. woods

Notes

Ask a volunteer to pantomime one or more of the vocabulary words, as the other children try to guess the word or words. You may want to explain what happens when you come into contact with poison ivy. Talk about what can be done to alleviate the itch (bathe in jewelweed juice, apply calamine lotion, don't scratch). Stress that it's best to know how to identify the plant and stay away from it.

Workbook page

The pictures provide clues for answering each question. Encourage the children to write the vocabulary words, but they can use other words as well, if they wish.

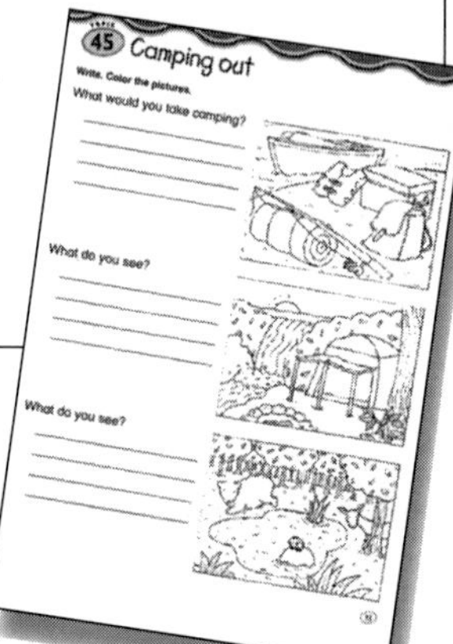
45 Camping out
Write. Color the pictures.
What would you take camping?
What do you see?
What do you see?

Stories

Components: Picture Dictionary (pp. 90–91), Cassette, Story (Topic 45).

See page xviii for techniques and strategies for presenting and practicing stories.

Look at that sunrise!
Wow! Camping is great!
Sleep in a tent. Cook on a grill.
Jump in the river, and
take a shower under a waterfall!

Listen to the frogs. R-r-ribbit! R-r-ribbit!
Hey, mister in the rowboat! Let's see
your fishing rod. O-o-o. A big fish!
Careful, Jasmin! That's poison ivy!

Sh-h-h. A deer is nibbling the bushes.
Who's been eating the garbage?
Must be a bear. Bet he's in the woods.
Hope he stays there!

Who's going boating after breakfast?
Sleeping bags off! Life jackets on!
Mm-m. Food smells good!
Bzz-z-z-z-z. What's that? Bugs!
Go away!

Story notes

Invite volunteers to describe their own experiences on hikes or camping trips. Ask the children to brainstorm about the variety of activities people can do in the woods: *camping, bird-watching, watching animals, hunting, fishing, gathering wild foods.*

Ask about the story:
Do the Lopezes like going camping? Where do they sleep? Do they sleep in beds? How do they make their breakfast? What is Grandpa doing? Who messed up the garbage? Where is the bear now? Is the deer eating garbage? What did the man catch? What will Jasmin wear in the boat?

Ask about your students:
Have you ever been camping? Would you like to go camping? What would you like to do on your camping trip? What would you need? Would you like to take a shower under a waterfall? How can you be safe? Why do people take tents? Where would you cook your food? What would you eat?

Dialogue

Components: Cassette, Topic 45 Wall Chart, Picture Dictionary (pp. 90–91).

See page xix for techniques and strategies for presenting and practicing dialogues.

Diego:	Whoa! This river is cold!
Boy:	Get under the waterfall, Diego! It's great!
Jasmin:	I see a nice big frog!
Mrs. Lopez:	Jasmin, watch out for the poison ivy! You almost stepped in it.
Jasmin:	I see it. Mama, look! That man in the rowboat caught a fish!
Mrs. Lopez:	If you want to go out in the boat after breakfast, put on your life jacket.
Jasmin:	All right!
Grandpa:	Somebody dumped the garbage. I bet it was a bear.
Grandma:	Oh, my. What a mess!
Grandpa:	Looks like he dragged the garbage off into the woods.
Grandma:	Is Vanessa still in the tent?
Mr. Lopez:	I think so.
Grandma:	Vanessa! Get out of your sleeping bag! Breakfast is ready! It smells so good. Come on, everyone. Let's eat!
Mr. Lopez:	Look at these bugs flying all around the food!
Grandma:	Shoo, bugs! Shoo! I guess the bugs want breakfast, too!

Dialogue notes

Encourage the children to invent their own dialogues based on a repeating pattern like this one:

First person:	Look out for the poison ivy! You almost stepped in it.
Second person:	I see the poison ivy. Look! That man in the rowboat has a fish!
Third person:	I see the fish. Look! ...

Once they are comfortable with the phrasing and words, encourage them to change to a series of comments on sounds, starting off with (for example):

First person:	Listen! The frogs are saying r-r-ribbit.
Second person:	I hear the frogs. Listen! ...

Beats!

Components: Cassette, Beats! (Topic 45).

See page xx for techniques and strategies for presenting and practicing Beats!

The sun is coming up!
There's a little bit of fog.
I hear the birds singing.
I see a frog!

Someone has a bunch of fish
lying side by side.
Someone has a rowboat.
Can we go for a ride?

Let's get our fishing rods
out of the tent.
I think I see a bear!
Where?
There!
Too late. He went.

The sun is going down.
One star is shining bright.
The bugs are buzzing all around.
Good night!

Beat notes

Practice this Beat as it is written until the children are comfortable reciting it. Then have them start again by lying down, as if they are in their sleeping bags. Act out rising and stretching during the first stanza, pantomime other activities during the two middle stanzas, and settle back down on the final *Good night!*

Worksheets

Worksheet 1: Camping out (p. 89)

Talk about the boy in the woods and the girl in the boat. Then have the children write the vocabulary words from the bottom of the page along with any other words they wish for things they see in the pictures.

Camping out

Name ____________

Write the missing words. Circle the things they see.

1. Where is he?
   He is in the ____________.
   What can he see?

2. Where is she?
   She is in a ____________.
   What can she see?

sunrise | waterfall | tent | sleeping bag
life jacket | rowboat | fishing rod | poison ivy
frog | deer | bear | woods

Topic 45 89

Worksheet 2: Camping out (p. 90)

Help the children read and follow the directions. You can suggest they use the Wall Chart or their Dictionary to help find the words, using the first letters as clues. They should underline *poison ivy, frog, deer,* and *bear.* You can discuss whether the word *woods* should be underlined.

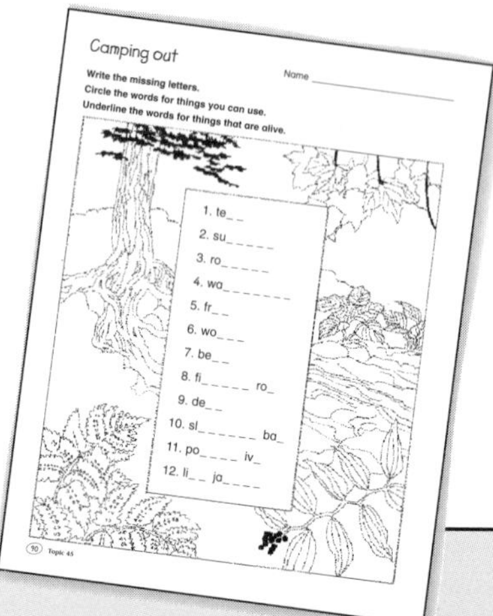

Camping out

Name ____________

Write the missing letters.
Circle the words for things you can use.
Underline the words for things that are alive.

1. te__
2. su____
3. ro____
4. wa______
5. fr__
6. wo___
7. be__
8. fi_____ ro_
9. de__
10. sl______ ba_
11. po____ iv_
12. li__ ja____

90 Topic 45

Activities

- Pack for a camping trip. Ask the children what they would need in order to spend a night away from home in the woods. Some of the ideas will probably be words from this topic, such as *tent* and *sleeping bag.* Other items may be suggested by the illustration, for example, *cups* and *plates.* Write each word on an index card and put it into a backpack or a box labeled as one. When the pack is full, pull the words out one by one and ask the children to identify them. Let them take turns pulling a card and challenging a friend to say the word.

- Work with a small group of children to make a play about camping. Suggest that they describe the setting first and decide on characters (ask *who* and *where* questions). You may want to write on a chart their characters and the description of the setting. Then ask, *What happens first? next? and then?* Schedule time for them to "play" the play for a while until they have a basic plot outline. Encourage them to take turns playing each part and trying different dialogue and action. Then ask them to stop and think about how the audience will know what is happening. Invite them to perform the play and welcome comments and discussion afterward.

- Play a campfire circle game. Start by introducing a clapping pattern (such as hands together twice, then hands on thighs once, and repeat). Begin the round-robin game with a simple phrase, for example, *I went to the woods and I saw a frog.* Then prompt your neighbor to repeat your words and add to the chant: *I went to the woods and I saw a frog and a deer.* Continue until each child has had a chance to add something, then repeat the entire chain of sights. Challenge the children to repeat the chain as well. Vary the game by beginning *I went to the woods and I heard ...,* or by limiting the add-ons to one category.

TOPIC 46 Bugs!

Content

- Insects
- Taking precautions

Language

- Identifying and describing insects and other small creatures: *The ants are marching in a line bringing food to their nest. The gray spider is spinning a beautiful silver web to catch other bugs.*
- Expressing positive and negative feelings about insects: *Look at the fireflies light up! They are beautiful! I don't like mosquitoes.*
- Describing the dangers of some insects: *Some kinds of ticks can make you sick. Bee stings hurt.*
- Suggesting actions for protection: *Wear long pants and long-sleeved shirts in the woods so ticks can't bite you. Use bug spray to keep mosquitoes away. Don't swat at bees; they might sting.*

It's twilight at the Lopez family campsite. They are having a wonderful time observing all the little insects, listening to the cicadas rubbing their wings together and the bees buzzing back to the hive. Jasmin is very excited by the fireflies flashing their lights. She is trying to catch one. Vanessa watches a spider spinning a beautiful silver web to catch other bugs. The children learn that the crawling caterpillar will spin a cocoon around itself and turn into a butterfly. Diego and a friend are looking through magnifying glasses. The friend is watching ants marching in a line, carrying bits of food. Diego's father is showing him a jar that has ticks in it. He is warning him that ticks are dangerous. Suddenly a swarm of mosquitoes appears. The children slap and scratch at their bodies. Mrs. Lopez comes quickly with bug spray to rub on their bare arms and legs.

Words

1. ant
2. spider
3. web
4. caterpillar
5. cocoon
6. butterfly
7. bee
8. ticks
9. firefly
10. mosquito
11. magnifying glass
12. bug spray

Labels

eggs
larva
pupa
adult

Additional Words

insect
cicada
beehive
anthill
scratch
itch
spin
rub
sting

Words

Components: Topic 46 Wall Chart, Picture Dictionary (pp. 92–93), Cassette, Word Picture Cards (Topic 46).

See page xiv for techniques and strategies for presenting and practicing words.

Bugs!

1. ant	6. butterfly	10. mosquito
2. spider	7. bee	11. magnifying glass
3. web	8. ticks	12. bug spray
4. caterpillar	9. firefly	
5. cocoon		

Labels

eggs larva pupa adult

Notes

After all the words have been introduced, let the children sort their word cards into various categories they invent, such as *fun to watch* or *be careful of these.*

Workbook page

Show the children how to find and record (check off) the bugs in the picture. For example, search the picture for the ant. When you find it, circle it; then make a mark in the box next to the clue art. In the match-and-write section, it may be easier for the children to match the sentences to the art after they use the internal clues to write the words.

46 Bugs!

Circle each bug and check the correct box.

ant spider tick caterpillar butterfly firefly mosquito bee

Match and write.

1. You can see bugs better with a ______ ______.

2. You can use ______ ______ to keep the mosquitos away.

3. Look! There is a spider in its ______.

Stories

Components: Picture Dictionary (pp. 92–93), Cassette, Story (Topic 46).

See page xviii for techniques and strategies for presenting and practicing stories.

Look through the magnifying glass! See the ants marching in a line? They're bringing food to their nest. Diego is looking at ticks. Those bugs can make you sick. Be careful!

The gray spider is spinning a beautiful silver web to catch other bugs! Zuzz-z! It's a bee! They sting, but they make honey, too. Listen to the cicadas, rubbing their wings together.

The funny fat creepy crawly thing is a caterpillar. It will spin a cocoon around itself. When it comes out, it will be a butterfly! How does it do that? Insects are really cool!

Jasmin sees little lights flying around! Fireflies! Flashing on and off. Fun! Fun! Catch one, but then let it go. Nnz-nnz-nnz. Mosquitoes! Ouch! Itch! Put on the bug spray!

Story notes

Ask the children to tell you what kinds of insects they have seen in the area where you live.

Ask about the story:

What does Diego's father have in the jar? Can ticks hurt you? What are the ants doing? Which insect flashes light? How can you keep mosquitoes away? What do spiders spin? Why do spiders make webs? How do cicadas make a noise? Where do butterflies come from?

Ask about your students:

Have you ever been bitten by an insect? What happened? Why do you think insects bite? What do you like about insects? What don't you like about them? Are insects good for anything? What are they good for? Do insects ever help people?

Dialogue

Components: Cassette, Topic 46 Wall Chart, Picture Dictionary (pp. 92–93).

See page xix for techniques and strategies for presenting and practicing dialogues.

Boy:	These ants are so little, but when you look through the magnifying glass they look so big!
Diego:	What are they doing?
Boy:	They're carrying big pieces of food.
Diego:	These ticks look mean. Dad, do ticks bite?
Mr. Lopez:	Yes, they do, but you can't feel it. That's why you have to be careful.
Diego:	Why?
Mr. Lopez:	Because sometimes their bite can make you sick. They can carry a sickness and give it to you.
Boy:	No thanks!
Mr. Lopez:	Well, ticks are usually in the woods, so wear long pants and shirts with long sleeves. And check your skin to be sure you don't have a tick on you.
Jasmin:	Look at the little lights flying around!
Mr. Lopez:	They're fireflies, Jasmin.
Jasmin:	Can I catch one?
Mr. Lopez:	Catch one if you can, but don't hurt it. And then let it go.
Diego:	Do all insects bite, Dad?
Mr. Lopez:	No, not all.
Vanessa:	Mosquitoes bite. Ouch! Where did they come from? They make me itch!
Mrs. Lopez:	Don't scratch. Here's some bug spray. Rub it on your arms and legs.
Vanessa:	That feels better. O-oh, I hear the cicadas in the trees. Bugs are fun.

Dialogue notes

Invent dialogues based on these exchanges:

Q: What is that?
A: They're fireflies.
Q: Can I catch one?
A: Catch one if you can, but don't hurt it.
And then let it go.

or

Q: What is that?
A: That's a tick.
Q: Can I catch one?
A: No, better not; a tick can make you sick.

Beats!

Components: Cassette, Beats! (Topic 46).

See page xx for techniques and strategies for presenting and practicing Beats!

Bugs are amazing
little things.
With feelers that talk
or wings that sing.

Some are artists
like the spider.
She spins a web
from silk inside her.

Some are magicians
that change shape and size.
Caterpillars turn into
butterflies!

Some are shiny and
some have fuzz.
Some are a nuisance!
Buzz! Buzz! Buzz!

Beat notes

Have the children practice the Beat as written, saying the last line in unison. Then you can suggest that the children recite the Beat, holding up each insect picture card as the particular insect is mentioned. They may want to try inventing new stanzas patterned on the structure *Some are ...*

Worksheets

Worksheet 1: Bugs! (p. 91)

Have the children identify each bug and write the vocabulary word(s) first. Demonstrate how to circle the first letter of a word. Then show students how to find the letters in the sections of the butterfly and use the code key to color it.

Name ________

Bugs!

Write.
Circle the first letter of each word.
Read the code to color the picture.

Code
Color "a" black.
Color "b" red.
Color "c" blue.
Color "f" orange.
Color "m" yellow.
Color "s" green.
Color "t" brown.

Topic 46 91

Worksheet 2: Bugs! (p. 92)

Help the children read the clues for the words across and write the words. The words down will then be complete, and they can write those words in the numbered spaces provided.

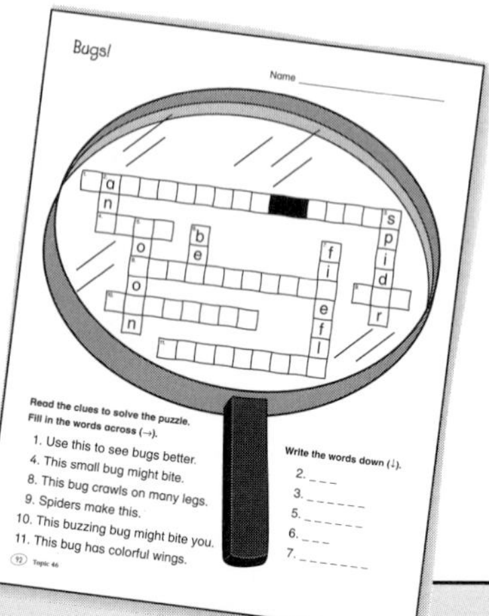
Bugs!

Name ________

Read the clues to solve the puzzle.
Fill in the words across (→).
1. Use this to see bugs better.
4. This small bug might bite.
8. This bug crawls on many legs.
9. Spiders make this.
10. This buzzing bug might bite you.
11. This bug has colorful wings.

Write the words down (↓).
2. ___
3. ______
5. _____
6. ___
7. _______

92 Topic 46

Activities

- Reproduce the picture-card insect images as small as possible—just large enough to be clearly identified with the help of a magnifying glass. Tape each tiny image onto a plastic counter or cardboard square. Divide a clear white paper mat into sections larger than the counters or squares, labeled with the bug names in this topic. Have the children examine each tiny bug (with or without a magnifying glass) and place it in the correct area on the mat.
- Make blown-paint webs. Place a fairly large dollop of wet poster paint in the middle of a piece of black construction paper. Using a plastic drinking straw, let the children blow from the center of the dollop to create the arms of the web. After the paint has dried, have the children add a spider made from four short pipe cleaners twisted together. Hang the webs on the wall and discuss ways how they are different from one another and how they are the same. If possible, present some pictures of real spider webs to compare with the children's webs.
- Explain that bees use dances, or body language, to communicate the location of a food source to other bees in the hive. Have the children work in small groups to invent a bee dance to direct each other to a specific location. Then ask all the members of a group but one to wait outside for a moment. Show the remaining member where a snack is hidden and challenge this child to use the bee dance (only) to give his or her hivemates directions.
- Provide magnifying glasses to the children, and let them take turns examining different objects or creatures. Ask the children to draw and label a picture of a tiny bug. Then ask them to imagine that they are looking at the same bug through a magnifying glass and to draw the magnified picture and label it appropriately.

Ranch in the desert

Content

- Southwestern environment
- Desert wildlife
- Ranch activities

Language

- Describing the southwestern landscape: *Tall cactuses grow in the desert. The mountains are purple.*
- Identifying desert plants and animals: *There's a lazy lizard lying on a rock. The buffalo are roaming on the plains. A prairie dog is poking its head out of its hole.*
- Describing actions: *The cowhands are going to rope cattle. The cowhand gave Alison a lasso. Alison is going horseback riding.*
- Expressing concern related to safety and warnings: *Watch out for rattlesnakes! Shake out your boots before you put them on; there may be scorpions inside.*

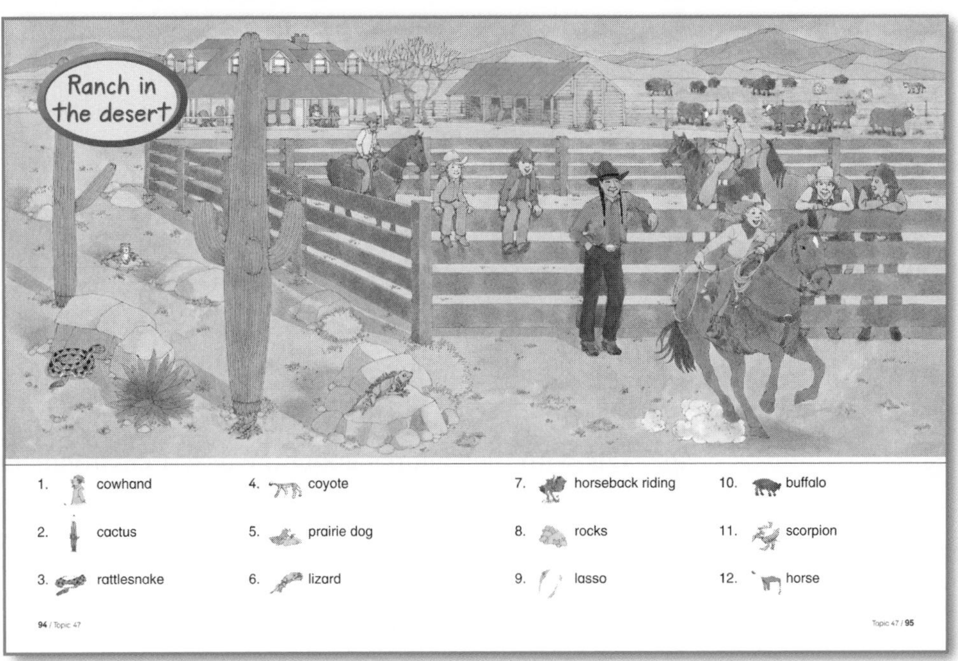

Words

1. cowhand
2. cactus
3. rattlesnake
4. coyote
5. prairie dog
6. lizard
7. horseback riding
8. rocks
9. lasso
10. buffalo
11. scorpion
12. horse

Additional Words

cattle
corral
saddle
rope
cowboy hat
spurs
iguana
ranch house
roam
howl
range
canyon
crawl

Alison's family is vacationing on a ranch in the Southwest. The landscape is beautiful. Cactuses stand tall in the pink, dry earth. The rocks are red, and behind the ranch house there are purple mountains. In the distance, a coyote runs across the desert. There are small herds of buffalo and cattle grazing. Nearby, a prairie dog is poking its head out of a hole. A lizard is lying on a rock. A scorpion and a rattlesnake are hidden among the cactuses and rocks. There are a stable and a corral, where cowhands are riding horses. Mr. and Mrs. Matthews are on the veranda of the ranch house watching, and Alison is on a horse ready to ride. She has on her riding boots and cowboy hat and is sitting in the saddle, holding the reins. A cowhand has just handed her a lasso. She is thrilled!

Words

 **Components:** Topic 47 Wall Chart, Picture Dictionary (pp. 94–95), Cassette, Word and Picture Cards (Topic 47).

See page xiv for techniques and strategies for presenting and practicing words.

Ranch in the desert

1. cowhand	6. lizard	9. lasso
2. cactus	7. horseback riding	10. buffalo
3. rattlesnake	8. rocks	11. scorpion
4. coyote		12. horse
5. prairie dog		

Notes

Model a series of questions and answers that prompt the children to use the vocabulary. Refer to the Wall Chart and ask, for example: *What is Alison riding? Alison is riding a horse. Where is the rattlesnake? The rattlesnake is under the rocks.* Encourage the children to make up their own questions to pose to each other. Shuffle a collection of picture cards. Invite volunteers to pick a card and ask a question using the vocabulary word shown on the card. You may want to explain why Alison is warned about rattlesnakes and scorpions. (Both animals protect themselves and paralyze their prey with poisons, administered by a rattlesnake's bite and a scorpion's stinger in its tail.)

Workbook page

Suggest that the children follow the cowhand's path with their finger or pencil. The words they need to label the picture are at the bottom of the page. To help the children answer the numbered questions, lead them to understand that she has a *lasso* in her hand and is going to go *horseback riding.*

47 Ranch in the desert
Write.
What does the cowhand see on her way to the horse?
cowhand
horse
1. What does she have?
She has a ________.
2. What will she do when she gets to the stable?
She will go ________.
cowhand, coyote, horseback riding, buffalo, cactus, prairie dog, rocks, scorpion, rattlesnake, lizard, lasso, horse

Stories

 **Components:** Picture Dictionary (pp. 94–95), Cassette, Story (Topic 47).

See page xviii for techniques and strategies for presenting and practicing stories.

Tall cactuses grow in the dry, pink earth of the desert, and the mountains are purple behind the ranch house. Buffalo roam the range, and coyotes howl at night.

Ch-ch-ch! Look quick! A prairie dog is poking out of his hole. And there's a lazy lizard lying on a rock. Some rocks are so old, you can see skeleton pictures inside!

Watch out for rattlesnakes! Shake out your boots before you put them on. There might be a scorpion inside! Ya-hoo! The cowhands are roping cattle in the corral.

And here comes Alison with her new saddle and spurs and cowboy hat! Here's a lasso for you, Miss! Yippee! Look at her ride that horse!

Story notes

Talk with the children about the desert environment. Direct their attention to the plants shown in the illustration, and ask what kinds of plants could grow in such a hot, dry place. Help them understand that plants that grow in the desert must be able to store water for long periods of time when there is no rain. You can also ask them what it would be like for humans and other animals to live in the desert, or you can ask them to compare the desert to a different environment.

Ask about the story:
What is Alison doing? Is anyone else riding a horse? Where are Alison's parents? What animals live in the desert? Do any plants live in the desert? What are the cowhands doing? Where are the cattle?

Ask about your students:
Have you ever seen a desert? How do you think the air feels in a desert? What would be hard about living in a desert? Would you like to ride a horse?

Dialogue

Components: Cassette, Topic 47 Wall Chart, Picture Dictionary (pp. 94–95).

See page xix for techniques and strategies for presenting and practicing dialogues.

Alison:	What's that sound?
Cowboy:	Ever see a prairie dog, Miss?
Alison:	No.
Cowboy:	Well, look quick! There's one just poking his head out of his hole.
Alison:	Oh, he's cute! And I see a lizard on the rocks.
Cowboy:	Yep, that's an iguana.
Alison:	Can I take some of those rocks home with me? They're a pretty color.
Cowboy:	Sure, Miss. Help yourself. And here's a new lasso for you.
Alison:	Oh! Thank you! I hope I can learn to throw it right, like all the cowhands do.
Cowboy:	You will. Now, then, what did I tell you about rattlesnakes?
Alison:	Watch out for rattlesnakes!
Cowboy:	Right. Just remember when you're riding, rattlesnakes like to hide under the cactus. And what did I tell you about your boots?
Alison:	Don't forget to shake out your boots!
Cowboy:	Right. Shake out your boots in the morning before you put them on. Scorpions like to hide in boots!
Alison:	I won't forget! Thanks again. Here I go! Yippee!

Dialogue notes

After listening to the dialogue a few times, invite the children to invent their own dialogues, focusing on plants and animals. The first speaker asks, *Did you ever see a prairie dog?* (or other plant or animal visible in the illustration on the Wall Chart or in the Dictionary). The second speaker answers, *No.* And the first speaker replies with a description of location or action to help identify the item, for example, *There's one sticking out of its hole.* Encourage the children to alternate roles and vary the phrase used to identify the items.

Beats!

Components: Cassette, Beats! (Topic 47).

See page xx for techniques and strategies for presenting and practicing Beats!

I'd like to be a buffalo
roaming on the plains.
I'd see you in the desert
where it almost never rains.

I could be a coyote,
always on the prowl.
I'd see you in the canyon.
At night I'd hear you howl.

I could be a rattlesnake.
In the cactus I would crawl.
Prairie dogs and scorpions
wouldn't bother you at all.

But I'm going to be a cowhand,
with a horse and saddle, too.
When I see you on the ranch,
I will come and ride with you.

Beat notes

Put the children into two groups to practice the Beat. Give each group a chance to recite the two parts. When the children are comfortable with the words and phrases, encourage them to take turns acting the parts of the animals described in the Beat, for example, crawling on the ground as rattlesnakes, or howling as coyotes.

Worksheets

Worksheet 1: Ranch in the desert (p. 93)

Review the animals in the scene by having the children compare the drawing on the worksheet to the illustration on the Wall Chart or in the Dictionary. They should recognize that the coyote, lizard, prairie dog, horse, and buffalo have four legs; the scorpion has more than four legs, and the rattlesnake and the cowhand have fewer than four legs. Some children may not include the cowhand as an animal.

Worksheet 2: Ranch in the desert (p. 94)

Point out that the number by each item the cowhand passes along the trail corresponds to the number of a space below, in which the children write the vocabulary word.

Activities

- Make a desert diorama. Provide empty boxes for small groups of children to use as a basis for a desert scene. Demonstrate how they can color or paint the interior of the box to look like the desert. Then help them make plants, animals, buildings and people, based on the Dictionary illustration and drawn on stiff paper and cut out (or made with modeling clay).

- Reconstruct a day on a ranch. Ask the children to pretend that they are on the ranch with Alison. Have them pantomime the actions you describe as you narrate. For example, you might begin with: *It's early morning. The sun is just coming up over the mountains. The people are just waking up.* Prompt the children to pantomime waking up, stretching, and shaking their boots to get rid of scorpions!

- Investigate horses. Share books and stories about horses. Some children might enjoy imagining that they have a horse. Encourage them to draw pictures, to give their horse a name, to find out what their horse likes to eat and how it sleeps, and to role-play taking care of and riding a horse. Encourage them to talk to one another as they play by modeling questions: *What does your horse look like? Is your horse very big?*

- Create a board game. Glue the picture cards face-up onto a large piece of cardboard in a random pattern, and draw a winding path that passes through each of the cards. Divide the path into sections. Tell the children that the object of the game is to collect as many word cards as they can. Invite the children to use a spinner (or roll a die) to move forward or backward whatever number of spaces they spin (or roll). Each time they land on a picture card, they have to say the word. If they say the correct word, they can collect the word card. Encourage them to invent their own variations to the game.

Theme 7: Animals

Topic 48 Dinosaur days
Topic 49 Who lives in the zoo?
Topic 50 I'm in Australia!
Topic 51 I'm in Africa!
Topic 52 I'm in Asia!

Theme Bibliography

Biggest, Strongest, Fastest
by Steve Jenkins.
Houghton Mifflin Co., 1997. ISBN 0395861365
Comparative facts and figures about the animal world are delightfully illustrated with cut-paper collage art in this book. As they read the simple text, students can identify familiar animals and learn new words to express comparisons. For children who want more information, a chart on the last page shows the size, weight, and diet of each animal and where it lives.

Birds
written and illustrated by Brian Wildsmith.
Oxford University Press, 1992. ISBN 0192721178
Fishes
written and illustrated by Brian Wildsmith.
Oxford University Press, 1996. ISBN 0192721518
These two books contain brilliant, exuberant paintings of birds and fishes, accompanied by traditional and invented collective nouns ("a stare of owls, a party of jays, and a stream of minnows, a hover of trout," etc.). The text not only extends students' familiarity with names and features of creatures in the natural world, it also generates a fun sense of wordplay.

Dinosaur Poems
compiled by John Foster; illustrated by Paul Korky.
Oxford University Press, 1997. ISBN 0192761269
Some of these bouncy, rhythmic, and lively poems can be used for reading in chorus or as springboards for role playing and inventing skits. Some of the language is British English; this may prompt discussion about differences in the language. Some of the dinosaurs featured in Topic 48 have poems about them in the book.

If I Were You
written and illustrated by Brian Wildsmith.
Oxford University Press, 1997. ISBN 0198490100
Starting with "I went to the zoo and I thought ...," this small book explores a child's imagination, using simple text and striking pictures. The repetitive structure "If I were ... I would..." can be used as a model in prompting students to express their own imaginative desires.

Kele's Secret
written by Tololwa M. Mollel;
illustrated by Catherine Stock.
Lodestar Books, 1997. ISBN 0525675000
This is the story of Kele the hen and the young boy Yoanes who must track down her secret nest of eggs. It is a charming introduction to Africa, and it can serve as a point of entry for students from Africa to share their home culture. The language in the story may need to be sheltered. The book also works well with Topic 44 from Theme 6 (Working on the farm), as it offers children another view of a farm, this one in a faraway place.

The King of the Birds
written and illustrated by Helen Ward.
Millbrook, 1997. ISBN 0761303138
Clear, colorful pictures of birds from all over the world illustrate this retelling of a traditional story about choosing a king. The text includes accessible vocabulary, although there are a few difficult words and sophisticated grammatical structures. In addition to generating discussion about bird identification and characteristics, the story can be used as a starting point for talking about group decision-making and expressing opinions.

The Lazy Bear

written and illustrated by Brian Wildsmith.
Oxford University Press, 1986. ISBN 0192721585
Wildsmith's colorful art ignites this moral tale of a bear who learns it isn't very nice to take advantage of his friends. While the birds and plants seem fantastical, many of the animals the children know from the Picture Dictionary are featured. The text offers simple past-tense language models that can be expanded, such as "He pushed the wagon up the hill."

Over in the Meadow

written and illustrated by Ezra J. Keats.
Scholastic Inc., 1992. ISBN 0590728091
This illustrated version of a well-known counting rhyme introduces the habitats of many animals living in a meadow and the noises that they make. The rhymes can be used for speaking activities. The illustrations can be used as prompts to teach motion verbs in the text. Many activities for counting, language learning, and identifying geography can start with this versatile book.

Rikki-Tikki-Tavi

written by Rudyard Kipling;
illustrated and adapted by Jerry Pinkney.
William Morrow and Co., 1997. ISBN 0688143202
This is the story of a brave little mongoose who protects his human family from a pair of menacing cobras. The simplified language and lush, detailed illustrations make Kipling's classic tale accessible to English-language learners. It is a great book to read aloud while students read along and collect new vocabulary words.

A Summertime Song

written and illustrated by Irene Haas.
Margaret McElderry, 1997. ISBN 0689505493
Animals and insects join Lucy in her dreamy adventure of a magic birthday party. The lush illustrations are filled with images of hidden animals, toys, and party paraphernalia that children will enjoy locating and identifying. There are many examples of language patterns that can be used to prompt student activities.

The Sweet and Sour Animal Book

by Langston Hughes; illustrated by students from the Harlem School of the Arts.
Oxford University Press, 1997. ISBN 0195120302
Langston Hughes takes children on a journey through the animal world with twenty-six short, clever poems; one for each letter of the alphabet. The illustrations for each poem are engaging examples of puppets, paper mache, clay, and painted constructions made by children. There is also a photo gallery of the artists, and an essay that discusses the process of creating art in response to poetry. Use this book to generate interest and excitement for making both poems and art.

The Trunk

written and illustrated by Brian Wildsmith.
Oxford University Press, 1982. ISBN 0198490070
Ask your children to identify the animals in this small, wordless picture book. It can be used as a great story-starter for your students' own stories.

What a Tale

written and illustrated by Brian Wildsmith.
Oxford University Press, 1982. ISBN 0192721607
Pleasing, funny pictures illustrate the adjectives introduced in this short book. It is well-suited for independent reading by young English-language learners. While reading aloud, children can try to guess the animal attached to each tail before its identity is revealed.

Wombat Divine

written by Mem Fox;
illustrated by Kerry Argent.
Harcourt Brace, 1996. ISBN 0152014160
Australian animals are the characters in this funny, sweet story of Wombat, who wants a part in the yearly Nativity Play. This Christmas story features repetitive, simple text and expressive illustrations. It can be used to generate talk about feelings as well as practice in identifying of places, animals, and things.

Dinosaur days

Content

- Prehistoric earth
- Dinosaurs
- Fossils

Language

- Using comparative and superlative adjectives: *The Diplodocus was longer than the Oviraptor. The Tyrannosaurus Rex is the biggest dinosaur in the picture.*
- Describing scenes: *The asteroid is falling to earth. The dinosaur is feeding her babies.*
- Expressing theories or speculations: *Maybe the asteroid killed the dinosaurs. The dinosaurs might have been different colors.*

Words

1. fossil
2. scientist
3. dinosaurs
4. Oviraptor
5. Pterosaur
6. Triceratops
7. Stegosaurus
8. Tyrannosaurus Rex
9. Diplodocus
10. asteroid
11. volcano
12. lava

Additional Words

paleontologist
erupt
crash
explode
herbivore
carnivore

Alison has found a fossil while on vacation in the Southwest. She is showing it to a scientist who is a paleontologist. She and Ting listen while he explains about the dinosaurs. Alison imagines herself and her friends in the last days of the dinosaur age. There are broken eggshells on the ground, and new baby Oviraptors are emerging. Their mother is feeding them pieces of an animal she has killed. A three-horned Triceratops is eating leaves. A Stegosaurus with bony plates on its back wants some, too. A huge Diplodocus is in the distance. Jackie has spotted a Pterosaur flying in the sky and points to it excitedly. Jo-Jo leans very casually against what he thinks is a tree, but it is the leg of a huge Tyrannosaurus Rex! An asteroid crashes into the earth, and a volcano erupts, spewing lava down its sides. Clouds of black dust cover the sun. This could be what killed the dinosaurs!

Words

Components: Topic 48 Wall Chart, Picture Dictionary (pp. 96–97), Cassette, Word and Picture Cards (Topic 48).

See page xiv for techniques and strategies for presenting and practicing words.

Dinosaur days

1. fossil	6. Triceratops	9. Diplodocus
2. scientist	7. Stegosaurus	10. asteroid
3. dinosaurs	8. Tyrannosaurus Rex	11. volcano
4. Oviraptor		12. lava
5. Pterosaur		

Notes

Talk about the fact that dinosaurs lived millions of years ago and are no longer alive anywhere in the world. Explain that *saurus* means *lizard*. Ask them to look for the word *saurus* (or part of it) in the names of the dinosaurs.

Workbook page

Help the children recognize that the first sentence is asking for the name of the entire group, *dinosaurs,* while the other picture clues are intended to prompt them to write specific dinosaur names. At the bottom of the page, the pictures are visual clues to help them unscramble the five words.

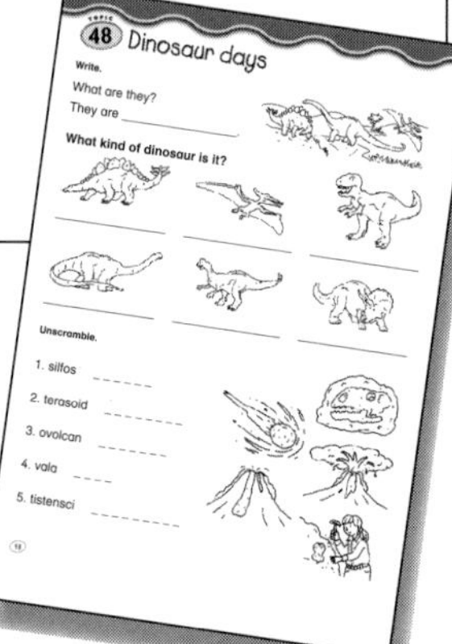

Stories

Components: Picture Dictionary (pp. 96–97), Cassette, Story (Topic 48).

See page xviii for techniques and strategies for presenting and practicing stories.

Has Alison found a dinosaur fossil?
Maybe. The scientist explains all about the dinosaurs, millions of years ago.
Imagine how the Earth was then. ...

Dinosaurs are everywhere!
Alison sees an Oviraptor feeding her babies. Ting sees a Triceratops eating leaves. A Stegosaurus with bony plates on its back wants some, too.

Jackie points to the sky. What's that?
A Pterosaur is flying high!
Jo-Jo leans against a tall tree. Tree?
It's the leg of a big Tyrannosaurus Rex!

Something explodes! Ka-boom!
An asteroid has crashed into the Earth!
A volcano erupts! Lava pours out.
Clouds of black dust cover the Sun.
What happens to the dinosaurs?

Story notes

Begin a discussion by saying that no one has ever seen a live dinosaur. Explain that the world was very different when the dinosaurs lived over sixty million years ago. There were no people living then. Some dinosaurs were very small, but some were bigger than a house. Ask the children how we can know about dinosaurs when we have never seen one. Encourage the children to offer suggestions about how we learn about something we've never seen.

Ask about the story:
What did Alison find? What were the Triceratops and the Stegosaurus eating? Was the Triceratops eating meat? What was Jackie pointing to? Why did Alison shout at Jo-Jo? What exploded? What comes out of a volcano? What happened to the asteroid?

Ask about your students:
Why won't you ever see a real dinosaur? Did you ever see a dinosaur in a museum? What kind of dinosaur do you like? Was a Tyrannosaurus Rex taller than you?

Dialogue

Components: Cassette, Topic 48 Wall Chart, Picture Dictionary (pp. 96–97).

See page xix for techniques and strategies for presenting and practicing dialogues.

Alison: Look at all these dinosaurs!
Ting: What strange-looking animals. The Triceratops and the Stegosaurus are eating leaves.
Alison: The Oviraptors aren't. The mother is feeding the babies an animal. Yuk!
Ting: I see a huge long, long dinosaur.
Alison: That's Diplodocus. He's a plant eater, too. He's eating that tree.
Ting: Hey! Jackie's pointing to something.
Alison: Yikes! He sees a flying Pterosaur!
Ting: Weird. Look! Jo-Jo's leaning against that dinosaur's leg.
Alison: Jo-Jo! Get away from there! Quick! Run! That's a Tyrannosaurus Rex. He's the worst, meanest dinosaur ever!
Alison: That must be the asteroid the scientist told us about!
Ting: The one that crashed into the earth?
Alison: That's the one!
Ting: Oh-h-h. Poor dinosaurs.

Dialogue notes

Practice this exchange:

Ting: I see a huge long, long dinosaur.
Alison: That's Diplodocus.

Then challenge the children to work in pairs to come up with another, similar exchange in which one child describes a dinosaur and the other names it. You can also encourage the children to practice phrases using comparative adjectives *(bigger, smaller, longer, shorter, meaner, stranger)* and superlative adjectives *(biggest, smallest, tallest, etc.)*.

Beats!

Components: Cassette, Beats! (Topic 48).

See page xx for techniques and strategies for presenting and practicing Beats!

Where, oh where did the dinosaurs go?
Does anybody know?
They used to wander all over the Earth,
but that was long ago.

Some were little,
and some were big.
Some were timid and shy.

Some were ferocious!
Some swam in the sea!
Some even flew in the sky!

Where, oh where did the dinosaurs go?
What happened so long ago?
Did they all get smashed
when an asteroid crashed?
We really would like to know!

Beat notes

Put the children into two groups and have them practice the Beat as written. Encourage the children to stomp around like dinosaurs for the first three stanzas and act out the words, for example, squinching down for *some were little,* and miming swimming or flying motions. Then they can fall to the ground for the lines *Did they all get smashed / when an asteroid crashed?* and jump back up to shout the final line shouted in unison.

Worksheets

Worksheet 1: Dinosaur days (p. 95)

The vocabulary words are all shown in the puzzle. You may suggest that as the children find and circle each vocabulary word, they cross out the word at the bottom of the page.

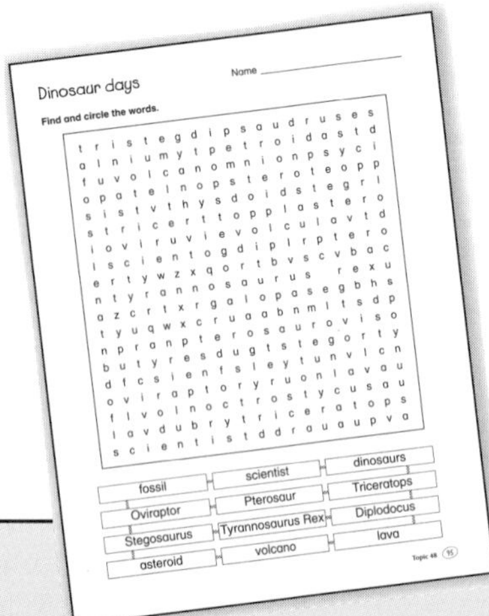

Dinosaur days

Name

Find and circle the words.

fossil	scientist	dinosaurs
Oviraptor	Pterosaur	Triceratops
Stegosaurus	Tyrannosaurus Rex	Diplodocus
asteroid	volcano	lava

Worksheet 2: Dinosaur days (p. 96)

Tell the children to write or dictate the words to label each picture. Then help them read and follow the coloring directions and name the dinosaurs at the bottom of the page.

Dinosaur days

Name

Write.

Color the biggest red.

Color the smallest brown.

What do you call it?

Activities

- Make a mural. Ask the children to suggest things they think would be in the dinosaurs' world, such as trees, big rocks, exploding volcanoes, lots of strange insects, and perhaps strange flowering plants. Ask questions such as *What color should the sky be? Were there plants then? Was there water?* Then have the children paint the mural—adding to the scene the dinosaurs of their choice.
- Make a felt board dinosaur world. Use the picture cards as pattern models (enlarged if possible) for cutting out felt dinosaurs. Also, cut out felt ferns and rocks and other elements of the environment. Have the children set up a scene on the felt board and dictate a story about it. The children can play together using the felt pieces to make other dinosaur stories.
- Make "fossils" by pressing different forms, such as a seashell, nut, or piece of uncooked pasta into rolled-out modeling clay to leave an impression. Place the "fossils" in the middle of a table, surrounded by the (randomly placed) objects used to make the impressions. Challenge the children to identify which object made which shape.
- Syllable Claps. This activity works with any of the topics, but it fits the dinosaur topic especially well because of the length of the words. Have the class say each word, clapping once for each syllable in it (for example, *Di-plo-do-cus* = four claps). After repeating the clapping patterns with the words, clap a pattern and ask the children which words have that pattern. That is, if you clap four times, the children could name *Diplodocus, Oviraptor,* or *Stegosaurus,* as they all have four syllables.

Who lives in the zoo?

Content

- Zoos
- Continent of origin of different animals
- Specific animal characteristics

Language

- Identifying and describing zoo animals: *Look at the zebra. The monkeys are climbing the tree.*
- Reading and interpreting signs: *The kangaroo comes from Australia. The animals from Africa are over there.*
- Categorizing animals: *Snakes are reptiles. An ape is a mammal; it isn't a bird.*
- Describing specific characteristics of animals: *That monkey's tail is long. An elephant's trunk can spray water. A gorilla's fur is thick.*
- Describing animal behavior: *Lions roar. Snakes wriggle, squirm, and slither. Tigers slink and stalk. Monkeys hang and swing.*

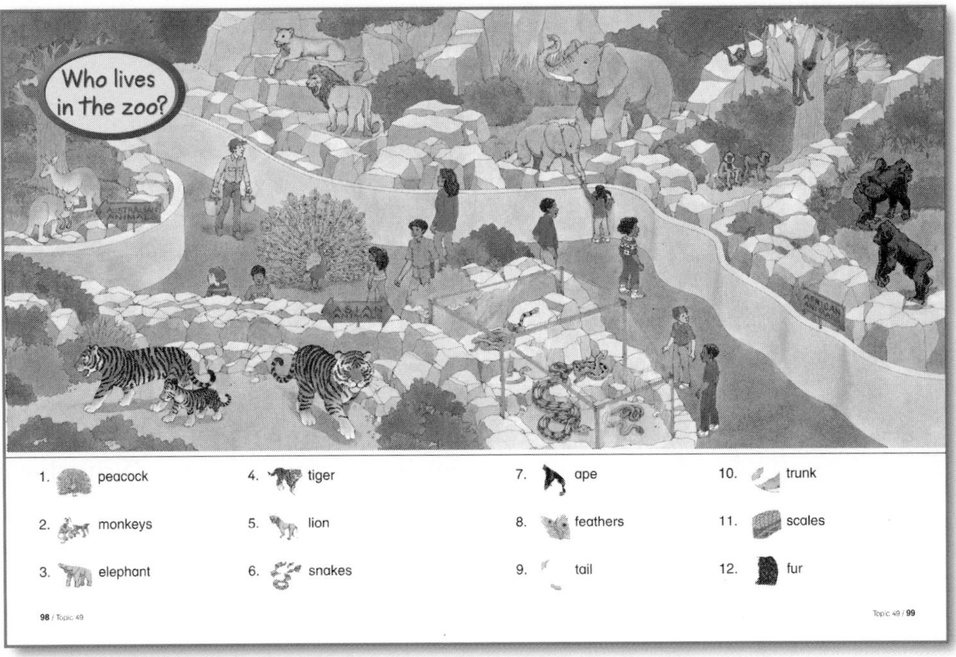

The Jacksons and Mrs. Young, Tommy, and Jim are at the zoo. The lions are roaring; the tigers are slinking back and forth; monkeys are hanging from the trees, swinging by their tails; and the snakes are wriggling between the rocks. Zoe loves the funny monkeys, and she's laughing at them. Nearby, Samantha pats the baby elephant's wrinkled trunk very gently. Jasmin is fascinated by the peacock spreading its beautiful tail feathers. She wants Diego to see it, but he's looking at the tigers and their cub. Tommy is looking around for the kangaroos. Jim and Marcus are busy watching the snakes and the gorillas—and the gorillas are busy watching Jim and Marcus!

Words

1. peacock
2. monkeys
3. elephant
4. tiger
5. lion
6. snakes
7. ape
8. feathers
9. tail
10. trunk
11. scales
12. fur

Additional Words

cub
calf
tusk
enclosure
reptile
mammal
primate
bird

Words

Components: Topic 49 Wall Chart, Picture Dictionary (pp. 98–99), Cassette, Word and Picture Cards (Topic 49).

See page xiv for techniques and strategies for presenting and practicing words.

Who lives in the zoo?

1. peacock	5. lion	9. tail
2. monkeys	6. snakes	10. trunk
3. elephant	7. ape	11. scales
4. tiger	8. feathers	12. fur

Notes

Write the words for characteristics on a chart: *feathers, tail, trunk, scales, fur.* Gather the children around the Wall Chart, and ask them to identify the animals in each enclosure in the zoo. Once all the animals have been named, point to each of the words on the chart in turn, and ask (for example), *Which of the animals in the zoo has a tail?*

Workbook page

The numbered pictures at the bottom of the page are the clues for filling in the missing letters and words in this crossword puzzle. You can have children work on this puzzle in pairs.

Stories

Components: Picture Dictionary (pp. 98–99), Cassette, Story (Topic 49).

See page xviii for techniques and strategies for presenting and practicing stories.

Zoos are fun! Where do all the wild animals come from? Africa, Asia, Australia ... all over the world. Watch! The animals are all different!

Jasmin watches a peacock.
Look at its feathers!
Zoe laughs at the monkeys.
They can hang by their tails!
Samantha pats an elephant's trunk.

Diego watches the big cats.
The tigers slink back and forth and the lions r-o-a-a-r-r-r!
Tommy is looking for kangaroos.
Where are they?

Jim and Marcus watch the squirming snakes with their shiny scales, and the apes with their thick black fur.
Hey boys! The apes are watching you!

Story notes

Invite volunteers to talk about their own experiences of visiting the zoo. Ask if any children can name some of the animals they saw at the zoo. Write down the animals they suggest, and compare the list to the topic words.

Ask about the story:
Which animals come from Africa? Are some animals from more than one continent? Which animals was Zoe watching? What were they doing? What did Jasmin see the peacock do? Can you find the kangaroos for Tommy? What was watching Jim and Marcus? Who was looking at the snakes?

Ask about your students:
Have you ever gone to the zoo? What animals did you see? Could you touch the animals in the zoo? Why do you think the animals are in enclosures? Who takes care of the animals? Would you like to visit a zoo? What would you like to see there?

Dialogue

Components: Cassette, Topic 49 Wall Chart, Picture Dictionary (pp. 98–99).

See page xix for techniques and strategies for presenting and practicing dialogues.

Tommy: Those lions sure can roar.
Diego: I'm watching the tigers!
Jasmin: Diego! Look at this big bird!
Diego: It's a peacock, Jasmin.
Jasmin: He's opening his feathers.
Diego: That's his tail.
Jasmin: Oh. He's opening his tail. Look, Diego, he's so beautiful!
Tommy: Where are the kangaroos? I'm going to look for the kangaroos.
Zoe: The monkeys are so funny! Watch them swinging by their tails!
Samantha: Look at this cute little elephant. Can I pat his nose, Zoe?
Zoe: That's his trunk, Samantha. Yes, you can pat him, but be careful. Don't pat him too hard.
Samantha: I won't. See? He likes it.
Marcus: I'm glad I'm not a snake. No feet.
Jim: They don't need feet. They can go fast, Marcus. Look at them wiggle.
Marcus: I like the apes better.
Jim: They must be hot with all that fur.
Marcus: I like this zoo. There's lots of space, and we can watch so many different kinds of animals.
Jim: Yeah, Marcus. And the animals can watch us. Look at those two big apes!
Marcus: Uh-oh!

Dialogue notes

Listen to the dialogue several times, and then ask the children to name the different animals mentioned. Write the names of the animals on the board or a piece of chart paper. Then ask the children to choose one animal to pay close attention to, and listen again. Ask: *Who can tell me more about the snakes? What did Marcus and Jim say about the snakes?* Review the characteristics of the pertinent animals in this way. Then encourage the children to have their own dialogues about animals they might see in a zoo.

Beats!

Components: Cassette, Beats! (Topic 49).

See page xx for techniques and strategies for presenting and practicing Beats!

I love the zoo!
I do, too!

Monkey, monkey!
Swinging in the trees!
Playing tricks.
You're a tease!

Peacock, peacock!
What a pretty sight!
Open up your feathers!
That's right!

Curly trunk
and wrinkles, too.
Elephant!
How old are you?

Listen! Listen!
Roar-r-r! Roar-r-r!
Lion! Lion!
Roar some more!

I love the zoo!
I do, too!

Beat notes

Divide the class into four groups, one group for each animal in the Beat. Then have each group divide in two and practice the lines as written. When they are comfortable with the words and phrasing, have each group take turns saying the first line of the refrain *(I love the zoo),* with the whole class responding, *I do, too!* Then prompt each group to recite its stanza. Continue in this way until the entire Beat has been recited, with the refrain repeated between the stanzas.

Worksheets

Worksheet 1: Who lives in the zoo? (p. 97)

Have a discussion about zoo animals and then brainstorm questions the group would like answered about how they are cared for. If you have a local zoo, consider sending these letters to the zookeepers. Use this opportunity to talk about the conventions of letter writing.

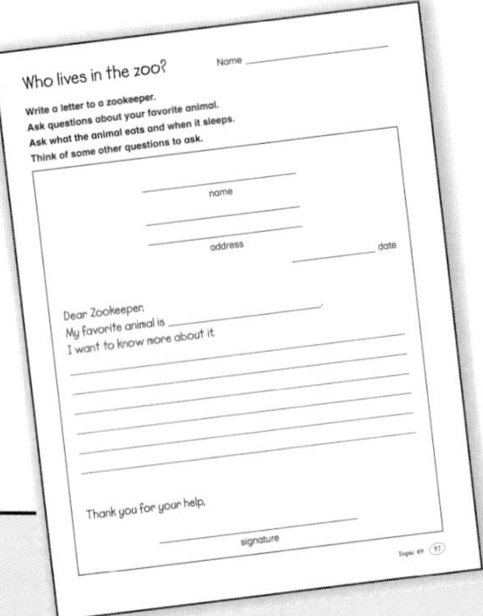

Who lives in the zoo? Name ____________

Write a letter to a zookeeper.
Ask questions about your favorite animal.
Ask what the animal eats and when it sleeps.
Think of some other questions to ask.

____________ name

____________ address

____________ date

Dear Zookeeper,
My favorite animal is ____________.
I want to know more about it.

Thank you for your help.

____________ signature

Topic 49 97

Worksheet 2: Who lives in the zoo? (p. 98)

Show the children how to trace a path from the sign to the enclosure for the animal it names. Encourage them to use vocabulary words to complete the lists for the questions at the bottom of the page, but they need not limit themselves to those words if they can think of other animals that fit the categories.

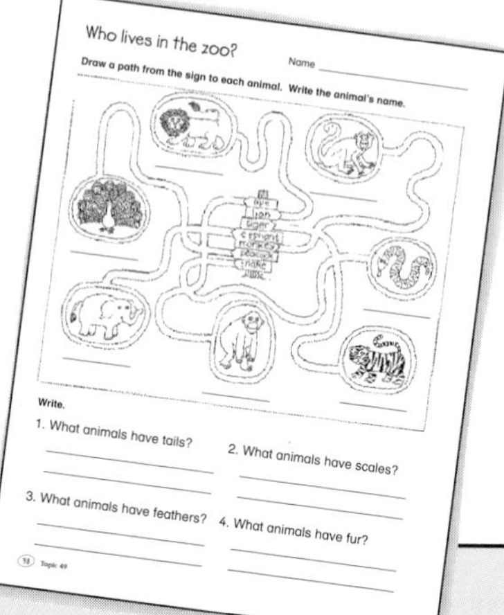

Who lives in the zoo? Name ____________

Draw a path from the sign to each animal. Write the animal's name.

Write.

1. What animals have tails?
2. What animals have scales?
3. What animals have feathers?
4. What animals have fur?

98 Topic 49

Activities

- Play a circle game. Model the pattern of statement, question, and response for the children. Use hand clapping or pantomime to enhance the game; for instance, you might begin *We're going to the zoo.* Prompt the children to repeat that line, *We're going to the zoo.* Then ask, *What do we see?* They repeat, *What do we see?* Say, *I see a peacock,* and prompt the group to reply, *We do, too!* Then begin the pattern again, repeating each time from the beginning as each child around the circle adds a new animal. Continue until each child has had a chance and all the animals have been named. Then repeat the entire list in unison. Vary the activity by changing the verb tense used, or by modeling *What do I hear?* in the opening refrain.

- Help the children to make animal riddle cards. Talk about riddles and how they work. Offer an example: *I am very big, I have a long trunk and a short tail. I have four legs. What am I?* Give each child an index card, and help them write a riddle about a zoo animal on one side. Then have them draw a picture of the animal on the other side and write the animal's name.

- Make a zoo bulletin board. Have the children work in small groups to study an animal. Help them find out such things as what the animal eats, whether it sleeps during the day or at night, and how it moves. Then give each group a piece of poster board on which they can display their information, pictures of the animals, and their own stories or observations.

- Move like the animals. Have the children stand in a circle and chant:

  Turn around, turn around, one, two, three.
  Who will we move like? What will we be?

  Say a sentence that describes an action *(Slither like a snake; Plod like an elephant; Chatter like a monkey).* Then lead the children around the circle while imitating the animals. The children can take turns being the leader once they know the game.

I'm in Australia!

Content

- Australian habitat
- Australian animals
- Specific animal characteristics

Language

- Identifying and naming Australian animals and their habitat: *Koala bears sleep high up in the trees. The dingoes are behind the bushes.*
- Describing specific characteristics of animals: *The parrot has colorful wings. The wombat digs with its sharp claws.*
- Discussing animal behavior: *The kangaroo keeps her baby in her pouch. The parrots fly away when they are scared.*

Tommy, with his toy kangaroo beside him, is dreaming of the Australian outback. In the distance, tall, skinny emus are running across the flat red earth. Dingoes lurk in the shadows. Jim is intrigued by a mother kangaroo with a pouch and a baby joey inside looking out. Other kangaroos are hopping away. A bright orange kangaroo is with them. Is it Tommy's toy kangaroo come to life? Nearby, high up in a gum tree, a koala is munching leaves it holds in its claws. In another tree, a kookaburra is laughing and screeching with its head thrown back. Two parrots have been scared by the kookaburra and are flying away. A few red and green feathers from their wings are floating in the air. At the foot of the tree, a little gray wombat is also leaving as fast as it can, scared off by the thumping kangaroos. In the red dirt, little white wichity grubs are wiggling. Tommy was watching them, but he has suddenly seen his orange toy kangaroo hopping with the other kangaroos! They are both so happy to see each other!

Words

1. emu
2. dingo
3. koala
4. kangaroo
5. joey
6. wichity grubs
7. wombat
8. kookaburra
9. parrot
10. claws
11. pouch
12. wings

Additional Words

outback
dust
lizard (goanna)
gum tree (eucalyptus)
platypus
creep/crept
munch
wiggle
waddle
thump

Words

Components: Topic 50 Wall Chart, Picture Dictionary (pp. 100–101), Cassette, Word and Picture Cards (Topic 50).

See page xiv for techniques and strategies for presenting and practicing words.

I'm in Australia!

1. emu
2. dingo
3. koala
4. kangaroo
5. joey
6. wichity grubs
7. wombat
8. kookaburra
9. parrot
10. claws
11. pouch
12. wings

Notes

Tell the children that these animal names are derived from words in Australian aboriginal languages. For example, *wichity* is from the word *wudjuta.*

Write the three vocabulary words for animal characteristics *(claws, pouch,* and *wings)* on a chart, and ask the children to tell you which animals have those characteristics.

Workbook page

The pictures are clues for completing the words. The first seven words are missing the letter *o*, the next two are missing the letter *u,* and the final three are missing the letter *w*. You can use this opportunity to play a game in which each child privately writes two words that have a vowel in common. The child writes the words on another paper with blank(s) in place of the common vowel, then challenges a partner to figure out what letter is missing.

Stories

Components: Picture Dictionary (pp. 100–101), Cassette, Story (Topic 50).

See page xviii for techniques and strategies for presenting and practicing stories.

Big skinny emus were running
across the red earth. Dingoes crept
in the shadows, and a koala high up in
a gum tree munched leaves in its claws.
A goanna was taking a sun bath.

Thump! Thump! Thump!
Look! Kangaroos! Jim laughed.
One had a pouch in front.
What was inside? A baby joey!

Tommy was watching wichity grubs
wiggling in the dust.
He looked up. Hey!
There was his orange kangaroo!

A scared little wombat waddled
away, fast! And a kookaburra laughed
so loud that two parrots flew up in
the air, dropping red and green
feathers from their wings.

Story notes

On a globe or map of the world, show the children where they are right now; then point out where Australia is. Plan an imaginary trip to Australia. Ask, *How could we get to Australia? Would it take a long time?* Collect travel information about Australia to share with the children.

Ask about the story:
What color was the ground? Did the emus walk slowly? Were the dingoes running? Which animal was creeping in the shadows? Who was high up in the gum tree? Why was the koala in the tree? What did Tommy see that made him feel happy? Who was carrying her baby? Where did she carry him? What scared the parrots?

Ask about your students:
Have you ever seen any of these animals? Are there animals like these where we live? Are there other animals with wings? Do birds around here have red and green feathers? What other animals have claws? Do some other animals have a pouch?

Components: Cassette, Topic 50 Wall Chart, Picture Dictionary (pp. 100–101).

See page xix for techniques and strategies for presenting and practicing dialogues.

Tommy:	Jim! There's a koala up in the gum tree. What's it eating?
Jim:	Leaves. That's the only thing it eats.
Tommy:	What's that noise?
Jim:	It's kangaroos! They're coming this way!
Tommy:	Why do they make so much noise?
Jim:	That's their big tails thumping on the ground when they hop.
Tommy:	They sure take big hops!
Jim:	Come on! Let's go!
Tommy:	I just want to watch these little wichity grubs for a minute.
Jim:	Come on! I think I see a baby kangaroo in the mother's pouch. Look at the baby joey!
Tommy:	Is his name "Joey"?
Jim:	No, that's what all "roo" babies are called.
Tommy:	Why does the mother have a pouch?
Jim:	To protect the baby and feed it ... and that's where she carries him. Koalas have pouches, too.
Tommy:	They do?
Jim:	And that little wombat does too.
Tommy:	You old kookaburra! You scared me! Hey! Look who I see! Jim! Look who's here! It's my kangaroo!

Dialogue notes

Listen to the dialogue several times, and encourage the children to invent dialogues beginning with the phrase *What's that noise?* Prompt the children to answer with the description of an animal's actions: *It's emus! They're running away!* or *It's a koala! She's eating leaves.*

Components: Cassette, Beats! (Topic 50).

See page xx for techniques and strategies for presenting and practicing Beats!

What's that noise?
Thump! Thump! Thump!
The kangaroos are coming!
Jump! Jump! Jump!

What's that noise?
Crunch! Crunch! Crunch!
The koala's in the gum tree
eating lunch!

What's that hiding?
in the mother's pouch?
A joey is riding.
Bounce! Bounce! Ouch!

Who's that crazy bird?
Ha ha! Ha ha! He-e-e-e!
A kookaburra's laughing
at you and me!

Beat notes

Separate the children into three groups. Have one group ask the opening question for each stanza, a second group make the sound effects, and a third group answer the question. Then have the children trade roles and repeat the Beat, until everyone has had a chance to do all three parts.

Worksheets

Worksheet 1: I'm in Australia! (p. 99)

Help the children cut and fold the little book. Then prompt them to choose one animal from Australia to draw and write about. You may need to help them find out more about the animals they choose by consulting reference materials.

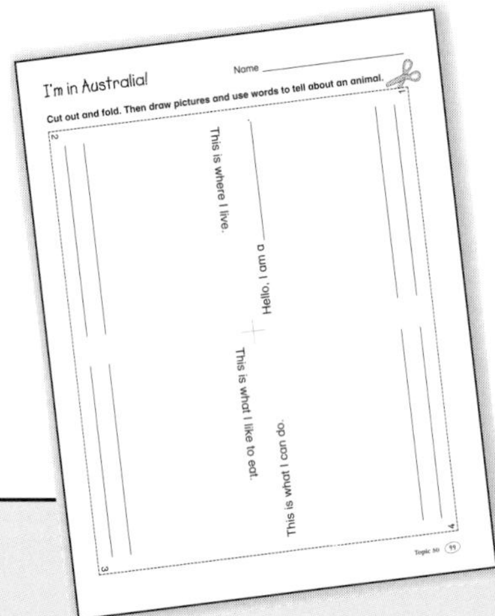

I'm in Australia! Name ___

Cut out and fold. Then draw pictures and use words to tell about an animal.

This is where I live.

Hello, I am a ___.

This is what I like to eat.

This is what I can do.

Worksheet 2: I'm in Australia! (p. 100)

Help the children read the clues and find the matching pictures. For example, the clue *I have wings* can be matched to the kookaburra, the parrot, and the emu (even though it doesn't fly); the clue *I live in trees* can be matched to the koala as well the parrot and kookaburra. Some children may say that the clue *My big tail helps me jump* can be matched to the joey as well as to the kangaroo.

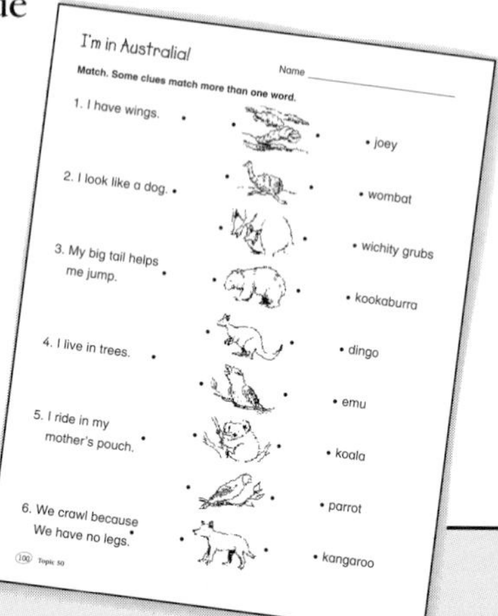

I'm in Australia! Name ___

Match. Some clues match more than one word.

1. I have wings.
2. I look like a dog.
3. My big tail helps me jump.
4. I live in trees.
5. I ride in my mother's pouch.
6. We crawl because We have no legs.

• joey
• wombat
• wichity grubs
• kookaburra
• dingo
• emu
• koala
• parrot
• kangaroo

Activities

Teach "The Kookaburra Song":

Kookaburra sits in the old gum tree.
Eating all the gumdrops she can see.
Laugh, Kookaburra. Laugh, Kookaburra.
Gay your life must be.

Then have the children stand or sit in a circle to sing the song. Have each child step into the center of the circle, name an animal, and act like that animal, as the rest of the group sings the song with the animal's name in place of "kookaburra." You may want to find out what each animal eats and place that in the song as well (for example, *Koala bear sits in the eucalyptus tree / eating all the fresh leaves he can see*).

Make stick puppets. Discuss each animal first, focusing on the characteristics that make it different from other animals. Ask questions such as *How do you know this is a kangaroo?* Then help each child make a stick puppet. You can make photocopies of the picture cards, and ask them to color the drawings and glue each to a stick or straw. Encourage the children to invent their own puppet show stories.

Make an Australian Animals Class Book. Give each child a piece of paper on which to draw a picture of one of the animals in the unit. Each child then writes or dictates some sentences about the animal. Help them to find out more information about the animal they have chosen. Bind all of the pages together in a book, and have the children make a cover.

Play a version of Twenty Questions. Let a volunteer silently choose an Australian animal he or she will "be." The other children ask *yes/no* questions, trying to guess what the animal is: *Do you hop? Do you eat gum leaves? Do you waddle? Do you wriggle? Do you fly?* Whoever guesses correctly chooses a new animal.

I'm in Africa!

Content

- African habitat
- African animals
- Specific animal characteristics

Language

- Identifying and naming African animals: *Lions live in the grasslands. Those zebras have stripes all over.*
- Describing specific animal characteristics: *The leopard's spots are black. The hippopotamus's jaws are huge.*
- Discussing animal behavior: *The gorilla thumps his chest. Lion cubs pounce and roll. Chimps and baboons play in the trees.*

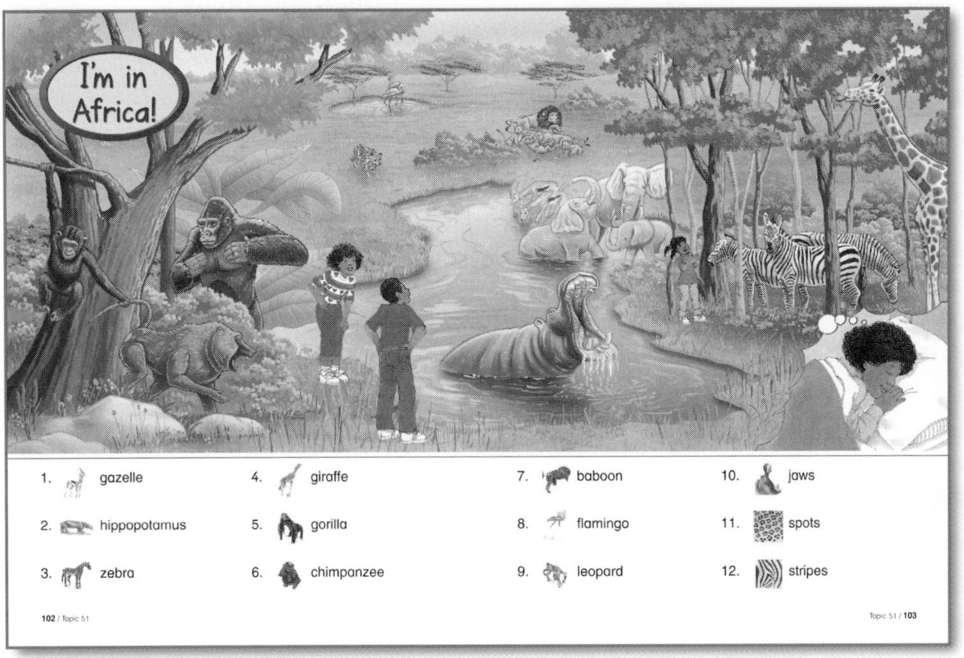

Words

1. gazelle
2. hippopotamus
3. zebra
4. giraffe
5. gorilla
6. chimpanzee
7. baboon
8. flamingo
9. leopard
10. jaws
11. spots
12. stripes

Additional Words

water hole
jungle
grassland
spray
squirt
hide/hid
rise/rose
chomp
thump
pounce
roll

Zoe is dreaming of Africa. A water hole is in the center of a jungle area. Behind it stretches a grassland with pink flamingoes, a black spotted leopard, and male and female lions asleep. Their cubs play, pouncing on each other in the grass. Three black-and-white striped zebras stand in the shadows of the big-leafed jungle trees. A giraffe is busy chomping leaves from the treetops. Samantha hides behind a tree, trying to see what the noise is overhead. On the other side of the water hole, a big black gorilla thumps its chest and roars. A chimpanzee teases a baboon and pulls its tail. In the water hole, two wrinkled gray elephants and their calf are having a wonderful time spraying water on each other. Some gazelles are drinking, ignoring the elephants. Zoe and Marcus are surprised by a hippo rising from the mud, dripping water and opening its huge jaws.

Components: Topic 51 Wall Chart, Picture Dictionary (pp. 102–103), Cassette, Word and Picture Cards (Topic 51).

See page xiv for techniques and strategies for presenting and practicing words.

I'm in Africa!

1. gazelle	5. gorilla	9. leopard
2. hippopotamus	6. chimpanzee	10. jaws
3. zebra	7. baboon	11. spots
4. giraffe	8. flamingo	12. stripes

Notes

Tell the children that the names of these animals are derived from words in African languages. Bring in pictures of African animals gathered from magazines and other sources. (Travel agencies often have large posters featuring African animals.)

Write the three words for animal characteristics *(jaws, spots, and stripes)* on a chart, and ask the children to tell you which of the animals have those characteristics. You may want to mention that hippopotami are often called hippos.

Workbook page

The pictures provide clues for the vocabulary words. Help the children read the clues and match the pictures to the characteristics before writing the words. (This is an opportunity to discuss the fact that all of the animals—and the children, as well—have jaws.)

Components: Picture Dictionary (pp. 102–103), Cassette, Story (Topic 51).

See page xviii for techniques and strategies for presenting and practicing stories.

Big gray elephants sprayed water.
The gazelles didn't mind, but
a huge hippo rose out of the mud
and opened its jaws wide!
Marcus and Zoe laughed.

Samantha hid in the jungle
among the zebras with their black
and white stripes. She listened.
Something was chomping leaves
from the treetops. A giraffe!

Who else was coming to the water hole?
Not the gorilla thumping its chest.
Not the chimpanzees, or the baboons,
or the pink flamingos.
The leopard with its black spots? Maybe.

Two golden lions were asleep, but
their cubs were awake, pouncing and
rolling over and over. When the lions
come to the water hole,
get out of the way!

Story notes

Ask about the story:

Where are the animals gathered? How do elephants spray water? What animal was hiding in the mud? Which animal has big jaws? Do other animals have jaws? Where was Samantha? What did she hear? What animal was eating leaves from the treetops? Who was asleep? Which animals were playing? Which animals have spots? Does any animal have stripes and spots?

Ask about your students:

Have you ever seen any of these animals? What did you see? What were they doing? Do you have jaws? Would you like to go to Africa? What would you like to do there?

Dialogue

Components: Cassette, Topic 51 Wall Chart, Picture Dictionary (pp. 102–103).

See page xix for techniques and strategies for presenting and practicing dialogues.

Zoe: This is much better than the zoo, Marcus!
Marcus: Yeah, those elephants are having fun squirting water through their trunks.
Zoe: That's a good way to take a shower! The elephants are so big, but the gazelles aren't afraid of them.
Marcus: No, elephants are friendly.
Zoe: The baboon is funny, but the gorilla is kind of scary.
Marcus: Wow! That hippopotamus really surprised me!
Zoe: What a big mouth!
Marcus: What huge jaws!
Zoe: I can't see Samantha anymore.
Marcus: She's still hiding in the trees with the zebras.
Zoe: All I can see are zebra stripes and shadows.
Marcus: Samantha's trying to see the top of the giraffe.
Zoe: It has such a long neck!
Marcus: We're lucky the lions are asleep. When they wake up, they'll be thirsty.
Zoe: Will they come to the water hole, too?
Marcus: You bet they will, and we'd better get out of here!
Zoe: What about the other animals? Will they stay?
Marcus: No way!

Dialogue notes

Put the children into three groups to practice the section of the dialogue beginning with *Wow! That hippopotamus really surprised me!* and ending with *What huge jaws!* When the children are comfortable with the phrasing and words, repeat this opening phrase with another animal in the place of the hippopotamus (for example, *Wow! That giraffe really surprised me!*). Prompt the groups of children to come up with two new responses (for example, *What a long neck!* and *What a small head!*). Let the children take turns choosing the animal to exclaim over and inventing their responses.

Beats!

Components: Cassette, Beats! (Topic 51).

See page xx for techniques and strategies for presenting and practicing Beats!

Something's in the shadows,
hiding in the bushes.
What's in the shadows
behind the trees?

Does it have spots?
It might be a leopard.
Does it have stripes?
It might be a zebra.

Is it a chimp?
Or a gorilla?
Or a hippopotamus?

Oh! Please!
It's only a giraffe,
eating leaves!

Beat notes

Let the children perform the Beat in groups, with one group asking the questions and the second group responding. Encourage the children to pantomime the actions of each animal as they name it.

Worksheets

Worksheet 1: I'm in Africa! (p. 101)

Point out that the numbers for the writing spaces correspond to the numbers in the picture. At the bottom of the page, the children's placement of animals in the two categories may vary.

I'm in Africa!

Name ____________

Follow the path. Write the animals in order.

1. ________ 2. ________ 3. ________
4. ________ 5. ________ 6. ________
7. ________ 8. ________ 9. ________

Write.

1. Which animals have spots?

2. Which animals have stripes?

Topic 51 101

Worksheet 2: I'm in Africa! (p. 102)

Take this opportunity to talk about postcard writing conventions. When the children have completed the page, they may wish to cut out the two halves of the postcards and glue them together, with a construction paper layer in-between to add strength. These can be kept in a collection to be shared by the class.

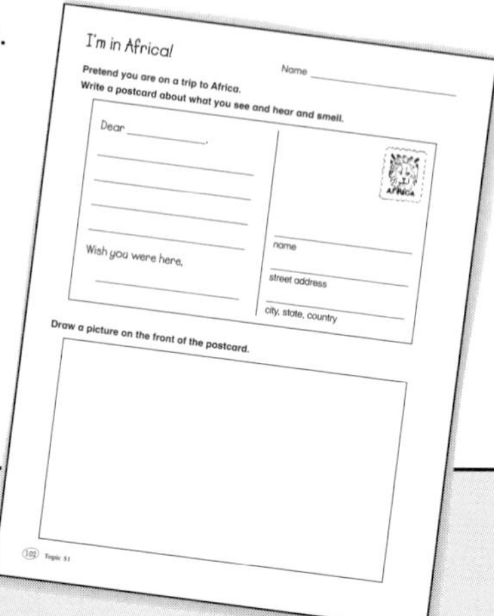

I'm in Africa!

Name ____________

Pretend you are on a trip to Africa.
Write a postcard about what you see and hear and smell.

Dear ________,

Wish you were here,

name

street address

city, state, country

AFRICA

Draw a picture on the front of the postcard.

102 Topic 51

Activities

- Model clay animals. Discuss the animals and, if possible, provide different pictures of each animal. Encourage the children to make animals out of play dough or modeling clay. Ask questions as they work to help them focus on specific features: *How many legs does a zebra have? Does a hippopotamus have a big head?*

- Play a word game. Write the alphabet on a piece of paper and put it where the children can all see it. Hold up a picture card, or point to one of the animals on the Wall Chart. On a separate chart, write blank spaces for the letters in the animal's name. Then let the children take turns picking a letter from the alphabet. If it's in that animal's name, write it in the correct space. (The letters don't have to be picked in the right order.) When all the letters are filled in, let the child who placed the last letter choose the next animal.

- Play a round-robin circle game. Begin by modeling the language: *I went down to the water hole and what did I see? I saw a gazelle looking at me.* Then prompt the child beside you to repeat your words, and add another animal (for example: *I went down to the water hole and what did I see? I saw a gazelle and a hippopotamus looking at me*). Continue in this manner until all the children have added an animal to the list. At the end, say *All together now,* and then repeat the entire list in order.

TOPIC 52

I'm in Asia!

Content

- Asian habitat
- Asian animals
- Specific animal characteristics

Language

- Identifying and naming Asian animals: *The panda is in the bamboo. The tiger is behind the plant.*
- Describing specific animal characteristics: *The rhinoceros's horn is very hard. The egret's beak is sharp.*
- Discussing animal behavior: *Orangutans can hang upside down. Pandas eat bamboo.*
- Asking and answering questions using *were* in the conditional: *If you were an orangutan, what would you do? If I were an orangutan, I'd splash a crocodile. If she were a panda, she would eat bamboo.*

Words

1. camel
2. orangutan
3. crocodile
4. cobra
5. rhinoceros
6. egret
7. panda
8. bamboo
9. humps
10. horn
11. beak
12. fangs

Additional Words

desert
coil
peck
stare
perch
march

Diego has been dreaming of Asia. In his dream, Jasmin is looking up into a grove of bamboo, excitedly watching a large black-and-white panda eating the bamboo. In another area, a cobra is coiled. An orange orangutan is hanging upside down from a tree branch, splashing water from a small stream onto a swimming crocodile. A rhinoceros with a single horn has an egret proudly perched on its back. The egret is pecking bugs out of the rhino's skin with its beak. In the distance, camels with double humps are walking across the desert sands. Diego is pushing back some big green leaves to get a better look at something moving there. What he sees through the leaves is a fierce black-and-orange striped tiger, staring at him, snarling and showing its fangs! Diego is so startled he wakes up.

Words

Components: Topic 52 Wall Chart, Picture Dictionary (pp. 104–105), Cassette, Word and Picture Cards (Topic 52).

See page xiv for techniques and strategies for presenting and practicing words.

I'm in Asia!

1. camel	5. rhinoceros	9. humps
2. orangutan	6. egret	10. horn
3. crocodile	7. panda	11. beak
4. cobra	8. bamboo	12. fangs

Notes

Point out that rhinoceri are often called *rhinos*, just as hippopotami are often called *hippos*. After introducing the vocabulary words, play a riddle game. Begin with: *I'm thinking of an animal that has two humps. What is it?* The children can either show their picture cards or say the name. Continue in this manner until the children can identify the animals easily by sight and can name them and some of their features *(fangs, beak, horn, humps)*. Encourage the children to take turns making up similar riddles. Make the game a little more complicated by posing riddles that have more than one answer *(I'm thinking of an animal with four legs; what is it?)* or by posing the riddle in a negative manner *(I'm thinking of an animal that doesn't have four legs; what is it?)*.

Workbook page

Help the children read and follow the directions. The pictures in the left column provide clues to the animal (and don't require matching); those in the right column provide clues for the characteristics identified in the middle. Tell the children to draw a matching line from each animal to its characteristic.

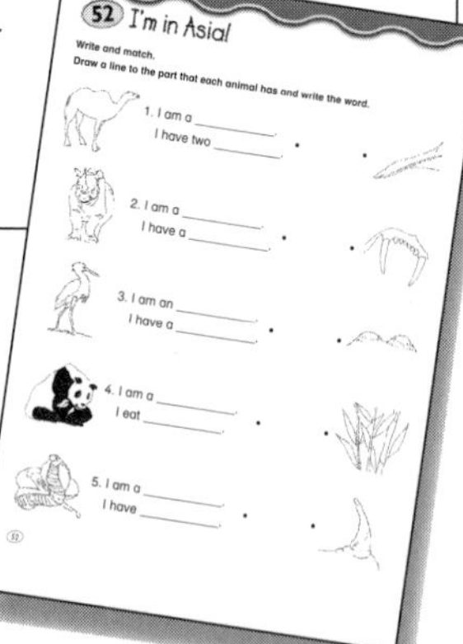

Stories

Components: Picture Dictionary (pp. 104–105), Cassette, Story (Topic 52).

See page xviii for techniques and strategies for presenting and practicing stories.

Far away, camels with big humps were crossing the hot desert sand. Nearby, a cobra coiled itself around a tree. An orangutan hung upside down splashing water on a crocodile.

A rhinoceros marched by. One great horn grew on top of its nose! A tiny egret perched on the rhino's back, pecking insects from the rhino's skin with its beak!

"Snap!" A furry black-and-white animal was eating bamboo. It was a big panda! A real panda! Jasmin was so excited! Where was Diego?

Diego was staring through the green leaves. What was in there? A huge tiger with white fangs stared back! Wake up, Diego! Wake up!

Story notes

On a map of the world or a globe, point out where the children are now. Then show them where Asia is. Explain that Asia is the largest continent in the world and that more people live in Asia than anywhere else in the world. There are many different countries and many different types of land in Asia.

Ask about the story:
What were the camels crossing? What do pandas eat? What did Jasmin see? Did the panda see Jasmin? Did the orangutan splash the rhinoceros? Which is bigger: the egret or the rhinoceros? Who was Diego staring at? Who was staring at Diego?

Ask about your students:
Have you ever seen any of these animals? Have you ever dreamed about animals? How would you feel if you saw a tiger? What noise do you think the tiger is making?

Components: Cassette, Topic 52 Wall Chart, Picture Dictionary (pp. 104–105).

See page xix for techniques and strategies for presenting and practicing dialogues.

Jasmin:	Diego! The orangutan is having fun. He's splashing a crocodile! Oooo, I see a snake!
Diego:	That's a cobra. Stay away from it. It's dangerous!
Jasmin:	What are you doing, Diego?
Diego:	Nothing.
Jasmin:	There's a great big rhino going by, and he's giving a tiny little bird a ride on his back.
Diego:	Uh-huh.
Jasmin:	Diego, what are you looking for?
Diego:	Oh, nothing.
Jasmin:	I hear something! It's going snap! snap! snap! Oh, Diego! I see it! Up in the tree! It looks like a big panda! It is a panda! It's a real panda! Diego! Diego, what are you doing? Are you looking for tigers?
Diego:	Sh-sh-sh-sh-sh!
Jasmin:	Diego, are you looking for tigers? Did you find one? Diego?
Diego:	What a dream!

Dialogue notes

Separate the children into groups of three, one to play the tiger (hiding in the bushes), the second to play Diego (looking for the tiger), and the third to play Jasmin (asking questions). Then let them practice a series of questions and responses, based on the dialogue:

Jasmin:	What are you looking for?
Diego:	Oh, nothing.
Jasmin:	Are you looking for a tiger?
Diego:	No, no.
Jasmin:	Did you find a tiger?
Diego:	Yes!

Have the child playing the tiger curl up and hide his or her face, while the two playing children's roles improvise the questions and answers until the "tiger" leaps out roaring.

Components: Cassette, Beats! (Topic 52).

See page xx for techniques and strategies for presenting and practicing Beats!

What's that panda doing?
Eating bamboo.
If you were a panda,
you would too.

If I were a camel,
would I have bumps?
Yes, you would,
but you'd call them humps!

What if I were a rhino
with an egret on my back?
You'd let him peck out all the bugs
and eat them for a snack!

If you were a tiger,
what would you do?
I'd run through the tall grass, and
I'D CATCH YOU!

Beat notes

Make up verses for other animals (for example: *If you were an orangutan, what would you do? If I were an orangutan, I'd splash you!*).

Worksheets

Worksheet 1: I'm in Asia! (p. 103)

Provide crayons and markers, and help the children follow the directions for coloring the picture. Then, prompt them to dictate or write the names of the animals that fit into each category at the bottom of the page. (The cobra is the only animal depicted that has no legs.)

I'm in Asia!

Name ______

Color the animal with a horn grey.
Color the animal with a beak blue.
Color the animal with fangs yellow.
Color the animal with humps brown.
Color the other animals any way you like.

Write.

Animals with legs	Animals with no legs

Topic 52 103

Worksheet 2: I'm in Asia! (p. 104)

Help the children unscramble the words, using the clues provided by the pictures. (The three animal words contained in the final scrambled word are *orangutan, crocodile,* and *camel.*)

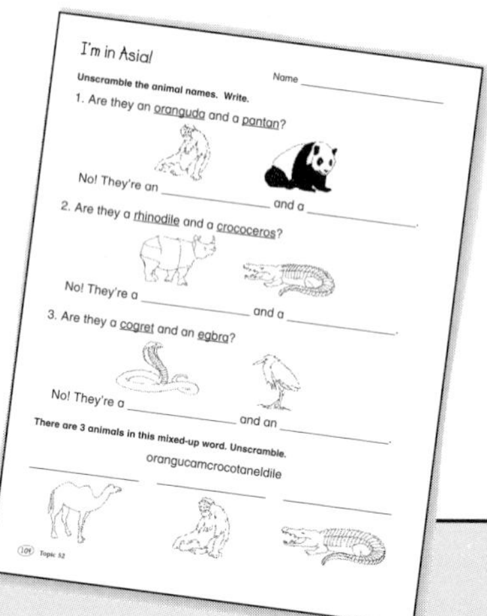

I'm in Asia!

Name ______

Unscramble the animal names. Write.

1. Are they an oranguda and a pantan?

No! They're an ______ and a ______.

2. Are they a rhinodile and a crococeros?

No! They're a ______ and a ______.

3. Are they a cogret and an egbra?

No! They're a ______ and an ______.

There are 3 animals in this mixed-up word. Unscramble.

orangucamcrocotaneldile

______ ______ ______

104 Topic 52

Activities

- Make animal face masks. Simple masks can be made from paper plates decorated with markers or glued-on construction-paper features. Talk about each animal and what makes it different from the rest. After all the masks are made, have the children put them on and act like the animal they represent. Ask: *What noises do you make? How do you move? What do you eat?*

- Make dioramas of an Asian scene. Children can create their scenes by drawing and gluing paper inside a box and using modeling clay for animals and other details. Encourage them to share their dioramas with the class and talk about what they have shown.

- Play Who Lives Where? Now that the children have been introduced to the animals of Australia, Africa, and Asia, challenge them to sort the animals according to their native habitats. Gather colorful pictures of the animals from all three areas. Divide a bulletin board or chalkboard into three sections, one for Australia, one for Africa, and one for Asia. Let the children take turns taping or gluing a photograph of an animal in the section where it belongs. (Remember to provide enough pictures so that animals that live in more than one continent can be placed in both sections.)

- Play a version of Red Rover, using all the animals studied in Topics 49 through 52. Let each child pick a card with the name and picture of an animal on it. Then stand at one end of the room and say, *Come over, come over. Let all the animals with feathers (with a tail, with horns, with four legs, etc.) come over!* Some clues can be references to only one specific animal, and others call for a number of animals. Once the children get the idea, let them take turns calling out clues.

Theme 8: Seasons

Topic 53 Spring is here!
Topic 54 We planted a garden!
Topic 55 Hot summer
Topic 56 Windy fall
Topic 57 Snowy winter

Theme Bibliography

Animal Seasons
written and illustrated by Brian Wildsmith.
Oxford University Press, 1991. ISBN 0192721755
Charming illustrations take the reader through the seasons. Using the present tense, the text characterizes each changing season by its effect on the lives and activities of plants, animals, and birds. The story and pictures present vocabulary also relevant to topics in Theme 7.

Changes
written by Marjorie N. Allen and Shelley Rotner;
photographs by Shelley Rotner.
Simon & Schuster Children's Books, 1995.
ISBN 0689800681
A simple, lyrical celebration of change begins and ends with the phrase: "All things go through changes as they grow." Clear color photographs illustrate this statement with examples from the world of nature. Children can compare pictures depicting different seasons or stages of development and discuss the changes they find.

The Cloud Book
by Tomie de Paola.
Holiday House, 1985. ISBN 0823405311
Using simple, declarative sentences, Tomie de Paola invites the reader to take a closer look at clouds. He explores the science of clouds and the role they play in folklore and metaphor. The book introduces and explains such colloquial phrases as, "She has her head in the clouds!" The cartoon-like illustrations amplify the text and add a bit of silliness that children will enjoy.

The First Snowfall
written and illustrated by Anne and Harlow Rockwell.
Simon & Schuster Children's Books, 1992.
ISBN 0689716141
This brightly illustrated book is a perfect expansion for Topic 57. Students will find familiar words from the Picture Dictionary in a new context. The pictures are full of crisp, primary colors that can be used in point-and-identify activities. The voice of the narrator, a young girl telling about her activities on the day of the season's first snowfall, can be a model for children telling or writing about their own experiences.

Flash, Crash, Rumble, and Roll
written by Franklin M. Branley;
illustrated by Barbara and Ed Emberley.
HarperTrophy, 1985. ISBN 0064450120
For children who want to know more about thunder and lightning, the book explains these phenomena with diagrams and cartoon illustrations. The material may be somewhat advanced for younger children. The bright, detailed pictures include tips on how to stay safe in a storm.

Gilberto and the Wind
written and illustrated by Marie Hall Ets.
Viking Press, 1978. ISBN 0140502769
Gilberto knows the wind well, in all its moods, and he describes it as his favorite playmate. The story explores what the wind can and cannot do: "He can't make the bubbles—I have to do that. But he carries them way up into the air for the sun to color." The illustrations are simple pencil on brown paper with touches of brown, white, and black. They are powerfully evocative, both of a lonely landscape and the emotional experience of a solitary child who has found a good friend in the wind.

From Seed to Plant
written and illustrated by Gail Gibbons.
Holiday House, 1993. ISBN 0823410250

Gail Gibbons invites young children to wonder at the nature of growing plants. With a clear, concise text and bright, detailed illustrations, the book offers basic information about the structure of plants and their life cycles—from seed to flower, from flower to fruit, and then to seed again. It also includes instructions for growing your own bean plants. You may want to bring in live plants or cut flowers so the children can compare them to the illustrations or to prompt the vocabulary words.

My Spring Robin
written by Anne Rockwell;
illustrated by Harlow and Lizzie Rockwell.
Aladdin Paperbacks, 1996. ISBN 0689804474

This book celebrates a young child's delight in the natural world. A young girl sets off to explore a spring garden to find the robin she heard last summer. She discovers a sense of the patterns and order in the seasons and nature. The softly colored pictures lend themselves to identifying items; many of them will be familiar words from Themes 7 and 8. There are one or two short sentences with each illustration. Grammatical structures in the text are repetitive and simple enough for English-language learners and beginning readers.

The Reasons for Seasons
written and illustrated by Gail Gibbons.
Holiday House, 1996. ISBN 0823412385

This book explains the science of the seasons by showing the effects of the Earth's tilt and orbit on the activities of people and animals. The text is simple and straight-forward, and the pictures and words can be used as a starting point for talking about change.

Snow is Falling
written by Franklyn M. Branley;
illustrated by Holly Keller.
HarperTrophy, 1986. ISBN 0064450589

More than just a story about snow, this book explores the science of a snowflake and the role of snow in the ecology. The simple cartoon pictures are cheerful and bright. The text is repetitive and appropriate for English-language learners and beginning readers. Children who want to know more about snow will love this book.

Storms
by Seymour Simon.
William Morrow & Co., 1989. ISBN 0688074138

This book may be too difficult for young children to read, but the spectacular photographs will lend themselves to discussion of storms, thunder, lightning, hurricanes, and tornadoes. Information in the text can be shared with the students to prompt discussion about their own feelings and experiences of stormy weather.

The Tiny Seed
written and illustrated by Eric Carle.
Little Simon, 1998. ISBN 0689819668

Illustrated with dazzling, colorful collages, this book tells the saga of a tiny seed, from its windblown fall to its germination, growth, and flowering, and ends with the mature plant releasing its own seeds into the wind. The story is full of the dangers that each seed faces. Younger students will be caught by the adventure of the story, as they learn the seasonal cycles and natural orders. The text, written in the present tense, has some good examples of comparisons, such as "The tiny seed is smaller than any of the others, and flies higher than the others."

Weather Words and What They Mean
written and illustrated by Gail Gibbons.
Holiday House, 1992. ISBN 082340952X

Like many of Gail Gibbons's books, this one is a treasure for English-language learners. Bright cartoons illustrate simple sentences about weather conditions and—without getting too complex—the science that explains them. Accompanying speech balloons show identifying words and examples of how people talk about the weather. The last page has a chart of interesting weather facts.

White Snow, Bright Snow
written by Alvin Tresselt;
illustrated by Roger Duvoisin.
William Morrow & Co., 1988. ISBN 0688082947

Snowfall comes to a rural community and the local residents (and rabbits) respond to it in variety of ways. This classic Caldecott Medal winner combines a slow and simple story, written in rhythmic verse, with gentle illustrations. The text and pictures can be used to prompt children to talk about how snow or other weather conditions affect them, their neighbors, and the world around them.

A Year in the City
written by Kathy Henderson;
illustrated by Paul Howard.
Candlewick Press, 1996. ISBN 1564028720

This book takes children on a month-by-month trip through the seasons in an urban setting. Vivid illustrations evoke city dwellers' seasonal behaviors, such as turning up collars in the winter cold or pouring into a park to get some fresh summer air, along with the changes in the weather and natural world. Children will enjoy pointing out distinct faces in the crowd scenes and identifying familiar vocabulary items from the Picture Dictionary.

Spring is here!

Content

- Spring
- Plants and animals
- Activities associated with spring
- Planting seeds

Language

- Identifying spring activities: *It's time for spring cleaning! We can plant a garden now.*
- Discussing plants and animals in the spring: *There are buds on the trees. The first flowers are blooming. The robin is building a nest.*
- Putting actions in sequential order: *First dig a hole. Now plant the seeds. Cover the seeds with dirt. Water the seeds each day.*
- Making and responding to invitations: *Who wants to plant seeds? I do. Can we plant seeds, too? Yes, you can.*

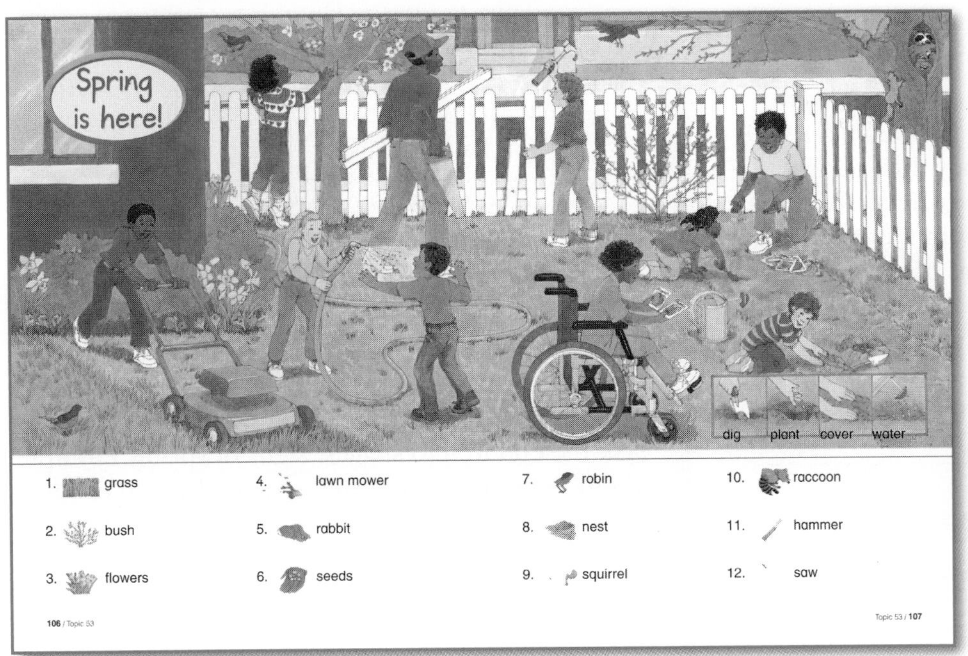

Words

1. grass
2. bush
3. flowers
4. lawn mower
5. rabbit
6. seeds
7. robin
8. nest
9. squirrel
10. raccoon
11. hammer
12. saw

Labels

dig
plant
cover
water

Additional Words

trowel
watering can
trunk
branch
buds
bloom
garden
lawn
chase

Spring has come to the Jacksons' garden. The grass has begun to grow, and the tree branches are covered with new green buds. Flowers are blooming, and robins have made a nest on a low tree branch. It has four blue eggs in it. Zoe is standing on tiptoe, looking at the eggs. Squirrels are chasing each other up and down the tree trunks. There is a raccoon den in the hollow of an old tree. The raccoons are asleep inside, with three new babies. Some big black crows are squawking, and a baby rabbit is hiding under a bush. Marcus is cutting the grass with the lawn mower. Mr. Jackson is fixing the broken fence with his saw and a piece of wood. Jim hands him the hammer. Mariah has given Tommy some seeds to plant. He has already dug holes, put seeds in each hole, and covered up one set of seeds, patting the soil carefully. He has a watering can ready to water the seeds. Samantha is digging with her trowel. Mrs. Jackson has a handful of seeds for her to choose from. Diego and Alison are playing with a hose, laughing.

Words

Components: Topic 53 Wall Chart, Picture Dictionary (pp. 106–107), Cassette, Word and Picture Cards (Topic 53).

See page xiv for techniques and strategies for presenting and practicing words.

Spring is here!

1. grass	5. rabbit	9. squirrel
2. bush	6. seeds	10. raccoon
3. flowers	7. robin	11. hammer
4. lawn mower	8. nest	12. saw

Labels

dig plant cover water

Notes

Prompt a discussion of the end of winter and the beginning of spring by reciting the saying *March comes in like a lion and goes out like a lamb.* Ask the children to talk about what they think it means. Use the Wall Chart or the Dictionary illustration as a referent, and ask the children to point out the things that let them know this is a picture of spring. As they identify the vocabulary words, you can reinforce their understanding by offering language models: *Yes, that is a lawn mower. The grass grows in the spring, and people cut it with a lawn mower.*

Workbook page

The words to label the pictures are at the bottom of the page. Help the children read and follow the directions for coloring the pictures. They color all the words except *nest.*

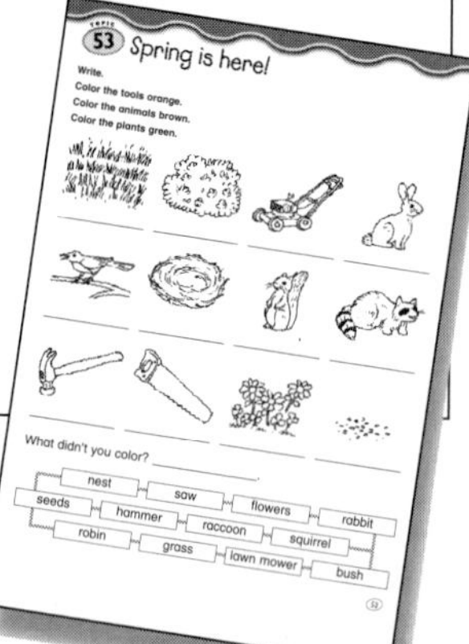

Stories

Components: Picture Dictionary (pp. 106–107), Cassette, Story (Topic 53).

See page xviii for techniques and strategies for presenting and practicing stories.

Spring is here! The grass is green again, flowers are blooming, and trees have new green buds. Robins have made a nest on a low branch. There are four blue eggs in it! Zoe looks. O-o-o!

Squirrels chase each other up and down the tree trunks. Noisy crows! Sh-h-h. A raccoon family is asleep in a tree hole. Oh! Look under the bush. A baby rabbit!

Time to cut the lawn! Here comes Marcus with the lawn mower. Mr. Jackson has to fix the fence. He has cut a piece of wood with his saw. Now where's that hammer? Jim has it. Thanks!

Who wants to plant seeds? Tommy does. So does Samantha. She's digging with her trowel. Vegetables or flowers? Both! We're going to have a beautiful garden!

Story notes

Ask the children to suggest signs of spring. Prompt them to think about both the natural world (buds, new growth, flowers, geese migrating) and things that happen in their own lives (putting away winter clothes, opening windows, using less heat, maybe eating different foods or playing different games). Make a chart of their suggestions.

Ask about the story:
How do you know it's spring by looking at plants? What are the squirrels doing? Who built a nest in the tree? How many eggs can Zoe see in the nest? Where is the baby rabbit? What jobs are people doing? How did Jim help Mr. Jackson?

Ask about your students:
How do you know when it's spring? How does the weather change in the spring? What are your favorite signs of spring? What would you plant if you had a garden? Where can you go to see buds on trees and bushes?

Components: Cassette, Topic 53 Wall Chart, Picture Dictionary (pp. 106–107).

See page xix for techniques and strategies for presenting and practicing dialogues.

Zoe:	O-o-o-o. Look at the blue eggs in the robins' nest!
Mr. Jackson:	How many are there?
Zoe:	Four.
Mr. Jackson:	Well, I guess we're going to have four baby robins soon. Be careful with the lawn mower, Marcus. I think there's a baby rabbit hiding under that bush. Don't scare it.
Marcus:	OK, Dad.
Jim:	Here's your hammer, Mr. Jackson.
Mr. Jackson:	Thanks, Jim, I've got to fix this fence!
Mrs. Jackson:	The squirrels are going crazy running up and down the trees!
Zoe:	They're happy because spring is here.
Mrs. Jackson:	We're all happy. Who wants to plant seeds?
Tommy:	I do!
Samantha:	Me, too!
Mrs. Jackson:	Now remember, first dig a hole. Then plant a few seeds in it. What comes next?
Samantha:	Cover the hole with dirt.
Mrs. Jackson:	Yes, put the soil over the seeds very, very carefully and pat it down a little.
Tommy:	And then, water them.
Mrs. Jackson:	Right, Tommy. Seeds need water to grow. Alison and Diego! Put down that hose now. You can water after we finish planting.
Alison:	Can we plant, too?
Mrs. Jackson:	Of course you can. We'll make a special garden for you right here.
Alison:	Oh, thank you, Mrs. Jackson! What fun! Then we can watch everything grow.
Samantha:	Mine's going to grow first!
Mrs. Jackson:	Wait and see!

Dialogue notes

Model a dialogue about planting seeds that children can practice in pairs. Let the two voices take turns giving directions and asking for the next step:

First dig a hole. What comes next?
Plant a few seeds in it. What comes next?

Components: Cassette, Beats! (Topic 53).

See page xx for techniques and strategies for presenting and practicing Beats!

The trees are getting leaves.
The grass is getting green.
  Are the robins back again?
Go and see!

I see a nest!
  I see it, too!
Four little robins' eggs.
  Blue, blue, blue.

Baby rabbits!
  Baby raccoons!
Where are the flowers?
  Soon, soon, soon.

Listen to the birds!
  Hear them sing?
It's time to plant the seeds!
  It's spring!

Beat notes

Encourage the children to practice the Beat as written, modeling the two emphatic claps heard on the cassette before the last line. Then, when they are comfortable with the words and rhythms, invite them to add sound effects. They can make bird sounds or baby animal squeaks, or simply clap their hands and stamp their feet rhythmically during the last line of each stanza.

Worksheets

Worksheet 1: Spring is here! (p. 105)

All of the words needed to complete the sentences can be found at the bottom of the page. You may want to have children work in pairs on this worksheet, asking and answering the questions modeled aloud as they fill in the missing words.

Spring is here! Name ________

Write the missing words.

1. The ________ are eating under the ________.
2. What is she using? She is using a ________.
3. What is she doing? She is using a ________ to fix the fence.
4. What is he doing? He is using a ________ to cut the ________.
5. What are they doing? They are building a ________.
6. The ________ in the tree sees the ________.

grass · bush · lawn mower · rabbits · robin · nest · squirrel · raccoon · hammer · saw

Topic 53 105

Worksheet 2: Spring is here! (p. 106)

Help the children read and follow the directions. Some children may underline *seeds* and *flowers* as things people use (along with the tools), rather than circling them as things that are alive. The vocabulary words are at the bottom of the page, but children don't have to limit themselves to these words.

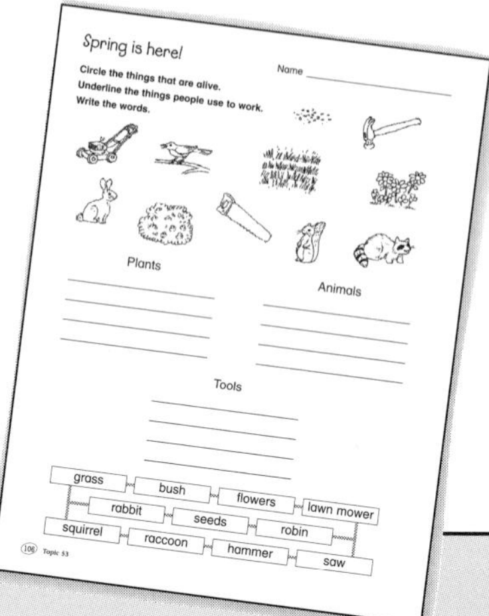

Spring is here! Name ________

Circle the things that are alive. Underline the things people use to work. Write the words.

Plants

Animals

Tools

grass · bush · flowers · lawn mower · rabbit · seeds · robin · squirrel · raccoon · hammer · saw

106 Topic 53

Activities

- Take a nature walk. Allow time for the children to observe grass shoots and buds on trees and bushes. Have them stop and close their eyes to listen for spring sounds. Record their observations. Provide the children with language models as you narrate what you see. Encourage them to draw pictures and write or dictate their descriptions of what they see for use in a class book.
- Bring spring indoors by planting seeds. Plant beans in resealable bags so the children can watch the roots develop. Grass seed strewn on a sponge sprouts rapidly; you can keep the sponge damp by placing it in a pie tin with water in the bottom. Plant mystery seeds in small paper cups, and watch to see what grows.
- Spring calendar. Make a calendar that shows each week of the months that are usually designated as spring months. Once a week, set aside time to talk about specific changes in the world outside, and help the children record their observations on the calendar. This activity can be extended by asking the children to find out the temperature every day, then record it and other weather changes on the calendar.
- Make Welcome Spring cards. Provide the children with seed catalogs or magazines. Have them cut out their favorite flowers or other pictures that signify spring, then glue them on the front of a card to take home to their families or give to friends. Inside, have them write or dictate a simple message about spring *(Spring is special because …)*.
- Introduce the children to some of the many stories about changing seasons in different cultural traditions, such as the Greek story about Persephone's kidnapping by Pluto, or the Wampanoag story of Glucksap and the people needing to be reminded to pay attention and honor the Sun. Invite the children to illustrate the stories and to make up their own stories.

We planted a garden!

Content

- Plants
- Parts of plants
- Patterns of growth
- Plant needs

Language

- Naming and describing plant characteristics: *The roots are growing under the soil. The stem grows above ground. The leaves grow from the stem.*
- Identifying the needs of plants: *Plants need water to grow. Plants can't grow without sunshine.*
- Expressing pleasure at watching things grow: *I see something! My daisies are growing! My plants have wiggly stems.*
- Comparing objects: *Jim's plant is bigger than mine. Samantha's plant is taller than Diego's plant.*

Words

1. sunshine
2. rain
3. soil
4. seed
5. root
6. sprout
7. stem
8. leaf
9. bud
10. flower
11. raincoat
12. umbrella

Additional Words

rainbow
puddle
dirt
daisies
sunflowers
pumpkin
underground

It's raining, but the Sun's rays are peeking from behind a cloud. The children are excitedly looking at the garden they planted. There are seed packets attached to sticks to identify the plants. Diego is disappointed. There is nothing growing in his space, but we can see tomato seeds growing roots underground. Zoe and Ting see six little daisy sprouts pushing through the soil. Alison's space has three snapdragon sprouts. Marcus's has four thin corn plant stems. Tommy is scratching his head in wonder. Those are his vinelike stems wriggling across the ground, but he forgets what he planted! Underground we can see that two pumpkin seeds have grown roots. Jim has three sturdy bean plants with thick green stems and leaves. Samantha is imagining the tall sunflower plant that will grow from her seed. She knows it will have a beautiful yellow flower with seeds in the middle. Alison comes running into the garden with her umbrella, pointing to the rainbow in the sky.

Words

Components: Topic 54 Wall Chart, Picture Dictionary (pp. 108–109), Cassette, Word and Picture Cards (Topic 54).

See page xiv for techniques and strategies for presenting and practicing words.

We planted a garden!

1. sunshine
2. rain
3. soil
4. seed
5. root
6. sprout
7. stem
8. leaf
9. bud
10. flower
11. raincoat
12. umbrella

Notes

Bring in old seed catalogues and magazines, so the children can cut pictures from them to make collages. Encourage them to find a picture to illustrate each vocabulary word. If they can't find a picture for any of the words, tell them they can draw a picture themselves. Invite them to talk about their pictures with one another.

Workbook page

Suggest that the children refer to the Wall Chart or Dictionary illustration as they complete this page. All the required words are given on the page. Help them understand that in the final exercise they are to circle only the things a plant needs, not all the vocabulary words.

54
We planted a garden!
Write.
root
stem
leaf
sprout
flower
seed
Circle the correct words.
What does a plant need?
raincoat
rain
soil
umbrella
sunshine

Stories

Components: Picture Dictionary (pp. 108–109), Cassette, Story (Topic 54).

See page xviii for techniques and strategies for presenting and practicing stories.

It's raining! It's raining!
Rain and sunshine make plants grow.
Have the seeds grown yet?
Put on your raincoats. Let's go see.

Where are Diego's tomatoes? Gone? No!
Wait. Roots are growing under the soil.
Zoe and Mariah see little sprouts
pushing through the soil. Daisies? Yes!
Alison's snapdragons have sprouts, too.

What are the thin stems? Marcus's corn.
What are the wiggly stems? Uh-oh.
Tommy can't remember.
Jim's beans have thick stems and leaves.
Oh! Samantha's sunflowers have buds!

They will be flowers with seeds in the middle!
Samantha can plant them next year.
Here's Alison with an umbrella.
And here comes the Sun. Hey! Look up!
There's a rainbow in the sky!

Story notes

Ask how many children have ever seen a rainbow. Explain that rainbows form when the Sun shines during or right after rainfall. The best time to see a rainbow is early in the morning or late in the afternoon.

Ask about the story:
Why are the children wearing raincoats? Which seeds have sprouted? What has happened to Diego's seeds? Whose seeds have roots but no stems? Are Jim's plants corn or beans? Whose plant has bigger leaves, Jim's or Marcus's? Who planted flowers? What is Samantha imagining? What does her plant look like?

Ask about your students:
Have you ever planted seeds? What foods do you eat that are seeds? What foods do you eat that are grown from seeds? How can you tell if a seed is growing into a plant? Which part of the plant grows underground? Which parts of the plant grow above the ground?

Dialogue

Components: Cassette, Topic 54 Wall Chart, Picture Dictionary (pp. 108–109).

See page xix for techniques and strategies for presenting and practicing dialogues.

Zoe:	I see something! They're little sprouts. My daisies are growing!
Marcus:	My corn has some tall stems, but they're thin.
Tommy:	My plants have wiggly stems, and they're lying down. Why don't they stand up?
Marcus:	What did you plant?
Tommy:	I don't remember.
Marcus:	Look at Jim's plants! They're bigger than mine.
Jim:	And I have leaves! I'm going to have beans soon.
Samantha:	Look at mine! Look at mine!
Everyone:	Wow!
Jim:	Samantha's are the tallest! They're huge! And they have buds!
Samantha:	When will they be flowers?
Jim:	In the summer. And guess what they'll have in the middle?
Samantha:	What?
Jim:	Seeds.
Samantha:	Seeds? Can I plant them?
Jim:	Sure. You can plant them next spring.
Diego:	Where are my plants?
Zoe:	Oh, poor Diego. His plants didn't grow!
Jim:	What did you plant, Diego?
Diego:	Tomatoes.
Jim:	Tomatoes are slower, that's all. They're growing roots under the soil. They'll be up soon.
Zoe:	Sing to them, Diego.
Diego:	Sing?
Zoe:	That's what my mama does. She says plants need sunshine and rain and love. So she sings to them.
Jim:	Hey, it's raining and the Sun is shining at the same time.
Alison:	Look! There's a rainbow in the sky!

Dialogue notes

Encourage the children to invent their own dialogues based on this exchange:

What did you plant? I planted corn. Did it grow?

Beats!

Components: Cassette, Beats! (Topic 54).

See page xx for techniques and strategies for presenting and practicing Beats!

Do you hear that?
Do you hear that?
Hear come the raindrops!
Pitter, pitter, pat!

Rain is good for plants.
It makes them grow.
The roots are growing
down below.

Rain is good for plants.
They'll grow some sprouts.
Drip, drop. Drip, drop.
The Sun is coming out!

Sun is good for plants.
They'll grow leaves by and by.
And then they'll grow flowers.
Hey! A rainbow in the sky!

Beat notes

Encourage the children to add hand and body motions as they practice this Beat. You can suggest, for example, that they make the motions of opening and shutting an umbrella, holding their hands out to check if it's raining, or pointing to an imaginary rainbow.

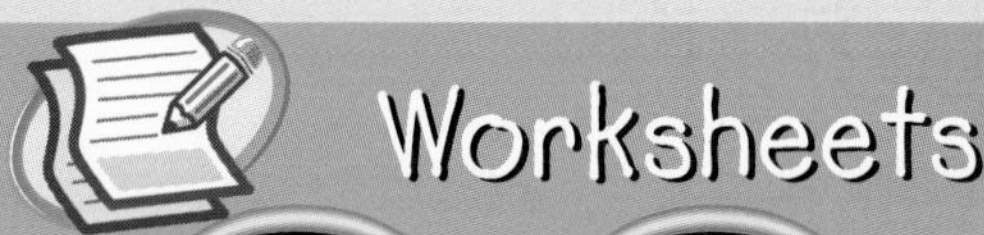

Worksheets

Worksheet 1: We planted a garden! (p. 107)

Help the children read the sentences and fill in the missing words. All the words are at the bottom of the page. You may want to do this as a group activity, reading the sentences aloud and encouraging volunteers to identify the missing words.

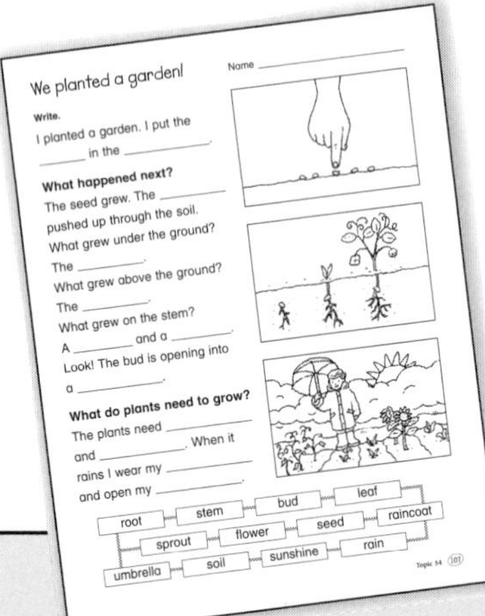

We planted a garden!

Name ______

Write.

I planted a garden. I put the ______ in the ______.

What happened next?

The seed grew. The ______ pushed up through the soil.

What grew under the ground?

The ______.

What grew above the ground?

The ______.

What grew on the stem?

A ______ and a ______.

Look! The bud is opening into a ______.

What do plants need to grow?

The plants need ______ and ______. When it rains I wear my ______ and open my ______.

root stem bud leaf sprout flower seed raincoat umbrella soil sunshine rain

Topic 54 107

Worksheet 2: We planted a garden! (p. 108)

For the unscrambling exercise, the vowels for each word appear in the left column, and the consonants in the middle. To write the words correctly, the children have to recombine the letters. Once they have rewritten the words, they can match them to the pictures. All the words can be found at the bottom of the page.

We planted a garden!

Name ______

Write the whole word.
Circle the picture.
Draw a line from the picture to the word.

oo	rt	______
e	stm	______
ea	lf	______
ou	sprt	______
oe	flwr	______
ee	sd	______
aioa	rnct	______
uea	mbrll	______
oi	sl	______
uie	snshn	______
ai	rn	______

root stem raincoat leaf sprout flower seed umbrella soil sunshine rain

108 Topic 54

Activities

- Seed sorting. Have the children classify a variety of seeds according to size, color, and shape. Suggest that they invent new categories. Include wheat berries, soy or mung beans, orange and apple seeds, bulbs, and even an avocado pit to show the wide variation of seeds in nature. Make a chart with the children to show the different categories. You can have them draw the seeds or glue samples to the chart.

- Plant a mystery garden. Invite the children to choose seeds from the seed collection and plant them in small pots or recycled plastic containers. Watch over the seedlings carefully and when leaves and flowers appear, challenge the children to identify and label the plants using seed catalogues or plant books. You can use the growing plants to practice comparative and superlative language: *These stems are shorter than those. This plant has the most leaves.*

- Share some books about growing plants, such as *Pumpkin, Pumpkin* by Jeanne Theringer or Eric Carle's *The Tiny Seed* (both Scholastic).

- Demonstrate how plants drink water by placing a stalk of celery in a cup of water. Add a few drops of food coloring to the water and watch with the class as the colored water travels up the stalk. Provide language models and help the children understand the information.

- Study a tree. Choose a tree or bush in the school yard or neighborhood, and make regular visits to observe the changes brought by spring. Record the changes you see. Ask the children to point out the parts of the tree or bush, such as stem, leaf, bud, and flower. Use this opportunity to encourage the children to use comparative words; if there are buds, ask, *Are the buds bigger or smaller than they were last week?*

Hot summer

Content

- Summer sports and activities
- Picnics
- Thunderstorms

Language

- Talking about summer sports and activities: *Let's have a picnic! Do you want to go swimming in the pool or play baseball?*
- Asking and answering questions about preferences: *Do you want a hamburger or a hot dog? I'd like a hot dog, please. Would you rather go swimming or skating? I'd rather swim.*
- Describing weather: *Wow! It's hot! Look at the dark clouds in the sky! What was that? Lightning! A storm is coming.*

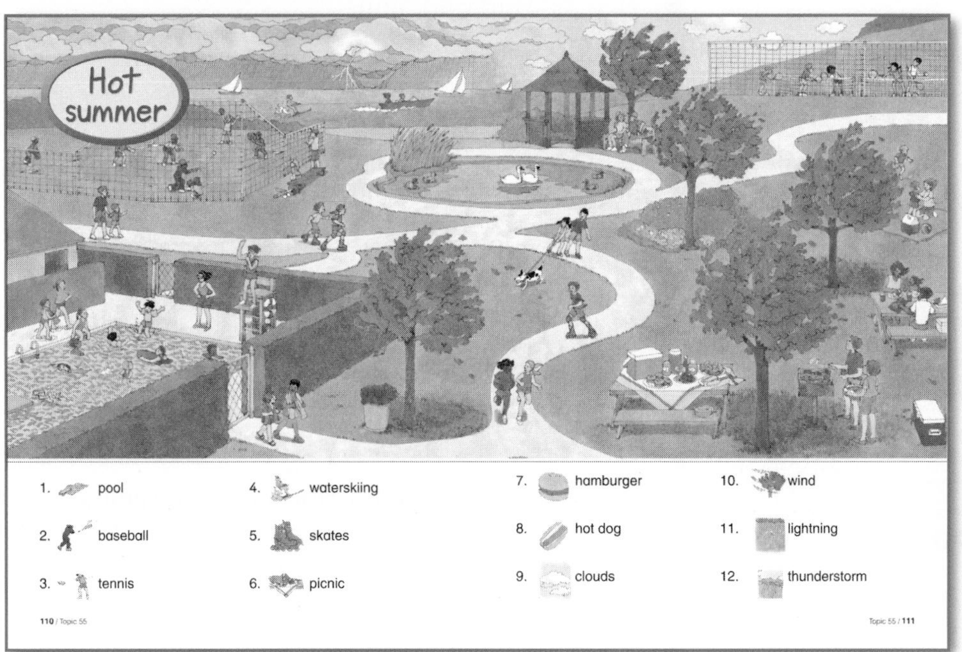

Words

1. pool
2. baseball
3. tennis
4. waterskiing
5. skates
6. picnic
7. hamburger
8. hot dog
9. clouds
10. wind
11. lightning
12. thunderstorm

Additional Words

cookout
lawn
duck
swan
pond
bay
whistle
thunder

It's summer in the town park. Everyone is having fun! People are swimming in the pool. Marcus is playing baseball. Zoe, Ting, and Alison are playing tennis. Henry's there, too. People are waterskiing out on the bay and having picnics on the lawn. The white swans are chasing the ducks on the pond. The Youngs are having a cookout. Mrs. Young and Uncle Pete are cooking hamburgers and hot dogs. Tommy and Diego are on their way! And Jim is hurrying on his skates. The trees are blowing in the wind and gray thunderclouds are building up in the sky. There's lightning! The lifeguard is blowing his whistle. Everyone out of the pool! A thunderstorm is coming!

Components: Topic 55 Wall Chart, Picture Dictionary (pp. 110–111), Cassette, Word and Picture Cards (Topic 55).

See page xiv for techniques and strategies for presenting and practicing words.

Hot summer

1. pool	6. picnic	10. wind
2. baseball	7. hamburger	11. lightning
3. tennis	8. hot dog	12. thunder-storm
4. waterskiing	9. clouds	
5. skates		

Notes

Encourage the children to choose word or picture cards of their favorite summer activities. Invite volunteers to show their picture cards and talk about them to the other children. With the children, brainstorm how summer is fun. Write a list of all the things suggested.

Thunderstorms are sometimes frightening to young children. This might be a good time to talk about those feelings and about things you can do to feel safe when there's a thunderstorm (such as staying out of water and taking shelter).

Workbook page

The pictures provide clues to the missing words. Have children work in pairs on this page, asking and answering the questions you model aloud as they complete the sentences. Encourage them to use the vocabulary words and other words to answer the questions at the bottom of the page.

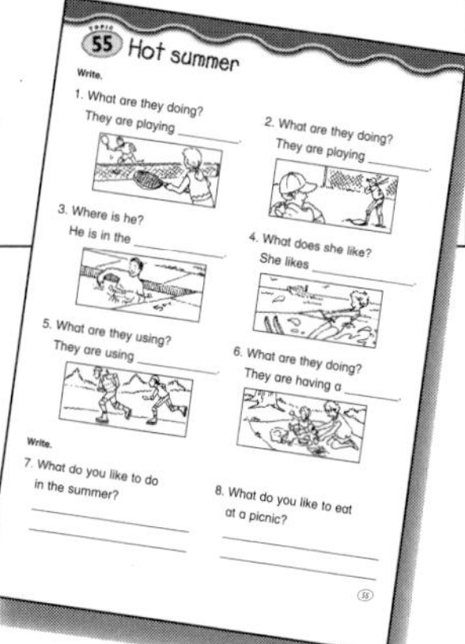
55 Hot summer

Write.

1. What are they doing? They are playing ______
2. What are they doing? They are playing ______
3. Where is he? He is in the ______
4. What does she like? She likes ______
5. What are they using? They are using ______
6. What are they doing? They are having a ______

Write.

7. What do you like to do in the summer?
8. What do you like to eat at a picnic?

Components: Picture Dictionary (pp. 110–111), Cassette, Story (Topic 55).

See page xviii for techniques and strategies for presenting and practicing stories.

Let's go swimming in the pool!
Let's play baseball.
Let's play tennis and have
a picnic later. OK!

Someone's having a cookout.
Mm-m. Smells good. It's the Youngs
cooking hamburgers and hot dogs!
There goes Jim on his skates.
Hurry up, Jim!

Everyone is having fun, even the
two white swans chasing ducks
in the little pond. Out on the bay
people are waterskiing and sailing.
Wow! It's windy!

Look at the dark clouds in the sky!
What was that? Lightning!
And listen! R-r-rumble-boom!
Oh no! It's a thunderstorm!

Story notes

Invite volunteers to describe a favorite summer activity. Encourage the other children to ask questions to draw the speakers out. Model language: *Where did you play baseball? Did you play on a team? How many people were on the team?*

Ask about the story:
What games could you play in the park? Who was on skates? What were the Youngs going to have for lunch? Why was the lifeguard blowing his whistle? How can you tell when a storm is coming? What do you think happened to the cookout?

Ask about your students:
Take a group survey and graph the children's responses to questions about summer activities *(Who likes to ride a bike?)* or favorite picnic foods *(What would you like to drink?)*. Help the children to understand how graphs can be used to show information.

Dialogue

Components: Cassette, Topic 55 Wall Chart, Picture Dictionary (pp. 110–111).

See page xix for techniques and strategies for presenting and practicing dialogues.

Tommy:	The pool was fun!
Diego:	Yeah, did you see me dive off the high diving board?
Tommy:	Yeah, you're good. I can't dive off the high board. I jump.
Diego:	Where is everyone?
Tommy:	Jim is skating. Some people are playing tennis.
Diego:	Marcus is playing baseball. Do you want to watch?
Tommy:	No. C'mon, let's eat.
Diego:	OK. I'm hungry.
Tommy:	My Uncle Pete is cooking hamburgers and hot dogs for us.
Diego:	Great! Hey, look at the sky! It looks like rain. Feel that wind!
Tommy:	I just saw lightning!
Diego:	Where?
Tommy:	In those dark clouds.
Diego:	Uh-oh. Thunder! We're going to have a thunderstorm!
Tommy:	Not before I get my hamburger! Hurry up! Run!

Dialogue notes

Use the Dictionary illustration or the Wall Chart as a referent, and invite pairs of volunteers to invent dialogues about the children in the story, based on the language modeled in this dialogue. You can give each child the name of one of the characters, and then prompt them to ask each other *where* questions *(Where's Alison? Alison's playing tennis. Where's Jim? Jim is skating).* Or prompt them to vary the format by asking, *What is Mrs. Young doing?*

Beats!

Components: Cassette, Beats! (Topic 55).

See page xx for techniques and strategies for presenting and practicing Beats!

There's a bright blue sky.
The sun is nice and warm.
Shall we swim in the pool?
Or picnic on the lawn?

We could play tennis,
or have a baseball game.
Where did the dark clouds come from?
It looks like rain!

Flash! goes the lightning.
Boom! goes the thunder.
Here comes a thunderstorm!
What can we get under?

Well, look at that!
The storm has moved away.
Let's go sailing.
It's a beautiful day!

Beat notes

After the children have become comfortable with the words and phrases in this Beat, encourage them to act it out as they recite, pantomiming the sports mentioned and their reactions to thunder and lightning.

Worksheets

Worksheet 1: Hot summer (p. 109)

You may want to encourage the children to read aloud the questions and answers once they complete the sentences. Help them understand that in the second set of exercises they circle only one ending to each sentence.

Hot summer Name ____

Write.

1. Can they feel the wind?
They can feel the ____.

2. Can he see the clouds?
He can see the ____.

3. Can she see the lightning?
She can see the ____.

Circle one.

If there is a thunderstorm I will

4. get in the pool. / get out of the pool.
5. stop playing tennis. / start playing tennis.
6. eat a picnic outside. / eat a picnic inside.
7. take off my skates. / put on my skates.
8. start playing baseball. / stop playing baseball.

Topic 55 109

Worksheet 2: Hot summer (p. 110)

The pictures provide clues for words the children can write or dictate. All the vocabulary words are found at the bottom of the page, but the children don't have to limit themselves to those words.

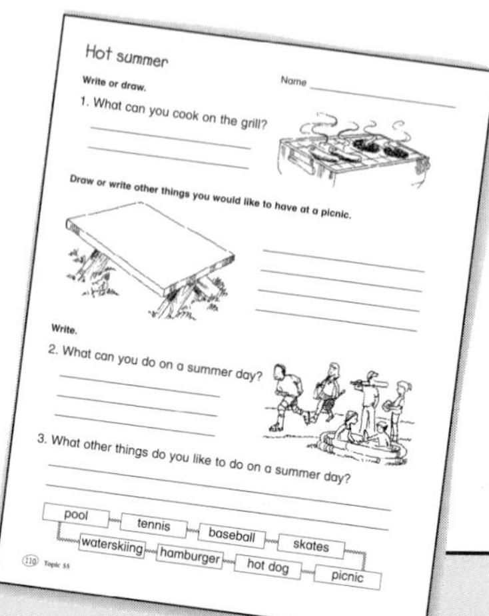
Hot summer Name ____

Write or draw.

1. What can you cook on the grill?

Draw or write other things you would like to have at a picnic.

Write.

2. What can you do on a summer day?

3. What other things do you like to do on a summer day?

pool tennis baseball skates waterskiing hamburger hot dog picnic

110 Topic 55

Activities

- Plan a picnic game. With the children in a circle, begin by establishing a clapping pattern. Then say, *We're going on a picnic and we will take hamburgers.* Prompt your neighbor to repeat your words, and add another item to take on the picnic. Continue around the circle, all the while keeping the rhythm with the clapping pattern, until it's your turn again. Recite the entire list, then challenge the children to repeat it.

- Teach your class the song "Eentsy Weentsy Spider." In conjunction with this song, talk about the water cycle: water vapor in the air cools, condenses and falls as rain, is then warmed, and evaporates to become water vapor in the air again.

The eentsy weentsy spider
went up the waterspout.
Down came the rain and
washed the spider out.
Out came the Sun and
dried up all the rain.
And the eentsy weentsy spider
went up the spout again.

- Make a play. Tell this popular folktale:
A stonecutter, feeling hot and inconsequential on the side of a rockface, wishes to be more powerful. He wishes to be the Sun and so becomes the Sun. But the clouds cover his face, so he wishes to be the clouds, and he is. But the wind blows the clouds away. So he wishes to be the wind, and he is. But the mountain stops the wind, so he wishes to be the mountain, and he is. But a tiny stonecutter is reducing the mountain to gravel, so in the end he wishes to be himself again.

Invite the children to act out the story, using actions and sound effects to show each step.

TOPIC 56 Windy fall

Content

- Fall activities and sports
- Seasonal changes
- Harvesting
- Plants and animals
- Tools and equipment used for fall chores

Language

- Identifying and describing fall activities and sports: *Let's rake the leaves. The bushes need clipping. The boys are playing football. We have a soccer game today.*
- Discussing animal behavior in the fall: *The robin's nest is empty. The squirrels are busy burying nuts.*
- Describing seasonal changes: *Look at the trees! The leaves have changed color. They're falling to the ground. The geese are flying south.*

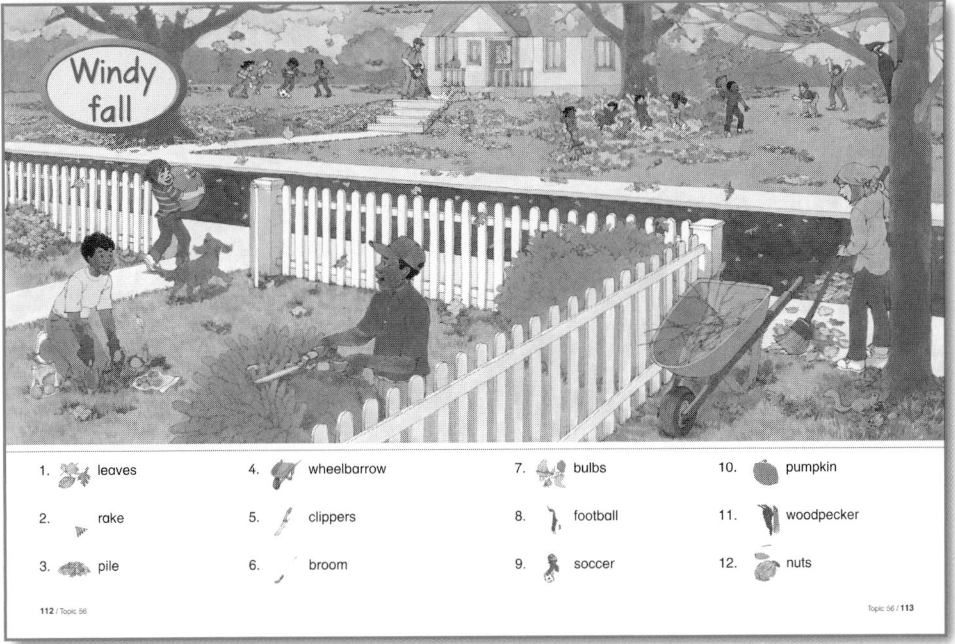

Words

1. leaves
2. rake
3. pile
4. wheelbarrow
5. clippers
6. broom
7. bulbs
8. football
9. soccer
10. pumpkin
11. woodpecker
12. nuts

Additional Words

leaf blower
sweep
path
hedge
clip
change
bury

It's fall in the Jacksons' neighborhood. The trees have turned bright orange, red, and gold, and there are leaves all over the ground. Everyone is raking and tidying up their gardens for winter. One neighbor is using a leaf blower. Another neighbor is putting broken branches in a wheelbarrow, and a third is sweeping her path with a broom. Two squirrels with very thick tails are burying nuts. A woodpecker is pecking at a tree, and the robin's nest is empty. The robins are gone, and the geese are flying south, where it's warmer. Mr. Jackson is trimming the bushes with clippers. Mrs. Jackson is planting bulbs. Tommy carries a huge pumpkin! It grew from the seeds he planted in the spring! Diego, Zoe, and Alison are playing soccer. Marcus and Jim are playing football. Samantha is attempting to rake more leaves into the leaf pile with a big rake, while Jasmin and the two Cheng twins jump in the pile of leaves.

Words

Components: Topic 56 Wall Chart, Picture Dictionary (pp. 112–113), Cassette, Word and Picture Cards (Topic 56).

See page xiv for techniques and strategies for presenting and practicing words.

Windy fall

1. leaves
2. rake
3. pile
4. wheelbarrow
5. clippers
6. broom
7. bulbs
8. football
9. soccer
10. pumpkin
11. wood-pecker
12. nuts

Notes

Review the cycle of the seasons with the children. Ask them to tell you the season that comes before fall and the one that comes after. Explain that another word for fall is *autumn*. If needed, review the words from other units, such as *squirrel, robin,* and *nest*; talk about the concept of planting bulbs in the fall to bloom in the spring. Play a game that prompts children to practice expressions of likes and dislikes. Shuffle a collection of word or picture cards and choose one. Show it to the children and model two responses: *I like _______* or *I don't like ______.* Then invite a volunteer to choose a card and give either a negative or positive response. As the children become more familiar with the vocabulary, ask them to elaborate their responses by stating a reason: *I like pumpkins because they are pretty* or *I don't like pumpkins because they are very heavy.*

Workbook page

Help the children read and follow the directions. As they locate the vocabulary word for each picture, they can color its space orange and make a mark on the picture. When they have found all the words, they will have colored a pumpkin and can identify it in the question at the bottom of the page.

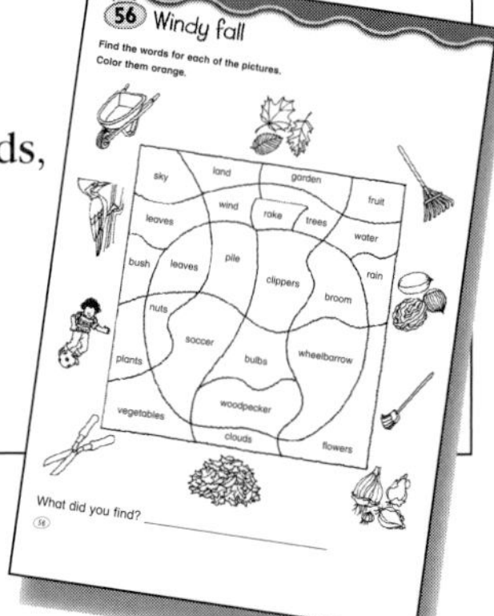

56 Windy fall
Find the words for each of the pictures. Color them orange.
What did you find?

Stories

Components: Picture Dictionary (pp. 112–113), Cassette, Story (Topic 56).

See page xviii for techniques and strategies for presenting and practicing stories.

Look at the trees! They've changed color!
Orange, red, gold! Beautiful!
Some leaves have fallen. Where's the rake?
Let's make piles and jump in them!

Get out the wheelbarrow and the clippers!
Bushes need clipping.
Leaves need raking.
Paths need sweeping with a broom.
Listen to that noisy leaf blower!
Time to plant bulbs for next year's flowers.

It's good football weather. And soccer, too.
Join the game, Tommy. Wow! What a huge
pumpkin! So that's what Tommy planted
in the Jacksons' garden last spring!

Look! The geese are flying south to
warmer places. The robins' nest is empty.
Woodpeckers are still here. Rat-a-tat!
Squirrels are busy burying nuts to eat.
Hurry scurry! Winter is coming!

Story notes

Invite volunteers to talk about changes they see around them that show the season has changed. Prompt them to think about both the natural world (falling leaves, ripe fruits, geese migrating) and things that happen in their own lives (wearing warmer clothes, closing windows, maybe eating different foods or playing different games). Make a chart of their suggestions.

Ask about the story:
What work is being done? What needs raking? Who is carrying the pumpkin? Why are the leaves on the ground? Why are the squirrels burying nuts? Where are the geese going? Which game is Diego playing?

Ask about your students:
Do leaves fall where you live? What color leaves have you seen? Have you ever raked leaves? What can you do with a pumpkin? How do you get ready for winter?

Dialogue

 **Components:** Cassette, Topic 56 Wall Chart, Picture Dictionary (pp. 112–113).

See page xix for techniques and strategies for presenting and practicing dialogues.

Samantha:	This rake is too big!
Jasmin:	You're making a good pile, Samantha.
Jo-Jo:	I love jumping in the leaves.
Samantha:	There! Go ahead, Jo-Jo. Jump!
Jo-Jo:	Here I come! Whe-e-e!
Mrs. Jackson:	I'm going to plant these bulbs here.
Mr. Jackson:	That's fine. Then we'll have beautiful daffodils next spring.
Mrs. Jackson:	Maybe Marcus can help you clip that hedge.
Mr. Jackson:	No, he's having a good time playing football. I just need a new pair of clippers.
Mrs. Jackson:	Will you look at your daughter playing soccer! She's good!
Tommy:	Hi, everyone!
Mrs. Jackson:	Oh! Hi, Tommy! Did you come for your pumpkin?
Tommy:	Yeah.
Mrs. Jackson:	There it is!
Tommy:	Where?
Mrs. Jackson:	Over there! The big one!
Tommy:	That's my pumpkin?
Mrs. Jackson:	Yes, that's yours! That's what you planted last spring!
Mr. Jackson:	It's heavy. Can you lift it?
Tommy:	Yes, I can do it! Thanks. I'll take it home. Hey, look everyone! Look at my pumpkin! I grew it!

Dialogue notes

After listening to the dialogue a few times, encourage the children to form groups of two or three. Have them choose characters from this dialogue and invent new dialogues they think those same children might have. For example, if the children in a group of three pretend they are Samantha, Jasmin, and Jo-Jo, they can make up dialogues about raking leaves into piles and jumping into them. Encourage the groups to create a small scene with dialogue that they can act out for their classmates.

Beats!

 **Components:** Cassette, Beats! (Topic 56).

See page xx for techniques and strategies for presenting and practicing Beats!

Look what's falling from the sky!
Red and yellow leaves!
They're not falling from the sky.
They're falling from the trees.

Where did the big fat pumpkins
come from?
Where did the flowers go?
The wind is whirling all the leaves.
Blow, wind! Blow!

Why are the rabbits in their holes?
They're keeping nice and warm.
Where's the robin in his nest?
Sorry! He's gone!

The flowers don't grow anymore.
The swallow doesn't call.
What's happening to everything?
It's fall! That's all.

Beat notes

As soon as the children become comfortable with the words and phrases in this Beat, put them into two groups. Have one group divide in half to recite the Beat as written, saying the final line in unison; the other group pantomimes the Beat (leaves falling, wind whirling, rabbits hiding).

Worksheets

Worksheet 1: Windy fall (p. 111)

You may want to help the children write the sentence fragments on separate pieces of paper so that they can manipulate them as they solve this puzzle. The questions in each section should help them put the sentences in order. You can demonstrate what to do with the first sentence by asking: *Who is this sentence about? What does the boy do? Where does the boy take* (or *put*) *the leaves?*

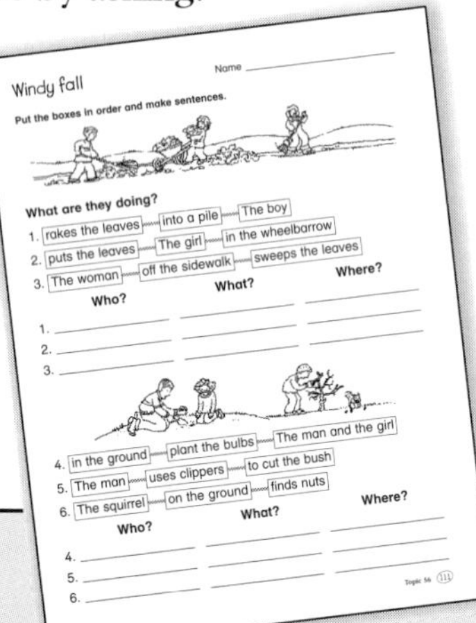

Windy fall Name

Put the boxes in order and make sentences.

What are they doing?

1. rakes the leaves — into a pile — The boy
2. puts the leaves — The girl — in the wheelbarrow
3. The woman — off the sidewalk — sweeps the leaves

	Who?	What?	Where?
1.			
2.			
3.			

4. in the ground — plant the bulbs — The man and the girl
5. The man — uses clippers — to cut the bush
6. The squirrel — on the ground — finds nuts

	Who?	What?	Where?
4.			
5.			
6.			

Topic 56 111

Worksheet 2: Windy fall (p. 112)

Point out that the spaces provided for writing the words correspond to the numbers next to each item in the picture.

Windy fall Name

Write the word for each number.

1. ______ 2. ______
3. ______ 4. ______
5. ______ 6. ______
7. ______ 8. ______
9. ______ 10. ______
11. ______ 12. ______

112 Topic 56

Activities

- Create leaf collages and prints. Gather leaves from different trees in the neighborhood or school yard, and make colorful collages to hang in the classroom and hallways. Show the children how to make a leaf rubbing by putting the leaf on a table with a piece of paper on top. Rub the paper with the side of a crayon using firm, even strokes. The outline of the leaf will appear on the other side of the paper.
- Fall is a good time to collect seeds from a variety of wild and garden plants, trees, and shrubs. Bring in some you collect, and invite students to bring in seeds they find. Put them in a shoebox or other container where the children can handle and examine them. Talk with the children about how these seeds provide the winter food for many birds and animals. Invite the children to name (and taste) seeds that people as well as animals eat, such as many nuts, pumpkin seeds, and sunflower seeds.
- Share books about fall with your students, such as *Red Leaf, Yellow Leaf* by Lois Eblert (Harcourt Brace), which tells the story of a sugar maple tree from seed to syrup through the seasons and through the years.
- Make an *Imagine That Garden Now* mural. Help the children recollect the Jacksons' garden in the spring. Work with the children to make a mural of what their garden would look like with all of the vegetables and flowers they planted now ready to harvest (beans, corn, pumpkins, tomatoes, snapdragons, daisies, sunflowers). Use seed catalogs or books about plants as references, and encourage the children to create a colorful, rich harvest.

Snowy winter

Content

- Winter activities and sports
- Snow

Language

- Identifying and describing winter activities and sports: *They're ice skating on the frozen pond. We can sled down the hill. They ski fast down the hill.*
- Discussing winter snowstorms: *Hooray! A blizzard! The snowflakes are coming down fast! Here comes the snowplow!*
- Expressing concern and asking about someone's well-being: *It's very cold, so wear a heavy jacket, and don't forget your gloves. Samantha just fell off her sled! Are you OK, Samantha?*

Words

1. snow
2. snowflakes
3. snowman
4. snowball
5. icicles
6. sled
7. ice skating
8. skiing
9. hat
10. jacket
11. gloves
12. scarf

Additional Words

frozen
blizzard
shovel
snowdrift
snowplow
sleigh riding
ski mask

It's winter in the park. Snowflakes are swirling all around. Icicles are hanging from rooftops. There are snowdrifts, and a snowplow is clearing the road. Alison and her mother are skiing. Samantha and Jasmin are going down a hill on their sleds, but Samantha has landed in a snowdrift at the bottom! Everyone is wearing heavy jackets, hats, and gloves. Ting and Zoe have just made a snowman with a carrot nose, a hat, and a scarf. Zoe is patting him, putting on the finishing touches. Ting has picked up her ice skates, ready to go ice skating. Vanessa is trying to catch a snowflake on her tongue. Who's throwing snowballs? Tommy, Diego, Jo-Jo, and Jackie! Jackie's snowball has hit Tommy in the back. Tommy's getting his snowball ready!

Words

Components: Topic 57 Wall Chart, Picture Dictionary (pp. 114–115), Cassette, Word and Picture Cards (Topic 57).

See page xiv for techniques and strategies for presenting and practicing words.

Snowy winter

1. snow	5. icicles	9. hat
2. snowflakes	6. sled	10. jacket
3. snowman	7. ice skating	11. gloves
4. snowball	8. skiing	12. scarf

Notes

Invite the children to make a winter mural. Draw a background, including a slope for skiing and sledding, a pond for skating, a flat area for snowball throwing and snowman building, and a house with eaves. Let the children add elements to the scene as you introduce and review the vocabulary words. They can glue shreds of cotton for snow, and silver foil for the ice in the pond and as icicles hanging from the eaves. Help them make cut-paper snowflakes to decorate the edge of the mural. Introduce the clothing as they add figures to the mural.

If you live in a warm climate, or have children who have never seen snow or experienced freezing weather, challenge them to think of "cold" words *(slick, smooth, icy, frozen, chilled, shiver, brrrr!)* or words that have to do with winter activities *(sliding, gliding, skating, slippery)*. Ask a child to choose a word or phrase, and have the group pantomime it.

Workbook page

Help the children read and follow the directions. The pictures provide clues for responding to the questions.

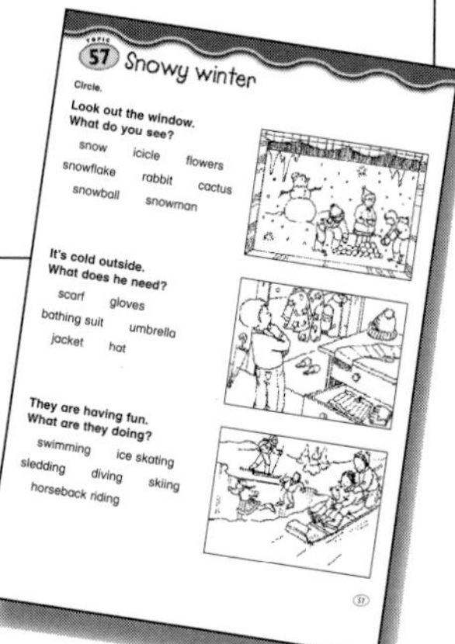

Stories

Components: Picture Dictionary (pp. 114–115), Cassette, Story (Topic 57).

See page xviii for techniques and strategies for presenting and practicing stories.

Look at the snow! Hooray! A blizzard!
The snowflakes are coming down fast!
Try to catch one on your tongue!
Let's make a snowman with a carrot
nose! Put a hat on him and a scarf.

Icicles are hanging from the rooftops.
The pond is frozen. It's really cold!
Want to go ice skating? Wear a heavy
jacket, and don't forget gloves!

Here's the snowplow to clear the road.
Is that Alison skiing down the hill?
She's good! Samantha and Jasmin are
on their sleds. Uh-oh! Samantha just
landed in a snowdrift!

Hey! Who threw that snowball?
Yo! Jackie! Here comes one right back!
Let's have a snowball fight!
That's the best thing about snow!

Story notes

Invite children to talk about what they like and what they don't like about winter. As they share their thoughts with the group, make notes on a piece of paper. Then organize your notes and share them with the children on a chart. Before showing the chart, ask the group if they think most people in their class like winter.

Ask about the story:
Who made the snowman? How did they make the snowman? What did they use for the snowman's nose? What is Alison doing? What happened to Samantha? Did Jasmin fall off the sled? Can Vanessa catch a snowflake?

Ask about your students:
What do you like to do in the snow? Have you ever gone ice skating? Would you like to ski? Why can you skate on a pond when it's very cold? What do you wear when you go out in the cold? Do you like snowball fights?

Dialogue

 **Components:** Cassette, Topic 57 Wall Chart, Picture Dictionary (pp. 114–115).

See page xix for techniques and strategies for presenting and practicing dialogues.

Zoe:	What a beautiful snowman we made!
Ting:	I like his carrot nose. Ugh-h. My gloves are all wet!
Zoe:	I hope Marcus doesn't see the hat and scarf.
Ting:	Why?
Zoe:	Because they're his!
Ting:	Let's go ice skating now.
Zoe:	OK. Vanessa! What are you doing?
Vanessa:	Catching snowflakes on my tongue. They taste good.
Ting:	Look! There's Alison skiing down the hill. That looks like fun. And there's Samantha!
Zoe:	Where?
Ting:	In the snowdrift! She just fell off her sled!
Zoe:	Samantha! Are you OK?
Samantha:	Yes!
Ting:	Uh-oh! A snowball fight! Let's get out of here!
Tommy:	Ouch! Who threw that snowball and got snow all over my jacket and down my neck? OK, Jackie, here comes one for you!

Dialogue notes

After listening to the dialogue a few times, invite the children to play a game. Whisper to one or two children a scene you want them to pantomime, for example, *You are ice skating on a slippery pond and you fall down*. Then, as the class watches, model language for inventing dialogues: *Look! What is he doing? He's ice skating. Oh no! What happened? He fell down.* Next, invite two volunteers to watch the pantomime first and then invent dialogues about what they are seeing as the mimes act it out a second time.

Beats!

 **Components:** Cassette, Beats! (Topic 57).

See page xx for techniques and strategies for presenting and practicing Beats!

Look at that!
Look at the snow!
    Wow! It's a blizzard!
    Let's go!

Grab your snowboard!
    Grab your sled!
Don't land in a snowdrift
on your head!

Who threw that snowball?
There's snow down my back.
    My gloves are frozen.
    That's enough of that!

Let's watch the ice skating.
Round and round they go.
    Let's watch the snowflakes.
    I love snow!

Beat notes

Separate the students into two groups to practice the Beat as written. Encourage students to pantomime throwing and being hit by snowballs, brushing snow off their gloves and clothing, ice skating, and sledding.

Worksheets

Worksheet 1: Snowy winter! (p. 113)

Help the children read and follow the directions. Point out that they should circle only one ending to each sentence. Encourage them to use vocabulary words in answering the question about what they like to do in the snow, but they should not limit themselves to those words. If your students have never been in a snowy place, ask what they would like to do in the snow.

Snowy winter

Name ____________

Circle one box for each sentence.

What are they doing?

1. The girl is making [a snowman.] [an icicle.]
2. The boy is throwing [a snowman.] [a snowball.]
3. The girl is pulling [a sled.] [a snowflake.]
4. She is wearing [a scarf.] [a snowball.]
5. They are playing [in the snow.] [in the sand.]
6. He is ice skating [on a street.] [on a pond.]
7. The woman is [skiing.] [swimming.]

Draw a face on the snowman.
Add a scarf, hat, and gloves.
Write.

What do you like to do in the snow?

____

Topic 57 113

Worksheet 2: Snowy winter! (p. 114)

After the children have completed the first set of words, ask them what word they wrote each time. You might want to take this opportunity to talk about compound words. The children can underline or circle the words *yes* or *no* in the last group of exercises.

Snowy winter

Name ____________

Write the missing letters.

____flakes ____man ____ball snow

ice skat___ ski___

What letters did you write each time? ___

Choose *yes* or *no*. Write the word.

Is this a jacket?
Yes. No. This is a ______.

Is this a scarf?
Yes. No. This is a ______.

Is this a hat?
Yes. No. This is a ______.

Are these gloves?
Yes. No. These are ______.

114 Topic 57

Activities

- Paint with ice cubes. Let the children sprinkle different colors of dry tempera paint on plain white paper. (You can fill salt shakers with the powdered paint or let them sprinkle it on paper using spoons.) Then provide an ice cube for each child, and show them how they can paint by moving the ice through the sprinkled paint. As the cube melts, it liquefies the paint and creates a design. Take this opportunity to talk about the properties of water in its different states.

- Follow the leader. Prepare cards with a phrase or picture of a winter activity *(You are a snowplow clearing a path; You are slipping and sliding on the ice; You're building a snowman; You're shoveling heavy snow.)*. Shuffle the cards and invite a child to draw a card and move accordingly. Tell the other children to watch, and when they think they know what the first child is doing, they can join in the motion. After a few minutes, ask the children what they are doing, and then ask the first child if that is what he or she was doing.

- Teach to the tune of "Row, Row, Row Your Boat":

  Blow, blow, blow, North Wind,
  biting at my nose.
  Slippy, drippy, nippy days.
  Feel the cold winds blow.

  Blow, blow, blow, North Wind,
  you're the one who knows
  why the flowers all are gone
  and where the summer goes.

- Make a winter felt board. Divide the board into indoor and outdoor areas. Cut two people and various items of clothing out of felt. Have the children prepare the people for a snowy day, send them "outside," and bring them "in" again.

- If you are fortunate enough to have both falling snow and a freezer, place a piece of black construction paper in the freezer for an hour. Then hold it outside to collect snowflakes. Provide magnifying glasses so that the children can examine them and watch how rapidly they melt.

Theme 9: Earth and Space

Topic 58 Up in the night sky
Topic 59 Out in space
Topic 60 My blue Earth

Theme Bibliography

Big Silver Space Shuttle
written and illustrated by Ken Wilson-Max.
Scholastic Inc., 1996. ISBN 0590100815
This interactive book attracts children like magnets, but the flaps and tabs must be treated gently. On every page of this simulated shuttle journey there are tabs to pull, pieces to push, and flaps to open. Some of the language is technical *(external fuel tank, cargo bay door)* but within the context of the story and art, it is easy for interested students to acquire.

Blast Off to Earth! A Look at Geography
written and illustrated by Loreen Leady.
Holiday House, 1992. ISBN 0823409732
In a cute and clever approach to geography, readers travel along with a group of robotic aliens on a visit to Earth. They first see the blue planet floating in space, then drop down to visit the oceans and continents. The illustrations are charming and full of details to notice and discuss. The language is conversational; short, declarative, and interrogative sentences are set in speech bubbles. The book can be used to prompt children to invent their own dialogues about visiting a new place.

Goodnight Moon
written by Margaret Wise Brown;
illustrated by Clement Hurd.
HarperCollins Children's Books, 1996.
ISBN 0060275049
For more than fifty years the magical pictures and repetitive text of this cherished classic have helped put children to sleep with a sense of security and belonging. It is a book English-language learners can read themselves about an experience we all share. For a good vocabulary activity, students can find items mentioned throughout the book in the pictures of the room.

How Much is a Million?
written by David M. Schwartz;
illustrated by Steven Kellogg.
Mulberry Books, 1993. ISBN 0688099335
Really, really big numbers are explored through simple, repetitive text and expressive pictures. The solid, detailed illustrations provide a glimpse of quantities difficult for anyone to conceive, even adults! The pages are filled with amusing detail for students to identify and ponder.

I See the Moon, and the Moon Sees Me
written by Jonathan London;
illustrated by Peter Fiore.
Puffin Books, 1998. ISBN 0140554874
A boy has an adventurous day in the country. He greets the world with joy and expectation. His busy day includes flying a kite at the beach, climbing high in the mountains, canoeing on a lake, and biking through meadows of flowers. This book will be welcomed by English-language learners because it is engaging yet easy to read. Each page features a different verse based on an old rhyme. The vibrant watercolors are soothing and the repetition of the text helps build vocabulary and language patterns.

Look At The Moon
written by May Garelick;
illustrated by Barbara Garrison.
Mondo Pub, 1996. ISBN 1572551429
A gentle, repetitive book in which a young girl asks if the moon she sees is the same moon seen by animals and people around the world. The pictures are soft and luminescent, as if lit by moonlight. The text gives children an opportunity to review the names of animals from around the world.

The Moon Seems to Change

written by Franklyn Branley;
illustrated by Barbara and Ed Emberley.
HarperTrophy, 1987. ISBN 0064450651

Bright cartoon illustrations of the moon in the night sky accompany a text that explains the moon's phases. There are illustrated instructions for experiments that students can perform to solidify the concepts covered. The class can act out the relationship between the Earth, moon, and Sun as a classroom activity.

My Place in Space

written by Robin and Sally Hirst;
illustrated by Roland Harvey with Joe Levine.
Orchard Books, 1992. ISBN 0531070301

A rude bus driver asks two children if they know where they live. Indeed they do! The children proceed to tell him in great detail, from street address to universe. The illustrations are a fascinating blend of ground-level human detail, with all manner of silly, wild narratives for children to talk about.

New Moon

written by Pegi Deitz Shea;
illustrated by Cathryn Falwell.
Boyds Mills Press, 1996. ISBN 156397410X

This beautiful book about the moon and its phases shows the loving relationship between a big brother and his little sister. Colorful illustrations express the joy of learning and sharing. The text combines dialogues and descriptive narratives. The book provides good material for question-and-answer exchanges with students about what is happening in the story and why.

Our Solar System

by Seymour Simon.
William Morrow & Co., 1992. ISBN 0688099920

Stunning photos accompany the text of this striking book, which expands on the vocabulary from Topic 59. The language is clear and concise. Interesting diagrams show the relative size of the planets and offer information about each. Children who are interested in learning more can read about asteroids, meteors, and other elements of our solar system.

Planets in Our Solar System

written by Franklyn Branley;
illustrated by Don Madden.
HarperTrophy, 1998. ISBN 006445178X

Like many of Branley's science books, this one has an activity for children to do, plus straightforward text filled with information about the solar system.

Stars in the Sky

by Alan Fowler.
Children's Press, 1996. ISBN 05160202200

Color photographs illustrate this book, excellent for both English-language learners and beginning readers. It uses straightforward declarative sentences. Scientific terms introduced in the text are contained in an illustrated glossary at the back of the book.

Under the Sun

written and illustrated by Ellen Kandoian.
Dodd, Mead & Co., 1987 ISBN 0399220259

Molly asks her mother where the Sun goes when it sets. Her mother's answer follows the Sun as it sets all over the world until it wakes up Molly again in the morning. The book includes a more scientific explanation of the Sun's movement across the sky, accompanied by a group experiment to demonstrate the Earth's motion. Students can use a map to locate each place mentioned in the text as it follows the path of the setting Sun. Many words will be familiar from the Picture Dictionary.

What Makes Day and Night

written by Franklyn M. Branley;
illustrated by Arthur Dorros.
HarperTrophy, 1986. ISBN 0064450503

Clear diagrams and pretty pictures of Earth illustrate a simple text that explains night and day in terms of Earth's rotation and relation to the Sun. There is a visit to the moon and a brief explanation of its phases. As with other books in this *Let's Read and Find Out* science series, there is an activity students can duplicate, this time with a lamp or a flashlight in a darkened room.

What the Moon Saw

written and illustrated by Brian Wildsmith.
Oxford University Press, 1987. ISBN 0192721577

The Sun brags about all he can see. In the process he introduces young readers to a list of adjectives as well as to many animals from around the world. The moon responds by pointing out the one thing she can see that the Sun never does—the dark. Brian Wildsmith's vibrant collages add exuberance to this book. The simple prose: "There is a... This is a..." is accessible to English-language learners. They can collect adjectives in a word bank and employ them in other contexts.

Up in the night sky

Content

- Objects in the sky
- Using a telescope

Language

- Identifying and naming objects in the night sky: *The moon is just above the houses. The stars are twinkling tonight. A meteor looks like a falling star.*
- Observing and speculating about astronomical phenomena: *A star is falling. The moon is full. Does anyone live on the moon?*
- Talking about using a telescope: *The telescope makes the moon look bigger. I can see a planet.*

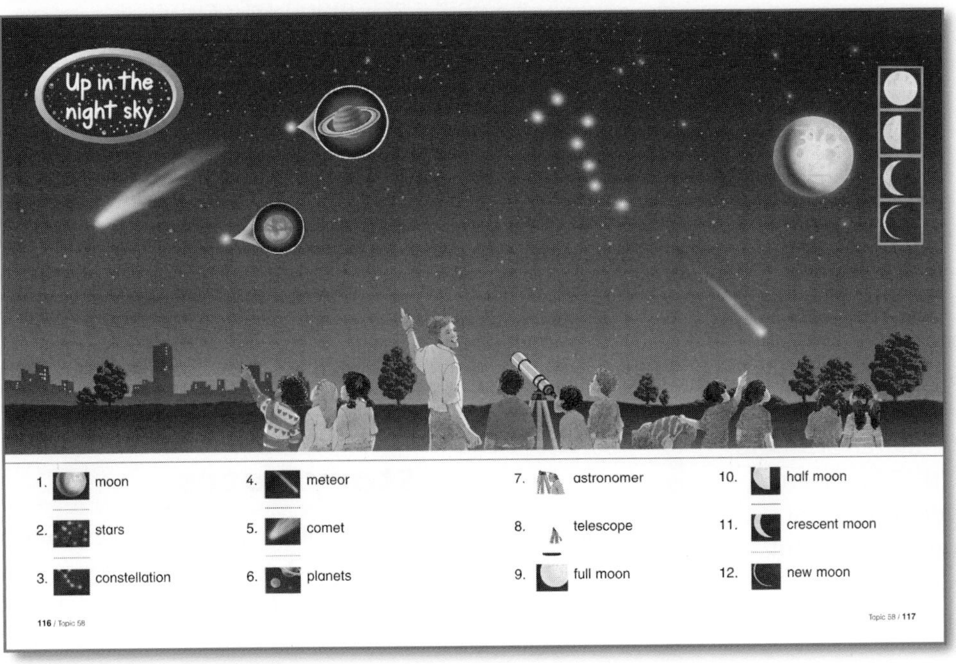

Words

1. moon
2. stars
3. constellation
4. meteor
5. comet
6. planets
7. astronomer
8. telescope
9. full moon
10. half moon
11. crescent moon
12. new moon

Additional Words

universe
galaxy
space
crater
magnify

The scene is a small park in the community, where the children are gathered to watch the night sky. There is a bright full moon with crater shadows, and a sky full of twinkling stars. Two of the "stars" are really the planets Saturn and Mars. The Big Dipper constellation is overhead. A fuzzy white comet with a long tail is visible, and a meteor streaks through the night sky. An astronomer is showing his telescope to the children. He is pointing out Saturn to Marcus, Jim, and Diego. Diego is looking through the telescope. Ting, Zoe, and Alison have their heads together looking up at the comet. Jo-Jo and Jackie are very excited. They see the meteor and are pulling on Tommy's shirt so that he will see it, too, but Tommy is busy looking upside down at the Big Dipper. Samantha and Jasmin are looking at the bright full moon, spellbound. (At the top of the illustration, four stages of the moon are shown: new moon, crescent moon, half moon, and full moon.)

Words

Components: Topic 58 Wall Chart, Picture Dictionary (pp. 116–117), Cassette, Word and Picture Cards (Topic 58).

See page xiv for techniques and strategies for presenting and practicing words.

Up in the night sky

1. moon	6. planets	10. half moon
2. stars	7. astronomer	11. crescent moon
3. constellation	8. telescope	12. new moon
4. meteor	9. full moon	
5. comet		

Notes

You may want to tell the children that *astro* means *star* and ask them if they have ever heard of another word made with *astro* (examples are *astronaut* and *astronomy*). When spelled out, this word may be a familiar cognate for Spanish native speakers. Invite four volunteers to stand in a line in the center of a circle of children. Then offer one child the *new moon* picture card. Ask the other children which card you should give to the next child *(crescent moon),* and continue until the four phases are represented in order of appearance. Then ask the children with the cards for the moon phases to form their own small circle, with their backs to each other. As the rest of the children walk in a circle around them, children call out each phase as they pass it. Ask the children which phase of the moon is shown in the Dictionary illustration.

Workbook page

Give the clue that the first two words, *constellation* and *stars,* are missing all of their consonants. The children can draw lines to match the pictures to the words. For the drawings of the phases of the moon, suggest that they use the Wall Chart or Dictionary as a reference.

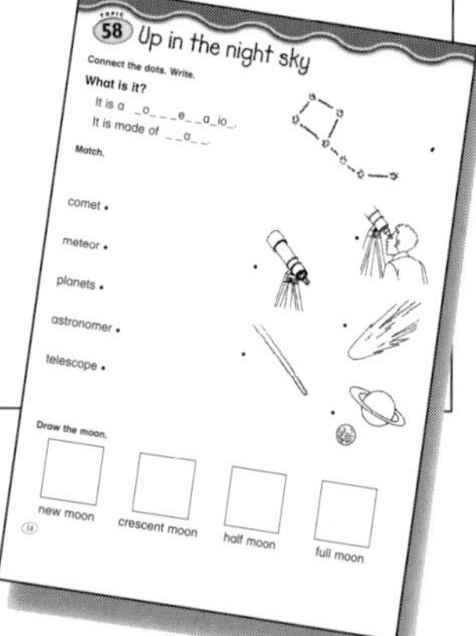

Stories

Components: Picture Dictionary (pp. 116–117), Cassette, Story (Topic 58).

See page xviii for techniques and strategies for presenting and practicing stories.

Look at all those stars!
Does anyone live on a star?
No, they're burning hot.
There's the Big Dipper!
That's a constellation of stars.

Look at the moon! It's bright!
That's because it's full. Sometimes
it's only a half moon, or a crescent.
Who lives on the moon? No one.

Look! Quick! A shooting star!
It's a meteor falling.
And there's a comet with a long tail.
What else is out there? Planets!
Look through the telescope. Wow!

Maybe someone lives on a planet.
Ask the astronomer. He knows.
Guess what! We live on a planet!
Earth is a planet, and the Sun is a star!

Story notes

Invite volunteers to talk about what they see when they look at the night sky where they live. Some children may have had the experience of looking at the night sky from places with less light obscuring the view. Ask them where they can see more stars. Some children may have seen the Hale-Bopp comet, or the aurora borealis. Encourage them to describe what they have seen.

Ask about the story:
What kind of scientist is the man? What does he use to see the stars better? What is another name for a shooting star? What is fuzzy and white and has a long tail?

Ask about your students:
Have you seen the moon? Did you see the moon last night? What does the moon look like? Have you ever seen a shooting star? Have you looked through a telescope? Can you see the stars in the daytime? Why can't we see the stars when it's raining?

Dialogue

Components: Cassette, Topic 58 Wall Chart, Picture Dictionary (pp. 116–117).

See page xix for techniques and strategies for presenting and practicing dialogues.

Diego:	What a lot of stars!
Astronomer:	You can see the planets, too. Here, Diego. Look through the telescope.
Diego:	Wow! Does anyone live out there?
Astronomer:	We don't know. Not on the stars, but maybe on the planets.
Marcus:	Astronomers can see way out in space with the big telescopes, can't they?
Astronomer:	Yes, and we can send people to the moon.
Samantha:	To that moon? That moon up there?
Astronomer:	Yes, that moon. Astronauts can walk on that moon.
Samantha:	I think I see someone up there now. I see a face.
Marcus:	You see the man in the moon. It just looks like a face, Samantha. It's not a real face.
Jo-Jo:	I see something! A star is falling!
Astronomer:	That's a meteor. Sometimes it's called a shooting star.
Diego:	Look over there! What's that?
Astronomer:	It's a comet. It looks white and fuzzy, and it has a long tail.
Zoe:	I see it!
Ting:	So do I!
Tommy:	Where's the Big Dipper?
Astronomer:	It's right up above you, Tommy. It's upside down. It looks like a big pot with a long handle. See it? That's a constellation.
Jasmin:	I like the moon the best. I'm going to the moon someday.
Astronomer:	Maybe we'll go with you!
Jasmin:	OK!

Dialogue notes

Ask the children to pretend they are looking at the night sky. They should invent dialogues in which they follow the pattern modeled by Diego and the astronomer: *Look over there! What's that? That's a* ________.

Beats!

Components: Cassette, Beats! (Topic 58).

See page xx for techniques and strategies for presenting and practicing Beats!

When it gets dark I like to look
far out in the sky.
You can see the moon and stars,
and planets way up high.

Look at the moon!
It gets bigger every night.
And then it gets smaller.
And then it's out of sight.

Have you seen a shooting star?
Or comet passing by?
When I look up, I like to find
star pictures in the sky.

Is anybody out there,
beyond the farthest star?
Maybe someone's out there,
but we don't know if they are.

Beat notes

Provide the children with rattles, bells, triangles, or other small, fairly quiet instruments to accompany this Beat. After practicing until they are comfortable with the words and phrases, invite them to join in rhythmically at the end of each stanza.

Worksheets

Worksheet 1: Up in the night sky (p. 115)

The picture at the top of the page helps children fill in the blanks. The pictures in the middle of the page provide clues for writing the name of each item that can be seen in the night sky. The boxed words can be found on the page. The exercise at the bottom of the page asks the children to write the names for the phases of the moon.

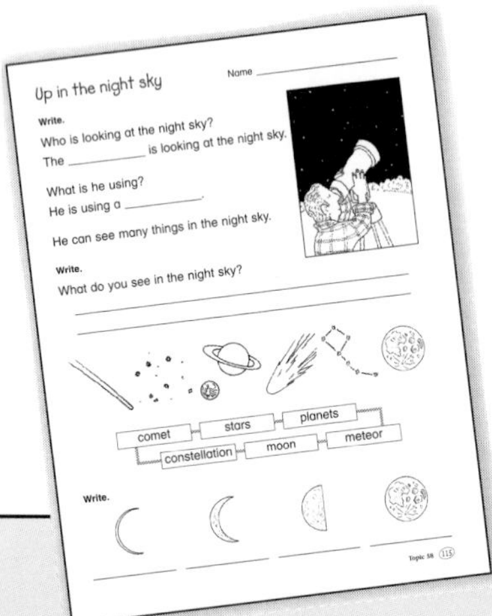

Up in the night sky Name ________

Write.

Who is looking at the night sky?

The ________ is looking at the night sky.

What is he using?

He is using a ________.

He can see many things in the night sky.

Write.

What do you see in the night sky?

comet stars planets constellation moon meteor

Write.

Topic 58 115

Worksheet 2: Up in the night sky (p. 116)

It may help the children unscramble the words if you suggest they write the letters in a straight line on a separate piece of paper. Once they have unscrambled and rewritten the words, they can match them to the pictures in the right-hand column.

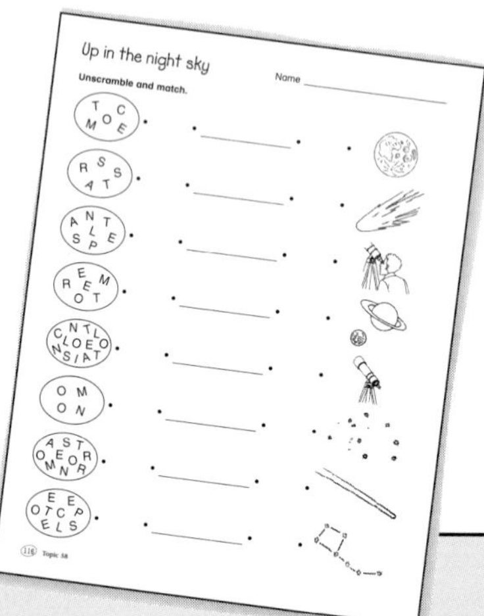

Up in the night sky Name ________

Unscramble and match.

T C O M E

R S S A T

A N T L S P E

E R E M O T

C N T L L O E O N S I A T

O M O N

A S T O E O R M N R

E E O T C P E L S

116 Topic 58

Activities

- Make a telescope. With markers, the children can decorate cardboard tubes from paper towel rolls. You can fit different sized tubes together, for "focusing." Have the children look through their telescopes and describe an imaginary night sky.
- Model orbits. One child can be the Sun and say, *I'm the Sun.* A second volunteer says: *I'm the Earth. I go around the Sun.* This child walks slowly around the Sun (leaving room for the moon to orbit the "Earth" in turn). A third child then says: *I'm the moon. I go around the Earth.* He or she walks slowly around the Earth as the Earth walks around the Sun. Give everyone a chance to play each role.
- Teach the song "Twinkle, Twinkle, Little Star":

  Twinkle, Twinkle, Little Star,
  how I wonder what you are,
  up above the world so high
  like a diamond in the sky.
  Twinkle, Twinkle, Little Star,
  How I wonder what you are.

- Share popular children's books, such as *Goodnight Moon* by Margaret Wise Brown (Clement Hurd) and the Moon and Little Bear series by Frank Ashe (*Mooncake, Moondance,* and *Moongame,* all published by Aladdin Paperbacks), to spark the children's imaginations and encourage discussion.

Out in space

Content	Language
Earth's Solar System	Identifying and naming the planets in Earth's Solar System: *The closest planet to the Sun is Mercury. Earth is the third planet from the Sun.*
Planets	Describing characteristics of the planets: *Saturn has rings around it. Jupiter has lots of moons. Earth has a lot of water.*
Space travel	Using superlatives and comparative adjectives: *Mercury is the fastest planet. Venus is hotter than Mercury. It is the hottest planet.*

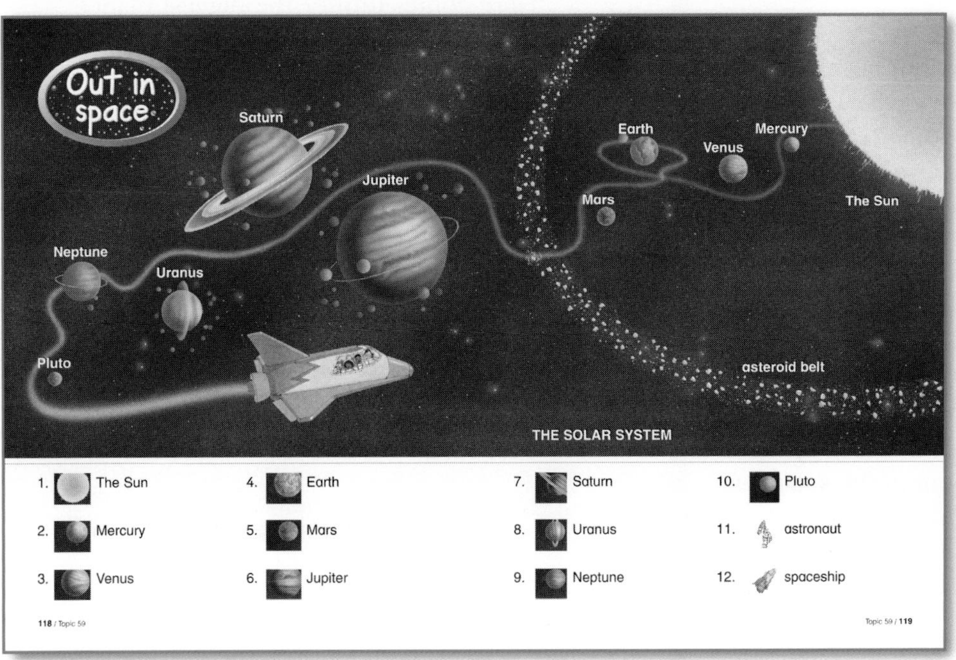

A spaceship carrying Captain Ting and her crew of astronauts—Marcus, Tommy, Diego, Alison, and Zoe—is traveling through the Solar System, leaving a trail that can be followed. It began in the vicinity of the Sun, passed Mercury (the fastest-moving planet) and Venus (the hottest planet), before circling Earth. Then it continued past reddish Mars, through the asteroid belt—where it bumped into an asteroid—and past Jupiter (the largest planet), marked by a red spot and many moons. The ship then passed Saturn, which is surrounded by thick rings and seventeen or more moons. Beyond Saturn, the astronauts passed a planet that looks as if it's lying on its side (Uranus), and then went on past Neptune and finally Pluto (the planet farthest from the Sun and notable because its moon may be bigger than it is). The ship almost leaves the Solar System, but then turns and heads back to Earth.

Words

1. The Sun
2. Mercury
3. Venus
4. Earth
5. Mars
6. Jupiter
7. Saturn
8. Uranus
9. Neptune
10. Pluto
11. astronaut
12. spaceship

Additional Words

universe
Solar System
satellite
crew
orbit
rocket
launch
sixteen
seventeen

Words

Components: Topic 59 Wall Chart, Picture Dictionary (pp. 118–119), Cassette, Word and Picture Cards (Topic 59).

See page xiv for techniques and strategies for presenting and practicing words.

Out in space

1. The Sun	5. Mars	9. Neptune
2. Mercury	6. Jupiter	10. Pluto
3. Venus	7. Saturn	11. astronaut
4. Earth	8. Uranus	12. spaceship

Notes

Look at the Wall Chart with the children, and ask them to help you assign a number to each planet, beginning with Mercury as number one because it's closest to the Sun. Tape the number over each planet, or tape numbers to the word cards for children to refer to. Then prompt the children to generate numbers. One way to do this is to ask two children to hold up (on the count of three) any number of fingers on one hand. Have the children add (or count) the fingers and call out the name of the planet with that number. Then, ask the two children to point to the planet on the Wall Chart. If the children come up with the number ten, tell them they are out of the solar system, and let them try again!

Workbook page

Help the children read and follow the directions. The planets and the Sun listed in the ship's log should then read in the same order as is indicated by the path in the picture.

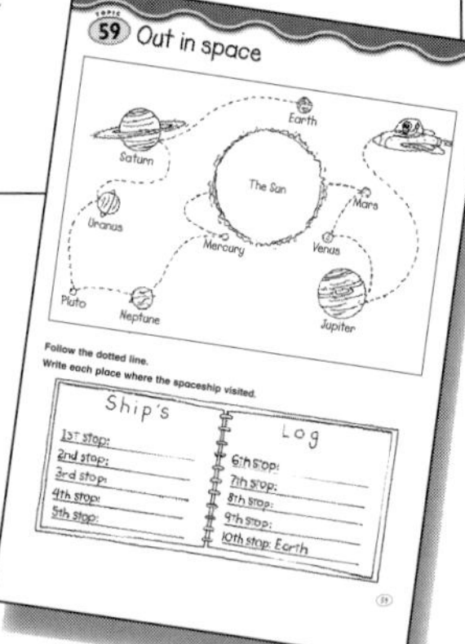

Stories

Components: Picture Dictionary (pp. 118–119), Cassette, Story (Topic 59).

See page xviii for techniques and strategies for presenting and practicing stories.

Calling Earth! This is Captain Ting.
Our spaceship has passed
the fastest planet, Mercury,
and the hottest planet, Venus. Phew!
We've orbited Earth. Now on to Mars!

Hey! Mars has two moons! Bump!
Oops! Hit an asteroid! We're OK.
Here comes Jupiter, the biggest planet,
with a big red spot.
It has sixteen moons!

Saturn next! What are these? Rings!
It has rings and seventeen moons.
Uh-oh. Uranus has fallen over!
Its rings go sideways.

We're moving fast, farther and farther.
Past Neptune and cold, cold Pluto and ...

Earth calling Ting! You astronauts are out
too far! Come back into the Solar System!
Come back!

Story notes

Talk about space travel. Help the children understand that space travel is possible now, but it isn't like what they may have seen on TV or in the movies. For instance, we don't know anything about the existence of aliens or any forms of life on other planets.

Ask about the story:
Which planet did the spaceship pass first? What caused the bump the children in the spaceship felt? Did the asteroid hurt the spaceship? What's the biggest planet? How many moons does Jupiter have? Which planets have rings? Does Mercury move faster or slower than Earth?

Ask about your students:
What do you see when you look up at the sky during the day? What do you see at night? Would you like to travel in space? How could you go into space? Where would you like to go? What would you see if you were in a spaceship?

Dialogue

Components: Cassette, Topic 59 Wall Chart, Picture Dictionary (pp. 118–119).

See page xix for techniques and strategies for presenting and practicing dialogues.

Ting:	Calling Earth! This is Captain Ting.
Mission Control:	Have a good trip, Captain Ting!
Ting:	We will!
Jim:	Look how fast Mercury is going around the Sun. Gosh. I'm glad we don't live on Mercury.
Zoe:	Venus is too hot. I'd hate to live on Venus.
Ting:	I'll just orbit Earth now.
Zoe:	Look! I see Mars! It has two moons. I like just one moon better. What was that?
Ting:	We just bumped into a little asteroid.
Marcus:	This next planet is huge. Be careful, Ting. It's Jupiter, and it's made of gas. You can't land on it.
Ting:	I'm not going to land.
Jim:	I can't believe it has so many moons!
Zoe:	Look what's coming next! Saturn, with a whole bunch of rings around it.
Jim:	Hey, Ting! You're going too fast! Are you sure you know how to fly this thing?
Marcus:	Yeah—we'll be out of the Solar System and then where will we go?
Ting:	Well, good-bye Uranus and Neptune and Pluto. ...
Mission Control:	Earth calling Ting! You astronauts are out too far! Come back into the Solar System! Come back!
Ting:	All right. Here we come! We're heading back to Earth!
Everyone:	Yay!!

Dialogue notes

After listening to the dialogue several times, invite volunteers to take turns being captain of an imaginary spaceship. Suggest that the children begin their dialogues by varying the phrase *Look! I see Mars!* to mention other planets and add a line of description *(It has two moons).*

Beats!

Components: Cassette, Beats! (Topic 59).

See page xx for techniques and strategies for presenting and practicing Beats!

We're flying in the Solar System,
heading toward the stars.
We see the planets Mercury,
Venus, Earth, and Mars.

On we go through the asteroids.
Our spaceship zooms!
Jupiter! Saturn! They're huge!
And they have a lot of moons!

Saturn has rings, and so does Uranus.
Look! It's on its side!
Next comes Neptune, last comes Pluto.
And that's the end of our ride!

Is anyone out here? Anyone else?
Guess we're all alone.
Let's head back to Planet Earth,
our home sweet home!

Beat notes

Say the Beat as a whole class, then in four groups (with each group saying one stanza), and then as a whole class again. Let the children add any actions they can: pointing to various planets, arms in a circle to represent rings, arms out to the side for flying or zooming, making an about-face and pointing for the line *head back to Planet Earth,* etc.

Worksheets

Worksheet 1: Out in space (p. 117)

Provide crayons or markers for the children to color the planets. You may suggest that they use the Wall Chart or illustration in the Dictionary as a reference. Then help them understand that they are to write the names of the planets from the Sun outwards. All of the planet names are given on the page. Finally, encourage the children to choose one planet and write or dictate a short story about visiting there.

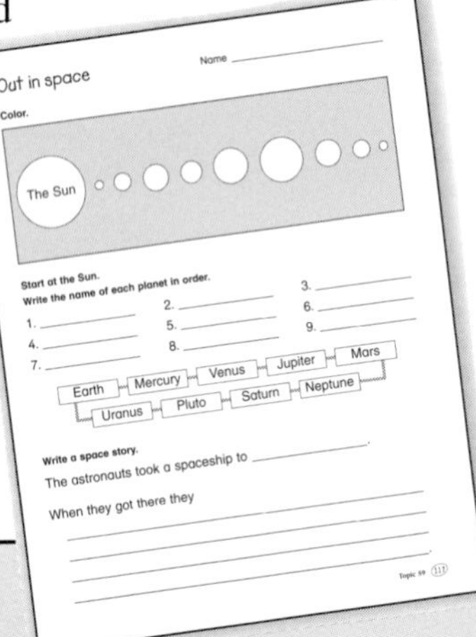

Out in space Name ____________

Color.

The Sun

Start at the Sun.
Write the name of each planet in order.

1. ________ 2. ________ 3. ________
4. ________ 5. ________ 6. ________
7. ________ 8. ________ 9. ________

Earth Mercury Venus Jupiter Mars
Uranus Pluto Saturn Neptune

Write a space story.
The astronauts took a spaceship to ____________.
When they got there they ____________

Topic 59 117

Worksheet 2: Out in space (p. 118)

Give the children the clue that the names for the planets and the Sun are written backwards and that, to unscramble them, they just have to write the last letter first, the next-to-last letter second, and so forth.

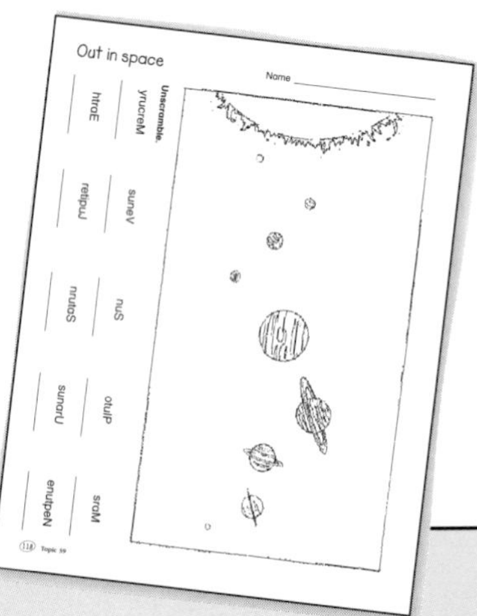

Out in space Name ____________

Unscramble.

yrucreM ____ htraE ____
suneV ____ retipuJ ____
nuS ____ nrutaS ____
otulP ____ sunarU ____
sraM ____ enutpeN ____

118 Topic 59

Activities

- Help the children build a spaceship. A large, sturdy refrigerator box works well. Cut a window and door and let the children take chairs inside and draw a control board. Or simply place two chairs side by side for the capsule and use a desk with a cardboard control panel. Encourage the children to elaborate on their space capsule and use it as a jumping-off point for dialogues and other projects.
- Play Toss the Spaceship. Have each child pick a word card from a shuffled deck (leave out *astronaut* and *spaceship*). Tell them to remember what they picked and then return the cards to the deck. Then stand in the center of a circle with a beanbag to represent the spaceship, and call out a destination (for example, Mars). Throw the beanbag into the air. The child who picked Mars catches (or retrieves) the bag and takes a turn in the center, calling out a different destination.
- Design planet hats. Have each child choose a planet (or the Sun). Make simple cone or folded-paper hats, and have the children decorate their hats to show something that distinguishes their planet. For example, Earth could be blue with white swirls; Mars would have swirling reds. Have the children write the name of the planet (or the Sun) on the front of the hat.
- Create planet mobiles. Have the children decorate circles of various sizes cut from construction paper or stiff cardboard to represent the planets and the Sun. Attach them to a long strip of stiff cardboard with yarn.

60 My blue Earth

Content

- The Earth
- Maps, globes, and photos of Earth from space

Language

- Describing Earth: *Look how blue the Earth is. The Earth is covered with oceans. There are no dividing lines.*
- Asking and answering questions about Earth: *Where are the different countries? You can't see them from space. Why is the Earth blue? That's because the oceans are blue.*
- Expressing opinions: *We're lucky to live on the Earth. I'm glad it's my Earth.*

Ting, Diego, Zoe, Tommy, and Alison are floating in their spacesuits in space looking down on the Earth. They can see the swirling white clouds and the blue of the oceans. The Earth from space looks serene, beautiful, and without borders or divisions.

Words

There are no vocabulary words in this topic.

Additional Words

oceans
planet
clouds
country
space
beautiful
dividing

Words

Components: Topic 60 Wall Chart, Picture Dictionary (pp. 120–121), Cassette.

See page xiv for techniques and strategies for presenting and practicing words.

Word notes

Although there are no vocabulary words in this unit, you may elicit language from the students by showing them a map of the world, a globe, and the illustration, or pictures of Earth from space. Ask them to describe the differences they see between the different versions of Earth. Make sure they understand that the globe and the maps have more colors than the photos because they are made to show the political divisions between countries. You may want to explain that the concept of a world without divisions is based on the words of astronauts looking at Earth from space for the first time.

Stories

Components: Picture Dictionary (pp. 120–121), Cassette, Story (Topic 60).

See page xviii for techniques and strategies for presenting and practicing stories.

That's my Earth! My blue Earth!
Covered with oceans,
and bright white clouds.

With no dividing lines
between countries.

No dividing lines
between people.

It looks like one big happy Earth!

Story notes

The story is inspired by the words of astronauts orbiting the Earth. If possible, show the children satellite or shuttle images of Earth. Talk with the children about the idea of borders or dividing lines that exist in human perception but are invisible from space.

Ask about the story:
Why do they call the Earth blue? Is the Earth only blue? What color do you think the ocean is? What are the dividing lines between people?

Ask about your students:
Would you like to see the Earth from space? Have you ever crossed a border or dividing line? Could you see it?

Dialogue

Components: Cassette, Topic 60 Wall Chart, Picture Dictionary (pp. 120–121).

See page xix for techniques and strategies for presenting and practicing dialogues.

Ting:	Look how blue the Earth is.
Tommy:	That's because the oceans are blue. That's why.
Zoe:	No other planet is blue like Earth.
Diego:	I like the white clouds. No other planet has white clouds, either.
Tommy:	Where are the different countries?
Diego:	You can't see them from space.
Zoe:	You can't tell one country from another. They all look the same.
Ting:	There aren't any lines like on a map.
Alison:	No, it all looks the same, and it all looks beautiful.
Ting:	It is beautiful. We're lucky we live on the Earth.
Tommy:	I'm glad it's my Earth.
Diego:	I'm glad it's my Earth, too.
Everyone:	Me, too.
Zoe:	It's my blue Earth.

Dialogue notes

After listening to the dialogue several times, ask the children to look at the illustration in the Dictionary and imagine they are floating in space along with the children in the picture, looking down at the Earth. Prompt them to make their own comments based on the language models in the dialogue.

Beats!

Components: Cassette, Beats! (Topic 60).

See page xx for techniques and strategies for presenting and practicing Beats!

Out in space
my Earth looks blue.
  Blue, blue,
  the oceans are blue.

Out in space
my Earth looks white.
  White, white,
  the clouds are white.

No lines
between the countries.
  No lines
  that we can see.

Wouldn't it be fun to be
one big happy family!

Beat notes

Divide the class into two groups. Let one group say the first two lines of each stanza and the second group say the third and fourth lines of each stanza. The last stanza can be said in unison. When the children are comfortable with the words and phrases, invite the children to join hands within their group, forming two circles, one inside the other. Then ask each circle to move, the inner circle to the right and the outer circle to the left, as they recite.

Worksheets

There are no worksheets for this topic.

Activities

- Explore globes. Prompt your children to compare flat maps, such as those in Topics 4 (Big world!) and 40 (Let's see the USA!), with globes. If possible, provide round blue balloons. Help the children blow up the balloons and tie them off, put on the continents with marker, and glue cotton to the surface to represent the cloud cover that can be seen from space.

- Make a peace chain. Cut strips of brightly colored construction paper for links. Ask students to write their names on one side of the strips and to write or dictate one thing they think people could do to help make the world more peaceful. Encourage the children to make as many links as they wish. Read each link aloud as you glue them together in a chain.

- Learn to say *I love you* in many different languages. Parents of class members, other children, or other adults can serve as resources for the correct words. Here is the phrase *I love you* as it is said in a few other languages in other countries:

Venezuela	*Te quiero*
China	*Wo ai ni* (Mandarin)
France	*Je t'aime*
Greece	*S'agapo*
Hawaii	*Aloha au la'oe*
Saudi Arabia	*Ana bibbak*
Germany	*Ich liebe dich*
Norway	*Jeg elsker deg*
Namibia	*Et het jou lief*
Tanzania	*Nakupenda*
Cambodia	*Kenyuh shroplang neak*
Ecuador	*Aehicata munai*
Israel	*Ani ohev otach*

Words

T

U

V

W

X

Y

Z

Verbs

Topic 6: Good morning!
brush
cook
eat
get dressed
sleep
wash

Topic 10: Here comes the school bus!
lean
push
sit
stand

Topic 11: Time for school!
ride
walk

Topic 12: What are you making?
build
cut
listen
look
paint

Topic 13: Where's my homework?
draw
read
think
write

Topic 15: What's new in the hall?
cry
frown
laugh
smile
yawn

Topic 16: Gym time!
crawl
hop
jump
skip
tumble

Topic 18: Let's play!
bounce
catch
climb
fall
kick
run
throw

Topic 19: What's the matter?
cough
lie down
sneeze

Topic 20: Music!
beat
blow
clap
sing

Topic 24: Let's go to the library!
check out
return

Topic 30: Nice evening!
help
play
practice
rest
talk
watch

Topic 39: Great restaurant!
chop
pour
serve
stir

Topic 41: Beach day
dive
float
swim

Topic 44: Working on the farm
drive
feed
milk
pick

Subjects

Animals

Topic 23: Can we have a pet?
bird
cat
dog
fish
kitten
mouse
puppy
turtle

Topic 41: Beach day
seagull

Topic 42: We found a tide pool!
clams
crabs
duck
geese
goose
minnows
pelican
snail

Topic 43: What's under the sea?
dolphin
jellyfish
octopus
sea horse
shark
whale

Topic 44: Working on the farm
cow
hen
pig
rooster
sheep

Topic 45: Camping out
bear
deer
frog

Topic 46: Bugs!
ant
bee
butterfly
caterpillar
firefly
mosquito
spider
tick

Topic 47: Ranch in the desert
buffalo
coyote
horse
lizard
prairie dog
rattlesnake
scorpion

Topic 48: Dinosaur days
dinosaurs
Diplodocus
Oviraptor
Pterosaur
Stegosaurus
Triceratops
Tyrannosaurus Rex

Topic 49: Who lives in the zoo?
apes
elephant
lion
monkeys
peacock
snakes
tiger

Topic 50: I'm in Australia!
dingo
emu
joey
kangaroo
koala
kookaburra
parrot
wichity grubs
wombat

Topic 51: I'm in Africa!
baboon
chimpanzee
flamingo
gazelle
giraffe
gorilla
hippopotamus
leopard
zebra

Topic 52: I'm in Asia!
camel
cobra
crocodile
egret
orangutan
panda
rhinoceros

Topic 53: Spring is here!
rabbit
raccoon
robin
squirrel

Topic 56: Windy fall
woodpecker

Body

Topic 3: Different faces
chin
ears
eyelashes
eyes
hair
mouth
nose
skin
teeth
tooth

Topic 14: Bodies and bones!
ankle
arm
back
buttocks
chest
elbow
feet
fingers
foot
hand
head
hip
knee
leg
neck
ribs
shoulder
skull
stomach
spine
toes
wrist

Clothing

Topic 8: What can I wear?
baseball cap
boots
dress
jeans
pajamas
skirt
sneakers
socks
sweater
sweatshirt
T-shirt
underwear

Topic 26: Who's at the hospital?
mask
rubber gloves

Topic 38: Carnival!
costume

Topic 41: Beach day
bathing suit

Topic 45: Camping out
life jacket

Topic 54: We planted a garden!
raincoat

Topic 57: Snowy winter
gloves
hat
jacket
scarf

Food

Topic 9: Who made breakfast?
bread
butter
cereal
eggs
juice

Topic 17: What's for lunch?
apple
carrot
cookie
egg roll
milk
salad
sandwich
sushi
taco

Topic 27: Busy supermarket!
bananas
broccoli
cheese
lettuce
meat
orange
pineapple
seafood

Topic 29: Dinner's ready
apple pie
beans
chicken
corn
melon
peas
potato
rice
roast beef
rolls
soup
tomato

Topic 31: Saturday at the mall
french fries
ice cream cone
pizza
soda

Topic 32: Happy birthday!
cake
candy

Topic 38: Carnival!
cotton candy
popcorn

Topic 55: Hot summer
hamburger
hot dog

Neighborhood Places

Topic 5: Where do you live?
apartment
house
street
yard

Topic 10: Here comes the school bus!
bus stop
corner

Topic 18: Let's play!
bars
seesaw
slide
swing

Topic 33: Sunday in the city
park

Occupations

Topic 10: Here comes the school bus!
bus driver

Topic 11: Time for school
crossing guard
librarian
nurse
principal
student
teacher

Topic 21: Can we cross now?
police officer

Topic 25: I'm sick!
doctor

Topic 26: Who's at the hospital?
paramedic

Topic 28: Errands in town
dentist
letter carrier

Topic 34: Street scene
artist
dancer
mime
musician

photographer
singer

Topic 35: New building going up!
carpenter
construction worker
electrician
plumber

Topic 36: Fire!
fire chief
firefighter

Topic 38: Carnival!
acrobat
clown
magician

Topic 39: Great restaurant!
chef
waiter

Topic 41: Beach day
lifeguard

Topic 44: Working on the farm
farmer

Topic 47: Ranch in the desert
cowhand

Topic 48: Dinosaur days
scientist

Topic 58: Up in the night sky
astronomer

Topic 59: Out in space
astronaut

Sport And Physical Activity

Topic 18: Let's play!
ball
bars
bounce
catch
climb
kick
run
seesaw
slide
swing
throw

Topic 32: Happy birthday!
baseball bat

Topic 37: Big harbor

sailboat

Topic 41: Beach day
dive
float
kite
surfboard
swim

Topic 43: What's under the sea?
fins
snorkel

Topic 45: Camping out
fishing rod
rowboat

Topic 47: Ranch in the desert
horseback riding
lasso

Topic 55: Hot summer
baseball
pool
tennis
waterskiing

Topic 56: Windy fall
football
soccer

Topic 57: Snowy winter
ice skating
skiing
sled

Stores And Services

Topic 21: Can we cross now?
barbershop
library
pet shop
police officer
sports store
toy store

Topic 28: Errands in town
bakery
bank
dentist
drugstore
gas station
hardware store
laundry
mailbox
post office
restaurant

Topic 31: Saturday at the mall
arcade
clothing store
movie theater
rest rooms
shoe store
snack bar

Topic 33: Sunday in the city
airport
factory
highway
railroad
subway

Topic 37: Big harbor
ferry

Tools, Machines, And Utensils

Topic 6: Good morning!
sink
stove

Topic 7: Busy bathroom!
bathtub
shower
toilet

Topic 9: Who made breakfast?
fork
knife
spoon

Topic 11: Time for school!
clock

Topic 12: What are you making?
crayons
glue
markers
pencil
scissors

Topic 17: What's for lunch?
garbage can
tray

Topic 19: What's the matter?
thermometer

Topic 24: Let's go to the library!
computer

Topic 25: I'm sick!
scale
stethoscope

Topic 34: Street scene
camera

Topic 36: Fire!
axe
fire extinguisher
hose
ladder

Topic 39: Great restaurant!
chopsticks
pots

Topic 42: We found a tide pool!
pail
shovel

Topic 46: Bugs!
magnifying glass

Topic 53: Spring is here!
hammer
lawn mower
saw

Topic 56: Windy fall
broom
clippers
rake
wheelbarrow

Transportation And Vehicles

Topic 11: Time for school!
bicycle
bus
car

Topic 21: Can we cross now?
motorcycle
taxi
truck

Topic 22: Look at the toys!
airplane
boat
train

Topic 26: Who's at the hospital?
ambulance
wheelchair

Topic 32: Happy birthday!
helicopter

Topic 33: Sunday in the city
garbage truck
highway
railroad
subway

Topic 35: New building going up!
backhoe
bulldozer
cement mixer
crane
dump truck
forklift

Topic 36: Fire!
fire engine

Topic 37: Big harbor
barge
ferry
sailboat
ship
tugboat

Topic 44: Working on the farm
tractor

Topic 45: Camping out
rowboat

Topic 47: Ranch in the desert
horse

Topic 55: Hot summer
skates

Topic 57: Snowy winter
ice skating
skiing
sled

Topic 59: Out in space
spaceship

Weather

Topic 54: We planted a garden!
rain
raincoat
sunshine
umbrella

Topic 55: Hot summer
clouds
lightning
thunderstorm
wind

Topic 57: Snowy winter
icicles
snow
snowflakes